PREFACE TO THE PRESIDENCY

PHOTO BY BARBARA KINNEY, THE WHITE HOUSE

PREFACE TO THE PRESIDENCY

Selected Speeches of Bill Clinton

1974–1992

Compiled and Edited by

Stephen A. Smith

THE UNIVERSITY OF ARKANSAS PRESS
FAYETTEVILLE ❖ 1996

Manufactured in the United States of America

00 99 98 97 96 5 4 3 2 1

Designed by Ellen Beeler

♾ The paper used in this publication meets the minimum requirements of the American National Standard for Permanence of Paper for Printed Library Materials Z39.48-1984.

Library of Congress Cataloging-in-Publication Data

Clinton, Bill, 1946–
Preface to the presidency : selected speeches of Bill Clinton, 1974–1992 / compiled and edited by Stephen A. Smith.
p. cm.
ISBN 1-55728-440-7 (alk. paper). — ISBN 1-55728-441-5 (pbk. : alk. paper)
1. Arkansas—Politics and government—1951– 2. United States—Politics and government—1989–1993. I. Smith, Stephen A., 1949– . II. Arkansas. Governor (1979–1981 : Clinton) III. Arkansas. Governor (1983–1992 : Clinton) IV. Title.
E838.5.C55 1996
976.7'053—dc20 96-22577
CIP

To the Arkansas Library Association
Intellectual Freedom Committee

ACKNOWLEDGMENTS

This volume of speeches came into being with the help of many people whose names do not appear on the cover, and I wish to gratefully acknowledge their assistance. Linda Pine, special collections archivist at the University of Arkansas at Little Rock, helped locate materials and provided the text of the 1976 speech in Russellville from the Doug Wallace Collection. The Democratic National Committee's Arkansas office supplied copies of Clinton's 1983 speech on education and his addresses to the 1984 and 1988 Democratic National Conventions. Kay Kelley Arnold collected and provided copies of numerous speech texts from the 1992 campaign, as well as providing assistance with research on some of the earlier speeches. Skip Rutherford, as always, was helpful in many ways. Prof. Paul Barefield of the University of Southwestern Louisiana went beyond the call of collegial assistance in finding data *obscura.*

At the University of Arkansas, Fayetteville, Miller Williams, director of the University Press, has been especially supportive of the project from its inception. Prof. Jimmie Rogers contributed to this volume in many untold ways since I first became his student as an undergraduate, and my colleagues on the communication faculty are always a source of wisdom, support, and too much fun. John Harrison, director of libraries, has made all of my research much easier in many ways but especially by his commitment to providing access to resources ranging from electronic databases to musty documents. Lindsley Armstrong Smith and Jill Robbins prepared much of the manuscript.

Of course, someone should finally acknowledge the nameless, overworked, and underappreciated staffers who have worked on speeches for Bill Clinton over the years, and I do so here and now.

Finally, I cannot fail to offer my personal appreciation for the love and support of the Smith family—Austin, Margaret, Nancy, Lindsley, Caleb, and Maggie. Just knowing them helps keep me from going sane.

CONTENTS

INTRODUCTION

Public discourse is not "mere rhetoric." It is the process by which we learn of the world, understand our past, construct social reality, articulate our humanity, shape our values, build our dreams, reach collective decisions, perform civic responsibilities, guard our liberties, transmit our culture, and speak to one another about the small events and grand schemes in the public sphere. It is important.

For as long as I can remember, I have been fascinated by the process of political communication, especially the role of public speaking by passionate citizens, candidates, and public officials. I watched and listened to Orval Faubus in full stride, enjoyed an academic education that valued rhetoric and trained me as a critic of discourse, and even sought and held public office.

For a brief period I had an opportunity to work with Bill Clinton, help craft his political speeches as a candidate and in office, and learn by observing a masterful communicator practicing the art in a variety of contexts. At first I collaborated as he would toss off an admirable final draft with a felt-tipped pen on a yellow legal pad. After coming to understand his style and his positions, I would sometimes produce full drafts and watch as he made refinements and revisions. Most often I would collect information and provide only a suggested outline, watching him bring it to life from the podium. It was an experience of which most political speech writers can only dream. Always, he was responsible for his own speeches, both in invention and in performance, and in my view he is at his best without a prepared text.

The demands of life on the stage of national politics does not allow the lead actors the same full attention to scripting their own roles or writing their own lines; however, I have seen enough evidence of Clinton's not-so-invisible hand in his speeches during the 1992 campaign to conclude that both he and his staff deserve more credit as principals than either are given by the national media or the public audience. It is also apparent that he continues to assume responsibility for his own words in important public speeches as president. Following his public address on the issue of race in America at the University of Texas on October 16, 1995, the day of the Million-Man March in Washington, White House Press Secretary Mike McCurry briefed reporters on the genesis of the speech:

> Several people have asked how the speech came together at the last minute for the President. I think you all have heard a lot about the work that he's done on this. One of the questions we had at the White House was whether, frankly, he would have the time necessary to really think through exactly what he wanted to say, and clearly, the President did. He has spent recent days talking to a wide variety of African Americans to get ideas and to get a sense of how he could best appropriately continue this conversation that he believes America needs to have about race. . . . His speech-writing team under Don Baer, the two speech writers who I think worked mostly with the President, were David Shipley and Terry Edmunds. There was somewhere a little wire item or something saying that there had been some question of which of the two of them worked on it—they actually worked on it together with Don Baer and with the President. The President, though, wrote, obviously, large portions of this himself. He was making blue felt-tip changes and rewriting passages until the early hours this morning, and then woke up about 7:00 A.M. this morning, worked on it some more. So obviously it is a speech very much from the heart.
>
> Question: How much sleep did he get?
>
> Not much, because his last pass-off of notes to the speech writers was about 3:00 A.M. and he was up working on it at 7:00 A.M. this morning. But the reason for that, I think it's clearly something he had thought about a lot and wanted to bring together in a speech that reflected in a very personal way some things he felt needed to be said both to black Americans and to white Americans, and he clearly directed those remarks in a personal way at both audiences today.

The process described by McCurry is one familiar to anyone who has ever been charged with working with Bill Clinton on a major speech, and it is one I doubt will change during his career in public life. In addition to the persistent pattern of speech writing, I think the speeches in this volume also reveal a surprising consistency in the basic themes and policy positions—over time, in varied contexts, and to vastly diverse audiences—articulated by Clinton during a relatively long rhetorical career from a twenty-seven-year-old candidate seeking a seat in Congress to a forty-six-year-old candidate claiming victory in a campaign for the presidency.

In the first speech in this collection, addressing the Democratic State Convention as the party's nominee for Congress in September 1974, he presented his philosophy of the government's role in solving economic problems, saying, "in the words of a friend of mine who works on the Scott County road crew, 'The people want a hand up, not a hand out.'" In the final selection, his speech accepting the results of the presidential election in November 1992, he told the audience, "It was a victory for the people who work hard and play by the rules, a victory for the people who feel left out and left behind but want to do better, a victory for the people who are ready to compete and win in the global economy, but who need a government that offers a hand up, not a hand out. That is what we offer, and that is what tomorrow we will begin to work to provide to all of you."

This volume was conceived on the fundamental premise that the words, messages, and rhetorical choices of public figures and political leaders are a window through which we can discern far more than their motives and immediate concerns; they are also a mirror that reflects the dialectic of a larger shared political reality in which we all participate as passive observers or, sometimes, as active players. The public speeches of Bill Clinton collected in this volume certainly tell us much about his aspirations and his communication skills within the context of a political career in Arkansas that spanned almost two decades before he became the president of the United States, but they are also valuable for other reasons as well. A close reading of these texts can reveal the power of language, the discovery and use of evidence, the preference for competing values, the vitality of ideas, the force of logical arguments, the appeals to emotion, the constraints of context, the choices among policy options, the requirements of audiences, the resonance of rhetoric, and the processes of continuity and change in the life of the republic. I invite you to engage them with a critical attitude, investigate their rhetorical nuances, examine the use of evidence, appraise the interplay of ideas, discern the imbedded meanings, and make your own informed judgments.

The Fight for Fairness and Justice

Democratic State Convention
Hot Springs, Arkansas
September 13, 1974

Less than a year after graduating from Yale Law School and returning to Arkansas, twenty-seven-year-old Bill Clinton announced in February 1974 that he would be a candidate for Congress. He led a field of four candidates with 44 percent and defeated veteran state senator Gene Rainwater with 69 percent two weeks later. In doing so he had also captured the attention of the Democratic Party. As a gesture of support the party scheduled its state convention in Hot Springs, Clinton's family home and one of the largest cities in the Third Congressional District, and slated him as the keynote speaker for the convention.

The speech, delivered to two thousand eager partisans in the Hot Springs Convention Center, was repeatedly interrupted with applause and was met with a standing ovation at the end. It was Clinton's first opportunity to address a statewide audience, and it was the only one of the campaign delivered from a written manuscript; however, it was essentially a distillation of the themes he had developed on the stump during the primaries and which he would take into a bold, but unsuccessful, fall campaign against the incumbent, John Paul Hammerschmidt.

❖ ❖ ❖

Ladies and Gentlemen, we have come together in the midst of one of our country's most difficult periods.

After two years of turmoil, a president of the United States has resigned his office.

His chosen successor, in whom Democrats and Republicans alike had at first placed such hope, has granted a "full, free, and absolute" pardon to the fallen president in advance of any charges being filed against him.

This pardon has again opened the wounds of Watergate. It has undermined respect for law and order. It has prejudiced pending trials. It has tormented the families of those already in prison for the administration's political crimes. It is yet another blow to that vast body of law-abiding Americans, whose faith in equal justice under law has been shaken, then repaired, and is now shaken again.

Rumbling beneath these headline events, even more troubling, are the twin evils of inflation and recession. For the first time, both plagues are afflicting our economy at once. Together, these relentless forces have a vice-like grip on those of us who have the least ability to resist them—small businessmen, family farmers, working men and women, the poor, and the elderly. These people are hurting. And who is responsible?

For six long years, the other party has held the White House and enough of the Congress to implement its policies. What have they brought? Record interest rates, record prices, record budgets, record deficits, and recession.

They have held back money from pressing human needs and still built the biggest deficits and the biggest bureaucracies in history.

They have taken a grain surplus that we needed at home and given it to the Russians. The Russians then sold it for a huge profit, while our food prices exploded.

They have kept prices high and profits high for the biggest corporations, while trying to hold down minimum wages and telling working people to tighten their belts.

They have driven up interest rates and dried up money—crippling small businesses, the housing industry, and savings-and-loan institutions—while Mobil buys Montgomery Ward, Gulf buys Barnum and Bailey Circus, and the big New York banks export billions of our dollars abroad to the highest bidder.

They have given away foreign aid, nuclear power, and three-million-dollar helicopters to the Arabs, who have quadrupled the price of oil and may cut off its supply again if it suits them.

In the face of this sorry record, if President Ford wants to pardon anybody, he ought to pardon the administration's economic advisors.

The question before us, my friends, is not what they have done, but what we can do for our people.

How can we restore the even-handed rule of law for which so many have fought and died since our Revolution?

How can we return to the people the prosperity and stability which they have earned by their efforts and their loyalty to our way of life?

We ought to go back to the roots of our democracy—the people. They have some ideas of their own about what the politicians ought to do.

For eight and a half months in my campaign for Congress, I have been with the people nearly every day—listening to their problems, their frustrations, their hopes. This is what they are saying:

We know that in every system of laws, because men are frail and fall short of the glory, justice must be tempered with mercy. But we want it remembered that—even for the favored few—mercy must also be tempered with justice.

We do not mind making sacrifices in the name of inflation, but we do mind suffering while others are making a killing from inflation because they have the power to keep the prices up and the people down.

We do not want to avoid our responsibility to pay fair taxes, but we do resent bearing the tax burdens that many, far wealthier, have the power to avoid.

We do not mind showing generosity to foreign countries, but we know that foreign friends cannot be bought. We want America's needs to be met first; charity begins at home.

We do not want the federal government to give up its attempts to protect our national security and promote domestic well-being, but we do want to cut back on wasteful spending and bloated bureaucracies. These middlemen of government meddle with our lives without increasing the common good.

In short, in the words of a friend of mine who works on the Scott County road crew, "The people want a hand up, not a hand out."

Our task, our obligation, is to extend that hand. It is a challenge the Democratic Party has met before.

Thomas Jefferson, our founder, said that because all men are created equal, democracy "requires equal and exact justice to all men of whatever state or persuasion, religious or political."

With particular relevance to our present plight, Franklin D. Roosevelt declared, "We have always known that heedless self-interest was bad morals. We now know that it is bad economics."

Let us listen to these voices, for, as Woodrow Wilson said, "The success of party means little except when the Nation is using that party for a large and definite purpose. No one can mistake the purpose for which the people now seek to use the Democratic Party."

As we meet today, the purpose of our party must be to restore justice and fairness—not just to the courtroom and the halls of government. We must bring it back to the farms and factories, the streets and stores, the homes and hearts of all Americans.

The good government we love has too often been made use of for private and selfish purposes. Those who have abused it have forgotten the people.

It is time to balance the budget, balance the burden of fighting inflation, and balance the scales of justice.

The Democratic Party in Arkansas is ready. It has fielded perhaps the finest array of leaders of any state in the nation:

Senator John McClellan, who has pioneered the development of the Arkansas River, fought organized crimes, and made the largest single contribution to the fight against inflation this year by bringing new economy to our defense budget without imperiling our security.

Senator Bill Fulbright, my old friend, who is in China today representing this nation in the struggle for world peace, for which he has labored so valiantly all his public life.

Our great governor, Dale Bumpers, who will bring to the Senate a new force for reconciliation and progress and who, we may hope, will reach an even higher level of service to his country.

Chairman Wilbur Mills, who has worked against Republican opposition for nearly forty years to bring real Social Security to our old and disabled, and who now needs our help in the face of an alleged progressive Republican onslaught that can do no better than bring in Ronald Reagan to tell the people of Arkansas how to vote.

Bill Alexander, who has led the fight to protect the privacy of farmers and to improve the quality of life in rural America in the face of this administration's determination to drive the small farmer out of business.

Ray Thornton, who, with courage and determination, has played a major role in protecting the American people from virtual dictatorship and in proving that, in spite of abuses of presidential power, we are still a government of laws.

Here in Arkansas, our new and retiring lieutenant governors, Joe Purcell and Bob Riley, who have been models of the kind of self-sacrifice and integrity every government needs to succeed.

Attorney General Jim Guy Tucker, whose long, at first lonely, battle against propane price gouging has earned him nationwide respect and the everlasting gratitude of the people in my district who depend upon propane for survival.

Those who have led our party in the past year, Brad Jesson and Nancy Balton, under whose guidance we have reunited to fight for the welfare of our people instead of against each other.

And the man we especially honor at this convention, David Pryor, who at his young age has devoted so many years to the people of Arkansas, in the state legislature, in Congress, and soon, in the State House. His demonstrated concern for those in need proves that he will be a great progressive governor.

But the greatest strength of our party is not in its leaders. It is in the people who rally to its standard. It is for you to keep the party committed to the fight for fairness and justice.

If you are looking for a battleground, go outside onto the streets where I grew up. Lift up your eyes to the hills of north and west Arkansas. There is a fight in this Third Congressional District which is a clear and unmistakable struggle between what we are for and what we are against. For, in the words of Harry Truman, when you strip away the "small talk and double talk, the combination of crafty silence and misrepresentation," you find this seat in Congress occupied by one of the strongest supporters of, and apologists for, the abuse of presidential power and policies which have wrecked the economy.

And why is he strong? Because of these, these questionnaires and letters and press releases that every congressman has an obligation to send and that the people pay for.

Let me ask you about these questionnaires, my friends in the Third Congressional District. When you received them, did you say in them that you wanted him to vote for high gas prices and low taxes on the big oil companies? I think not, but he has.

Did you tell him that you wanted him to support agricultural policies like the Russian wheat deal which would break the small farmers in our district? I think not, but he has.

Did you tell him, with sewage running over in the streets in some of the little towns in my district, that you wanted him to vote to keep the water and sewer money out of our district and away from our people? I think not, but he has.

Did you tell him, every mother of a schoolchild out there, that you wanted him to vote three out of the four past years to keep federal funds away from your schoolchildren? I think not, but he has.

And did you tell him in that questionnaire that you wanted him to defend and uphold and refuse to criticize this unforgivable pardon? I think not, but he has.

I want my gift to this party, to you, to be the return of this seat in Congress to our people. With your help, I will make that gift. Together, we must show the people of Arkansas that we will abide by principles and take positions which will restore their faith in government and their prosperity.

Today, we must deliberate. Tomorrow, we must take out of this hall the will to set things right. Let us begin!

The Guardian of the People's Interest

River Valley Democratic Rally
Russellville, Arkansas
April 10, 1976

During the fifteen months since almost winning a seat in Congress, Clinton had maintained his political organization in northwest Arkansas and expanded it statewide by working for the state Democratic Party, and he was far better known than either of his opponents for attorney general. The River Valley Rally, sponsored by the Arkansas Democratic Women, is the traditional kick-off for the primary campaign. It is held on the first weekend following the filing deadline, and, fortuitously for Clinton, it is held at Russellville in the heart of the Third Congressional District, and the audience was dominated by the party regulars who had backed him and come to admire him in 1974.

Speaking to about five hundred enthusiastic Democrats on the campus of Arkansas Tech University, it was clear from the personal tone of his remarks that Clinton was talking to an audience of friends and supporters. Seven weeks later he would win the primary with 56 percent of the vote, carrying seventy-three of the state's seventy-five counties, and, without an opponent in the general election, he became the attorney general-elect at the age of twenty-nine.

❖ ❖ ❖

For a long time, I have looked forward to this night, for here, two years ago, is when it all began.

Tonight I come again, seeking your help to become attorney general. The office is one of the most important the people have within their gift. The attorney general must be the guardian of the people's interest as well as the lawyer for their government.

In the next two years, I want the attorney general's office:

- to provide every possible assistance to all our law-enforcement officials in enforcing our entirely new body of criminal law;

- to work to ensure that those convicted of violent crimes serve definite minimum sentences;
- to help establish a program which will provide compensation to victims of those crimes who don't have the resources to return to a normal life and who are too often forgotten in their suffering;
- to see that there is an "ombudsman," or public listener, who will be available at all times to help any citizen with any problem with any branch of state government;
- to urge passage of an amendment to the Consumer Protection Act which will give each one of you the right to go into your local courts to help yourself if you suffer a loss as a result of unfair or deceptive practices;
- to be willing and able to contribute to the deliberations of state and national regulatory agencies to ensure not only that our people pay only their fair utility rates but that we also have a sensible and adequate energy policy;
- to give you an office which embodies the highest standards of professional excellence and ethics—one open to serve you all.

These are lofty goals. They demand an attorney general who is dedicated to the law and to justice. They demand a deep compassion and sensitivity to the needs of the people. I want to meet those demands, but I need your help to do it.

Help me to prove that a devotion to excellence and hard work and progressive leadership do have a place in our politics. As we have in the past, help me to hold to the high road in the face of the negative forces which continue to erode the quality of public and private political activity within our state. Help me to improve the lives of our people by moving forward in this campaign on what we have built before with so much toil and sacrifice and joy.

This morning as I drove up Highway 7 from Hot Springs, in the breathtaking beauty of our Arkansas spring, I thought of all the long roads so many of us have walked together, up and down this river valley—not just through the main towns, but also to the hamlets of which so many others are but dimly aware—to Houston, Casa, and Adone; Havana, Briggsville, and Chickalah; Coal Hill, Hartman, and Lamar; Hector, Appleton, and Dover, and more. I know them all, and they are home to me because of you.

I believe there is an unbreakable bond between us, and I have tried to keep faith with it.

Now I need you once more to fight another battle. If you will do it, it will be an exhilarating reaffirmation of the work to which I have given the fullest measure of my time and strength and spirit. If you will do it, we will bring home a great victory that will surely belong to us all.

God bless you.

To Bring Out the Best in All of Us

Announcement of Candidacy for Governor
Little Rock, Arkansas
March 6, 1978

On a chilly morning before a crowd of about two hundred and fifty supporters, Atty. Gen. Bill Clinton appeared on the steps of the Old State House at Center and Markham streets in downtown Little Rock, accompanied by his wife, his mother, and his brother, and announced that he would be a candidate for governor of the State of Arkansas. The thirty-one-year-old candidate delivered this speech, then boarded an airplane to repeat the announcement in Texarkana, El Dorado, West Memphis, and Fayetteville before the day was over. He was immediately acknowledged as the front-runner, and he went on to defeat four opponents, capturing 59 percent of the primary vote, and to an easy victory with 63.4 percent of the vote in the November election.

❖ ❖ ❖

Today I want to ask all of you to help me become the next governor.

While this decision has not come easily to me, I know it is right.

As a people, we have come a long way in a little time. We have put aside so many of the fears and prejudices which crippled us in the past. But we have held fast to our heritage of proud individualism, love for nature's bounty, and firm faith in hard work, discipline, and respect for each other.

Because of what we have kept and what we have put aside, we have reached a point of truly remarkable possibility: Our best days are before us if we will forge our own destiny.

To do that, we must have leadership. More than anyone else, the governor must provide it. The governor can capture the spirit of our state. He can call forth and channel the energies of our people to the tasks at hand.

There is so much to be done.

We need more jobs and better incomes for our people, in new opportunities, expansion of existing operations, and opening new markets abroad, so that the thousands of young Arkansans who leave us unwillingly every year can stay with their roots.

We need a decent road program for our workers and farmers, our businesses and industries.

We need to do more to improve the education of our children, especially to give them the best possible start and a stronger grasp of the fundamentals of learning.

We need to do what we can here at home to preserve our family farms and to promote sales of their products around the world.

We need to provide the best quality of life we can to our senior citizens and others who are being swamped by inflation and do not have enough to live on.

We need to give the people a new constitution to carry us into the future. But we must not abandon the strongest point of our present one—that we pay as we go and live within our means.

To achieve these goals, we need a governor who will move on the problems, make decisions, bring fine people into government, and run an open, responsive, and balanced administration.

I want to be that governor.

As attorney general, I have gained priceless experience in the workings of all levels of government. I have tried to protect the legal interests of the state and to keep faith with the people. I have fought utility policies and rate increases I thought were wrong. I have worked to protect consumers and small businessmen from those who abuse the marketplace. I have been particularly concerned with the legal and economic difficulties of our senior citizens. Throughout, I have tried to be fair with everyone.

As governor, I know I cannot be a miracle worker, but I will be a worker, and a doer, and I will strive to see that our limited tax dollars are not wasted.

Most important of all, I will try to bring out the best in all of us.

From this day forward, I will campaign with that goal in mind. I will continue to do my job with that goal in mind. I will try to be honest about what cannot be done, but I will direct our visions toward what must be done.

I will try to make the people of Arkansas as proud of me as I am of them. I will try to be worthy of the love and devotion of my family and friends who are here, and those who are gone but who linger on in my memory, without whom I could not have come to this place today.

I will make one promise: If you will let me be your governor, no one will love this state more, care more about our people's problems, or work harder to see that we become what we ought to be.

A New Era of Achievement and Excellence

First Inaugural Address
Little Rock, Arkansas
January 9, 1979

After a primary campaign in which he defeated four other candidates with 59 percent of the vote and a convincing 64 percent victory in the general election, Clinton became, at thirty-two, the nation's youngest governor. His first inaugural address, the most eloquent of the five he would eventually deliver, was essentially a typed reading copy of a first draft he had written by hand on a yellow legal pad during the previous evening, but it was also an articulation of the political aspirations developed and campaign promises made during his five years in Arkansas politics.

Earlier in the day Clinton had taken the oath of office and delivered brief remarks to a joint session of the legislature. The formal inaugural address, lasting only nine minutes, was presented that evening from the east front of the state capitol on live television and to a crowd of about 250 who braved the subfreezing temperature for the outdoor ceremony. True to the genre, the inaugural presented the new governor's vision for the state, while the specific policy proposals and legislative details would come the following week in the State of the State speech to the general assembly.

❖ ❖ ❖

Mr. Chief Justice, Governor Faubus, constitutional officers of this state, members of the general assembly, Reverend Clergy, ladies and gentlemen:

At the outset, I wish to acknowledge what we all know well: I did not come here alone. I was carried by the people of our state, through the efforts of those who have known and nourished me, in the hope that together we might make a difference to the future of Arkansas. Without the sacrifices, affection, and inspiration of my family, my friends, and my staff in political combat and public service, I would be elsewhere tonight. Without the love, courage, patience, and counsel of my wife, I might not be worthy to be here tonight. To all of you and to the people at large, I am grateful, and humbly so, for the gift of this precious office.

As we celebrate this new beginning, I want to explain as clearly as my command of the language will allow what kind of governor I will try to be.

The exercise of authority over the people's business is a hard job. Its essence is the making of decisions which no one else has the authority to make—decisions requiring choices among people and policies and conflicting interests. Sometimes, all the available choices will be less than fully acceptable. Sometimes, there will be more than one good choice. Sometimes, we hope, the best choice will present itself plainly. Regardless, the decisions will have to be made. Inevitably, I will be compelled to say "No" more often than I can say "Yes," even to those of you who have stood by me in defeat and victory.

In this work, I will seek and often will follow advice and counsel, but in the end, I will have to decide alone. I wish I could please you all, but I cannot. I wish I could avoid errors, but I cannot. I will do all that I can, in good faith and humility, to exercise your power well. I must ask you to abide with me, through differences and disappointments, for only then can we move our state forward in these promising but difficult times.

Like anyone else, I will tend to make decisions that reflect the values and principles I have come to cherish over the years of living and struggling to grasp what understanding I can of the human condition.

For as long as I can remember, I have believed passionately in the cause of equal opportunity, and I will do what I can to advance it.

For as long as I can remember, I have deplored the arbitrary and abusive exercise of power by those in authority, and I will do what I can to prevent it.

For as long as I can remember, I have rued the waste and lack of order and discipline that are too often in evidence in governmental affairs, and I will do what I can to diminish them.

For as long as I can remember, I have loved the land, air, and water of Arkansas, and I will do what I can to protect them.

For as long as I can remember, I have wished to ease the burdens of life for those who, through no fault of their own, are old or weak or needy, and I will try to help them.

For as long as I can remember, I have been saddened by the sight of so many of our independent, industrious people working too hard for too little because of inadequate economic opportunities, and I will do what I can to enhance them.

Today, we begin anew the people's business in a time that is confusing, uncertain, and sometimes difficult to understand. In the recent past, we have learned again the hard lesson that there are limits to what government can do—indeed, limits to what people can do. We live in a world in which limited resources, limited knowledge, and limited wisdom must grapple with problems of staggering complexity and confront strong sources of power, wealth, conflict, and even destruction, over which we have no control and little influence.

Let us not learn too much of this lesson, however, lest caught in the thrall of what we cannot do, we forget what we can and should do. We are a people of pride and hope, of vision and skill, of vast capacities for work. We have the prospect, for which we have waited so long, of economic growth which does not require us to ravage our land and so to reject our heritage. We have the immeasurable benefit of living in a state in which the population is sufficiently small and widely dispersed for people of all kinds still to know and trust each other, still to believe in and work together for the elusive common good.

We have an opportunity together to forge a future that is more remarkable, more rich, and more fulfilling to all Arkansans than our proud past, and we must not squander it.

There is much to be done.

In education, we have lingered too long on or near the bottom of the heap in spending per student and in teacher salaries. We must try to reverse that. However, we must be mindful that higher quality education will not come from money alone. The money must be but part of a plan which includes better accountability and assessment for students and teachers, a fairer distribution of aid, more efficient organization of school districts, and recognition of work still to be done in programs for kindergarten, special education, and gifted and talented children.

In energy, we have been too undisciplined and tardy in our efforts to provide for future energy supply that we need for sustenance and growth at prices the people can afford. The energy department I have proposed will attempt to marshal and intensify our efforts to promote conservation, develop alternative energy sources, and develop more effective and fairer utility regulatory policies.

In human services and health care, we have a great deal to do, especially for those at the far ends of life's spectrum—our senior citizens and children. The proposals of this administration will provide to senior citizens tax relief, a uniform probate code, greatly expanded and improved home health care, and advances in nursing-home care. For children, we will seek to complete an effective care network for those who are emotionally disturbed and to create a system of perinatal care that will be a model for the nation.

In economic development, we must move quickly to intensify advances all across our state and to make more efforts for more development in the areas of our state that need it the most. The economic development department I have proposed will lead this effort with its new emphasis on marketing our products abroad, expanding existing enterprises at home, and more vigorous attempts to help local communities help themselves. But every other agency of government, from the Employment Security Division to the highway department to the Department of National and Cultural Heritage, will be asked to do its part.

In the general conduct of the government, there is a crying need for more effective management, more efficient delivery of basic services, and a renewed spirit of dedication on the part of all of us who work for the State of Arkansas. I expect the Department of Finance and Administration and the new cabinet group on waste and inefficiency in government to move us forward in these areas. But today, I ask the thousands of fine people who serve our government all across the state, many of whom could command greater compensation elsewhere, to join with me in this effort. Let us resolve that every person with whom we deal, from the governor's office to the local welfare and revenue offices, will be treated with courtesy and kindness and will leave us knowing that we are doing our best to handle their business with fairness and dispatch.

Last evening, after our gala, a friend of mine from Washington, who travels this country and speaks to many groups in many places, said that he felt in that crowd two emotions which are not found in other places: pride and hope. Pride and hope. With these two qualities, we can go a long way. We can bring on a new era of achievement and excellence—we can fashion a life here that will be the envy of our nation. The future lies brightly before us. With pride and hope, and the grace of God to take our hands and lead us on, we shall not fail!

Thank you, and God bless you all.

Discipline, Courage, and Devotion to the People

Connecticut Democratic Convention
Hartford, Connecticut
July 18, 1980

Clinton presented this speech to more than one thousand delegates and guests at the Connecticut State Democratic Convention meeting in the Bushnell Convention Center at Hartford. He was the keynote speaker at the two-day convention that nominated Rep. Christopher J. Dodd for the U.S. Senate seat being vacated by Abraham A. Ribicoff. Clinton's invitation came from Gov. Ella Grasso, his friend from the National Governors' Association, who attended the convention in her first public appearance at a major event since her surgery and cancer treatments earlier in the year.

The speech provides an early version of many of Governor Clinton's views on the challenges facing the national Democratic Party, a topic to which he returned often in speeches around the nation while serving as governor, as a founder of the Democratic Leadership Council, and as a candidate for president.

❖ ❖ ❖

Thank you very much, Governor O'Neal, for that very flattering and mercifully brief introduction. Senator Ribicoff, my wonderful and brave friend and boss in the Democratic governors, Governor Grasso, Senator-to-be Dodd, distinguished platform guests, and Democrats of Connecticut. It is a great honor for me to be here tonight. This is the first time in the seven years that have elapsed since I finished Law School that I have had the pleasure to be in the State of Connecticut. But for three wonderful, exciting, and difficult years I was a student not only at Yale Law School but a student of the Democratic Party of the State of Connecticut where I participated in its brawls, its victories, and its defeats on behalf of friends of mine and friends of yours, some of whom are here with us tonight. I am more honored than I can say to be here.

I am determined, however, to make this trip something more than a keynote speech and perhaps something less. Some of the reporters have asked me whether I could afford to be away from home for a day because of the terrible crisis that is racking our state, costing us about a half a billion dollars in farm income in this heat wave and, even more tragically, having killed a hundred of our citizens. I hope that I can afford it. I think it is important to be here. But I am not going to give what you normally hear in a keynote address, because I have been watching the television the last couple of days, and I have heard enough simple, simplistic, simple-minded speeches to last me a lifetime.

I called a friend of mine today who is about fifty-five, a marvelous woman, who is sort of a barometer for me of how the people of Arkansas think. I said, "What did you think of the Republican convention? Did you watch it?" She said, "I watched every minute of it." I said, "Well, what do you think? Have we got a chance?" She said, "You know, Mr. Reagan gives a wonderful speech. I just went to school in Arkansas and took basic math, but for the life of me I can't figure out how we are going to cut taxes, raise defense spending, and balance the budget."

I know a lot of people are worried about the Reagan-Bush ticket, but let me just remind you about one thing and you think about it every day. In Ronald Reagan's first movie, Gabby Hayes got the girl.

Well, Gabby Hayes got the girl then but, you know it, and let's face it: the people of this country are disillusioned with us today. Many of us, from our president on down, have tried very hard. Sometimes I think of President Carter with great sympathy and try to muster a little humor when he tries so hard to meet some of our difficulties and things don't seem to work out right, and I am reminded of one of my favorite jokes. I find myself in this position sometimes, too, and I think Jimmy Carter and Bill Clinton and some of the rest of us in politics are like the hero in the story of the conductor on the train who had worked for twenty years and excelled at his job and had a lapel full of pins and commendations, had never been criticized, and never failed to do his job well. One day he was on his train and he saw a lady get on. He just saw the back of her head. She seemed to be the only person in the passenger car that he was passing through, and so he didn't pay much attention to her. A few minutes later a man got on and sat down across from the lady, discarding all the empty seats in the car. He noticed that she was rocking her little baby. I am very sensitive about that since I have a little baby now. He looked at this lady with her child, and he said, "Lady, I hate to tell you this, but that is the ugliest kid I ever laid my eyes on." She was startled. She didn't know what to say. He said, "Really, I don't mean to be rude, but I am just about to get sick looking at that kid of yours, it is so ugly." And like any self-respecting parent she was infuriated. She rang the bell for our conductor friend who was trying hard to please. He came and said, "Lady, what can I do for you?" She said, "I don't know what kind of train you fellows are running here, but I want you to know that this bum got on this car and totally unsolicited sat down across from me with all these vacant seats here and proceeded to hand me the worst insult of my life, and if you don't do something about it I am going to sue you and sue the railroad company and do everything I can to ruin your reputation with everybody I know." Our conductor friend was mortified and embarrassed, and he said, "Lady, I promise you I am going to make it right for you. I am going to throw this guy off the train right now. I am going to give you your ticket money back. I am going to let you spend the night in the pullman car for free. I am going to give you a free steak dinner in the dining car, and before I do one other thing, I am going to go right this second and get a banana for that baboon of yours." Sometimes, no matter how hard you try, it doesn't come out very well.

To be serious, and to return to the point, the people of this country are wondering whether they should trust the leadership of the Democratic Party. The Democrats are divided about what that leadership should be. Beyond the reach of party politics we see in the last eight to twelve months reflected in the public opinion polls an astonishing trend never before noted by our pollsters: a profound and deeply entrenched alienation. For the last year and for the first time ever, a solid majority of the people of this country when asked say that the present is worse than the immediate past was and that they expect the future to be worse than the present. Always before, the American people have fundamentally been optimistic, believing the present to be better than the past and believing in the future. This is a fact of profound political significance not only for the Democrats but for the future welfare of the American nation.

The reasons are not hard to find. In my state, unemployment is 8 percent. Inflation is there just as it is everywhere else, and more than half the people are literally having a hard time making ends meet. Our patriotic and proud citizens are frustrated by Iran and Afghanistan, by the hold on our economy that OPEC has, by our inability in many places in the world to deal with the Russians, and by our inability to compete with the Germans, the Japanese, and others at home.

The difficulties we face today are particularly painful for us, the diehard Democrats, who can remember what happened in the Great Depression and how the Democratic Party came to the aid of the country and constructed a system which guaranteed throughout the forties, the fifties, and the sixties low unemployment, low inflation, and ever-increasing productivity. Along the way, our party dealt with the racial crisis in our nation, kept the southern and northern factions of its party throughout united, and overcame its own mistakes in Vietnam. Today, we see clearly what we should have seen before, perhaps, and that is at least for a decade the system we constructed in the Great Depression has been breaking down. We have had inflation that is too high, unemployment that is too high, and declining productivity. Even those of us who live in the Sunbelt who do not have oil and gas to make us rich overnight are caught in the undertow of national economic forces. More important than all these present economic difficulties, I believe that the majority of the people in this country are alienated today because they feel powerless to do anything about it, because they do not see where we are going, and they cannot spot the proverbial light at the end of the tunnel.

I also believe that we do not need to be as alienated or as pessimistic as we are. I believe that this country today is in a time of profound transition under fundamental stress in economic and environmental areas among others. And I believe that our challenge today as Democrats is to recognize that this is the time of transition and respond to it.

The Republicans say that government is the problem, that if it weren't for government we wouldn't have any problems. You have heard them over and over and over again in the past several days. Give us less government. Cut the taxes. Balance the budget. But, by the way, increase defense spending at the same time, and if we'll just talk tough, everybody in the world will do what we want. I don't believe the American people believe that. I don't believe that the Republican platform represents a return to traditional values. In my traditional values there is a place for the feelings of Thomas Jefferson and the other founding fathers who said that all of us had an obligation to respect everybody else's values, and what they believe, and how they wanted to live, and I don't find that in that platform.

I don't believe the American people think that that is a particularly attractive alternative. The question is not are the people turning to the Republicans. The question is, are they going to turn against us or are we going to do what we did in the Great Depression. Are we going to meet this profound transition, these great challenges, by finding solutions to give expression to the values that the Democratic Party has stood on since the time of Thomas Jefferson?

We should not try to escape the blame for all that has gone wrong with our country. We should not try to promise complete solutions. All we have to do is to show the country that we know what the real questions are and that we know what direction we need to take and that we are prepared to talk sense about the specific, concrete, and continuing dilemmas the people of this country face and I believe they will stay with us.

The first thing that I think we need to do is to correct the attitude of our people. Most of us who are in this hall tonight became adults in the 1940s, the 1950s, or the 1960s. Most of us were conditioned to believe in the myth that we and our party helped to foster: that the American system broke down in the depression, we fixed it up in the New Deal and World War II, and it would run like a top from then on. We will never be able to do that. Tonight we need the help of those of you who are in this audience whose memories can reach back beyond to the days of the Great Depression, who know that times have been much worse in this country than they are today, and that the people met the challenges of those times by sticking together and working on their problems in a way that was good for the majority of the people. We need to bring that spirit again today. We do not have a single problem in this country today that we don't have the human and material resources to deal with. We do have a lousy attitude for dealing with our plight. And part of it is, I am convinced, our own disappointment because we really believed that we should always be prosperous. We are being challenged and we are going to have to change. But those of you who lived through the depression can help us to put our heads on straight and open our minds and our hearts.

The second thing we need in this country today that at least the Democrats are moving toward, which is more than the other party can say, is a realistic energy policy. Every economist of both political parties or outside the political parties says that half the inflation rate today is due to the cost of oil and the rapid increase in energy prices, and I am convinced that until we become more and more and more serious about energy conservation and the development of alternative energy sources we will not see the end of the dilemmas we are presently confronting. I am an unabashed advocate of the so-called "soft-path," not to the exclusion of traditional energy sources but simply in recognition of the fact that we are still wasting untold opportunities to conserve. We are still squandering opportunities to use alternative sources. And while the Department of Energy's budget this year only calls for expending about 14 percent of its total on energy conservation and new energy sources, believe me, that is a whole lot better than the Republicans would recommend if they were in power.

In my state, we were the biggest users of gasoline per registered vehicle in America, because people love to live in the country and work in the city. This year, for the last three-month period, our gasoline consumption is down 9.6 percent. We have 1 percent of the nation's population in Arkansas, but we produce 5 percent of the total energy which is produced by the burning of solid waste, and we have projects in motion right now that will more than triple our output when they are completed. The energy department tells me that in 1978 we had next to the worst energy conservation record in America and today we are the ninth best. And I say that only to point out that we have made a beginning: a halting, pitifully limited beginning, but a beginning nonetheless. And, if the Democrats will seize the issue and press it through and talk sense to the people about it, it is an issue on which we can win.

The third element of our efforts to reconstruct the Democratic coalition and meet the challenges of the eighties is a sensible environmental policy. Whatever you may think about the inadequacies of our present environmental policy, listen to the rhetoric of the opposition about the alternatives. It's government regulation; it's government interference; it's breaking down the economy. That is not true. And if we don't continue to fight to protect the water and the air and the land, to deal with the problems of hazardous chemicals, to meet all the environmental challenges of modern times, we will all live to regret it, and our children and grandchildren won't have a country that is nearly as worthy to live in as ours. That's an important issue in this race.

In the last five years, the Japanese, who for years basically adopted the principles that the opposition party is running on in environmental areas, to the extent that they got rich in a hurry but you couldn't breathe in Tokyo and it was unsafe to live in many parts of the country, have spent more money per capita for anti-pollution equipment than we have, and they have still out-performed us economically. So, it can be done, and we do not have to sacrifice the health of our economy to protect our precious heritage. We must not.

The fourth element of our politics should be a clear definition of what the role of the federal government is going to be to meet the challenges of 1980. My friends, I honestly believe the issue is not less government and the issue is not more government. The issue is what kind of government we are going to have. You look at the countries that out-performed us economically in the 1970s. Look at Germany, look at Japan. Do they have weaker governments than we do? No. Do they have lower taxes than we do? No, they do not. In Germany the effective tax rates are higher, and they have a national health system, and they still produce a vital economy. Why? Because the role of government is defined in such a way and is related to the private sector, both business and labor, in a way that promotes the growth and health of the economy. That is what we have to do more of in this country. Government needs to have policies to revitalize our basic industries: automobiles, steel, and other industries that have lagged in productivity. We need to have a monetary policy which recognizes that we can't continuously inflate the money supply, but it should be implemented gradually and not overnight in a way that bankrupts small businessmen or farmers or other people who are vulnerable to high interest rates if they are imposed immediately.

We need to recognize that government policies, whether they are under Democrats or Republicans, are going to affect the pattern of our lives. No government policy has so dramatically affected the pattern of life in America as that which created the interstate highway system under the Republican president Dwight Eisenhower. So it is difficult to conceive that in this year, in 1980, a major party can take to the American people a platform which says that government is the whole problem and that we could have less government and everything will be all right. From the party that had more to do with the existing pattern of living in this country perhaps even than we did, that is naive indeed. That is not to say there is not waste in government and that we should not eliminate it. That is not to say that there are not bad programs that don't need to be continued, but let's look at the world the way it is. Let's look at all the other countries that we must compete with. Let's look at the nations that have gone through stages of maturation that we are about to go through and recognize that the issue is what kind of government we are going to have and not whether we are going to have one.

The fifth thing we need to be concerned about is the role in our society of business and the role of labor, their responsibility for productivity in their relationships with their government. No element of our country is blameless. But the Republican platform just says that if government will get out of the way and if we could just break all the unions in the country, the economy would flower. This obviously is not an answer and is not anywhere found in the industrialized world in the lives of working people or business people or government employees. We need to worry about how we can expand the economy without destroying the environment, but we cannot do it. We cannot do it by blaming the government and the working people and by letting those who make the decisions about investments and management in this country do what they want and accept no responsibility for our present problem.

The greatest Republican president who ever lived, Lincoln, tried to tell the Republicans something that I wish they would remember today, which is that we cannot build up one element of our society by tearing down another, and that is what our opposition is attempting to do today, and that is what we must not let happen. Let me just give you one example: in my state the Reynolds Metals Company has six factories. They are all unionized. They just opened a factory which makes rolled aluminum. This is an esoteric subject, perhaps, for a keynote speech but one of fundamental importance to our future economy. The aluminum industry is one of the most energy intensive industries in America and because the company management was willing to make a massive investment in improved technology, rolled aluminum is now being manufactured in the State of Arkansas at an energy savings of an astonishing 35 percent, and you will not find the technology anywhere else in the world except in one plant in France. Why did it happen? Because management made a decision for the future and was willing to sacrifice present benefits and next-quarter profits for the future welfare of the shareholders, the workers of Reynolds Metals, and the people of this country, and we need more of that, and we can only do it if we all work together.

Finally, I believe the Democratic Party must stand for policies which will fulfill the hunger of the American people to have more control over their lives on a daily basis. When my wife and I had our baby recently, we went through a Lamaze class. We had two truck drivers, somebody that worked for a railroad, the manager of our capital city zoo, a doctor, a hospital administrator, and the governor. Why? Because all of us wanted to have some control over the most fundamental happening in our lives. In every city in this country, including cities in my state, there have been remarkably successful experiments in the last few years in reducing the crime rate. There is only one common element in all of them: community control and responsibility for preventing crime, neighborhood watches, walks, working together.

We see today all over the country a hunger to make communities more beautiful, to rid them of litter. The people of Maine recently were asked to vote on repealing their "burdensome" bottle deposit bill. Do you remember how they voted? Eighty-four percent to keep it. Eighty-four percent. Why? Why did they do that? Whatever you may think about the merits of the bill, why did they do that? Because they felt they had some control in making their state a cleaner and lovelier place more consistent with their values. The whole energy movement today in renewable resources and conservation is designed in part to save people money and in part to give them more control over their lives. We recently had an alcohol fuels fair in my state where over a thousand farmers came to learn to make alcohol for themselves, and I know that some of them were so poor they actually had to borrow the money to get there, longing to exert some control over their lives in an area of importance to them.

This is not a prescription for solving all the problems of the country. What I have said leaves wide open areas for debate, for conservative and liberal positions within each of these areas. But this is a course that will enable the Democratic Party to meet the challenges of this time as we did in the depression and for thirty years thereafter. A test of leadership for our party today is whether we can show the people not immediate results, not the end of inflation, while we are still struggling and strangling in the grip of OPEC, but a course which will lead us to economic security and an improved quality of life.

I would ask you to remember tonight one final thing. Through all of our difficulties there are many people who believe that this is a good and great country. I have been personally acquainted, as you might imagine, in recent days with the difficulties which are associated with the dramatic influx of Cuban refugees. But let me just ask you this, whatever you think about that problem, isn't it interesting to you that after we have criticized ourselves in the open for so many years and after our nation has been reviled around the world for all of our shortcomings for so long that one hundred thousand people are breaking their necks and risking their lives to get to this shore? Isn't that interesting?

Many years ago, when I was in high school, a great president of the United States that Connecticut helped to send to the White House, John Kennedy, went to the Berlin Wall, another symbol of oppression, and looked out at teeming tens of thousands of people, and he said something that I would like for you to remember tonight. He said, "Freedom has many difficulties, our Democracy is far from perfect, but we never had to put up a wall to keep our people in." Pray God we never will. And we never will, if today, in our time, we can tear the walls inside our minds and hearts down and confront the 1980s as they are and offer the American people not a panacea, not overpromising, not immediate solutions, but a way out of the difficult times with discipline and courage and a devotion to the interests of all the people of our great country.

Thank you very much.

We Must Speak to America

Democratic National Convention
New York City, New York
August 14, 1980

Clinton's first opportunity to speak to a nationwide audience came in 1980 as the spokesman for the Democratic Governors' Association on the final night of the Democratic National Convention in Madison Square Garden. The speech was scheduled in early prime time before President Carter's acceptance speech, but Clinton, speaking with wide gestures and an urgent tone, managed to capture the attention of the restless capacity crowd and drew several rounds of applause from the delegates.

The speech was not carried in full by the networks, cutting away to display their commentators and consultants speculating with each other about what Carter would have to say, but it was one of the most thoughtful of the entire convention. It is historically important because it shows that Clinton had already developed many of the political conclusions about the Democratic Party's challenges and many of the themes that he would stress in his own campaign twelve years later.

❖ ❖ ❖

Thank you very much. Ladies and gentlemen of the convention, I come tonight to speak in behalf of the thirty-one Democratic governors, in behalf of Jimmy Carter and Walter Mondale, in behalf of the ideals and compassion of Senator Kennedy and his family, and for the interests, concerns, and burdens of the people of my beloved state and this nation.

For four days we have worked hard to bring together again the core of our party, through the delegates in this hall and those they represent. But now we must go on to an even more important task. We must speak to the millions of Americans who are not here—who do not even watch us on television or listen to us, who do not care, who will not bother to vote, or, if they do, will probably not vote for us. For it is these people who will decide the election of 1980. And they cannot be moved by the symbols and accomplishments of the Democratic Party of the past.

For four days I have listened to speakers come to the rostrum and shout at the top of their lungs to be heard, trying to find some way to speak to the heart of America, to reach to the heart of our problems—trying, trying, to restore the faith of our people in this party. Tonight I received a telegram from a constituent of mine which I would like to read. It says this: "Energize us. Renew our flickering faith that leadership does care and that government can respond. America waits."

And I ask you tonight, my fellow Democrats, what is America waiting for? We have proved that our party is more sensitive than the Republicans to equality and justice—to the poor and the dispossessed. But now we must prove that we offer more in the way of creative and realistic solutions to our economic and energy and environmental problems and that we have a vision that can withstand the erosion of special-interest politics that is gripping our land.

Those in this country that are alienated from us tonight are asking some very gnawing questions. They want to know why they should participate in a system that does not work for them. They want to know why, if they do vote, they should return to office a president and a party that has presided over a time of high inflation, high unemployment, and lagging productivity. They want to know what is at the root of our misery, and what we as Democrats are going to do about it. They wonder if there is anyone in this whole land with a clear vision of where we are going.

These questions must be answered. *Jimmy Carter and this administration cannot win this election simply by putting together the old elements of the Democratic coalition and repudiating Ronald Reagan. It is not enough.*

But there are answers to these questions. There are answers which will ring true to millions and millions of Democrats and independents and thoughtful Republicans. They can be found in the words and work of a new generation of Democratic leaders in Congress and state houses and city halls across this land. And yes, they can be found in the policies of President Jimmy Carter.

This is a painful time of transition of our nation. The economic arrangements, the cheap energy, the abundant natural resources, the lack of foreign competition on which our stability and prosperity depended for years are gone, and they are gone forever. Facing this reality is particularly painful to almost every adult in this hall. For most of us came of age in the forties, fifties, sixties, and seventies. We were brought up to believe, uncritically, without thinking about it, that our system broke down in the Great Depression, was reconstructed by Franklin Roosevelt through the New Deal and World War II, and would never break again. And that all we had to do was to try to reach out and extend the benefits of America to those who had been dispossessed: minorities and women, the elderly, the handicapped, and children in need.

But the hard truth is that for ten long years through Democratic and Republican administrations alike, this economic system has been breaking down. We have seen high inflation, high unemployment, large government deficits, the loss of our competitive edge. In response to these developments, a dangerous and growing number of people are simply opting out of our system. Another dangerous and growing number are opting for special-interest and single-interest group politics, which threatens to take every last drop of blood out of our political system.

Those of you who are here who are older, who can remember back to the Great Depression and before, can teach us a few lessons which we would do well to heed tonight. First of all, we should remember that things have been much worse than they are. Second, we must remember that we have no right to expect that this or any system will be permanently prosperous, free of all crises. For thirty years, the system worked as we set it up, and that is a long time to avoid the kind of problems we must now face today. Finally, we must realize that it does not matter whether Jimmy Carter or some perfect miracle worker, and there is none, is president: We did not get into these difficulties overnight, and we will not emerge from them immediately. It is not in the cards.

It seems that everyone in this convention and half the people at the Republican convention quoted Franklin Roosevelt. Everyone can quote him, but his words out of context mean little. And they do very little to illuminate what was really significant about his leadership. When Franklin Roosevelt ran for reelection in 1936, the election to which I hope this one will prove analogous, he was returned to office, but not because the depression was over, not because people were not unemployed, not because all the problems in the country had been solved. Far from it. We were still in the teeth of the depression. Why was he returned to office? Because people knew what sort of vision he had for America. They knew what action he was taking to transform the country. And they were willing, most important, to accept hardship for the present, because they believed they were part of a process that would lead them to a better tomorrow.

Jimmy Carter and our Democratic Party face that sort of challenge today.

If we meet it, we can win this election, in spite of the appeal of Ronald Reagan, in spite of the appeal of John Anderson, and most importantly, in spite of the fact that millions of Americans are turned off and not listening at all to us.

But let us not underestimate Ronald Reagan. His voice is clear, consistent, and committed. His appeal is strong. Listen to it. He says first of all, all of our problems can be solved without any sacrifice on your part, because you are not any part of the problem. All of our problems are caused by the federal government and by the Democrats which have run it, and we can have our solutions in hand if only we will cut taxes, increase defense spending, and thereby miraculously balance the budget, reduce inflation, reduce unemployment, and become so strong that everybody in the world will do exactly as we please. I do not believe the American people believe that. Ronald Reagan says energy conservation is more a joke than a serious response to our energy crisis and that the development of alternative and renewable energy sources is not worth the time, effort, and money. He says that environmental protection is often doing more harm than good in dragging down our economic system by lowering productivity. I do not believe the American people believe that. It is not that they believe everything Ronald Reagan says. It is simply that they do not know what our vision is and whether it will make any difference if our president and our party are returned to the White House.

John Anderson's message has great appeal to some. What is it? He offers relief from the words and wars of these two old parties that so many people think are irrelevant now. He is articulate and thoughtful. But be not deceived, a vote for Anderson is not a vote which reflects a real choice about the course for America in the 1980s, and in all probability it is a vote for Ronald Reagan.

But now comes the hard part. What do we say in response? What is our vision? What is our hope? What must we speak to the American people who do not listen tonight? First, we must say forthrightly that we are in a time of transition, a difficult and painful time, from which no one can escape the burden and in which no one can avoid a responsibility to play a part. Secondly, we must say we are committed to the economic revitalization of America, but it will require far, far more than a big tax cut for big business. It will require a redefinition of the relationship between the federal government and big business and labor. It will require a revitalization of our basic industrial structure. It will require us to admit we need to do more to increase risk taking and job creation in the small and new and growing businesses of our land. It will require us to work hard when it is difficult, to see that our agricultural sector continues to grow and export and save us in the international economic arena while we rebuild the rest of our economy.

It will, equally important, require us to recognize that our economic recovery and our very quality of life depends on having a sensible, safe, sane energy and environmental policy. Conservation matters, and it will work. Alternative sources of energy matter, and they can be developed. And we can develop our native sources of energy if only we are willing to pay the environmental price to do so. We must speak with a clear voice that we will not sacrifice the future of our nation by ruining the air, the water, the land because it seems expedient now and because we are having these troubles. And if we will speak with this voice, I believe we can be heard.

Finally, we must say something pretty strong to the millions and millions of middle-class and upper-middle-class people who are so alienated from this process, even though they have educations, even though they have jobs in this country, that they are not bothering to vote, and they are not bothering to consider these issues seriously. We must say to them, you have no right to do that. That is a violation of this heritage of yours. This country deserves your best effort, now, and this crisis of our generation can be the exhilarating accomplishment of your lives if you will give that effort instead of drop out and cop out.

I became a Democrat many years ago because of the values and the influence of my wonderful grandfather, who ran a country store in a black neighborhood in a small town in southwest Arkansas. But I remain a Democrat today because of my love and concern for the welfare of my six-month-old daughter. I know in my soul, whatever the faults of our party, this administration, and this president, and there are some, they still offer her a better hope for a safe and prosperous and good and decent world than the alternative, and I mean to do what I can to take that message to the American people.

Most of the people of this country know it's still the finest place in the world. Most people know in their hearts there must be some way out of our present dilemmas. It is for us here to come alive tonight to the needs of the people who aren't here, aren't looking, aren't listening, and go out of this hall determined to rekindle the spirit and vision of this party and our country, in a time of unprecedented but imminently solvable problems. If we do that, our cause is finished, and our course is run. We must do it—for your children and mine.

Thank you, and God bless you.

Hard Times and the Promise of Our Tomorrows

Second Inaugural Address
Little Rock, Arkansas
January 11, 1983

Narrowly defeated for reelection in 1980, Clinton regained the governorship in 1982, after winning a hard-fought primary and defeating Gov. Frank White with 55 percent of the vote in November. This speech was delivered to an audience of thirty-five hundred citizens, the largest inaugural crowd in memory, at noon on the east steps of the state capitol. Lasting twenty minutes and interrupted six times by applause, the inaugural address was less inspirational and much more focused on the specific problems facing the state than his first one, reflecting both his political experiences and the new tone of his administration as he promised to "give the people a government that solves problems and seizes opportunities."

❖ ❖ ❖

Today we are engaged in a new battle with an old and familiar enemy: hard times. Hard times dominate the long history of Arkansas. For generations our families have been forced to endure them and struggle to overcome them. The most moving story of my childhood was that of my grandfather coming home on Good Friday afternoon during the depression and crying on his knees to my mother because he could not afford a two-dollar Easter dress.

Today's hardship grows out of a national recession made worse by the national Republican economic policies, and out of problems especially burdensome to Arkansas which have given us pockets of real depression: our farmers have had three bad years in a row; too many of our workers are tied to automobiles and housing; other jobs have been lost to foreign competition and automation; we have not been competitive in the education and training of our people and in other areas; and the state's budget has been weakened, even in its ability to take care of the "truly needy" because of federal budget cuts, state revenue shortfalls, and deficit spending in the prison system.

Obviously, we must practice austerity. I have recommended the elimination of two government departments and one state agency and other substantial cuts. All offices can sustain some cuts, and I have recommended that we operate the governor's office budget below current spending.

But austerity is not enough.

We must give the people a government that solves problems and seizes opportunities; a government that will fight for the people's interest, not just respond to the special interest; most importantly, a government that will give our people a better chance to fight for themselves.

Our first priority must be to put the people back to work: by bringing new jobs; reopening closed plants; providing more investment capital for housing, agriculture, and business development; marketing more of our products; and training our people—some of them while on unemployment—to do the better jobs that are growing in numbers, as the jobs they have been doing move overseas or are absorbed by machines.

Over the long run, education is the key to our economic revival and our perennial quest for prosperity. We must dedicate more of our limited resources to paying teachers better; expanding educational opportunities in poor and small school districts; improving and diversifying vocational and high-technology programs; and, perhaps more important, strengthening *basic education.* Without competence in basic skills our people cannot move on to more advanced achievement.

In addition to our efforts in economic development and education, we must give our people some relief from spiraling electric rates brought on largely by excessive expenditures for power plant construction and general operations and from coming big increases in gas and telephone rates brought on by misguided federal policies.

Our citizens don't understand how the same state government that bragged about cutting highway taxes sixteen million dollars in 1981 approved utility rate increases of two hundred and twenty-seven million dollars in the same year. The utilities say they needed the money but so did teachers, state employees, businessmen, and farmers—but the state didn't mandate that kind of increase in income or profits for them, so they cut back and did without.

We need comprehensive utility reform: a law which requires the Public Service Commission to take into account the people's ability to pay larger increases and empowers the commission to defer or phase in our needed rate increases in hard economic times; stronger oversight of fuel charges and operations costs; strict review of demand charges and installation, repair, and deposit costs; and election of the PSC by the people. Nothing so clearly demonstrates what is wrong with the established order as the recent study by the Industrial Research and Extension Center which reviewed all utility rate-making systems and concluded that our present system of appointing the PSC is better government, even though the elected commissions have generally given proper, quicker decisions at less cost, with lower rates in the end. The people *do* have enough sense to elect our PSC, and a clear majority want the chance to do so. We should give it to them.

Finally, we have to do something about the prison system. Its budget is increasing dramatically because of a rapidly increasing population and longer sentences for repeat offenders. We must keep longer sentences for repeat offenders. However, we can reverse the trend of diverting more and more tax dollars from education and other needed services to prisons, but only if we make a determined effort to see that the thirty-eight hundred incarcerated men and women work more productively and pay more of their own way. This can be done with a comprehensive, diversified prison industry and agricultural program. The prison can be more self-supporting. In the short run, it will cost some money and take some time, but we must *begin now*.

Some of our needs do require more tax money than we have, but we *can* move on the basic problems facing us with the resources now available.

Many people say we can do nothing significant without large tax increases. I am not ready to concede that. If there is one thing my wife and I learned again in this campaign it is that there are hundreds of thousands of hard-working people who feel they are never represented by the established leaders in government. One man in Nashville asked me only to spend his dollars as if I lived like him on one hundred and fifty dollars a week take-home pay. Another, finishing construction on the Excelsior—a great monument to our possibilities—asked me to remember that, while we need more taxes, he was in his last day on the job and did not have another waiting.

It will not be easy to balance the complex and often competing forces at work in our state to forge a forward march, but we can do it.

Too often in the past, we have helped our old foe hard times to defeat us by working against ourselves—by fighting among ourselves, by thinking too little of ourselves and what we can achieve.

Admittedly, I have set an ambitious agenda for Arkansas in hard times. It has been criticized by those who say it is too full of promises. But politics is about the promises of today and tomorrow.

It is far better to fall short of a lofty goal than to stand by in self-satisfaction while good people are pained by present conditions.

On a very personal note, I must thank all the many thousands of people who fought to bring this administration to life with a faith that we could do what had never been done before and with a passion and dedication unequaled in our political history. They labored so that together we might lift our vision and move forward again. My family and I are humbly grateful for those that gave us this second chance.

Now the election is over, and we are one people again. I ask for your prayers and good wishes. I will work to give the people the kind of government that will face up to our problems. That is what Arkansas wants, needs, and deserves.

God bless you all.

Making All the Difference

Special Joint Session of the Arkansas General Assembly
Little Rock, Arkansas
October 4, 1983

During the summer, Hillary Clinton had headed a governor's task force on educational standards, holding public hearings across the state and developing a plan for educational reform, and in September Governor Clinton had addressed the people of Arkansas on statewide television from his desk in the governor's office, building further public support for his program of far-reaching educational reforms. Having called the legislature into a special session to deal only with education issues, he addressed a joint session of the 135 members of the House and Senate in the House of Representatives Chamber at 6:30 P.M., with his remarks again carried live on television.

The legislature listened with what one reporter described as "an attentive but somber mood," applauding only at the end of his thirty-minute speech when they gave him a standing ovation. Afterward, Clinton said, "I wanted them to listen. I tried not to slow down because I wanted them to hear each point I had to make. I thought they were exceedingly attentive, more than in any other speech I've given."

❖ ❖ ❖

In the life of our state, as in the life of a person, there are times of growth and decline, times of joy and sadness, times of triumph and tragedy, and times of ordinary getting along. Much of what life brings is a matter of circumstance beyond our control. Yet always our will makes some difference, and sometimes our will can make all the difference.

We are here tonight in such a time. All across America, people understand that the deep problems of our education system must be faced and overcome if we hope to restore economic growth and prosperity for our country. Here in Arkansas, the urgent national need has sparked a vigorous response, because we know we need to catch up and move ahead, and we see in the changing nature of the economy new opportunities long denied to Arkansans. Circumstances now open to us the best jobs—not because of cheap labor, low taxes, and weak environmental laws, but because of the productivity of our people, the quality of our environment and lifestyle, and the aggressive partnership we wish to establish for economic growth. Only one thing is missing: our determination to catch up in educational investment and to move to the front of the class in improving the quality of education.

Other states are moving, especially in the South. Even Mississippi, long dormant, has raised its standards and raised taxes—sales, severance, and income—to pay to implement them.

It is past time for us to catch up and move ahead. We can, but only if you and I act now. For too long, we have denied individual Arkansans a full, fair chance at self-development, and in so doing, we have denied our state its most valuable asset in the struggle for a better life for all.

Always before, we in public life have been able to make excuses for our inaction in education. We have convinced ourselves to take the easy way out. We have said education doesn't make much difference in promoting economic development, that people are against taxes and so we can't make the necessary investment, that we don't really know quite what to do, that maybe times will get better and the economy will grow and generate enough new tax revenues for us to do the job. Now we know these excuses don't hold water. And the people we represent know it, too.

Our people are sick of excuses. They want action. They want better education, and they are willing to pay for it. They are willing to do it because the higher standards are right for Arkansas, because we have to catch up and we can move ahead.

Two weeks ago I outlined my program of improvements for public schools, adult and vo-tech education, and higher education. Since then I have presented the program in greater detail to legislative committees and to almost all of you individually. Tonight I would like to review the program in brief and respond to some objections which have been raised against it.

The program has five basic components:

First, there is a new school formula, which has been developed pursuant to the Supreme Court's decision last May ordering us to equalize the spending between the districts which have less property wealth per child and those which have more.

Second, there are new school standards and other reforms for public education. These standards are the product of months of hard work by a committee of distinguished Arkansans, working without pay, chaired by my wife. If implemented they will put Arkansas among a handful of states with the most precise, comprehensive, demanding standards in the country. Some of the standards can be implemented now; others should be approved by the board of education in March for gradual implementation over the next three years. We can move now to provide for more years of school attendance, from six to sixteen years, with no more dropping out after eighth grade; for more time within the school day devoted to basic instruction; for a slightly longer school year for students and longer contract periods for teachers and administrators; for student testing for all students in the third, sixth, and eighth grades; and for uniform discipline standards. However, we should leave school districts more time to achieve the mandates of smaller classes in the early grades, more required courses for graduation, and more required course offerings for schools, because these will be costly and will require careful planning and the training or retraining of teachers in shortage areas.

In addition to the standards, I have proposed that we establish a special commission, like the Education Standards Committee, to review and make recommendations by January 1985 on the education, certification, and evaluation of teachers and administrators. Also, I propose to require an inventory testing of all presently certified teachers and administrators in basic learning skills and in the subject areas in which they are certified. My bill will require all certified personnel to take, during the 1984–85 school year, a test in basic skills such as the NTE Pre-professional Skills Test (PPST) and to take a test in their subject areas. Those who have taken and passed the NTE since 1980, when we first required it of college seniors who want to be teachers, will be exempt. Those who have not taken it will have until June 1987, the date all the standards become effective, or until their certifications expire, whichever is later, to pass the test.

Finally, I have proposed specific programs to improve our efforts in reading instruction; increase the effectiveness of our use of computers; expand opportunities for gifted and talented children; fund more adequately the handicapped education programs; recognize and reward outstanding students, teachers, and schools; and increase the involvement of parents in the schools.

Third, there is an Adult and Vocational Education Program, which is designed (a) to triple the number of adults being served in adult education, thus reducing adult illiteracy and making thousands of unemployed Arkansans more employable; (b) to expand vocational training opportunities for handicapped Arkansans; (c) to improve the quality and relevance of programs now being offered in the post-secondary vocational technical schools; (d) to provide schools the funding to start new programs or expand existing ones in areas where there are jobs available for those with the necessary skills; (e) to provide more modern equipment to both high schools and post-secondary vocational programs; and (f) to establish an industrial equipment pool, to provide expensive, high-technology equipment for all vo-tech schools, to use as needed in meeting training needs of new and expanding industries.

Fourth, there is a program for the institutions of higher education, which provides for more money to offset the relative budget losses of the last few years and to reduce pressure on the institutions to raise tuition, which has increased 72 percent in the past five years. The additional money must be spent in areas of greatest need or greatest opportunity, under budget plans which must be filed with the Department of Higher Education and made available to my office and the legislature before the money is spent. This will provide a measure of accountability which has been too uncommon in the past. Among other things, we must replace instructional equipment and buy new equipment to keep up with rapid changes brought on by the technological revolution; develop a more accurate maintenance schedule to preserve the hundreds of millions of dollars we have in capital investment; increase investment in libraries; raise faculty salaries to the regional average to stop the turnover rate, which is, for example, twice the national average at the University of Arkansas at Fayetteville; and fund the projects that are most critical to our economic development: the engineering school at UAF and the engineering technology facility at UALR.

Fifth, there is a tax package. To pay for these changes, I propose the largest increase in investment in education in our state's history: an increase in the state sales tax of one cent; an increase in the natural gas severance tax to 5 percent with a ten-cent per thousand cubic feet cap to protect gas consumers in western and northwestern Arkansas who use the bulk of the high-priced Arkansas gas; an increase in the corporate income tax from 6 to 7 percent for corporations with an income in excess of one hundred thousand dollars; and certain other minor changes in our sales tax laws.

Understandably, a program this broad in scope has been subject to some criticism and has drawn some opposition. I would like to review the objections to each element in the program.

(1) The formula. The proposed formula in its present form attempts to obey the Supreme Court order to equalize funding among the districts and their children. There are three controversial elements in it:

(a) The formula provides that districts which do not levy sixteen mills, about the state average, by 1987 will lose state aid in the amount of one-sixteenth for each mill the district is below sixteen mills.

There has been a legitimate concern as to whether the penalty will be constitutional or fair to the districts with Pillages below the state average, or more importantly, fair to the children in those districts. To allay that concern we are considering alternative penalties. I am, however, convinced, and I believe a majority of both houses of the legislature is convinced, that we should have some form of penalty while we might be flexible about the means.

(b) There is a concern that because the formula makes a strong effort to equalize spending per child as the Supreme Court ordered, twenty-nine districts will lose money even if we put another one hundred million dollars into the formula because their local wealth per child is so far above the state average. I do believe we must phase out state aid to these districts. However, I am prepared to delay the phase-out for one year and to reduce the percentage reduction below 25 percent in the first year of the phase-out. In that way, all but a small handful of these districts will be back in the formula by the third year because of ordinary revenue growth. We can follow the mandate of the court order without hurting some of our good schools and their programs.

(c) Perhaps the most emotional of all the formula issues has been the question of how to fund the small school districts. Today if a school district has fewer than three hundred and sixty students, it receives money as if it had more students than it does. Historically this "weighting" has been justified on the theory that it costs more per child to educate children in a very small district. That's true, but those who oppose small-school weighting argue that districts get the subsidy solely because of size, regardless of whether they are located in a remote area of our state or right next door to a larger district, and that it is not right for the state's taxpayers to pay extra for a district's choice to remain small. This argument has particular force now, when many of our school districts which have more than three hundred and sixty students but are still small and are faced with the obligation of improving education and meeting the higher school standards without the extra subsidy from the state.

The proposed formula phases out the small-school weighting over three years. Since the one hundred and ten weighted districts are really like the twenty-nine districts with more property resources per child in as much as both categories of districts are receiving aid for students that aren't really there, I would be prepared to treat both categories of schools identically. That will provide more solid revenue relief for the smallest districts who are going to try to meet the standards without compromising the principle that we must treat both categories equally and follow the mandate of the court order to equalize funding.

There has been a lot of discussion in the last few days about implementing the school formula and when it should begin. I must say that I have been somewhat surprised by the amount of opposition which has surfaced to implementing the formula in January and the support that is there for waiting until June.

I am still recommending that we adopt the formula that was voted out of the joint interim committee and begin implementing it in January, because that is consistent with the Supreme Court order of last May which upheld a lower court decision in 1981 ordering us to equalize and because no districts would lose money if we give the poorest ones six months of extra help to comply with the formula and court order.

I understand the opposition to the starting date. I want to make my position clear. I believe that all the money, the whole fifty million dollars, must be spent to improve public education in a manner that is consistent with the order which is largely responsible for bringing us here. If we can reach agreement on an alternative which provides the funds to the public schools and is consistent with the Supreme Court order, I will consider it. But I do not believe that we should spend this money in a way that disregards the purpose of raising the tax money in the first place and the mandate of the court order to equalize.

(2) The standards and other reforms. The main objection to the standards has been that they are too tough, too expensive, and likely to force consolidation.

Well, the standards are tough. But we have to get tough, and we have to spend money to pay for them. While the education problems cannot be solved by money alone, I know that no member of this legislature believes they cannot be solved without money.

Doubtless some districts will not be able to meet the standards and will be forced to consolidate in 1987. We have twice as many districts as any other southern state, and I would expect that some consolidation would flow from these standards. I have offered legislation that will permit districts who decide before 1987 that they cannot meet the standards to consolidate their high schools only and keep their grade schools and junior high schools if they meet the standards.

There has been some concern about the mandatory kindergarten standard. Many parents say they can prepare their children for first grade better at home. On the other hand, the evidence is overwhelming that most children, especially those from disadvantaged families, derive great benefits from kindergarten. Therefore, I ask you to remove the prohibition on mandatory kindergarten but to allow the state board of education to mandate it after some provisions have been made for those families who wish to and are able to prepare their children for first grade at home.

The most controversial of the education reforms is the proposal to test existing teachers and administrators. Frankly, no other state in America does it. I have received expressions of violent opposition to the testing idea on the grounds that a test will not identify whether or not a person is a good teacher; that the particular testing method I recommend is unfair and inadequate; and that it is an insult to teachers and administrators who have been working for years to ask them to take the test.

I agree that any test is no measure of whether a person would be a good teacher. That is not the purpose of the test. The purpose of the test is to determine whether those taking it have that threshold of basic skills and knowledge in their course area sufficient to continue in the classroom without being required to make a further effort to upgrade their skills and increase their knowledge. I have also proposed a committee on teacher education, evaluation, and certification which will involve teachers in developing a system that will enable us to identify good teachers. And I have proposed that we adopt the standards committee recommendation that we experiment with performance-based pay so that we can identify and properly compensate good teachers.

With regard to the fairness of the test, I have found general agreement even among teachers who don't like the idea that the PPST exam is a fair measure of very basic skills. The NTE subject matter tests are given today to college seniors who want to become teachers and to those who seek recertification in other areas. The legislation I present contains alternative means of testing, but I find it unusual that a system we use today is deemed to be unfair.

To those who feel insulted by the test, I can only reply that I think it is a small price to pay in exchange for the biggest tax increase for education in Arkansas history and for the contribution the testing process would make in our efforts to restore the teaching profession to the position of public trust and esteem that it deserves. I believe it is the most important profession of all.

(3) The tax program. The objections to the tax program are that we can't afford more taxes; that the education problem is not a money problem; that we should raise taxes but in a different way; that we should raise more taxes; that we should put off a tax increase until after reappraisal, and until all the standards are required because the Supreme Court didn't really order us to spend more money in the poorer schools as I have repeatedly said.

To these I reply: Taxes are always a burden, but they can be an investment. In this case, with even Mississippi out-spending us in education and all states out-taxing us, we have no choice if we want to catch up and move ahead.

Many favor a tax increase but want the money to be raised in a different way. Some say the sales tax is regressive because it falls too heavily on the working class and the poor. Others say the corporate income tax at the upper level will deter economic growth in Arkansas. To the first group I reply that this education program will benefit the children and grandchildren of the working class and the poor more than any other people in the state. The adult and vocational programs will benefit the unemployed. The higher education programs will bring more jobs, including blue-collar jobs, to Arkansas. With the sales tax, all will pay for a program from which all will benefit.

The corporate income tax increase will apply only to corporations with incomes in excess of one hundred thousand dollars. The rate will be raised 1 percent, from 6 to 7 percent, the same rate which now applies to individual incomes over twenty-five thousand dollars. This will be the second-highest rate in the region, but must be considered in terms of all other business tax burdens and benefits. According to the recent Troutman study, business share of the total tax burden in Arkansas is the lowest of any of the states in our region. When we take into account the substantial federal tax cuts of the last three years, the federal deduction for state income-tax payments, and the fact that corporations will benefit greatly from a better educated and trained work force, this tax increase is both modest and appropriate.

Our gas severance tax is the lowest in America by far and simply should be raised.

I could never hope to satisfy everyone with the form of the tax package. It is human nature to want someone else's ox to be gored. Improving education is a program for all Arkansans, and all Arkansans should help to finance it.

There are those who say we should raise more money because we might need it to implement the standards. I say no one knows how much we will need but we will be making a great mistake to raise too much money and lose all incentive to share local resources, make appropriate local effort, and find other ways to do what needs to be done in the most efficient manner.

Perhaps the most curious and indefensible objections to the tax program are those that cluster under that awful word *WAIT*: Wait because the Supreme Court didn't really order us to spend more money in the poorer districts. Wait because the standards don't have to be in place until 1987. Wait because reappraisal might provide enough money. Wait because lightning might strike the economy and provide enough money.

The only way we could meet the Supreme Court order to equalize school funding without giving more money to the poorer districts is to take money from almost all our school districts and put it in the bank. That would equalize by making everyone as poor as the poorest. That is absurd. I think raising more money is the better way.

This concludes the summary of my program.

Now I ask that you embrace it, to make it your program, to make it our program. Many members of this body have labored for years to advance education—in committees, on the floor, in regional and national organizations. Many of you have contributed already to the program I have put before you and the people. Now is the time when you must act.

All the work that has been done by the Quality Education Committee which was chaired by my wife, Hillary, and by all others will be for nothing if you do nothing. I recognize your duty to scrutinize this program but I urge you to move with dispatch to do that duty.

As the National Commission on Excellence in Education said so well: "History is unkind to idlers." And history has been brutal to Arkansas. For too long we have been a land of lost opportunities.

For all of us this session is an opportunity to claim a place in Arkansas history. To do it will require a determination to reconcile opposing views, the willingness to put the state's interest above our own, and for some of us, the courage to risk our political careers to do what is right.

Justice Oliver Wendell Holmes, who served on the United States Supreme Court with vigor and distinction until the age of ninety-three, said: "I think that, as life is action and passion, it is required of a man that he should share the passion and action of his time at peril of being judged not to have lived."

For you and for me the action and passion of this time demands involvement in the fight for better education. This is a magic moment for us and for Arkansas. It is worth whatever the effort and the risk to get the job done.

We are at the crossroads. We are going to move ahead or fall behind. I close with the words of Robert Frost, and ask you to keep them in mind as you cast each vote in this session. I close with the theme with which I began.

> Two roads diverged in a wood, and I—
> I took the one less traveled by
> And that made all the difference.

I ask you to join with me in making the difference for our beloved state. Thank you, and God bless you all.

Campaign Stump Speech

Benton County Farm Bureau Political Forum
Bentonville, Arkansas
June 16, 1984

Governor Clinton received a standing ovation from the crowd of three hundred rural voters attending the Saturday afternoon barbeque and political forum in Benton County, a Republican stronghold in northwest Arkansas. The Republican nominee for governor, Woody Freeman, had spoken earlier in the day and had already left the area for another event. Both candidates addressed the same audience from a raised podium in the south end of a large metal building at the fair grounds.

Speaking without notes and in a style that one local reporter described as "reminiscent of an old-time Southern preacher," Clinton delivered his fourth speech of the day, unusual for that point in the general-election campaign but not with regard to the candidate's activity and energy on the hustings. The text is included in this collection not because of its stylistic qualities or policy insights but because it represents Clinton running as an incumbent and addressing his Arkansas constituents at a nonpartisan campaign event. Clinton won reelection in November with 64 percent of the vote.

❖ ❖ ❖

Thank you very much. Thank you, thank you.

Thank you very much, ladies and gentlemen of the Farm Bureau.

First of all, let me express my appreciation to all of you for giving us this opportunity to come here, and let me say I'm very glad to be here today. This is my fourth stop; I've been in southeast Arkansas and Little Rock and northeast Arkansas and now here today. And it's good to see that a lot of people still care enough about their state to come out and be part of an experience like this.

Can I take my coat off? Thank you. I'm the hottest person here, so I'll do that.

It's early in the campaign, and I don't know if I can give a powerful speech, but I'd like to give a straightforward talk to the people of Benton County. I recognize that historically a majority of the people in this county have voted Republican in state and federal races, and I am here to ask all of you to consider voting for me for governor without regard to what your party is, for several reasons.

First of all, I think I've been responsive to the people of this county. This is the ninth trip I have made to Benton County since I've been governor, and I'd be very surprised if any previous governor, regardless of party, has come to Benton County nine times in a year and a half.

Secondly, I have made a number of appointments and funded a lot of community projects here and have tried to be fair and responsive to this county without regard to partisan considerations, and I think most of your Republican *and* your Democratic representatives will tell you that that is the case. I think that the farmers of this state support my reelection. The Farm Bureau representatives say that when I was governor last year, during the regular session of the legislature, we were in serious danger of having dramatic cutbacks in agricultural research and extension activities, and together with the Farm Bureau we came up with legislation to save the services that are very important to people in rural Arkansas all over this state. And I want to commend the Farm Bureau for their support, and I think they would tell you that I give agriculture my support. I'm the first governor in the history of the state ever to hire a practicing farmer to come off the farm and work in my office as an agricultural liaison. And he's worked—the man from Arkansas County—has worked long and effectively, I think, for the farmers of our state to try to do what we could to help the farmers.

Third, I am a member of the National Governors' Association Agriculture Committee, and it's been very, very active in trying to help develop a bipartisan farm policy on behalf of the farm state governors, to try to do what we can to influence considerations not only in the White House, but also in the Congress for the benefit of the farmers throughout our country, and I think we're making some progress on that. My message to you is very simple and very direct. I've been in office a year and a half—not a very long time. Arkansas is going in the right direction. We need continuity. We need to continue what we're doing. Now is not the time to make a change.

Let me just mention two important general areas. First, in the area of the economy and jobs, we have the most vigorous program our state has ever had recruiting new industry, and trying to help retain the industries we have, and trying to train people for the jobs that we have today and can bring into our state tomorrow. Let me just cite some industries that I've worked with in this county. Ask Lee Keller, down at the Sibley Company in Rogers; ask the people at McKee-Bacon; ask the people at Pelfreez. Ask them if they've been satisfied with their relationship with the current administration, whether we have worked with them to help them expand jobs and move the economy of the state forward and the economy of northwest Arkansas forward. I think they will tell you that they are satisfied.

Let me just give you some interesting statistics. Last year, in my first year as governor, we had twice as many new jobs committed to our state as we did in the year before I took office. The Department of Labor—the National Department of Labor—just came out with statistics on the economy going from March of 1983 to March of 1984. There are two absolutely astonishing statistics in that whole mass of figures. Your state, Arkansas, in the last year was in the top five states in America in the percentage growth of new jobs, from last year to this. Your state—this to me is even more amazing—*your state* was in the top five states in America in the percentage growth of per-capita income, along with the high-technology states, Massachusetts, Connecticut, New Hampshire. And the business leaders that work with me day in and day out, I think, will tell you that my administration is good for business in Arkansas. We are aggressive, we are moving forward, we are making progress, and now is not the time to make a change.

The second thing I want to say is that I believe that you should retain my administration because of the progress we have made, and are making, and will make in education. Over the long run, no issue will so affect the future of the state of Arkansas as the issue of education and the question of whether we have the will and the ability and determination to give our state a genuinely competitive system of education for our people. If we can't compete in the educational training of our people from kindergarten to the adult education program, we can never hope to have an economy which is strong and prosperous, where unemployment is low—not just here in northwest Arkansas, but along the Mississippi Delta and eastern Arkansas—and where people can look forward to growing up in Arkansas and not having to leave to find a decent job.

We have made real progress. The record is clear on this, and I'd like to just run down the statistics. We've made more progress in education in the last year and a half than we have in the previous generation, and my distinguished Republican opponent—and I wish he were still here—has taken issue with me in every significant area. In the area of the sales tax increase, he says, "Well, maybe we shouldn't have raised the sales tax and I supported it, but Bill Clinton shouldn't have done it because he said he wouldn't when he ran."

Getting on both sides of the issue. Let me tell you what I said when I ran. I said I'd do everything I could to avoid a tax increase. Then the Supreme Court threw out our system of financing the schools, and we had two choices—raise the sales tax or take money away from one hundred and fifty school districts in this state, some of our best school districts. And I refused—and we were already dead last in spending per child, dead last in teacher salaries—to cut the budgets of one hundred and fifty school districts, including three school districts in this county. It would have been wrong.

So you can't have it both ways. My Republican opponent voted *twice* as a member of the board of higher education, twice, to ask me to *raise* the sales tax. And now he says I shouldn't have done it. The school standards are important. To have them enforced is important. My opponent says he's for the standards, but he doesn't think they should be enforced against the districts that can't meet them. I'm for enforcement. We've done everything we could to help districts avoid consolidation—given them three years to meet the standards, given them more money, given them the opportunity to go into educational quality, but in the end the child growing up in the smallest town in rural Arkansas needs the same national, competitive system of educational opportunity as the child in the biggest city in the richest house. And I'm going to give it to them if I stay in office.

And finally, let me say that even though it is very controversial, I believe there is objective evidence which supports my position on the controversial teacher testing law, and I am not going to change it. I am not going to change it. My opponent is committed to changing it; you can ask any legislator here, including the Republican legislators. If I am defeated, the first thing the legislature will do is repeal that law anyway. But his position is we ought to give it, and then turn the test over to the school board, and if they want to do something with it, it's fine, and if they don't, that's fine. If the school boards of this state and the administrators of this state had been able to do the job effectively, we wouldn't need to give the test in the first place. So I'm going to stick with it; I'm going to hang tough.

And I'm going to say this in closing. When I spoke at a university commencement not very long ago, a lady who had been teaching in Rogers stopped as she was going across the podium to get her degree and came up to me, and she said, "I just want you to know that not all of us are against you on this; I think you're right. Bear down and go on." That's what I intend to do, and I hope you'll give me another term to do it.

Thank you very much.

Remembering Truman: Be Bold in Fighting for America's Future

Democratic National Convention
San Francisco, California
July 16, 1984

The big speeches of this night belonged to New York governor Mario Cuomo and former president Jimmy Carter, but for most Arkansas delegates the main event of the night belonged to their own governor. Although Clinton had waited until June to endorse Walter Mondale, his prime-time television convention speech was seen as a vote of confidence by the Mondale campaign, confidence in Clinton's future political prospects.

Clinton's early prime-time remarks followed a biographical film of Pres. Harry S. Truman to celebrate the centennial of his birth and to remind delegates of the greatest Democratic upset victory of modern times. While his tough words calling for the party to forget its nostalgic past and look to the future may not have captured the attention or remained in the memory of the five thousand convention delegates in the Moscone Center, it was a hit with the Arkansas delegation. Harold Jinks told one reporter, "Oh, I think it was a hell of a speech. Bill usually just stands up and talks to us when we're down home, but this time he made a national speech. It was a wonderful speech."

❖ ❖ ❖

Harry Truman. The very mention of his name evokes feelings of pride and nostalgia, especially among Democrats. It is so easy to turn away from our present problems and think of him.

We live in a time which rewards glamour and charisma. He thought it was more important to be a good citizen, and my people in Arkansas thought of him as one of them, a friend.

We live in a time when politicians often hedge their bets in language that leaves their options open. He spoke plainly and he meant what he said.

We live in a time when politicians mouth words written by others, that reflect the ideas and learning of others. Harry Truman spoke for himself, thought for himself, and prepared himself for his work through a lifetime of reading and study.

We live in a time when politicians too often fear decisions, especially if they break new ground, alienate entrenched groups, or carry the possibility of error. Harry Truman could make a decision.

We live in a time when millions of Americans believe that the Democratic Party's greatest days are behind it, that we are no longer the party of progressive change. Harry Truman fought for change, for new ideas, for the future. He began the Democratic Party's historic commitment to civil rights and brought the United States into peacetime cooperation with other nations.

Ah, Harry Truman. A great president. A great statesman. If only he were here today.

If he were here today, he'd give a speech that would take our hides off.

He'd speak from the heart, not the teleprompter.

He'd say again that a "statesman is a dead politician."

He'd remind us that in 1948 he was further behind and the Democrats were more divided than is the case today, and he'd tell us to scrap the nostalgia and quit whining about our internal problems and get on with the business of taking our message to the country.

He'd remind us that 1948, like 1984, was a time of change, when new realities required new ideas and a willingness to stand up to interest groups both within and outside our party when the public interest demands it.

He'd tell us that you can't please everybody in tough times and you shouldn't try.

He'd tell us that you can't win an election when you're out of office by just complaining about what the other guy has done. If you want the buck to stop here, you have to say what you'll do with it when you get it.

Harry Truman would be mad tonight because the Democratic Party, to which Americans have turned when they needed constructive change, is now seen by millions of Americans who have no memory of Harry Truman as the party of the past. Even when they agree with us, they see us as trying to preserve the gains of the past—in social security, environmental protection, and civil rights.

Harry Truman would tell us to forget about 1948 and stand for what America needs in 1984. That's the way to attract the millions of Americans who feel locked out and won't vote because they think we're irrelevant. That's the way to attract millions more, mostly young and well educated, who intend to vote against us because they think we have no program for the future.

Harry Truman would say:

America has a productivity problem. What are we going to do about it?

America is getting its brains beaten out in international economic competition. What are we going to do about it?

America has millions of people who want to work but whose jobs have been lost because of competition from low wages abroad or the necessity to automate at home. What are we going to do about it?

America is mortgaging its future with high deficits, driving interest rates too high, making our dollar too expensive and our trade deficit enormous. What are we going to do about it?

America is losing its family farms. What are we going to do about it?

America is drowning in a sea of illegal drugs. What are we going to do about it?

America is pricing itself out of affordable health care. What are we going to do about it?

America needs an invigorated education system based on high standards and real accountability, as well as more money. What are we going to do about it?

America needs both a strong defense and a strong effort to aggressively reduce the chances of nuclear war. What are we going to do about it?

If Truman were here, that would be his challenge to us. I believe our party and its leaders are capable of meeting that challenge. They have the values, the experience, and the ability to do it. America will be watching to see whether we have the will to do it.

Harry Truman would be very proud tonight that his party and Walter Mondale are leading the way in giving a great woman the opportunity to run for vice-president.

But he would want us to be equally bold in fighting for America's future.

The real way to honor Harry Truman is to wage a campaign that would make him as proud of us as we are of him.

Access to Opportunity

Third Inaugural Address
Little Rock, Arkansas
January 15, 1985

After winning the primary by 64 percent over three opponents and garnering 63 percent of the vote in the general election, Clinton became only the third person in the state's history to be sworn in for a third term as governor. Having achieved major reforms in the educational system during a special legislative session in 1983, Clinton declared that his third term would be dedicated to working on issues of economic development.

He again spoke at noon in an outdoor ceremony from the east steps of the state capitol. His eighteen-minute inaugural address was delivered to an audience of fifteen hundred, who interrupted only once with applause when he noted that his investiture coincided with the celebration of the birth of Martin Luther King Jr.

The text reveals several themes that Clinton would again raise in his future presidential campaign, including that environmental concerns and equal opportunity were not inconsistent with economic growth and that the established dogmas of both national political parties were inadequate to meet contemporary problems.

❖ ❖ ❖

My fellow citizens, I am honored to begin today my third term as governor. I am humbled by the renewal of your trust in my administration and I will do my best to be worthy of it.

Because I believe so much in our state and its possibilities, I have thought hard about what I should say at the beginning of this new term. I am well aware of the limitations of speech, especially in our time. The other night someone told me not to worry too much about my address because no one would pay attention no matter what was said and in the end all that would count is what appeared for a few seconds on the television news. That may be. But we live in a complex and challenging time, the essence of which cannot be quickly grasped, a time in which swift currents of change are sweeping through our state and nation, drawing us inexorably into a future very different from even the immediate past. In this time, I believe strongly that we have the chance to move forward on some of the most difficult problems facing America today. If we understand our situation, and act on it, we can go far beyond where we are, and what we do here can be an example to the rest of the nation.

There are some basic principles which should guide our way.

First, we must believe in ourselves and our ability to shape our own destiny. Too many of us still expect too little of ourselves and demand too little of each other because we see the future as a question of fate, out of our hands. But the future need not be fate; it can be an achievement.

Second, we must be clear that our primary goal is growth: More jobs and higher incomes. We will not sacrifice our commitment to equal opportunity, a clean environment or other important objectives to achieve growth but all our policies should be directed toward maximizing it. Work is the ultimate source of social welfare, and we must have more of it for all our people.

Third, we must understand that the established dogmas of both national political parties are inadequate to the needs of the present. The Democratic Party has been too concerned with dividing the fruits of our labors when the real need is to increase them, too receptive to the demands of its individual interest groups when the real need is to go beyond them in the public interest. The Republican Party has been too concerned with returning power to the states when some problems, like the farm crisis, require a national solution, too willing to leave people and places behind that are unprepared to compete in the world marketplace.

We may want the government off our backs but we need it by our sides. No other advanced nation leaves the economic welfare of its people solely to device of the world market and what other governments do to distort it. It is good to remember today that America's reigning business heir, Lee Iacocca, would never have saved Chrysler without the aid of a government loan guarantee.

We say we are one nation under God; we know there will always be problems that no government with a conscience, no people with a heart can turn its back on. It is time to go beyond the prison of past thinking. Our democracy has lasted longer than any other because in times of crisis our system permitted change when the alternative was defeat, and our people worked for change.

Fourth, we must be prepared to pay the price of time. The process of reforming our education system, retraining our work force and restructuring our economic base cannot occur overnight. We will need a decade of dedication to reap the full benefits of our efforts. This will not be easy to sustain. We live in a nation which craves instant gratification and has difficulty maintaining long attention spans. We live in a state which has for too long viewed politics as a sport rather than a pathway to tomorrow. We have had rewarding victories in education and economic development, and we will have more. But the real triumphs are in the long haul. And for that we must be patient as well as aggressive.

In order to succeed our government must act according to these basic principles, and as a people, we must believe in them.

To promote responsible growth, we must have a government that operates in practical partnership with the private sector, a government that fosters economic diversity and risk taking and helps to unleash the ideas and energy of our people. The progress in education and economic development of the last two years would not have been possible without the financial support and active involvement of the Arkansas business community. The recent announcement that International Paper will not close the Camden mill and will invest two hundred million dollars in an expansion of the Pine Bluff mill is an example of what we can do together. Agreement came after more than a year of intense cooperative efforts by the company's management and labor, the state and local governments and utilities. Working together works. We must do more of it.

We must have a government that operates its own programs with a commitment to excellence and accountability. Our successful efforts to reduce errors in the food stamp rolls, increase the involvement of victims in the criminal justice process, improve the productivity of the prison farms and implement innovative systems of student, teacher, and administrator testing in public education are all examples of that commitment to excellence and accountability.

We must have a government that is committed to increasing the participation of our people in making important decisions. This is especially important in the area of taxation, the process by which government takes money from people and spends it on something the people could not or would not finance on their own. The people are entitled to know, before a tax is imposed, what the need is and exactly how the money will be spent. They also deserve a fair chance to tell their representatives whether they support more taxes for that purpose, how much of an increase they support, and what kind of tax they prefer.

Public servants should not be dogmatic in opposition or support of tax measures without first serving as investment counselors to the people and getting their guidance. This is both good politics and good government.

Our administration will not propose a major tax increase this term and will not support any tax unless convinced the people at large, not just organized groups, support the amount and type of tax and know clearly how the money will be spent.

Our administration will pursue an ambitious agenda for Arkansas's future, an agenda based on our commitment to economic growth, our commitment to excellence in education, and our commitment to increased security and stability for our people.

Our economic program is designed to be as comprehensive and effective as the education program. When fully implemented it will make us competitive with all other states in the quest for more and better jobs. The program is designed to increase dramatically the capital available for all kinds of business investment, in companies small and large, high tech and traditional; in startups and expansions; and in basic and applied research. We want to create an environment for entrepreneurs second to none. We want to encourage more risk taking. And we are prepared to take some reasonable risks ourselves. For too long we have been on the short end of the old adage "nothing ventured, nothing gained." Given a fair chance to compete, the people of Arkansas can be America's best bet.

Our program will provide more and better job-training opportunities to unemployed adults and vocational students. It will give us the tools to better recruit new industry and promote expansions. It will present Arkansas to the business world more visibly and positively than ever before. No more will we have to worry about being held back because of the misconceptions and lack of knowledge about Arkansas beyond our borders. America will know where we are, what we stand for, what we have to offer, and what we are doing to improve our capacity to do the jobs of today and tomorrow.

Our education program has a simple goal: To retain the progress of the special session on education and build on it.

We must not weaken the standards or repeal the testing laws. We must provide opportunities to improve basic skills to those educators whose test results indicate the need to do so. We must establish a statewide network of educational cooperatives to assist school districts to meet the math, science, vocational, and other standards they cannot meet alone but can meet working together. We must pass a budget which preserves both the new sales tax revenues and the proper share of our other tax dollars for education. We must continue the push for greater involvement and business participation in the schools. We must increase the capacity of our schools to utilize educational television and computers to serve our students. We must implement a statewide system for evaluating teachers in the classroom and continue to support better pay for our fine teachers. We must never forget that no matter what the rest of us do, the real magic of education is what can occur in the classroom between teacher and student.

Of both our economic and education programs one further point needs to be made on this January 15, Martin Luther King's birthday. Dr. King dreamed that one day his four children would be judged not by the color of their skin but by the content of their character. His dream cannot be fully realized here until all children, regardless of race, have an education which provides them the ability to read, write, speak, and continue to learn; until all people have a fair chance to get into business and succeed or fail. Our administration will make strenuous efforts to assure that all our people have access to the opportunities our economic and educational programs afford.

Our program for the security and stability of our people grows largely out of the fine work of the task forces on criminal justice, child abuse, and indigent care. We propose to increase the personnel and pay of the state police and to provide a new communication system; to provide further for the interest of the victims of crime; to crack down on child sexual abuse; to establish an indigent-care trust fund, and to increase health-care coverage to thousands of poor children and their mothers.

With all our concentration on economic growth and education, we must not forget that many of our people have problems with daily life that a responsible and caring government cannot leave unattended.

This is our program for Arkansas. It can help to bring prosperity and opportunity to our people. But it cannot succeed without the strong support of all our people, regardless of party, region, race, age, or economic situation. If we share a belief in ourselves and our future, if we are willing to act on that belief, if we are willing to try, to fail, to get up and try again, we will move forward.

We have a historic opportunity, especially because during the coming term we will celebrate the one hundred and fiftieth birthday of our state. We will try to give every Arkansan the opportunity to participate in that celebration. We will welcome every Arkansan around the world to come home and take part. There is so much in our rich past to be proud of, to learn from, to honor.

Still, the best way to pay our respects to the past is to make the most of the present and prepare the way for a better future.

In honor of our one hundred and fiftieth birthday, let us resolve to do something those who came before us did not do. Let us move Arkansas from the economic backwaters to the crest of prosperity and opportunity in America.

My fellow Arkansans, that is the path I urge for us today. We may fail. We have done that before. But if our vision is as clear as our purest stream, our will as strong as our hardest rock, our dreams as lofty as our highest peak, I believe we will succeed. We owe it to ourselves and to our children to try.

Good Beginnings, Good Schools, Good Jobs

Fourth Inaugural Address
Little Rock, Arkansas
January 13, 1987

Having been elected to a fourth term in campaigns with a 61 percent victory in the primary against a field of three that included former governor Orval Faubus and a general election landslide of 64 percent over former governor Frank White, Clinton now began a four-year term as governor.

The seventeen-minute inaugural address was presented on the east steps of the state capitol at noon on a mild, sunny day and was interrupted three times by audience applause. Although he began the speech by calling the occasion "a day for decision," it was clearly the inaugural address of an incumbent seeking to further programs already begun and continue the policies of his previous tenure in office. Nonetheless, he reminded his audience, "No one can stand still in the middle of the stream. Either we press ahead or we are pushed back. There is no status quo."

❖ ❖ ❖

Far more than most such occasions, this is a day for decision.

For four years we have worked to give our children nationally competitive educational opportunities. We have made dramatic advances, but we must do more.

For four years we have worked to overcome the depression on the farm and the loss of factory jobs to overseas competition. Twice we have been in the top-ten states in the rate of job growth, but we must do more.

Our problems are clear: The collapse of agriculture, high rural unemployment except in areas immune to international pressures, increasing numbers of poor children with uncertain futures, too many unskilled workers. Today in Arkansas, as in so many other states, state revenues are insufficient to meet our basic responsibilities and to implement our new school standards on time.

What may not be so clear, but is far more important, is our opportunity, indeed our obligation to continue to prepare our people for and move our state toward the twenty-first century.

Before, in hard times, we have tightened our belts and waited for things to improve. We have put off progress in favor of survival.

That will not work today. Survival *requires* progress. We are swept along on currents of change which are too swift and too strong. No one can stand still in the middle of the stream. Either we press ahead or we are pushed back. There is no status quo.

Before, in hard times, we have cut back on our common investments in education and human development.

That will not work today. In our highly integrated, highly competitive world economy, we cannot succeed individually without overall economic growth and opportunity based on greater investment in people, greater cooperation between the public and private sectors, and a stronger sense of community based on principles of shared sacrifice and success. Every time a child is born with an avoidable problem, fails to learn to read, drops out of school, falls prey to drug abuse, enters the work force illiterate, your future and mine are diminished. We are in the struggle for tomorrow together.

As we enter the fifth year of our common effort to modernize our economy and our educational system, it has become clear that what our children need, what we all need, to make Arkansas work are three things: good beginnings, good schools, and good jobs.

Every child needs a good start in life but more and more of them don't get it. The dramatic rise in the number of children who are born to very young poor mothers is well documented and much lamented. The time has come for our state and every other one to do something about it.

Unless present trends can be altered, even the best school program will only reach 75 percent of our children. The rest will drop out. Many more will start behind and finish there.

This will not only hurt our conscience, it will hurt our pocketbook. Every child who gets a good start, who grows up to be a productive citizen contributes to our well-being. Every child who doesn't, costs us more down the line. Enough of them could prevent regions of Arkansas from ever emerging from their economic problems. Enough of them could cost America its standard of living and its economic political and military leadership in the world.

I will propose a comprehensive program designed to guarantee our children good beginnings by (1) implementing our indigent health-care plan, which increases the care of at-risk poor mothers and their children, starting before childbirth, to lower infant mortality and reduce avoidable damage to newborns; (2) improving parenting education for the mothers of at-risk children; (3) increasing special educational opportunities in early childhood; (4) implementing the recommendations of the Child Care Task Force to increase the availability of affordable quality child care; (5) strengthening child-support enforcement; (6) making an aggressive effort to reduce teen pregnancy, which produces most of the low-birth-weight at-risk children in Arkansas.

All these initiatives are affordable within the present tight budget and are far less expensive than neglect.

Above all else, we must implement the school standards on time, by the beginning of the next school year. Because of the decline in state revenues, it will cost more money to do it. I said that in the election of 1986. No secret was made of the fact that we would have to raise more money.

When Governor Conway gave Arkansas's first inaugural address in 1836, he said: "We have ample means for the early establishment of such institutions of learning as will be calculated to insure universal education to the youth of our country. Knowledge is power. It is the lever which sways everything in a popular government."

One hundred and fifty years later, in our sesquicentennial election year, our people agreed. We reaffirmed our support of the school program. We know more courses are being offered, class sizes are down, and masteries of the basics are up in the early grades, and our state is among the nation's leaders in opportunities for gifted children and the use of computers to aid all children. Now we have to finish the job.

As Governor Conway said so long ago, we have the means to do it, if we have the will.

In addition to implementing the standards on time, we will try to secure their benefits to all our children by aggressive efforts to prevent drug and alcohol abuse among our young people and to reduce the school dropout rate, which, at 23 percent, is the lowest in the South, yet unconscionably high.

Finally, we must dramatically expand our efforts to combat adult illiteracy. While we have tripled the number of Arkansans being served since 1983, we have only scratched the surface of what must be done. Most of the people who will be in the work force in the year 2000 are there now. Our new initiatives will offer all who will participate the chance to acquire the reading skills necessary to be competitive and productive.

The ultimate test of all our efforts is whether we provide jobs for our people after we educate them. During the election last year, a man in one rural county told me there was no point in spending all this money on education; all the better educated young people would still have to leave the county because no new jobs would ever be developed there.

I cannot accept that defeatist attitude for any place in Arkansas. For four years, I have spent far more of my personal time trying to create new jobs or save existing jobs than on any other endeavor. With better training programs, more help from higher education, the new Science and Technology Authority, more financial assistance through grants, loans, and tax incentives, new markets, like those provided by our work with the Wal-Mart "Buy American Program," and remarkable local leadership, we have often succeeded against all odds.

Over the next four years, we must refine and intensify these efforts. We must remember the basics: most new jobs will be created by people who are already here, in units of fifty or less, in the private sector, in communities with strong local leadership. We should work to improve the business climate, increase specific support services, and target areas that need our help most.

Specifically, I will propose (1) a package of insurance reform legislation designed to control costs and hold down rates; (2) a modification of our corporate code to make Arkansas more attractive to new companies and, hopefully, to bring some companies incorporated elsewhere home; (3) targeting a larger percentage of the resources of the AIDC and other agencies to rural areas and depressed communities least able to turn things around on their own; (4) sending job development teams to areas of high unemployment for extended periods to make sure the people there understand all available state economic programs, develop their own specific plans, and carry them out; (5) creating an economic development subcabinet to make sure all our state agencies are working together to address the needs of local communities; (6) increasing job-training opportunities for people with literacy problems, dropouts, displaced factory workers, minority and disadvantaged youth, farmers, and welfare recipients; (7) increasing financial and technical assistance to small business; (8) encouraging private-sector initiatives such as the Southern Bancorporation to create development capital pools for rural and small businesses; (9) requiring welfare recipients with children three or over to sign a contract committing themselves, in return for government assistance, to a course of independence and work, through literacy and job training and employment.

This is the agenda I propose for the next four years: good beginnings, good schools, good jobs.

Only the school standards carry a major cost, although we must pay for these other initiatives and meet our basic responsibilities.

How will we pay for them?

First, we must cut all possible costs in state government by consolidation of programs and control of personnel expense through an early retirement program coupled with tight control on hiring.

Already we have budgeted many state agencies for next year at levels below where they started this year. We should stop contributing tax money to retirement systems in amounts of millions of dollars over the recommendations of actuaries and in violation of sound business principles already enacted in the private sector.

Second, we should do a better job of collecting the tax now owed and by protecting the existing revenue base, by changing the system of sales tax collections, increasing enforcement on out-of-state purchases and a tax amnesty program. We should not lower the capital-gains tax rate after the Congress has just raised it.

Third, we should raise new revenues in ways that promote tax fairness and broaden the tax base. I propose we do that by repealing income tax deductions already eliminated by Congress; by enacting a modest severance tax on newer natural gas, much of which is going out of state; and by repealing one-half of the four cents exemption on the sales tax now accorded a few products and many services at retail. This will broaden the tax base to account for the relative growth of the service sector of the economy. By adjusting our tax structure to the realities of economic activity, we will reduce the pressure to raise property, income, and general sales taxes in the years ahead.

Most important, this program will allow us to meet our obligations to our children and to our future. It is not easy, but it will take us where we need to go.

My fellow Arkansans, I ask for your prayers and your support. I ask you to support and encourage your state legislators who will have to make the difficult decisions to save our school program and secure our future. I ask you to embrace the present difficulties with enthusiasm. When we are tested we have the opportunity to enlarge our lives, to be faithful to our heritage, to make a difference.

Let us now gladly take responsibility for our own future. When the history of this year is written, let it be recorded that we did our duty and moved our state forward into a brighter day.

Nomination of Michael Dukakis

Democratic National Convention
Atlanta, Georgia
July 20, 1988

In his third ritual address to a Democratic National Convention, Clinton, who had considered seeking the nomination himself, was given the publicity plum of making the prime-time nominating speech for his friend and fellow governor, Michael Dukakis. Clinton knew even before the speech that his task was going to be one of his most difficult rhetorical performances. "I wouldn't feel anything like this if I was just asked to say where we should go, give the keynote address," he said while finishing the seventh draft of the speech the previous evening. He faced the problem of crafting a message for three different audiences and three different demands—the convention delegates in the hall wanted a battle cry, the nationwide television audience wanted to know more about the nominee, and the party leadership wanted to assess Clinton's abilities and his potential for the future. An additional challenge was to enter Dukakis's name and to refocus the attention of the convention on Dukakis after Jesse Jackson's speech the night before, and he had to do it alone, since there would be no seconding speeches.

Clinton stepped to the podium shortly after 9:30 P.M. before a capacity crowd of 12,500 in the Omni Coliseum. The restless delegates on the floor initially gave the speech a warm reception, but, as Clinton suppressed his usually enthusiastic extemporaneous delivery and began reading almost every word of the nineteen-page text in a flat style, he lost the audience within the first couple of minutes. As the speech passed the scheduled limit of fifteen minutes and went on for thirty-two minutes, NBC shifted to commentary from the floor, ABC to cut away to a mini special on Dukakis's early political career, CBS showed shots of delegates drawing their forefingers across their necks and chanting "Get the hook," and CNN focused its cameras on the red podium light.

"Are people listening to this?" NBC's news correspondent Tom Brokaw asked Chris Wallace, who replied, "He has completely lost this crowd." The media commentary assured that Clinton also lost the national audience and the confidence of the party's grassroots leaders as well. "It was the worst speech I ever heard in my life," said Congressman Norman Dicks. "It was an embarrassment. It was terrible. It should have been half as long. Half? A third! There was two minutes of Dukakis at the beginning, forty minutes of Clinton in the middle, and two minutes of Dukakis at the end."

Leaving the podium, Clinton told reporters that he had practiced the talk repeatedly and it had never lasted more than fifteen minutes. It ran twice as long, he said, because of the cheers and chants of the enthusiastic Dukakis delegates. In directing the floor response, Dukakis delegate tracker Tad Devine had advised his crew, "When Clinton is introduced, I want to start turning the volume up. We should build it and build it. Anytime he says Dukakis, we want applause." During the speech, Devine sent additional orders to start a chant, "We want the Duke," to be followed by "Duke, Duke, Duke." Still not satisfied, he commanded his floor contacts to "turn up the juice."

Clinton said he mistook the chants of "Duke, Duke" for boos and conceded that the speech was a "comedy of errors" and a "bust in the hall," but he said the Dukakis staff had wanted him to give a serious speech and had cleared it before delivery. Realizing that he had lost his immediate audience, he considered cutting it short but decided to be "a good soldier" and march on in the manner approved by the presidential nominee. Dukakis aides were clearly disappointed, saying the problem was caused by Clinton making an eleventh-hour decision to lengthen his speech.

The national political fallout did not seem to hurt Dukakis in the polls, but Clinton's political future seemed at the time to be over. The *Washington Post* called the speech "Windy Clinty's Classic Clinker." The *Los Angeles Times* dubbed it "The Speech That Ate Atlanta," and said the Democratic Party's rising star had committed "nationally televised political suicide." The *New York Times* observed, "When he finally finished, his reputation as an orator was in ruins and all of the enthusiasm in the hall had been dissipated." Appearing on the "Tonight Show" a week later, Clinton told Johnny Carson, "My sole goal was achieved, however. I wanted so badly to make Dukakis look great, and I succeeded beyond my wildest dreams."

❖ ❖ ❖

I'm honored to be here tonight to nominate my friend Michael Dukakis for president of the United States. America has a lot riding on this election. We face big challenges, big problems, big opportunities. The fundamental fact of 1988 is that we can't take our success for granted anymore in this competitive world economy. We'll have to work harder and smarter to preserve the American dream. We'll have to have new economic policies and new people policies. And we'll need new leadership to take us where we want to go.

Mike Dukakis can provide that leadership. I want to talk about what he wants to do and what he expects us to do.

And I want to talk about Mike Dukakis. He's come so far, so fast that everybody wants to know what kind of person he is, what kind of governor he's been, and what kind of president he'll be.

He's been my friend a long time. I want you to know my answers to those questions, and why I believe we should make Mike Dukakis the first American president born of immigrant parents since Andrew Jackson.

The other day a friend of mine back home asked me if I were really excited about the prospect of Michael Dukakis becoming president. When I said I was, he said, "Bill, I can understand why you think he should be president, but how can you get *excited* about a guy who's so clean he squeaks when he walks and who mows his yard with a hand-powered mower?"

Well, I thought about it. And I decided that's one reason I *was* excited.

He's old-fashioned all right: he's the kind of man who plays it straight, keeps his word, and pays his bills.

In Arkansas, we say he's the kind of man you can "tie to."

Don't misunderstand me. He's not perfect. I have to confess right here in the Omni, home of the Atlanta Hawks, that he loves the Boston Celtics. During the playoffs, he even watched them while making campaign phone calls.

Still, I think Michael Dukakis should be president because he has the *character*, the *record*, and the *vision* America needs at this moment in our journey. And Michael Dukakis should be president because he is the right man for our times.

His character is steadfast and consistent. He wakes up in the same world every day, a trait of no small importance in a president.

I have found him self-confident, but willing to listen to other people. That's a lesson he and I learned the hard way—we got beat over the head with it. Both of us were elected, defeated, then given a rare second chance by our people. That does wonders for your sensitivity to others and their views.

Mike and I met after our defeats. He was teaching at the Kennedy School and I was the youngest ex-governor in American history. I was struck even then by his lack of bitterness, his eagerness to learn, and his continuing, genuine commitment to public life, in or out of office.

As someone who's worked with him on hard issues in the National Governors' Association, who's hammered out compromises with him, disagreed with him, and fought battles by his side, I can tell you one thing: when he needs to be, Michael Dukakis is tough as nails.

Of course, if he hadn't been tough, he never could have come back from his defeat. When that happens to most people, they pull the shades, rip the phone off the wall, and pack it in. Not Mike Dukakis. He hangs in there.

Mike Dukakis has unshakable integrity. One of his Massachusetts political opponents said of him, "He's got the strongest moral core of any man I ever met in public life."

He believes actions are more important than words. He has a passionate sense that performance matters. That's why two years ago his fellow governors, including the Republicans, voted him the "most effective" governor in America. When the Republicans take out after him, I'm going to remind them of that vote.

When Michael Dukakis speaks out for the American family, you can believe him. I have never known anyone more devoted to his wife and children. He and Kitty are different, but they're wonderful together. They're great role models for our young people. And Kitty will be a first lady who will make America proud and win the world's respect.

Mike's *record* is as strong and solid as his character.

For many years, I have watched him as governor. He has also been a soldier, a lawyer, a teacher, a legislator.

He has excelled in all these roles, because of his fine mind and his keen interest in other people.

He can speak to more Americans in their native tongues than anyone our party has ever nominated: in his own Greek, French, Italian, and, as millions now know, in Spanish.

As governor, he hasn't just played with issues, he's wrestled them to the ground. He has made the hard decisions: to balance budgets, create jobs, fight crime and drug abuse, move people from welfare to work, expand day care and health care, increase housing, and improve education.

Michael Dukakis knows how to translate ideas into action. One of our major news magazines called him the "master of innovation."

More than any other governor, he has worked to bring good jobs to his poor communities and poor people. Long before he knew he would be a presidential candidate, Michael Dukakis told me he couldn't believe there was no national plan, no leadership effort to give the depressed areas of our country the same opportunities his people in Massachusetts enjoy.

He believes that all citizens should lead productive lives. His welfare reform program "E.T." has been a model for the national welfare-reform effort for one simple reason: it has taken people off of welfare rolls and put them on payrolls.

He knows from his own experience that government cannot solve problems alone. But unlike the present administration, he also knows government cannot leave them alone. That's why he's broken new ground by building partnerships—partnerships with business, with labor, with educators, with local governments, with anyone willing to work with him to solve problems and seize opportunities.

He's worked with welfare recipients like Ruby Sampson, a single parent dependent on welfare for fourteen years, to help her get the education and training she needed to land a job as an operating-room technician. She now makes more than twenty thousand dollars a year.

He's worked with local officials like the mayor of Taunton, Massachusetts, to lower the city's unemployment rate from over 14 percent to under 4 percent.

He's worked with troubled companies like Diamond International and Morse Tool, to keep them open, saving the jobs of hundreds of his people.

He knows we may want the government off our back, but we sure need it by our side.

Michael Dukakis knows that working together works. And he's proved that once again by bringing us together in magnificent unity at this convention.

Michael Dukakis is a man with a vision, a shining *vision* for America—a country with good jobs at good wages; a country where all Americans can send their children to good public schools and can afford to send them to college; a country where working parents have access to good child care and health care for their kids; one where people can get decent long-term care without going to the poorhouse; a country with a clean environment and, yes, a clean government devoted once again to the rule of law.

He wants a country that can compete and win in the world economy and one that will seek a safer world, an enduring peace for ourselves and our children. Michael Dukakis will continue to work for arms control across the table from Mr. Gorbachev and, as commander in chief, he will make sure American interests are strongly represented around the globe.

In any time, because of his character, his record, and his vision, Michael Dukakis would be a proud standard-bearer for our party.

But at *this time* in our history, Michael Dukakis is *the* man for America.

The post–World War II era, when America dominated the world, economically, politically, and militarily, is over. For the rest of our lives we will have to compete with people in other countries for new jobs, new business opportunities, and technological breakthroughs. As we have learned painfully in the last decade, we won't win if we're not prepared.

The Republicans' main claim to the White House this year is that in the face of competition and adversity the administration produced a five-year recovery. Well, that recovery left a lot of people and places behind, was financed by a sea of borrowed money, and ignored or aggravated some harsh realities: the rise of huge budget and trade deficits; the loss of our competitive position in low-wage, low-skill, and import-sensitive industries, in agriculture, energy, and mining, and in some high-tech areas, too; the growth of a vast new class of poor people, most of them young women and their little children; an epidemic of social problems; and a decline in real wages.

Left unattended, these difficulties could threaten not only our children's future, but our own.

In the first half of the 1980s, for the first time in my lifetime, only 40 percent of our people had an increase in their incomes, while 20 percent stood still, and 40 percent actually suffered a reduction in real wages. We used to believe a rising economic tide lifts all boats. Today's tide is drowning four in ten of our people who have fallen off the boat, and the Republican crew won't even throw a life raft to the women and children.

There are those who see these developments as evidence that our nation is in decline. Best-selling books predict a downhill slide that we either cannot or will not stop.

Michael Dukakis doesn't believe that for a minute. He believes America's best days lie ahead. He reminds us that we've faced even greater challenges in the past. He is an apostle of hope.

Last night when Jesse Jackson gave that awesome, wonderful speech, many of you waved signs with his slogan: "Keep Hope Alive." In his own way, Mike Dukakis will never let us forget that admonition. We all must be apostles of hope. As the Scripture says: "Let us not grow weary in doing good, for in due season we shall reap, if we do not lose heart."

Michael Dukakis is a builder who wants to build a bridge to tomorrow: strong enough to carry our heaviest load; wide enough for all of us to walk across together; long enough to take us into the twenty-first century.

He's got a big job to do. And we have to help him.

His economic challenge is to reduce our debt; to nourish our entrepreneurs and small-business people who create most of our jobs; to promote new relationships between business and labor in which risk, loss, and gain are shared; to reduce the scandalous waste of money consumed by hostile mergers and takeovers that cost jobs; to get much more cooperation from our major competitors in Europe and Japan in making economic and defense policies; to fight for a fair trading system that gives us the chance to sell more as well as buy more; and to reduce the debt of the developing nations in Latin America whose futures are so tightly bound to our own.

This is an ambitious agenda, but Michael Dukakis has great ambitions for America.

Yet, even if he carries it off, America still could be in trouble.

Why? Because compared to all the world's major economic powers, we do the worst job of developing our most precious resource—our people.

We let more babies die than others do. A child born in Costa Rica has a better chance of living to be a year old than one born tonight in our nation's capitol.

We stand by while more of our children have children than others do, swelling the number of our "truly disadvantaged."

We accept far more adult illiteracy than others do, though we know 80 percent of the work force in the year 2000 will be composed of people who are already working and that sooner or later our workers' inability to read will catch up with them and catch up with us.

We tolerate more homeless children than others do, degrading the most blameless among us.

We live in the only *advanced* country that's still in the Dark Ages when it comes to child care.

Our school dropout rates are more than twice those of our major competitors.

When our kids do get out of school, they have about two years less learning than young people in Germany and Japan who are competing for those good jobs Mike Dukakis wants them to have.

A lot of our young people want to go on to college, but can't afford to, so they go right to work in a tough world economy that pays young unskilled workers 25 to 40 percent less than fifteen years ago.

What's all this got to do with you if you're not poor, your kids are in college, you have a job, and your company's doing fine?

I'll tell you what—all these people in trouble are growing as a percent of our population. If they can't do the jobs of today and tomorrow, we'll all be in trouble.

I want Michael Dukakis to be president because he knows we don't have a single person to waste.

I want Michael Dukakis to be president because he cares that one in four of our children under five is living in poverty and that without good child health programs and preschool for those who need it, we are cheating their future—and ours.

I want Michael Dukakis to be president because he understands that today it costs a middle-class family much more of its income to send a child to college than it did when he and I went a generation ago, and that government has to help make up the difference.

I want Michael Dukakis to be president because he knows one big reason hundreds of thousands of parents and children are homeless is that this administration has cut government housing starts by 800 percent since 1980.

I want Michael Dukakis to be president because he feels the pain of a mother who leaves for work every day worried sick about her children not being in a good affordable day-care center, partly due to the government's feeble efforts in child care.

I want Michael Dukakis to be president, not just because he knows and cares about these problems, but because he's tackled them in his state, and he's proved—time and again—that he can make a difference in people's lives.

When the Republicans gather in New Orleans next month, they'll talk about these family problems, too. They'll feature some of their good governors. Just remember, they had the White House for eight long years and did nothing.

Just as he did in Massachusetts, President Dukakis will insist that we all become partners in the fight for America's future, that we share the responsibility of forging it so that we can share the glory of achieving it.

He'll have business partners like Eugene Lang, a wealthy businessman who decided to "keep hope alive" at his old elementary school in Harlem. He gave the poor children there a dream of their own by promising all who would stay in school a scholarship to college. Michael Dukakis will share and spread that dream.

He'll have teaching partners like Jaime Escalante, the hero of the movie *Stand and Deliver,* whose entire class of poor students in east Los Angeles stunned the education world by passing the Advanced Placement Calculus test, under the guidance of a teacher who believes that all children can learn, and that students will perform at the level of our expectation. My friends, when it comes to education, Michael Dukakis will stand and deliver.

He'll have public service partners like Marian Edelman, the president of the Children's Defense Fund, who has fought a courageous, bipartisan battle in Congress for early investment in children, reminding us all that we can invest in them now or pay a much higher price for our neglect later. Michael Dukakis knows we must invest in our children while they still have a future.

He'll have political partners like Lloyd Bentsen, who built a successful business then went back into politics to keep our free-enterprise system and our nation's defenses strong so that others could have the same chance he had to succeed and who has had a lifetime commitment to the principle that *everybody* should have that chance.

Michael Dukakis will have political partners like Jesse Jackson, who in 1977, long before it was popular, went with me into the Arkansas public schools to plead with the students to say "no" to drugs, to "open their brains and not their veins." Like Jesse Jackson, Michael Dukakis has fought for drug-free schools with his Governor's Alliance against Drugs. Like Jesse Jackson, Michael Dukakis knows it's not enough to urge our children to "Just Say No" to drugs. They must be able to say "Yes" to life, too.

Not long ago, police in Detroit broke the biggest crack ring in that city. It was being run by two brothers from the Mississippi Delta area of Arkansas. They had brought over one hundred other young men up from their home county to help them peddle dope. The news reports said these country boys were more reliable than the street-smart city kids. They gave a good day's work for a good day's pay.

The unemployment rate in the county those boys fled is almost 20 percent. For black teenagers, it's more than twice that. Most farmers and business people there are too broke to help get them off the street. Those kids could make more money in a month in Detroit than they could in a year back home.

I wonder if their decision to deal misery for money would have been different if President Dukakis had had eight years to make good on his commitment to good schools and good jobs for all our people in all our communities. I think they might have been able to say "No to drugs" and "Yes to life."

My friends, we are moving into a future which richly rewards learning, achievement, and innovation. It punishes ignorance and waste and the pursuit of short-term profits at the expense of long-term growth.

We need a president who understands the future and its challenges. Michael Dukakis does.

This is one of those pivotal moments in our history. The issue is not whether we move left or right; it is whether we move ahead or fall behind. It's impossible to stand still in the strong currents of change which engulf us.

In these times of change, the Democratic Party has a place for all Americans who share our vision of the future and want to do their part: Democrats, Republicans, and Independents. Michael Dukakis has proved he will reach out to bring us all together.

The strength of his message rests on two simple but powerful ideas.

The first is that we are all in this fight for the future together. Whether they know it or not, the future of the California entrepreneur and the New York investment banker is tied to the drought-stricken, debt-ridden farmer in North Dakota and the poorest black schoolchild in Mississippi.

We're all in this together.

The second idea is that we must be willing to do what it takes today to guarantee our children's tomorrow.

I had a college professor who taught me that the key to America's success over more than two hundred years is that our people have always believed the future can be better than the present and that each individual has a personal, moral responsibility to make it so. He said we were in college because our parents preferred our future to their own present. He said, "As long as the American people prefer their children's future to their present, we're going to be all right, but if we ever reach the point where they don't, we've had it, and don't you ever forget it."

Michael Dukakis won't ever forget it. His whole life is a tribute to the enduring strength of the American dream. He knows that unless that dream is real for all our children, it is not secure for any of them. And he'll help us seize the future and make it ours.

In closing, I want you to remember that in November, when Michael Dukakis is elected president, we will observe the twenty-fifth anniversary of President Kennedy's death.

But Mike's victory will be a tribute to the life and legacy of John Kennedy, to the boundless optimism, the grace, the courage, and the sheer joy with which he urged us forward.

The great Israeli statesman Abba Eban began his memorial tribute to President Kennedy with this simple, stirring statement, "Tragedy is the difference between what is and what might have been."

Michael Dukakis has spent his entire public life closing the gap between what is and what might have been. That is why he should be president of the United States.

And so my fellow Democrats, I proudly place into nomination the name of the man who will become the forty-first president of the United States, Michael Dukakis.

A New Partnership for a Better Arkansas

Arkansas General Assembly
Little Rock, Arkansas
January 15, 1991

After winning election to a fifth term as governor, receiving 58 percent of the vote over Sheffield Nelson, Clinton took the oath of office at a time when Arkansas National Guard units were poised for war in the Persian Gulf and President George Bush was enjoying record popularity in national opinion polls. The inaugural tradition in the state was that the governor would appear before a joint session of the general assembly in the House of Representative chamber at ten o'clock in the morning, take the official oath of office, and make a few brief remarks, later taking the oath again in a public ceremony and delivering the formal inaugural address before the citizens assembled to witness the event.

The text below is that of the legislative address, which in this instance ran twenty-eight minutes—seven minutes longer than the formal inaugural address Clinton would deliver at noon in the capitol rotunda. Speaking from handwritten notes but without a prepared text, he stood behind the reading clerk's podium on the Speaker's dais and presented an enthusiastic extemporaneous message about his policy goals to an audience of six hundred people that included the other constitutional officers, his family, both houses of the legislature, and government staffers in the chamber, citizens seated in both galleries, and others crowded outside the House chamber watching through the doors.

Clinton opened his remarks by noting that every inauguration "is a little different," but an editorial reprise in the *Arkansas Gazette* noted that even twelve years after first taking office "he still manages to make it convincing." Veteran political columnist Ernest Dumas, who had been observing state government for more than twenty years, said Clinton's address "was like each of the others—sweeping vision, perfect tone, masterly delivery, and more impressive for its seeming to be so effortless."

❖ ❖ ❖

Every inauguration is a little different. It will be noted that this year I did know my right hand from my left, but the chief justice almost took my speaking notes away.

Mr. Foster reminded me that I should always speak from the heart and never from notes. The last time I spoke from a written text, it didn't work out so well.

When I walked up the stairs today with Senator Howell, I looked at him, and he looked at me, and I said, "We've made this trip a lot of times together." It's always been a good trip, but I hope never a better one than today.

I just came from a dedicatory church service over at my church, Immanuel Baptist Church, where the music raised the roof and the preaching and prayers made us all think a little more about our responsibilities. My pastor said at that service that at a time like this, we should focus not only on the time and how much we have, and whether the timing is right to do what we need to do and want to do, but also whether we have the opportunity to do anything that is timeless. And he reminded us that sometimes those things which are timeless are simple and not complex but profoundly important. And he ended, ironically, his remarks which lasted two minutes and lasts down to the present age, contrasting it with a two-hour speech given by the man who preceded President Lincoln and that no one remembers now but was very popular at the time.

Today, I pledge myself to a new partnership for a better Arkansas with you. All across this state, during the last campaign, I reminded people over and over again that one of the things that I had learned in the last ten years is that, by themselves, governors don't really do too much. That is, as my daughter says, once when she was five and was asked what I do for a living, she said, "Well, my dad makes speeches, drinks coffee, and talks on the telephone." So, by themselves, governors don't do too much, but together there is very little that we cannot do.

I feel very energized today. I feel more excitement about the prospect of this coming session than I have for any one since I first took office way back in 1979. And I have especially looked forward to this partnership with this new legislature. I have watched with admiration the decisions of your leadership, the changes in the rules, facing already some difficult choices which had to be made, the openness and progressive attitude that has been displayed by people without regard to party or to region.

And on Martin Luther King's birthday, it would be inappropriate not to note that today, for the first time in our history, we have a legislature which more nearly reflects the racial composition and diversity and richness of the people of Arkansas. And I ask all of you, without regard to race, in these difficult economic times, with many pressures on our social fabric and racial tensions heightening in some places in our state and throughout our country, to dedicate yourselves on this day to working together in a spirit of harmony and brother- and sisterhood for what is best for all of our people, to set an example for people throughout the state so that all may see that we can come into this capitol together to do the people's business in a way that the Constitution mandates and that morality and good sense dictate.

This is a day of celebration, and I think Dr. King would be very happy to know that this new legislature is sending its governor off to duty on January 15.

We owe the people nothing less than our best. We've been through a tough decade, a decade that was really tough on all of the rural areas of the country, especially the South, tough on the farmers, tough on the low-wage, low-skill factory workers, brutal on the small towns that depended on them for production. A decade in which, literally, 40 percent of the American people and at least half the people in our states had declines in their real income after you adjust for inflation.

There were some bright spots, to be sure. For four years, we led all the states around us in new job growth, and we've had some real achievements in education. Despite all the talk about our financial problems, and they're manifold and real, our little state that is forty-eighth in per-capita income is seventeenth in high-school graduation rate.

We see a big increase in the college-going rate as our children began to take the courses they should have been taking a long time ago, but they are now. We are moving in the right direction.

The nineties, I believe, will be more of the same, only more rapid. We will be tested over and over and over again by a very high standard of international competitiveness, and we have to decide whether we want to play.

Much of our future, I believe, is in our own hands. Therefore, our best, which is what we owe the people, cannot be timid or cautious even though these are troubled and uncertain times. Our best does not permit us to deny our problems or to ignore our possibilities, and if all of us would be perfectly honest, we've done too much of both as a state for too long.

Our best requires us to accept a few simple but powerful truths. I believe these things, and I believe each of you do, too.

I think more than any other time in our past, our destiny is in our own hands. I believe that because, when we are as healthy and as well educated as the rest of the country, our incomes will rise to the national average and our opportunities will broaden to those available to any other state in this country because we are living in a global economy where what you can earn depends on what you can learn, and no one can stop that from occurring.

On the other hand, if we decide we are not willing or we cannot afford to become as well educated and as healthy as most of the people in this country and the global economy in which money and jobs are mobile and what you can earn depends on what you can learn, then no one can help us, either.

Our destiny is in our own hands.

Whether we like it or not, we are a community, a community in which we will go forward together or not at all, in which we will rise together or in which none of us will ever see our beloved state come to the point to which we all want.

Now, if it is true what I've said, then we can go about the business of building this new future. What are the elements of it?

First, there must be more investment. One of my little rules of politics I've picked up along life's way is that whenever someone tells you it's not a money problem, they're almost always talking about someone else's problem.

It is a money problem. We do need to increase our investment if we want to increase opportunity.

So, day after tomorrow when I come back here to make the State of the State speech and go over with you bill by bill the bills in the administration's package, I will ask you to create an education trust fund, as we did in 1983 to promote opportunity for all of our people and to put every penny of the new general revenues I ask you to raise into that trust fund for education;

To provide adult literacy programs that will make us at the end of four years perhaps the first state in the country to make the claim that we have taught all of our work force to read at an acceptable level. If we teach everybody in this state to read at the high-school level, the income of the state would rise in the next couple of years. It's the least expensive thing we could do in the short run;

To provide apprenticeship programs for the young people who don't go on to college. We're the only country in the world that has no real system for moving the kids who don't go to college into decent jobs. That's why only workers without a college education or at least two years of post–high-school education have experienced such dramatic declines in their earnings in the last ten or fifteen years. They can't bring more in a global economy, but they're not stupid, and Lord knows they're not lazy.

The average wage earner is working more hours a week than he or she was fifteen years ago. It has nothing to do with stupid, it has nothing to do with lazy. It has to do with the lack of leadership and the lack of a system to give people a chance to compete in a world in which what you can earn depends on what you can learn, and we have got to do it.

We have got to put some more investment into our two-year programs, into our community colleges, our vocational programs, the things which train people to do the jobs of today and tomorrow.

We need to put more into our colleges and we need to do some more things in our public schools, and I'll just mention two or three.

We'll never become first in the world in math and science instruction until we make sure our teachers can do the job. I'm going to give you a program that I hope you will adopt to retrain our math and science teaching force.

And we'll never have the school we want until we have children showing up for school who are mentally and physically able to learn. Two years ago I asked and I will ask again for you to fund a preschool program that will give every county in this state a good parent-involved, parent-led preschool program that will prepare our children to succeed in school.

Let me just mention one other thing. I hope that you will adopt the Arkansas Academic Scholarship proposal that I will make patterned on the so-called Taylor plan in New Orleans, which would commit our state to give a tuition scholarship to every graduate of a high school in this state who comes from a family with an income of twenty-five to thirty thousand dollars, depending on the number of dependents in the household, who makes a B average or better and takes the recommended college core curriculum.

It would be the best investment we ever made. It would reduce remedial education by giving the children the courses they ought to take; it would send more people to college; it would enable more people to stay in college; and it would make a statement that we believe that government has a responsibility to the working people as well as to the poor. And I hope you will adopt it.

We cannot do those things without funds, and I hope you will be willing to adopt a plan to raise teacher pay which is far less expensive than one which would put all the money into the distributional formula at 56 percent for the teachers and 44 percent for the schools, but it will still cost money.

We cannot . . . we cannot ever hope to have the education system we want if we try to add new standards, new programs, and new opportunities on the backs of the schoolteachers. They have done all that they can do, and they have produced for you more results with less money than any state in the United States of America. And we should reward them, not just for the ones who are there now but because teaching is a dynamic enterprise.

Different people come and go every month, every year. And if you want to make a real commitment to teaching excellence, we must make the first real commitment in eight years, since the special session of 1983, to raise the pay for our schoolteachers.

The second major investment I think we need to adopt is one which has been widely chronicled in the press in the last few weeks, and that is the investment in the health care of our people, especially in our children but in others as well. You will have before you a proposal to raise a very large amount of money—three-quarters of it from the federal government in Medicaid, and of the last quarter, one-half from Medicaid providers and one-half from the general revenues of the state—to give our state the most progressive, comprehensive health-care program of any state in the South beginning with maternal and child health care for pregnant women and children up to 185 percent of the federal poverty level and going all the way through to the working poor, reaching in to the elderly people to provide the Elderchoices program and improved care in later years.

Unless we can access rural health care, unless we can keep alive health care in rural areas, our rural areas will die on the vine. And we will never be able to realize the economic potential of the people who live there because they will be too sick or too scared.

I don't know how many meetings I attended—all across the state, from high unemployment areas to low ones—where working people would come up to me and say, "You know, I get so tired of going to work every day, doing my best, living in mortal fear that my children will get sick and I have no health-insurance coverage."

Representative Roberts has pre-filed some bills that I strongly support that will provide some alternatives for health-care coverage. We will cover more children with this program, but I will say again what I've said before: We're the only country in the world with an advanced economy that doesn't provide some health-care access to everybody, and we spend a higher percentage of our income on health care than any country in the world.

We'll never get where we need to go in cost control, quality, and coverage until the national government takes some leadership in this but we cannot afford to wait, so I urge you to pass the health-care program to save the health-care network in rural Arkansas and to expand the benefits to our children and to our future.

And, finally, we have to invest more money in our economic development. That's roads and highways and bridges, to create four-lane networks throughout the state so that we can compete with these other states that are moving to do that, so that rural areas can maintain the network that they have, and it's very important.

The other states around us—Tennessee, Mississippi, Louisiana, Oklahoma—they're moving ahead. Unless we move, too, in the not-too-distant future, in northwest Arkansas, there'll be a toll road which dead ends at the Arkansas line, there'll be another four-lane which dead ends at the Missouri line, there'll be another four-lane which will dead end at the Louisiana line.

The tourism development we want in the Delta will not occur because people won't go in and out; it will be too much trouble. I can give you example after example after example. We need to face our responsibilities in this area.

I will give you some innovative small-business finance programs, minority business finance programs that companies will have access to starting out. And I hope you will adopt it.

There are some investment requirements in the environmental area, principally related to solid waste. The task force which Representative Gibson chaired has already pre-filed the bills. I hope you will look at those carefully; some of them will be controversial. But that's going to be our biggest environmental and economic-environmental headache of the 1990s. This program rests on three pillars: recycling, waste reductions, and regional solutions to the problems. We need to do it, and we need to do it now, get ahead of the curve, set up a system that we can live with for the next decade while other people gnash and tear their teeth.

Now, that's what we need to spend money on.

What I have to tell you is I don't believe money is enough. If we're going to have a real new sense of community, the people who are paying the bill have got to be convinced that government is taking the money only to do those things which government can do best and that we are holding ourselves accountable for the way we're doing business.

When I went around the state for eight months and had hundreds and hundreds and hundreds of community meetings, I never got any spontaneous applause for the stuff I just told you. You know what the spontaneous applause lines were? Let me give them to you.

Number one, I'm sick and tired of people having children out of wedlock and walking off and leaving them and not trying to support their children, and if you elect me, I will stiffen the child-support laws and move as close as I can to automatic wage withholding for people who father children out of wedlock and leave all of the burden on women. Governments don't raise children, people do. And the people would applaud.

Number two, I think it's a crying shame we spend seventeen thousand dollars a year putting people in the penitentiary, four times what we spend on children in schools, when a third of them are nonviolent offenders. They ought to be in boot camps or in community work centers where they're out cleaning the streets or building parks and paying us back for what they did to us instead of being rewarded with another seventeen thousand dollars of our money.

Number three, I believe very strongly that not just poor children but the children of working families should have access to college scholarships.

College costs are three times or more as a percentage of family income. And those people deserve our help, too; it would be the best money we've ever spent.

And number four, if you reelect me, I'll make it so you don't have to have an engineering degree to get a car license.

Now, what do those things say? Those were the applause lines. What do they say? What is the common sense of the people telling you? Do something for the working people who need help, too, and who are paying their taxes and getting up every day and killing themselves. Do something for them.

If you're going to help people with public money, hold them responsible for their own actions. You cannot expect the community to be responsible for people who will not behave responsibly.

You know, first-time nonviolent offenders want a chance to reclaim their lives and pay like the rest of us instead of take from the rest of us to the end of time.

And treat taxpayers like customers and change government the way it makes sense to change it. We need *perestroika* in government in America, and we need the kind of restructuring American corporations have had all during the eighties in government and education and health care. And so I say to you, you can spend all the money, and I want you to do it, but if you do it and you ignore the imperatives of the modern world and what the voters are saying, the demands they're making for more choice in the decisions they make when they elect a government and more responsibility on the part of the people who are the beneficiaries of government money and for more accountability from us in government, then we will not do our best.

So money alone is not enough.

I want you to expand the school choice program without running the risk of resegregating the schools, and we can do it. I want you to pass the Elderchoices program that gives older people a choice of how their tax money is going to be spent, whether they're taken care of in a nursing home or staying out of a nursing home.

We have more people in this state today growing older who have fine minds and good imaginations who are simply losing the physical strength that they need to get around. And nothing is more demeaning to them than to have somebody else tell them what they've got to do and how they've got to live and when to move and when not. This Elderchoices is not just an economic decision, it is a civil rights opportunity for the older people of this state.

In the area of responsibility I've already told you I hope you will adopt the child-support strengthening that Dr. Elders has been out speaking about. I hope you will adopt the expansion of the boot-camp program. I hope you will vote for Representative [Jodie] Mahony's bill to strengthen our driver's license requirement, and I hope you'll go home and ask your school superintendent to enforce it.

West Virginia was the first state, Arkansas was the second state to pass a bill that says that kids who drop out of school for no good reason lose their driver's licenses. The West Virginia graduation rate soared because they enforced the law more vigorously at the local level. We must have that kind of commitment here.

I hope you will adopt the new domestic-abuse law. I hope you will adopt the mandatory seat-belt law. Read the letter from the director of the Arkansas Automobile Dealers' Association about the money we are spending to pay for other peoples' decisions not to use their seat belts. It is not a personal decision; it is a social decision. We pay the bill.

I hope you will adopt Senator Snyder's anti-smoking bill to protect children from overexposure at an early age. Most people start smoking when they're young. That's not just an individual decision, either. We pay that bill, too.

I hope you will adopt Senator Dowd's bad-actor law so that our state will have the clear legal authority to tell people who have miserable records in environmental protection with a bunch of money, comply on paper with our rules and regulations and get a permit to do business in Arkansas. If they've done wrong somewhere else, that's a pretty good inference they'll do it to us if they get a chance, and we should be able to say no.

These are elemental responsibilities that we should expect our fellow citizens to assume. And in the area of government accountability, I'll be very brief, but I hope you will adopt the tax-reform proposal that I will recommend.

We still take too much of our tax money from the working poor and the near poor, people who don't get government assistance and pay their bills, people who, remember, are working more hours on average than they were fifteen years ago and getting less for it.

I hope you will adopt a bill to make us, the constitutional officers, more accountable in the way we account for public funds.

I hope you will adopt the comprehensive bill that will permit us to continue to restructure our school system, to change the mission of the Department of Education from a regulatory to a support body, to go to school-based management, to weed out middle layers of unnecessary bureaucracy and give us the modern, effective schools we need with the teachers and principals in control.

And I hope you will support the quality management initiatives that we are trying to make in state government to change state government from a top-down, rule-oriented bureaucracy-heavy system of delivering services which is the characteristic of every government in the United States of America today to one which mirrors the changes that are being made in the private sector, and I hope you will begin by simplifying car license procedures.

Now if we do these things together, we will be giving our best.

Let me say this in closing. There will be people who will say that the difficulty of the moment for our country and the foreboding we have, which I pray to God will be resolved by when we leave here, in the Persian Gulf, and the fact that by the end of the day, this day, it will be lawful under international law for the United States and our allies to make war on Iraq—that those things are so overwhelming that we should somehow sit by until they are resolved before we do anything.

I strongly disagree. With all respect, nothing that happens in the Persian Gulf can change the underlying economic, social, and political realities of where we are as a people at this point in our history. Nothing that happens there can make us smarter or more ignorant, richer or poorer, in the long run.

And so, I would ask you to remember that if the world is a dangerous and uncertain place, it is dangerous and uncertain in many ways, and our allies in the Persian Gulf are our competitors for the future we all want to have. And if we decide not to educate our people so we can compete for that future, have we done anything to enhance the national security? I think not.

The best thing we could do in this legislative session for America is to do Arkansas's part to guarantee that we can compete with anybody anywhere for anything that's worth having. And the best thing we can do for all those wonderful men and women from this state who are in the Persian Gulf today, the very best thing we can do, is to give them a better Arkansas to come home to.

Thank you.

A Campaign for the Future

Announcement for President
Little Rock, Arkansas
October 3, 1991

When Atty. Gen. Bill Clinton announced his candidacy for governor in March 1978, the thirty-one-year-old candidate chose to do so on the south portico of Arkansas's antebellum Old State House, a classic symbol of the state's traditional political heritage. On a beautiful fall day in 1991, the forty-five-year-old governor again stood in the same place, with his wife and daughter at his side and before a background of American flags, and announced at noon that he was a candidate for the Democratic nomination for president of the United States.

Whereas his gubernatorial announcement had been delivered to only two hundred and fifty people and had to compete with morning rush-hour traffic noises, this time the audience included forty-five hundred enthusiastic Arkansas supporters, the national media corps, and the national audiences watching live on C-SPAN and CNN, and the background noise was that of gospel choirs and the Hope High School Band. The thirty-two-minute speech introduced Clinton to the nation, presented his message of middle-class hope for the future of the nation, and established the issues on which he hoped to contest the primaries and the general election in November, and after he finished speaking, the sound system blared Fleetwood Mac's "Don't Stop (Thinking about Tomorrow)," a theme that would become the campaign anthem.

❖ ❖ ❖

Thank you all for being here today, for your friendship and support, for giving me the opportunity to serve as your governor for eleven years, for filling my life full of blessings beyond anything I ever deserved.

I want to thank especially Hillary and Chelsea for taking this big step in our life's journey together: Hillary, for being my wife, my friend, and my partner in our effort to build a better future for the children and families of Arkansas and America; Chelsea, in ways she is only now coming to understand, has been our constant joy and reminder of what our public efforts are really all about: a better life for all who will work for it, a better future for the next generation.

All of you, in different ways, have brought me here today, to step beyond a life and a job I love, to make a commitment to a larger cause: preserving the American dream, restoring the hopes of the forgotten middle class, reclaiming the future for our children.

I refuse to be part of a generation that celebrates the death of communism abroad with the loss of the American dream at home.

I refuse to be a part of a generation that fails to compete in the global economy and so condemns hard-working Americans to a life of struggle without reward or security.

That is why I stand here today, because I refuse to stand by and let our children become part of the first generation to do worse than their parents. I don't want my child or your child to be part of a country that's coming apart instead of coming together.

Over twenty-five years ago, I had a professor at Georgetown who taught me that America was the greatest country in history because our people believed in and acted on two simple ideas: first, that the future can be better than the present; and second, that each of us has a personal, moral responsibility to make it so.

The fundamental truth has guided my public career and brings me here today. It is what we've devoted ourselves to here in Arkansas. I'm proud of what we've done here in Arkansas together. Proud of the work we've done to become a laboratory of democracy and innovation. And proud that we've done it without giving up the things we cherish and honor most about our way of life—solid, middle-class values of work, faith, family, individual responsibility, and community.

As I've traveled across our state, I've found that everything we believe in, everything we've fought for, is threatened by an administration that refuses to take care of our own, has turned its back on the middle class, and is afraid to change while the world is changing.

The historic events in the Soviet Union in recent months teach us an important lesson: National security begins at home. For the Soviet empire never lost to us on the field of battle. Their system rotted from the inside out, from economic, political, and spiritual failure.

To be sure, the collapse of communism requires a new national-security policy. I applaud the president's recent initiative in reducing nuclear weapons. It is an important beginning. But make no mistake—the end of the Cold War is not the end of threats to America. The world is still a dangerous and uncertain place. The first and most solemn obligation of the president is to keep America strong and safe from foreign dangers and promote democracy around the world.

But we cannot build a safe and secure world unless we can first make America strong at home. It is our ability to take care of our own at home that gives us the strength to stand up for what we believe around the world.

As governor for eleven years, working to preserve and create jobs in a global economy, I know our competition for the future is Germany and the rest of Europe, Japan and the rest of Asia. And I know that we are losing America's leadership in the world because we're losing the American dream right here at home.

Middle-class people are spending more hours on the job, spending less time with their children, bringing home a smaller paycheck to pay more for health care and housing and education. Our streets are meaner, our families are broken, our health care is the costliest in the world and we get less for it.

The country is headed in the wrong direction fast, slipping behind, losing our way, and all we have out of Washington is status quo paralysis. No vision, no action. Just neglect, selfishness, and division.

For twelve years, Republicans have tried to divide us—race against race—so we get mad at each other and not at them. They want us to look at each other across a racial divide so we don't turn and look to the White House and ask, Why are all of our incomes going down? Why are all of us losing jobs? Why are we losing our future?

Where I come from we know about race baiting. They've used it to divide us for years. I know this tactic well, and I'm not going to let them get away with it.

For twelve years, the Republicans have talked about choice without really believing in it. George Bush says he wants school choice even if it bankrupts the public schools, and yet they are more than willing to make it a crime for the women of America to exercise their individual right to choose.

For twelve years, the Republicans have been telling us that America's problems aren't their problem. They washed their hands of responsibility for the economy and education and health care and social policy and turned it over to fifty states and a thousand points of light. Well, here in Arkansas we've done our best to create jobs and educate our people. And each of us has tried to be one of those thousand points of light. But I can tell you, where there is no national vision, no national partnership, no national leadership, a thousand points of light leaves a lot of darkness.

We must provide the answers, the solutions. And we will. We're going to turn this country around and get it moving again, and we're going to fight for the hard-working middle-class families of America for a change.

Make no mistake. This election is about change: in our party, in our national leadership, and in our country.

And we're not going to get positive change just by Bush bashing. We have to do a better job of the old-fashioned work of confronting the real problems of real people and pointing the way to a better future. That is our challenge in 1992.

Today, as we stand on the threshold of a new era, a new millennium, I believe we need a new kind of leadership, leadership committed to change; leadership not mired in the politics of the past, not limited by old ideologies; proven leadership that knows how to reinvent government to help solve the real problems of real people.

That is why today I am declaring my candidacy for president of the United States. Together I believe we can provide leadership that will restore the American dream, that will fight for the forgotten middle class, that will provide more opportunity, insist on more responsibility, and create a greater sense of community for this great country.

The change we must make isn't liberal or conservative. It's both, and it's different. The small towns and main streets of America aren't like the corridors and back rooms of Washington. People out here don't care about the idle rhetoric of "left" and "right" and "liberal" and "conservative" and all the other words that have made our politics a substitute for action. These families are crying out desperately for someone who believes the promise of America is to help them with their struggle to get ahead, to offer them a green light instead of a pink slip.

This must be a campaign of ideas, not slogans. We don't need another president who doesn't know what he wants to do for America. I'm going to tell you in plain language what I intend to do as president. How we can meet the challenges we face—that's the test for all the Democratic candidates in this campaign. Americans know what we're up against. Let's show them what we're for.

We need a new covenant to rebuild America. It's just common sense. Government's responsibility is to create more opportunity. The people's responsibility is to make the most of it.

In a Clinton administration we are going to create opportunity for all. We've got to grow this economy, not shrink it. We need to give people incentives to make long-term investment in America and reward people's money. We've got to invest more money in emerging technologies to help keep high-paying jobs here at home. We've got to convert from a defense to a domestic economy.

We've got to expand world trade, tear down barriers, but demand fair trade policies if we're going to provide good jobs for our people. The American people don't want to run from the world. We must meet the competition and win.

Opportunity for all means world-class skills and world-class education. We need more than "photo ops" and empty rhetoric; we need standards and accountability and excellence in education. On this issue, I'm proud to say that Arkansas has led the way.

In a Clinton administration, students and parents and teachers will get a real education president.

Opportunity for all means preschool for every child who needs it, and an apprenticeship program for kids who don't want to go to college but do want good jobs. It means teaching everybody with a job to read and passing a domestic GI Bill that would give every young American the chance to borrow the money necessary to go to college and ask them to pay it back either as a small percentage of their income over time or through national service as teachers or policemen or nurses or child-care workers.

In a Clinton administration, everyone will be able to get a college loan as long as they're willing to give something back to their country in return.

Opportunity for all means reforming the health-care system to control costs, improve quality, expand preventive and long-term care, maintain consumer choice, and cover everybody. And we don't have to bankrupt the taxpayers to do it. We do have to take on the big insurance companies and health-care bureaucracies and get some real cost control into the system. I pledge to the American people that in the first year of a Clinton administration we will present a plan to Congress and the American people to provide affordable, quality health care for all Americans.

Opportunity for all means making our cities and our streets safe from crime and drugs. Across America, citizens are banding together to take their streets and neighborhoods back. In a Clinton administration, we'll be on their side—with new initiatives like community policing, drug treatment for those who need it, and boot camps for first-time offenders.

Finally, opportunity for all means we must protect our environment and develop an energy policy that relies more on conservation and clean natural gas so all our children will inherit a world that is cleaner, safer, and more beautiful.

But hear me now. I honestly believe that if we try to do these things, we will still not solve the problems of today or move into the next century with confidence unless we do what President Kennedy did and ask every American citizen to assume personal responsibility for the future of our country.

The government owes our people more opportunity, but we all have to make the most of it through responsible citizenship.

We should insist that people move off welfare rolls and onto work rolls. We should give people on welfare the skills they need to succeed, but we should demand that everybody who can work go to work and become a productive member of society.

We should insist on the toughest possible child-support enforcement. Governments don't raise children, parents do. And when they don't, their children pay forever, and so do we.

And we have got to say, as we've tried to do in Arkansas, that students have a responsibility to stay in school. If you drop out for no good reason, you should lose your driver's license. But it's important to remember that the most irresponsible people of all in the 1980s were those at the top—not those who were doing worse, not the hard-working middle class, but those who sold our savings and loans with bad deals and spent billions on wasteful takeovers and mergers, money that could have been spent to create better products and new jobs.

Do you know that in the 1980s, while middle-class income went down, charitable giving by working people went up? And while rich people's incomes went up, charitable giving by the wealthy went down. Why? Because our leaders had an ethic of get it while you can and to heck with everybody else.

How can you ask people who work or who are poor to behave responsibly when they know that the heads of our biggest companies raised their own pay in the last decade by four times the percentage their workers' pay went up? Three times as much as their profits went up. When they ran their companies into the ground and their employees were on the street, what did they do? They bailed out with golden parachutes to a cushy life. That's just wrong.

Teddy Roosevelt and Harry Truman and John Kennedy didn't hesitate to use the bully pulpit of the presidency. They changed America by standing up for what's right. When the Salomon brothers abused the treasury markets, the president was silent. When the rip-off artists looted our S&Ls, the president was silent. In a Clinton administration, when people sell their companies and their workers and their country down the river, they'll get called on the carpet. We're going to insist that they invest in this country and create jobs for our people.

In the 1980s, Washington failed us, too. We spent more money on the present and the past and less on the future. We spent five hundred billion dollars to recycle assets in the S&L mess, but we couldn't afford five billion dollars for unemployed workers or to give every kid in this country the chance to be in Head Start. We can do better than that, and will.

A Clinton administration won't spend our money on programs that don't solve problems and a government that doesn't work. I want to reinvent government to make it more efficient and more effective. I want to give citizens more choices in the services they get and empower them to make those choices. That's what we've tried to do in Arkansas. We've balanced the budget every year and improved services. We've treated taxpayers like our customers and our bosses, because they are.

I want the American people to know that a Clinton administration will defend our national interests abroad, put their values into our social policy at home, and spend their tax money with discipline. We'll put government back on the side of the hard-working middle-class families of America who think most of the help goes to those at the top of the ladder, some goes to the bottom, and no one speaks for them.

But we need more than new laws, new promises, or new programs. We need a new spirit of community, a sense that we are all in this together. If we have no sense of community, the American dream will continue to wither. Our destiny is bound up with the destiny of every other American. We're all in this together, and we will rise or fall together.

A few years ago, Hillary and I visited a classroom in Los Angeles, in an area plagued by drugs and gangs. We talked to a dozen sixth graders whose number-one concern was being shot going to and from school. Their second worry was turning twelve or thirteen and being forced to join a gang or be beaten. And finally, they were worried about their own parents' drug abuse.

Nearly half a century ago, I was born not far from here in Hope, Arkansas. My mother had been widowed three months before I was born. I was raised for four years by my grandparents, while she went back to nursing school. They didn't have much money. I spent a lot of time with my great-grandparents. By any standard, they were poor. But we didn't blame other people. We took responsibility for ourselves and for each other because we knew we could do better. I was raised to believe in the American dream, in family values, in individual responsibility, and in the obligation of government to help people who were doing the best they could.

It's a long way in America from that loving family which is embodied today in a picture on my wall in the governor's office of me at the age of six holding my great-grandfather's hand to an America where children on the streets of our cities don't know who their grandparents are and have to worry about their own parents' drug abuse.

I tell you, by making common cause with those children we give new life to the American dream. And that is our generation's responsibility—to form a New Covenant—more opportunity for all, more responsibility from everyone, and a greater sense of common purpose.

I believe with all my heart that we can make this happen. We can usher in a new era of progress, prosperity, and renewal. We can. We must. This is not just a campaign for the presidency; it is a campaign for the future, for the forgotten hard-working middle-class families of America who deserve a government that fights for them, a campaign to keep America strong at home and around the world. Join with us. I ask for your prayers, your help, your hands, and your hearts. Together we can make America great again and build a community of hope that will inspire the world.

A New Covenant: Responsibility and Rebuilding the American Community

Georgetown University
Washington, D.C.
October 23, 1991

In the first major policy speech since his announcement in Little Rock and one in which he hoped to define his campaign premises, Clinton began to explain the parameters of his proposed "New Covenant" between the people and their government. He delivered the speech to about four hundred students and faculty in Gaston Hall at his alma mater, Georgetown University, but the 11 A.M. address was also covered by the national media and intended for an audience beyond that in the hall. Clinton invoked the legacies of Franklin Roosevelt and John Kennedy and stressed the theme of citizen responsibility, yet his presentation was in many ways quite unlike that of the typical challenger. The speech was intended to clarify Clinton's political assumptions about personal responsibility and the nature of community, setting up two future speeches in the series that would provide more attention to specific issues.

❖ ❖ ❖

Thank you all for being here today. You are living in revolutionary times. When I was here, America sought to contain communism, not roll it back. Most respected academics held that once a country "went communist," the loss of freedom was permanent and irreversible. Yet in the last three years, we've seen the Berlin Wall come down, Germany reunified, all of Eastern Europe abandon communism, a coup in the Soviet Union fail, and the Soviet Union itself disintegrate, liberating the Baltics and other republics. Now the Soviet foreign minister is trying to help our secretary of state make peace in the Middle East. And in the space of one year, Lech Walesa and Vaclav Havel both came to this city to thank America for supporting their quest for freedom. Nelson Mandela walked out of a jail in South Africa he entered before I entered Georgetown in 1964. He now wants a Bill of Rights like ours for his country. We should be celebrating. All around the world, the American dream—political freedom, market economics, national independence—is ascendant. Everything your parents and grandparents stood for from World War II on has been rewarded.

Yet, we're not celebrating. Why? Because our people fear that while the American dream reigns supreme abroad, it is dying here at home. We're losing jobs and wasting opportunities. The very fiber of our nation is breaking down: Families are coming apart, kids are dropping out of school, drugs and crime dominate our streets. And our leaders here in Washington are doing nothing to turn America around. Our political system rotates between being the butt of jokes and the object of scorn. Frustration produces calls for term limits from voters who think they can't vote incumbents out; resentment produces votes for David Duke—not just from racists, but from voters so desperate for change, they'll support the most anti-establishment message, even from an ex-Klansman who was inspired by Adolf Hitler. We've got to rebuild our political life together before demagogues and racists and those who pander to the worst in us bring this country down.

People once looked to our president and Congress to bring us together, solve problems, and make progress. Now, in the face of massive challenges, our government stands discredited, our people disillusioned. There's a hole in our politics where a sense of common purpose used to be.

The Reagan-Bush years have exalted private gain over public obligations, special interests over the common good, wealth and fame over work and family. The 1980s ushered in a gilded age of greed, selfishness, irresponsibility, excess, and neglect. S&L crooks stole billions of dollars in other people's money. Pentagon contractors and HUD consultants stole from the taxpayers. Many big corporate executives raised their own salaries when their companies were losing money or their workers were losing their jobs. Middle-class families worked longer hours for less money and spent more on health care, housing, education, and taxes. Poverty rose. Many inner-city streets were taken over by crime and drugs, welfare and despair. Family responsibility became an oxymoron for deadbeat fathers who were more likely to make their car payments than pay their child support. And government, which should have been setting an example, was even worse. Congress raised its pay and guarded its perks while most Americans were working harder for less money. Two Republican presidents elected on a promise of fiscal responsibility advanced budget policies that more than tripled the national debt. Congress went along with that, too. Taxes were lowered on the wealthiest people whose incomes rose and raised on middle-class people whose incomes fell.

And through it all, millions of decent, ordinary people who worked hard, played by the rules, and took responsibility for their own actions were falling behind, living a life of struggle without reward or security. For twelve years, the forgotten middle class watched their economic interests ignored and their values run into the ground. Nothing illustrates this more clearly, in the 1980s, than the fact that charitable giving by middle-class families went up as their incomes went down, while charitable giving by the wealthiest Americans went down as their incomes went up. Responsibility went unrewarded and so did hard work. It's no wonder so many kids growing up on the street think it makes more sense to join a gang and deal drugs than to stay in school and go to work. The fast buck was glorified from Wall Street to Main Street to Mean Street.

To turn America around, we need a new approach founded on our most sacred principles as a nation, with a vision for the future. We need a New Covenant, a solemn agreement between the people and their government, to provide opportunity for everybody, inspire responsibility throughout our society, and restore a sense of community to this great nation. A New Covenant to take government back from the powerful interests and the bureaucracy and give this country back to ordinary people.

More than two hundred years ago, the founders outlined our first social compact between government and the people, not just between lords and kings. More than a century ago, Abraham Lincoln gave his life to maintain the Union the compact created. Sixty years ago, Franklin Roosevelt renewed that promise with a New Deal that offered opportunity in return for hard work.

Today we need to forge a New Covenant that will repair the damaged bond between the people and their government and restore our basic values—the notion that our country has a responsibility to help people get ahead, that citizens have not only the right but a responsibility to rise as far and as high as their talents and determination can take them, and that we're all in this together. We must make good on the words of Thomas Jefferson, who said, "A debt of service is due from every man to his country proportional to the bounties which nature and fortune have measured to him."

Make no mistake, this New Covenant means change—change in our party, change in our national leadership, and change in our country. Far away from Washington, in your hometowns and mine, people have lost faith in the ability of government to change their lives for the better. Out there, you can hear the quiet, troubled voice of the forgotten middle class, lamenting that government no longer looks out for their interests or honors their values—like individual responsibility, hard work, family, community. They think their government takes more from them than it gives back and looks the other way when special interests only take from this country and give nothing back. And they're right. This New Covenant can't be between the politicians and the established interests. It can't be another back-room deal between the people in power and the people who keep them there. This New Covenant can only be ratified in the people in the 1992 election. And that's why I'm running for president.

Some people think it's old-fashioned to talk like this. Some people even think I am naive to suggest that we can restore the American dream through a covenant between people and their government. But I believe with all my heart after eleven years of work as governor, working every day to create opportunity and jobs and improve education and deal with all the problems that we all know so much about—I believe that the only way we can hold this country together, and move boldly forward into the future, is to do it together with a New Covenant.

Over twenty-five years ago, Professor Carroll Quigley taught in his Western civilization class here at Georgetown that the defining idea of our culture in general and our country in particular is "future preference," the idea that the future can be better than the present, and that each of us has a personal, moral responsibility to make it so.

I hope they still teach that lesson here, and I hope you believe it, because I don't think we can save America without it.

In the weeks to come, I will come back to Georgetown and outline my plans to rebuild our economy, regain our competitive leadership in the world, restore the forgotten middle class, and reclaim the future for the next generation. I will put forth my views on how to promote our national-security and foreign-policy interests after the Cold War. And I will tell you in clear terms what I believe the president and the Congress owe the people in this New Covenant for change.

But I can tell you, based on my long experience in public life, there will never be a government program for every problem. Much of what holds us together and moves us ahead is the daily assumption of personal responsibility by millions of Americans from all walks of life. I can promise to do a hundred different things for you as president. But none of them will make any difference unless we all do more as citizens. And, today, I want to talk about the responsibilities we owe to ourselves, to one another, and to our nation.

It's been thirty years since a Democrat ran for president and asked something of all the American people. I intend to challenge you to do more and to do better.

We must go beyond the competing ideas of the old political establishment: beyond every man for himself on the one hand and the right to something for nothing on the other.

We need a New Covenant that will challenge all our citizens to be responsible. The New Covenant will say to our corporate leaders at the top of the ladder: We'll promote economic growth and the free market, but we're not going to help you diminish the middle class and weaken the economy. We'll support your efforts to increase profits and jobs through quality products and services, but we're going to hold you responsible to be good corporate citizens, too.

The New Covenant will say to people on welfare: We're going to provide the training and education and health care you need, but if you can work, you've got to go to work, because you can no longer stay on welfare forever.

The New Covenant will say to the hard-working middle class and those who aspire to it: We're going to guarantee you access to a college education, but if you get that help, you've got to give something back to your country.

And the New Covenant will challenge all of us in public service: We have a solemn responsibility to honor the values and promote the interests of the people who elected us, and if we don't, we don't belong in government anymore.

This New Covenant must begin here in Washington. The New Covenant will literally revolutionize government and fundamentally change its relationship to people. People don't want some top-down bureaucracy telling them what to do anymore. That's one reason they tore down the Berlin Wall and threw out the communist regimes in Eastern Europe and Russia.

Now, the New Covenant will challenge our government to change its way of doing business, too. The American people need a government that works at a price they can afford. The Republicans have been in charge of the government for twelve years. They've brought the country to the brink of bankruptcy. Democrats who want the government to do more—and I'm one of them—have a heavy responsibility to show that we're going to spend the taxpayer's money wisely and with discipline.

I want to make government more efficient and more effective by eliminating unnecessary layers of bureaucracy and cutting administrative costs and by giving people more choices in the services they get and empowering them to make those choices. That's what we've tried to do in Arkansas—balancing our budget every year, improving services, and treating taxpayers like our customers and our bosses, giving them more choices in public schools, child-care centers, and services for the elderly.

The New Covenant must challenge Congress to act responsibly. And here again, Democrats must lead the way. Because they want to use government to help people, Democrats have to put Congress in order: Congress should live by the laws it applies to other workplaces. No more midnight pay raises. Congressional pay shouldn't go up while the pay of working Americans is going down. Let's clamp down on campaign spending and open the airwaves to encourage real political debate instead of paid political assassination. No more bounced checks. No more bad restaurant debts. No more fixed tickets. Service in Congress is privilege enough.

We can't go on like this. We have to honor, reward, and reflect the work ethic, not the power grab. Responsibility is for everybody, and it begins here in the nation's capital.

The New Covenant will also challenge the private sector. The most irresponsible people in the 1980s were those in business who abused their position at the top of the totem pole. This is my message to the business community: As president, I'm going to do everything I can to make it easier for your company to compete in the world, with a better trained work force, cooperation between labor and management, fair and strong trade policies, and incentives to invest in America's economic growth. But I want the jetsetters and the feather bedders of corporate America to know that if you sell your companies and your workers and your country down the river, you'll get called on the carpet. That's what the president's bully pulpit is for.

All of you who are going into business, it is a noble endeavor. It is the thing that makes this country run. The private sector creates jobs, not the public sector. But you have to know that the people with the responsibility in the private sector should think it's simply not enough to obey the letter of the law and make as much money as you can. It's wrong for executives to do what so many did in the eighties. The biggest companies raised their pay by four times the percentage their workers' pay went up and three times the percentage their profits went up. It's wrong to drive a company into the ground and have the chief executive bail out with a golden parachute to a cushy life.

The average CEO at a major American corporation is paid about one hundred times as much as the average worker—compare that to two countries doing much better than we are in the world economy. In Germany it's 23 to 1, and in Japan, which just completed fifty-eight months of untrammeled economic growth, it's 17 to 1. And our government today rewards that excess with a tax break for executive pay, no matter how high it is. That's wrong. If a company wants to overpay its executives and underinvest in the future, it shouldn't get any special treatment from Uncle Sam. If a company wants to transfer jobs abroad and cut the security of working people, it shouldn't get special treatment from the treasury. In the 1980s, we didn't do enough to help our companies to compete and win in a global economy. We did too much to transfer wealth away from hard-working middle-class people to the rich without good reason. That's got to stop. There should be no more deductibility for irresponsibility.

The New Covenant will also challenge the hard-working middle-class families of America. Their challenge centers around work and education. I know Americans worry about the quality of education in this country and want the best for their children. The Clinton administration will set high national standards based on international competition for what everybody ought to know, and a national examination system to measure whether they're learning it. It's not enough to put money into schools. We need to challenge the schools to produce, and we've got to insist on results.

I just came from Thomas Jefferson Junior High School here in Washington, and the principal of that school, Vera White, I think is here with me today. I've been to that school three times in the last five years. That school is in a building that was built when Grant was president. They have the plaster models of the Jefferson Memorial in the school auditorium. But every time I've been in that school, you could eat lunch off every floor in the school. There is a spirit of learning that pervades the atmosphere. Almost everyone in the school comes from an ordinary family in Washington—it's almost 100 percent minority. But in several years that school has won the National Math Council's competition going all the way to the finals for junior-high-school performance in math. And every time I go there I'm just overwhelmed by the spirit that exists from a teacher's and principal's point of view, because they know that they're going to produce, and they don't make excuses for the problems that the kids bring to the classroom; they open those kids to a brighter world. We need more of that.

But we also have to recognize that teachers can't do it all. We must challenge all parents and children to believe all children can learn. And here is the biggest challenge of all: Too many American parents raise their kids to believe that how much they learn depends on the IQ that God gave them and how much money their family makes. Yet in the countries we are competing against for the future, children are raised to believe that how much they learn depends on how hard they work and how much their parents encourage them to learn.

The New Covenant will challenge students of America to stay in school. Students who drop out of school or fail to learn as much as they can are not just letting down themselves and their families. They're failing their communities, because from that point on, chances are they're subtracting from society, not adding to it. In Arkansas, we've tried to enhance responsibility for students by saying that if they drop out for no good reason, they lose the privilege of a driver's license.

The New Covenant means new challenges for every young person. I want to establish a system of voluntary national service for all Americans. In a Clinton administration, we'll put forth a domestic GI Bill that will say to the middle class as well as low-income people: We want you to go to college, we'll pay for it, it will be the best money we ever spent, but you've got to give something back to your country in return. As president, I'll set up a trust fund out of which any American can borrow money for a college education, so long as they pay it back either as a small percentage of their income over time or with a couple of years of national service as teachers, police officers, child-care workers—doing work our country desperately needs.

And education doesn't stop in school. Adults have a responsibility to keep learning so they can stay ahead of the competition, too. All of us are going to have to work smarter in the years to come, and that will require new forms of cooperation in the workplace between management and workers and a continuing effort to move toward high-performance work organizations.

There's a special challenge in the New Covenant for the young men and women who live in America's most troubled urban neighborhoods, the children like those I met in Chicago and Los Angeles who live in fear of being forced to join a gang or getting shot going to and from school.

Many of these young people believe this country has ignored them for too long, and they're right. Many of them think America unfairly blames them for every wrong in our society—for drugs, crime, poverty, the breakup of the family, and the breakdown of the schools—and they're right. They worry that because their face is of a different color, their only choice in life is jail or welfare or a dead-end job, that being a minority in an inner city is a guarantee of failure. But they're wrong, and when I'm president, I'm going to do my best to prove they're wrong.

I know these young people can overcome anything they set their mind to. I believe America needs their strength, their intelligence, and their humanity. And because I believe in them and what they can contribute to our society, they must not be let off the hook. All society can offer them is a chance to develop their God-given abilities. They have to do the rest. Anybody who tells them otherwise is lying, and they know it.

As president, I'll see that they get the same deal as everyone else: they've got to play by the rules, stay off drugs, stay in school, and keep out of the streets. They've got to stop having children if they're not prepared to support them. Governments don't raise children. People do.

And for those young people who do get into trouble, we'll give them one chance to avoid prison, by setting up community boot camps for first-time nonviolent offenders—where they can learn discipline, get drug treatment if necessary, continue their education, and do useful work for their community. A second chance to be a first-rate citizen.

The New Covenant must be pro-work. That means people who work shouldn't be poor. In a Clinton administration, we'll do everything we can to break the cycle of dependency and help the poor climb out of poverty. First, we need to make work pay by expanding the earned income tax credit for the working poor, creating savings accounts that make it easier for poor people even on welfare to save, and supporting microenterprise grants for those who want to start a small business. At the same time, we need to assure all Americans that they'll have access to health care when they go to work.

The New Covenant can break the cycle of welfare. Welfare should be a second chance, not a way of life. In a Clinton administration, we're going to put an end to welfare as we know it. I want to erase the stigma of welfare for good by restoring a simple, dignified principle: no one who can work can stay on welfare forever.

We'll still help people who can't help themselves and those who need education and training and child care. But if people can work, they'll have to do so. We'll give them all the help they need for up to two years. But after that, if they're able to work, they'll have to take a job in the private sector or start earning their way through community service. That way, we'll restore the covenant that welfare was first meant to be: to give temporary help to people who've fallen on hard times.

If the New Covenant is pro-work, it must also be pro-family. That means we must demand the toughest possible child-support enforcement. We need an administration that will give state agencies that collect child support full law-enforcement authority and find new ways of catching deadbeats. In Arkansas, we passed a law this year that says if you owe more than a thousand dollars in child support, we're going to report you to every credit agency in the state. People shouldn't be able to borrow money before they take care of their children.

Finally, the president has the greatest responsibility of all—to bring us together, not drive us apart. For twelve years, this president and his predecessor have divided us against each other—pitting rich against poor, black against white, women against men—creating a country where we no longer recognize that we're all in this together. They have profited by fostering an atmosphere of blame and denial instead of building an ethic of responsibility. They had a chance to bring out the best in us and instead they appealed to the worst in us.

Nothing exemplifies this more clearly than the battle over the Civil Rights Act of 1991. You know from what I've already said today that I can't be for quotas. I'm for responsibility at every turn. That bill is not a quota bill. When the Civil Rights Act was in place from 1964 to 1987, I never had a single employer in my state say "it's a quota bill." We need rules of workplace fairness for the 70 percent of new entrants in our work force who will be women and minorities in the decade of the nineties. That's what that bill is for.

Why does the president refuse to let a civil rights bill pass? Because he knows that the people he is dependent on for his electoral majority—white, working-class men and women, mostly men—have had their incomes decline in the 1980s, and they may return to their natural home, to someone who offers them real opportunity. And so he is dredging up the same old tactic that the hard Right has employed in my part of the country, in the South, since I was a child. When everything gets tight, and you think you're going to lose those people, you find the most economically insecure white people, and you scare the living daylights out of them.

That is wrong. This president turned away John Danforth, who shepherded Clarence Thomas's nomination through the Senate. John Danforth begged him for a civil rights bill. He said no. He turned away the Business Roundtable, an organization of corporate executives, largely Republican, who said we need a civil rights bill. He said no. And today, in the press it's reported that he turned away his own minority leader in the United States Senate, Senator Bob Dole, who wanted a civil rights bill.

This man does not want a bill. He wants an issue to drive a stake into the heart of America, and it's wrong. And I won't let him get away with it.

I pledge to you that I'm not going to let the Republicans get away with this cynical scam anymore. A New Covenant means it's my responsibility and the responsibility of every American in this country to fight back against the politics of division and bring this country together.

After all, that is what's special about America. We want to be part of a nation that's coming together, not coming apart. We want to be part of a community where people look out for each other, not just for themselves. We want to be part of a nation that brings out the best in us, not the worst. And we believe that the only limit to what we can do is what our leaders are willing to ask of us and what we are willing to expect of ourselves.

Nearly sixty years ago, in a famous speech to the Commonwealth Club in the final months of his 1932 campaign, Franklin Roosevelt outlined a new compact that gave hope to a nation mired in the Great Depression. The role of government, he said, was to promise every American the right to make a living. The people's role was to do their best to make the most of it. He said: "Faith in America demands that we recognize the new terms of the old social contract. In the strength of great hope we must all shoulder our common load."

That's what our hope is today: A New Covenant to shoulder our common load. When people assume responsibility and shoulder that common load, they acquire a dignity they never knew before. When people go to work, they rediscover a pride that was lost. When fathers pay their child support, they restore a connection they and their children need. When students work harder, they find out they all can learn and do as well as anyone else on Earth. When corporate managers put their workers and their long-term profits ahead of their own paychecks, their companies do well, and so do they. When the privilege of serving is enough of a perk for people in Congress, and the president finally assumes responsibility for America's problems, we'll not only stop doing wrong, we'll begin to do what is right to move America forward. And that is what this election is really all about—forging a New Covenant of change that will honor middle-class values, restore the public trust, create a new sense of community, and make America work again.

Thank you.

A New Covenant for Economic Change

Georgetown University
Washington, D.C.
November 20, 1991

In the second in a series of major policy speeches defining his campaign message, Clinton delivered this forty-minute address to students, faculty, and the national media at Georgetown University's Gaston Hall. Laying the blame for the nation's economic woes on both President Bush and the Congress, he said his campaign was "a crusade to restore the forgotten middle class" and that it was time to "lay George Bush off, and put America back to work."

The *Washington Post* said Clinton brought "Clear and incisive thinking" to the nation's long-term economic future, and the *Los Angeles Times* called it "a detailed program" proposing "a restructuring of the American economy that is expected to form the core of his campaign for the Democratic presidential nomination." While demonstrating that the campaign felt the economy was the main issue of the campaign—"It's the Economy, Stupid" would become the internal slogan—Clinton here argued that economic solutions must also include proposals for restructuring the related systems of education and health care, putting people first.

❖ ❖ ❖

Thank you for being here today. A better future for your generation—a better life for all who will work for it—is what this campaign is about.

But I come here today convinced that your future—the very future of our country—the American dream—is in peril. This country is in trouble. As I've traveled around this country, I've seen too much pain on people's faces, too much fear in people's eyes. We've got to do better.

This month, I visited with a couple from New Hampshire named David and Rita Springs. He's a chemical engineer by training; she's studying to be a lab technician. They told me that a month before his pension was vested, the people who ran his company fired him to cut their payrolls. Then they turned around and sold the company, and bailed out with a golden parachute while David Springs and his family got the shaft.

Last week, at a bowling alley in Manchester, I met a fireman who was working two jobs and his wife who was working fifty hours a week in a mill. They told me they were worried that even though both of them were working like this and their son was a straight-A student, they still wouldn't be able to afford to send him to college because of the rising cost of college education and because they were too well-off to get government help.

At a breakfast in a cafe in New Hampshire, I met a young man whose twelve-year-old child had had open-heart surgery, and now no one will hire him because they can't afford his health insurance.

The families I met are from New Hampshire, but they could be from anywhere in America. They're the backbone of the country, the ones who do the work and pay the taxes and send their children off to war. They're a lot like people I've seen in Arkansas for years, living with the real consequences of our national neglect. These are the real victims of the Reagan Revolution, the Bush Succession, and this awful national recession.

During this administration, the economy has grown more slowly and fewer jobs have been created than in any administration since World War II. People who have jobs are working longer hours for less money; people who don't are looking harder to find less. Middle-class people are paying more for health care, housing, education, and taxes, when government services have been cut.

And as these hard-working middle-class families look to their president to make good on his promises, his answer to them is: Tough luck. It's your fault. Go buy a house or a car.

Just this week, George Bush said we don't need a plan to end this recession —that if we wait long enough, our problems will go away. Well, he's right about that part: If he doesn't have a plan to turn this country around by November of 1992, we're going to lay George Bush off, put America back to work, and our problems will go away.

We need a president who will take responsibility for getting this country moving again, a president who will provide the leadership to pull us together and challenge our nation to compete in the world and win again.

Ten years ago, America had the highest wages in the world. Now we're tenth, and falling. Last year, Germany and Japan had productivity growth rates three and four times ours because they educate their people better, invest more in their future, and organize their economies for global competition, and we don't.

For twelve years of this Reagan-Bush era, the Republicans have let S&L crooks and self-serving CEOs try to build an economy out of paper and perks instead of people and products. It's the Republican way: every man for himself and get it while you can. They stacked the odds in favor of their friends at the top, and told everybody else to wait for whatever trickled down.

And every step of the way, the Republicans forgot about the very people they had promised to help—the very people who elected them in the first place—the forgotten middle-class Americans who still live by American values and whose hopes, hearts, and hands still carry the American dream.

But Democrats forgot about real people, too.

Democrats in Congress joined the White House in tripling the national debt and raising the deficit to the point of paralysis. Democrats and Republicans in Congress joined the White House on the sidelines, cheering on an S&L boom until it went bust to the tune of five hundred billion dollars.

For too many Americans, for too long, it's seemed that Congress and the White House have been more interested in looking out for themselves and for their friends, but not for the country and not for the people who make it great.

And, now, after twelve years of Reagan-Bush, the forgotten middle class is discovering that the reward for twelve years of sacrifice and hard work is more sacrifice and more hard times: They've paid higher taxes on lower incomes for service cuts, while the rich got tax cuts, while poverty increased, and the president and Congress got pay raises and health insurance.

We've got to move in a radically different direction. The Republicans' failed experiment in supply-side economics doesn't produce growth. It doesn't create upward mobility. And most important, it doesn't prepare millions and millions of Americans to compete and win in the new world economy.

And we've got to move away from the old Democratic theory that says we can just tax and spend our way out of any problem we face. Expanding government doesn't expand opportunity. And big deficits don't produce sustained economic growth, especially when the borrowed money is spent on yesterday's mistakes, not tomorrow's investments.

Stale theories produce nothing but stalemate. The old economic answers are obsolete. We've seen the limits of Keynesian economics. We've seen the worst of supply-side economics. We need a new approach.

For twelve years, we've had no economic vision, no economic leadership, no national economic strategy. What America needs is a president with a radical new approach to our economic problems that will give new life to the American dream.

We need a New Covenant for economic change, a new economics that empowers people, rewards work, and organizes America to compete and win again. A national economic strategy to liberate and energize the abilities of millions of Americans who are paying more taxes when the government is doing less for them, who are working harder while their wages go down.

This New Covenant isn't liberal or conservative. It's both, and it's different. The American people don't care about the idle rhetoric of left and right. They're real people, with real problems, and they think no one in Washington wants to solve their problems or stand up for them.

The goals of our New Covenant for economic change are straightforward: We need a president who will put economic opportunity in the hands of ordinary people, not rich and powerful special interests; a president who will revolutionize government to invest more in the future; a president who will encourage the private sector to organize in new ways and cooperate to produce economic growth; a president who will challenge and lead America to compete and win in the global economy, not retreat from the world. That's how we'll turn this country's economy around, recapture America's leadership in the world, and build a better future for our children. That's how we'll show the forgotten middle class we really understand their struggle. That's how we'll reduce poverty and rebuild the ladder from poverty to the middle class. And that, my friends, is why I'm running for president of the United States.

Our first responsibility under this New Covenant is to move quickly to put this recession behind us. Last week, I released a plan for what I would do right away to help working people and get the economy moving again. I'd not only extend unemployment benefits, as Congress and the president have finally done, but I'd push through a middle-class tax cut, an accelerated highway bill to create forty to fifty thousand new construction jobs over the next six months, and an increase in the ceiling on FHA mortgage guarantee so half a million families could pump up the economy by buying their first home. I do think good credit-card customers should receive a break from the 18 and 19 percent rates of banks, which have cut the rates the customers get paid on their deposit accounts. And I'm proud to say that four of the ten banks charging the lowest credit-card rates nationwide are in my state.

I would also make sure federal regulators send a clear signal to the financial community not to call in loans that are performing and not to fear making good loans to local businesses.

But even if we did all those things tomorrow, it wouldn't change the fundamental challenge of the 1990s. We need to get out of this recession, and soon. But we also need a long-term national strategy to create a high-wage, high-growth, high-opportunity economy, not a hard-work, low-wage economy that's sinking when it ought to be rising.

It doesn't have to be that way. I believe we can win again. In the global economy of the 1990s, economic growth won't come from government spending. It will come instead from individuals working smarter and learning more, from entrepreneurs taking more risks and going after new markets, and from corporations designing better products and taking a longer view. We're going to reward work, expand opportunity, empower people, and we are going to win again.

Empowering Every American

There are two reasons why middle-class people today are working harder for less pay. First, their taxes have gone up; but that's only 30 percent of their problem. The other 70 percent of the problem is America's loss of economic growth and world economic leadership.

If we're going to turn this country around, we've not only got to liberate ordinary people from unfair taxes, we've got to empower every American with the education and training essential to get ahead.

Let me make this clear: Education is economic development. We can only be a high-wage, high-growth country if we are a high-skills country. In a world in which money and production are mobile, the only way middle-class people can keep good jobs with growing incomes is to be lifetime learners and innovators. Without world-class skills, the middle class will surely continue to decline. With them, middle-class workers will generate more high-wage jobs in America in the nineties.

Empowering everybody begins with preschool for every child who needs it, and fully funding Head Start. It includes a national examination system to push our students to meet world-class standards in core subjects like math and science, and an annual report card for every state, every school district, and every school to measure our progress in meeting those standards.

Empowerment means training young people for high-wage jobs, not dead-end ones. Young Americans with only a high-school education make 25 percent less today than they would have fifteen years ago. In a Clinton administration we'll have a national apprenticeship program that will enable high-school students who aren't bound for college to enter a course of study, designed by schools and local businesses, to teach them valuable skills, with a promise of a real job with growing incomes when they graduate.

Empowerment means challenging our students and every American with a system of voluntary national service. In a Clinton administration we will offer a domestic GI Bill that will say to middle class as well as low-income people: We want you to go to college, and we're glad to pay for it; but you've got to give something back to your country in return. As president, I'll ask Congress to establish a trust fund out of which any American can borrow money for a college education, so long as they pay it back either as a small percentage of their income over time or with a couple of years of national service as teachers, police officers, child-care workers—doing work our country urgently needs. The fund would be financed with a portion of the peace dividend and by redirecting the present student-loan program, which is nowhere near as cost-effective as it should be. This program will pay for itself many times over.

But in an era when what you can earn depends largely on what you can learn, education can't stop at the schoolhouse door. From now on, anyone who's willing to work will have a chance to learn. In a Clinton administration, we'll make adult literacy programs available to all who need it, by working with states to make sure every state has a clear, achievable plan to teach everyone with a job to read, to give them a chance to earn a GED, and wherever possible, to do it where they work. In Arkansas we had fourteen thousand people in adult education programs in 1983. Today we have over fifty thousand. By 1993, we'll have over seventy thousand. Every state can do the same for a modest cost with a disciplined plan and a flexible delivery system.

And we will ensure that every working American has the opportunity to learn new skills every year. Today, American business spends billions of dollars on training—the equivalent of 1.5 percent of the costs of their payrolls—but 70 percent of it goes to the 10 percent at the top of the ladder. In a Clinton administration, we'll require employers to offer every worker his or her share of those training dollars or contribute the equivalent to a national training fund. Workers will get the training they need, and companies will learn that the more you train your workers, the more your profits increase.

We need special efforts to empower the poor to work their way out of poverty. We'll make work pay by expanding the earned income tax credit for the working poor, and by supporting private and public partnerships to give low-income entrepreneurs the tools to start new businesses, through innovative institutions like Shore Bank in Chicago and its rural counterpart, the Southern Development Bancorporation in Arkansas. We've got to break the cycle of dependency and put an end to permanent dependence on welfare as a way of life, by really investing in the development of poor people and giving them the means, the incentives, and the requirement to go to work.

Finally, empowering working Americans means letting them keep more of what they earn. Ronald Reagan and George Bush raised taxes on the middle class. I'm going to cut them. In a Clinton administration, we'll cut income-tax rates on the middle class: an average family's tax bill will go down 10 percent, a savings of three hundred and fifty dollars a year. And the deficit won't go up—instead, those earning over two hundred thousand dollars a year will pay more, though still a smaller percentage of their incomes than they paid in the seventies, not to soak the rich but to return to basic fairness.

A Revolution in Government

Besides empowering citizens, we must lead a revolution in government so it becomes an engine of opportunity again, not an obstacle to it. Voters who went to the polls in this month's elections sent us a clear message: People want more for their money. The experts in Washington think that is a contradiction. But I think the experts are wrong and the people are right. People want a better deal from government, and they'll get it in a Clinton administration.

Too many Washington insiders of both parties think the only way to provide more services is to spend more on programs already on the books in education, housing, and health care. But if we reinvent government to deliver new services in different ways, eliminate unnecessary layers of management, and offer people more choices, we really can give taxpayers more services with fewer bureaucrats for the same or less money.

Every successful major corporation in America had to restructure itself to compete in the last decade, to decentralize, become more entrepreneurial, give workers more authority to make decisions, and offer customers more choices and better products.

That's what we're trying to do in Arkansas—balancing the budget every year, improving services, and treating taxpayers like our customers and our bosses, because they are. Arkansas was the first state to initiate a statewide total-quality-management program. We've dramatically reduced the number of reports the Department of Education requires of school districts, slashed bureaucratic costs in the Department of Human Services and put the money into direct services that help real people, and speeded up customer services in the revenue department. We measure the job-placement rate of graduates from vocational-technical programs, and if a program can't show results, we shut it down.

So I know it can be done. But let us be clear: Serious restructuring of government for greater productivity is very different from the traditional top-down reorganization plans that have been offered over the last twenty years, including in this campaign. Those require a lot of time and energy and generally leave us with more of the same government, not less.

What I am proposing is hard, unglamorous work. It will require us to reexamine every dollar of the taxpayers' money we spend and every minute of time that the government puts in on business. It will require us to enlist the energies of front-line public servants who are often as frustrated as the rest of us with bureaucracy. And if we do it in Arkansas, which has among the lowest taxes in the country, imagine how much more important and productive it will be at the federal level. In a Clinton administration, we'll make government more effective by holding ourselves to the same standard of productivity growth as business and insisting on 3 percent across-the-board cuts in the administrative costs of the federal bureaucracy every year.

If we're going to get more for our money, we ought to have a federal budget which invests more in the future and spends less on the present and the past. As president, I'll throw out last year's budget deal, which brought us the biggest deficits in American history and the fastest-growing spending since World War II. In its place, I'll establish a new three-part federal budget: a past budget for interest payments, a present budget for spending on current consumption, and a future budget for investments in things that will make us richer.

Today the federal government spends only 9 percent of the budget on investing in the future—in education, child health, environmental technology, infrastructure, and basic research. We'll double that in a Clinton administration. We'll begin to finance the future budget by converting resources no longer needed for national defense to the investments needed to rebuild our economic security and by controlling health-care costs.

We can bring the deficit down over time, but only if we control spending on current consumption programs by tying overall increases to real revenue increases, not estimates. I propose to limit overall increases in the consumption budget to increases in personal income, so that the federal budget can't go up any faster than the average American's paycheck. Making Congress and the president live by this rule will cut the deficit drastically in five years, in a dramatic budget reform.

Finally, if we're serious about reinventing government, we must reinvent the way we deliver health care in this country. We spend 30 percent more than any other country on health care and do less with it. For many Americans, the rising cost of health care and the loss of it is the number-one fear they face on a daily basis. Thousands of American businesses are losing jobs because health-care costs are a 30 percent handicap in the global marketplace. Two-thirds of the strikes today are about health care, and no matter how they come out, both sides lose. We are the only nation in the world that doesn't help control health-care costs.

We could cover every American with the money we're spending if we had the courage to demand insurance reform and slash health-care bureaucracies and if we followed the lead of other nations in controlling the unnecessary spread of technology, stopping drug prices from going up three times the rate of inflation, and forcing the people who send bills and the people who pay them to agree on how much health care should cost. We don't need to reduce quality; we need to restructure the system. And no nation has ever done it without a national government that took the lead in controlling costs and providing health care for all.

In the first year of the Clinton administration, Congress and I will deliver quality, affordable health care for all Americans.

A Revolution in the Workplace

These changes are vital, but American workers and American businesses are going to have to change, too; the private sector is where the jobs are created. Many of the most urgent changes cannot be legally mandated, but we know they're overdue after a decade in which the stock market tripled and average wages went down.

Old economic arrangements are holding America back. It's time for a revolution in the American workplace that will radically raise the status of the American worker and tear down the Berlin Wall between labor and management.

It's been years since the U.S. could outproduce the rest of the world by treating workers like so many cogs in a machine. We need a whole new organization of work, where workers at the front lines make decisions, not just follow orders, and entire levels of bureaucratic middle management become obsolete. And we need a new style of management, where front-line workers and managers have more responsibility to make decisions that improve quality and increase productivity.

Dynamic, flexible, well-trained workers who cooperate with savvy, sensitive managers to make changes every day are the keys to high growth in manufacturing and in the service sector, including government, education, and health care, areas where productivity growth was very weak in the 1980s.

Everyone will have to change, but everyone will get something in return. Workers will gain new prosperity and independence, but they'll have to give up nonproductive work rules and rigid job classifications and be more open to change. Managers will reap more profits but will have to manage for the long-run, train all workers, and not treat themselves better than their workers are treated. Corporations will reach new heights in productivity, growth, and profitability, but CEOs will have to put the long-term interests of their workers, their customers, and their companies first.

We should restore the link between pay and performance by encouraging companies to provide for employee ownership, profit-sharing for all employees, not just executives. And executives should profit when their companies do. We should all go up or down together. We'll say to America's corporate leaders: No more taking bonuses for yourselves if you don't give bonuses to everybody. And no more golden parachutes if you don't make good severance packages available for your workers.

It's wrong for executives to do what so many did in the eighties. Executives at the biggest companies raised their pay by four times the percentage their workers' pay went up and three times the percentage their profits went up. It's wrong to drive a company into the ground and have the boss bail out with a golden parachute to a cushy life.

The average CEO at a major American corporation is paid eighty-five times as much as the average worker. And our government today rewards that excess with a tax break for executive pay, no matter how high it is, or whether it reflects increased performance. If a company wants to overpay its executives to perform less well, and underinvest in the future, it shouldn't get any special treatment from Uncle Sam.

If a company wants to transfer jobs abroad and cut the security of working people, it shouldn't get special treatment from the treasury. In the 1980s, we didn't do enough to help out companies to compete and win in a global economy. We did too much to transfer wealth away from hard-working middle-class people to the rich without good reason and too much to weaken our country with debt that wasn't invested in America. That's got to stop. There should be no more deductibility for irresponsibility.

I believe in business. I believe in the marketplace. I believe that the best jobs program this country will ever have is economic growth. Most new jobs in this country are created by small businesses and entrepreneurs who get little help from the government.

Too often, especially in this environment, banks and other investors won't take a chance on good ideas and good people. I want to encourage small business people and entrepreneurs. In a Clinton administration, we'll offer a tax incentive to those who take risks by starting new businesses and developing new technologies. Instead of offering a capital-gains tax cut for the wealthy who will churn stocks on Wall Street anyway, we'll put forth a new-enterprise tax cut that rewards those with the patience, the courage, and the determination to create new jobs. Those who risk their savings on new businesses that create most of the jobs in the country will receive a 50 percent tax exclusion for gains held more than five years.

And I want to encourage investment here in America in other ways—by making the R&D tax credit permanent, by taking away incentives for companies to shut down their plants in the U.S. and move their jobs overseas, and by offering a targeted investment tax credit to medium- and small-size businesses who'll create new jobs with new plants and equipment.

A New Strategy to Compete and Win

Finally, we owe American workers, entrepreneurs, and industry a pledge that all their hard work will not go down the drain.

We must have a national strategy to compete and win in the global economy. The American people aren't protectionists. Protectionism is just a fancy word for giving up; we want to compete and win. That is why our New Covenant must include a new trade policy that says to Europe, Japan, and our other trading partners: we favor an open trading system, but if you won't play by those rules, we'll play by yours. That's why we need a stronger, sharper "Super 301" bill as the means to enforce that policy.

I supported fast-track negotiations with Mexico for a free-trade agreement, but our negotiators need to insist upon tough conditions that prevent our trading partners from exploiting their workers or by lowering costs through pollution to gain an advantage. We should seek out similar agreements with all of Latin America, because rich countries will get richer by helping other countries grow into strong trading partners.

We also need a new energy policy to lower the trade deficit, increase productivity, and improve the environment. We must rely less on imported oil and more on cheap and abundant natural gas and on research and development into renewable energy resources. We must achieve European standards of energy efficiency in factories and office buildings. That will free up billions of dollars to invest in the American economy.

If we want to help U.S. companies keep pace in the world economy, we need to restore America to the forefront not just in inventing products, but in bringing them to market. Too often, we have won the battle of the patents but lost the war of creating jobs, profits, and wealth. American scientists invented the microwave, the VCR, the color TV, and the memory chip, and yet today the Koreans, the Japanese, and other nations make most of those products.

The research and development arm of the defense department did a great job of developing products and taking them to production because we didn't want them produced overseas. We should launch the civilian equivalent, an agency to provide basic research for new and critical technologies and make it easier to move these ideas into the marketplace. And we can pledge right now that for every dollar we reduce the defense budget on research and development, we'll increase the civilian R&D budget by the same amount. We should commit ourselves to a transitional plan for converting from a defense to a domestic economy in a way that creates more high-wage jobs and doesn't destroy our most successful high-wage industrial base, and with it the careers of many thousands of our best scientists, engineers, and workers.

We must do all these things and something more. The economic challenges we confront today are not just a matter of statistics and numbers. Behind them are real human beings and real human suffering. I have seen the pain in the faces of unemployed workers in New Hampshire, policemen in New York and Texas, computer company executives in California, middle-class people everywhere. They're all showing the same pain and worry I hear in the voices of my own people in Arkansas, including men and women I grew up with who played by the rules and now see their dreams for the future slipping away.

That's why we're offering a new radical approach to economics. Economics as if people were really important. If we offer these hard-working families no hope for the future, no solutions to their problems, no relief for their pain, then fear and insecurity will grow, and the politics of hate and division will spread. If we do not act to bring this country together in common cause to build a better future, David Duke and his kind will be able to divide and destroy our nation. Our streets will get meaner, our families will be devastated, and our very social fabric—our goodness and tolerance and decency as a people—will be torn apart.

The politics of division which the Republicans have parlayed into the presidency will turn on even them. George Bush has forgotten the warning of our greatest Republican president, Abraham Lincoln: A house divided cannot stand. Lincoln gave his life for the American community. The Republicans have squandered his legacy.

I want to be a president who will unite this country. This morning, here at Georgetown, the Robert Kennedy Human Rights Awards ceremony was held. Twenty-five years ago, when I was president of my class here, Robert Kennedy accepted our invitation to come to Georgetown to give a speech. In that same year, he gave a very different description of what American politics should be all about. And I would like to read that to you today and ask you how long it's been since you heard an American president say and believe these things:

> Each time a man stands up for an ideal or acts to improve the lot of others or strikes out against injustice, he sends forth a tiny ripple of hope, and crossing each other from a million different centers of energy and daring, those ripples build a current that can sweep down the mightiest walls of oppression and resistance.

That is the spirit I seek to bring to the presidency. The spirit of renewal of America. I believe with all my heart that the very future of our country is on the line. That is why these are not just economic proposals. They are the way to save the very soul of our nation.

This is not just a campaign. This is a crusade to restore the forgotten middle class, give economic power back to ordinary people, and recapture the American dream. It is a crusade not just for economic renewal, but for social and spiritual renewal as well. It is a crusade to build a new economic order of empowerment and opportunity that will preserve our social order and make it possible for our country once again to make the American dream live at home and to be strong enough to triumph abroad.

A New Covenant for American Security

Georgetown University
Washington, D.C.
December 12, 1991

In his third and final speech in the series of "New Covenant" addresses, Clinton became the first of the Democratic presidential hopefuls to stake out a comprehensive foreign-policy position that was more than just vaguely disagreeing with the policies of the past twelve years. He delivered this detailed forty-two-minute speech to his alma mater, the Georgetown School of Foreign Service, before five hundred and fifty students and faculty who received his remarks with applause throughout the speech in the Multicultural Center Auditorium.

Realizing that foreign policy was Bush's only strong suit and that a southern governor would be questioned on experience and expertise in foreign affairs, he used this venue to present his ideas, showing that he was prepared to challenge Bush in this area and distinguishing himself from the rest of the Democratic challengers. It appeared to be a successful strategy, because the site reinforced his educational background in the field and assured national media coverage of the speech. The *Atlanta Constitution* opined, "One speech does not, to be sure, make a foreign-policy expert. But at a time when other Democratic candidates have been giving Bush a wide berth in the field and concentrating on what they charge is neglect of domestic needs, Clinton at Georgetown made a strong beginning toward diminishing the criticism that he would be no match for George Bush beyond the water's edge."

❖ ❖ ❖

I was born nearly half a century ago at the dawn of the Cold War, a time of great change, enormous opportunity, and uncertain peril, at a time when Americans wanted nothing more than to come home and resume lives of peace and quiet, our country had to summon the will for a new kind of war—

containing an expansionist and hostile Soviet Union which vowed to bury us. We had to find ways to rebuild the economies of Europe and Asia, encourage a worldwide movement toward independence, and vindicate our nation's principles in the world against yet another totalitarian challenge to liberal democracy.

Thanks to the unstinting courage and sacrifice of the American people, we were able to win that Cold War. Now we've entered a new era, and we need a new vision and the strength to meet a new set of opportunities and threats. We face the same challenge today that we faced in 1946—to build a world of security, freedom, democracy, free markets, and growth at a time of great change.

Anyone running for president right now—Republican or Democrat—is going to have to provide a vision for security in this new era. That is what I hope to do today.

Given the problems we face at home, we do have to take care of our own people and their needs first. We need to remember the central lesson of the collapse of communism and the Soviet Union. We never defeated them on the field of battle. The Soviet Union collapsed from the inside out—from economic, political, and spiritual failure.

Make no mistake: foreign and domestic policy are inseparable in today's world. If we're not strong at home, we can't lead the world we've done so much to make. And if we withdraw from the world, it will hurt us economically at home.

We can't allow this false choice between domestic policy and foreign policy to hurt our country and our economy. Our president has devoted his time and energy to foreign concerns and ignored dire problems here at home. As a result, we're drifting in the longest economic slump since World War II, and, in reaction to that, elements in both parties now want America to respond to the collapse of communism and a crippling recession at home by retreating from the world.

I have agreed with President Bush on a number of foreign-policy questions. I supported his efforts to kick Saddam Hussein out of Kuwait. I think he did a masterful job in pulling together the victorious multilateral coalition. I support his desire to pursue peace talks in the Middle East. I agree with the president that we can't turn our back on NATO. And I supported giving the administration fast-track authority to negotiate a sound and fair free-trade agreement with Mexico.

But because the president seems to favor political stability and his personal relations with foreign leaders over a coherent policy of promoting freedom, democracy, and economic growth, he often does things I disagree with. For example, his close personal ties with foreign leaders helped forge the coalition against Saddam Hussein, but also led him to side with China's communist rulers after the democratic uprising of students. The president forced Iraq out of Kuwait, but as soon as the war was over, he seemed so concerned with the stability of the area that he was willing to leave the Kurds to an awful fate. He is rightfully seeking peace in the Middle East, but his urge to personally broker a deal has led him to take public positions which may undermine the ability of the Israelis and the Arabs to agree on an enduring peace.

In the aftermath of the Cold War, we need a president who recognizes that in a dynamic new era, our goal is not to resist change, but to shape it. The president must articulate a vision of where we're going. The president and his administration have yet to meet that test—to define the requirements of U.S. national security after the Cold War.

Retreating from the world or discounting its dangers is wrong for the country and sets back everything else we hope to accomplish as Democrats. The defense of freedom and the promotion of democracy around the world aren't merely a reflection of our deepest values; they are vital to our national interests. Global democracy means nations at peace with one another, open to one another's ideas and one another's commerce.

The stakes are high. The collapse of communism is not an isolated event; it's part of a worldwide march toward democracy whose outcome will shape the next century. If individual liberty, political pluralism, and free enterprise take root in Latin America, Eastern and Central Europe, Africa, Asia, and the former Soviet Union, we can look forward to a grand new era of reduced conflict, mutual understanding, and economic growth. For ourselves and for millions of people who seek to live in freedom and prosperity, this revolution must not fail.

And yet, even as the American dream is inspiring people around the world, America is on the sidelines, a military giant crippled by economic weakness and an uncertain vision.

We face two great foreign-policy challenges today. First, we must define a new national-security policy that builds on freedom's victory in the Cold War. The communist idea has lost its power, but the fate of the peoples who lived under it and the fate of the world will be in doubt until stable democracies rise from the debris of the Soviet empire.

And second, we must forge a new economic policy to serve ordinary Americans by launching a new era of global growth. We must tear down the wall in our thinking between domestic and foreign policy.

We need a coherent strategy that enables us to lead the world we have done so much to make and that supports our urgent efforts to take care of our own here at home. We cannot do one without the other.

We need a New Covenant for American Security after the Cold War, a set of rights and responsibilities that will challenge the American people, American leaders, and America's allies to work together to build a safer, more prosperous, more democratic world.

The strategy of American engagement I propose is based on four key assumptions about the requirements of our security in this new era: First, the collapse of communism does not mean the end of danger. A new set of threats in an even less stable world will force us, even as we restructure our defenses, to keep our guard up. Second, America must regain its economic strength to maintain our position of global leadership. While military power will continue to be vital to our national security, its utility is declining relative to economic power. We cannot afford to go on spending too much on firepower and too little on brainpower. Third, the irresistible power of ideas rules in the Information Age. Television, cassette tapes, and the fax machine helped ideas to pierce the Berlin Wall and bring it down. Finally, our definition of security must include common threats to all people. On the environment and other global issues, our very survival depends upon the United States taking the lead.

Guided by these assumptions, we must pursue three clear objectives: First, we must restructure our military forces for a new era. Second, we must work with our allies to encourage the spread and consolidation of democracy abroad. And third, we must reestablish America's economic leadership at home and in the world.

Restructuring Our Military Forces

When Americans elect a president, they select a commander in chief. They want someone they can trust to act when our country's interests are threatened. To protect our interests and our values, sometimes we have to stand and fight. That is why, as president, I pledge to maintain military forces strong enough to deter and when necessary to defeat any threat to our essential interests.

Today's defense debate centers too narrowly on the size of the military budget. But the real questions are, what threats do we face, what forces do we need to counter them, and how must we change?

We can and must substantially reduce our military forces and spending, because the Soviet threat is decreasing and our allies are able to and should shoulder more of the defense burden. But we still must set the level of our defense spending based on what we need to protect our interests. First let's provide for a strong defense. Then we can talk about defense savings.

At the outset of this discussion, I want to make one thing clear: the world is still rapidly changing. The world we look out on today is not the same world we will see tomorrow. We need to be ready to adjust our defense projections to meet threats that could be either heightened or reduced down the road.

Our defense needs were clearer during the Cold War, when it was widely accepted that we needed enough forces to deter a Soviet nuclear attack, to defend against a Soviet-led conventional offensive in Europe and to protect other American interests, especially in Northeast Asia and the Persian Gulf. The collapse of the Soviet Union shattered that consensus, leaving us without a clear benchmark for determining the size or mix of our armed forces.

However, a new consensus is emerging on the nature of post–Cold War security. It assumes that the gravest threats we are most likely to face in the years ahead include

- First, the spread of deprivation and disorder in the former Soviet Union, which could lead to armed conflict among the republics or the rise of a fervently nationalistic and aggressive regime in Russia still in possession of long-range nuclear weapons.
- Second, the spread of weapons of mass destruction, nuclear, chemical, and biological, as well as the means for delivering them.
- Third, enduring tensions in various regions, especially the Korean peninsula and the Middle East and the attendant risks of terrorist attacks on Americans traveling or working overseas.
- And finally, the growing intensity of ethnic rivalry and separatist violence within national borders, such as we have seen in Yugoslavia, India, and elsewhere, that could spill beyond those borders.

To deal with these new threats, we need to replace our Cold War military structure with a smaller, more flexible mix of capabilities, including

- *Nuclear deterrence.* We can dramatically reduce our nuclear arsenals through negotiations and other reciprocal actions. But as an irreducible minimum, we must retain a survivable nuclear force to deter any conceivable threat.
- *Rapid deployment.* We need a force capable of projecting power quickly when and where it's needed. This means the army must develop a more mobile mix of mechanized and armored forces. The air force should emphasize tactical air power and airlift, and the navy and marine corps must maintain sufficient carrier and amphibious forces, as well as more sealift. We also need strong special-operations forces to deal with terrorist threats.
- *Technology.* The Gulf War proved that the superior training of our soldiers, tactical air power, advanced communications, space-based

surveillance, and smart weaponry produced a shorter war with fewer American casualties. We must maintain our technological edge.

- *Better intelligence.* In an era of unpredictable threats, our intelligence agencies must shift from military bean-counting to a more sophisticated understanding of political, economic, and cultural conditions that can spark conflicts.

To achieve these capabilities, I would restructure our forces in the following ways:

First, now that the nuclear arms race finally has reversed course, it's time for a prudent slowdown in strategic modernization. We should stop production of the B-2 bomber. That alone could save twenty billion dollars by 1997.

Since Ronald Reagan unveiled his "Star Wars" proposal in 1983, America has spent twenty-six billion dollars in futile pursuit of a fool-proof defense against nuclear attack. Democrats in Congress have recommended a much more realistic and attainable goal: defending against very limited or accidental launches of ballistic missiles. This allows us to proceed with R&D on missile defense within the framework of the ABM treaty—a prudent step as more and more countries acquire missile technology.

At the same time, we must do more to stop the threat of weapons of mass destruction from spreading. We need to clamp down on countries and companies that sell these technologies, punish violators, and work urgently with all countries for tough, enforceable, international nonproliferation agreements.

Although the president's plan does reduce our conventional force structure, I believe we can go further without undermining our core capabilities. We can meet our responsibilities in Europe with less than the one hundred and fifty thousand troops now proposed by the president, especially as the Soviet republics withdraw their forces from the Red Army. We can defend the sea lanes and project force with ten carriers rather than twelve. We should continue to keep some U.S. forces in Northeast Asia as long as North Korea presents a threat to our South Korean ally.

To upgrade our conventional forces, we need to develop greater air and sea-lift capacity, including production of the C-17 transport aircraft. But we should end or reduce programs intended to meet the Soviet threat. Our conventional programs, like the new air force fighter and the army's new armored systems, should be redesigned to meet regional threats.

The administration has called for a 21 percent cut in military spending through 1995, based on the assumption, now obsolete, that the Soviet Union would remain intact. With the dwindling Soviet threat, we can cut defense spending by over a third by 1997.

Based on calculations by the Congressional Budget Office, my plan would bring cumulative savings of about one hundred billion dollars beyond the current Bush plan. If favorable political and military trends continue, and we make progress on arms control, we may be able to scale down defense spending still more by the end of the decade. However, we should not commit ourselves now to specific deeper cuts ten years from now. The world is changing quickly, and we must retain our ability to react to potential threats.

Also, we must not forget about the real people whose lives will be turned upside down when defense is cut deeply. The government should look out for its defense workers and the communities they live in. We should insist on advanced notification and help communities plan for a transition from a defense to a domestic economy. Thirty-one percent of our graduate engineers work for the defense industry. They and other highly skilled workers and technicians are a vital national resource at a time when our technological edge in a world economy must be sharper than ever before. I have called for a new advanced research agency—a civilian DARPA—that could help capture for commercial work the brilliance of scientists and engineers who have accomplished wonders on the battlefield.

Likewise, those who have served the nation in uniform cannot be dumped on the job market. We've got to enlist them to help meet our many needs at home. By shifting people from active duty to the National Guard and reserves, offering early retirement options, limiting reenlistment, and slowing the pace of recruitment, we can build down our forces in a gradual way that doesn't abandon people of proven commitment and competence.

Our people in uniform are among the most highly skilled in the areas we need most. We need to transfer those human resources into our work force and even into our schools, perhaps in part by using reserve centers and closed bases for community-based education and training programs.

The defense policy I have outlined keeps America strong and still yields substantial savings. The American people have earned this peace dividend through forty years of unrelenting vigilance and sacrifice and an investment of trillions of dollars. And they are entitled to have the dividend reinvested in their future.

Finally, America needs to reach a new agreement with our allies for sharing the costs and risks of maintaining peace. While Desert Storm set a useful precedent for cost-sharing, our forces still did most of the fighting and dying. We need to shift that burden to a wider coalition of nations of which America will be a part. In the Persian Gulf, in Namibia, in Cambodia, and elsewhere in recent years, the United Nations has begun to play the role that Franklin Roosevelt and Harry Truman envisioned for it. We must take the lead now in making their vision real—by expanding the Security Council and making Germany and Japan permanent members; by continuing to press for greater efficiency in U.N. administration; and by exploring ways to institutionalize the U.N.'s success in mobilizing international participation in Desert Storm.

One proposal worth exploring calls for a U.N. rapid deployment force that could be used for purposes beyond traditional peacekeeping, such as standing guard at the borders of countries threatened by aggression, preventing attacks on civilians, providing humanitarian relief, and combating terrorism and drug trafficking.

In Europe, new security arrangements will evolve over the next decade. While insisting on a fairer sharing of the common defense burden, we must not turn our back on NATO. Until a more effective security system emerges, we must give our allies no reason to doubt our constancy.

Promoting Democracy around the World

As we restructure our military forces, we must reinforce the powerful global movement toward democracy.

U.S. foreign policy cannot be divorced from the moral principles most Americans share. We cannot disregard how other governments treat their own people, whether their domestic institutions are democratic or repressive, whether they help encourage or check illegal conduct beyond their borders. This does not mean we should deal only with democracies, or that we should try to remake the world in our image. But recent experience from Panama to Iran to Iraq shows the dangers of forging strategic relationships with despotic regimes.

It should matter to us how others govern themselves. Democracies don't go to war with each other. The French and British have nuclear weapons, but we don't fear annihilation at their hands. Democracies don't sponsor terrorist acts against each other. They are more likely to be reliable trading partners, protect the global environment, and abide by international law.

Over time, democracy is a stabilizing force. It provides nonviolent means for resolving disputes. Democracies do a better job of protecting ethnic, religious, and other minorities. And elections can help resolve fratricidal civil wars.

Yet President Bush too often has hesitated when democratic forces needed our support in challenging the status quo. I believe the president erred when he secretly rushed envoys to resume cordial relations with China barely a month after the massacre in Tiananmen Square; when he spurned Yeltsin before the Moscow coup; when he poured cold water on Baltic and Ukrainian aspirations for self-determination and independence; and when he initially refused to help the Kurds.

The administration continues to coddle China, despite its continuing crackdown on democratic reforms, its brutal subjugation of Tibet, its irresponsible exports of nuclear and missile technology, its support for the homicidal Khmer Rouge in Cambodia, and its abusive trade practices. Such forbearance on our part might have made sense during the Cold War, when China was a counterweight to Soviet power. But it makes no sense to play the China card now, when our opponents have thrown in their hand.

In the Middle East, the administration deserves credit for bringing Israel and its Arab antagonists to the negotiating table. Yet I believe the president is wrong to use public pressure tactics against Israel. In the process, he has raised Arab expectations that he'll deliver Israeli concessions and fed Israeli fears that its interests will be sacrificed to an American-imposed solution.

We must remember that even if the Arab-Israeli dispute were resolved tomorrow, there would still be ample causes of conflict in the Middle East: ancient tribal, ethnic, and religious hatreds; control of oil and water; the bitterness of the have-nots toward those who have; the lack of democratic institutions to hold leaders accountable to their people and restrain their actions abroad; and the territorial ambitions of Iraq and Syria. We have paid a terrible price for the administration's earlier policies of deference to Saddam Hussein. Today, we must deal with Hafez Assad in Syria, but we must not overlook his tyrannical rule and domination of Lebanon.

We need a broader policy toward the Middle East that seeks to limit the flow of arms into the region, as well as the materials needed to develop and deliver weapons of mass destruction; promotes democracy and human rights; and preserves our strategic relationship with the one democracy in the region: Israel.

And in Africa as well, we must align America with the rising tide of democracy. The administration has claimed credit for the historic opening to democracy now being negotiated in South Africa, when in fact it resisted the sanctions policy that helped make this hopeful moment possible.

Today, we should concentrate our attention on doing what we can to help end the violence that has ravaged the South African townships, by supporting with our aid the local structures that seek to mediate these disputes and by insisting that the South African government show the same zeal in prosecuting the perpetrators of the violence as it did in the past when pursuing the leaders of the anti-apartheid movement. The administration and our states and cities should only relax our remaining sanctions as it becomes clearer that the day of democracy and guaranteed individual rights is at hand. And when that day does dawn, we must be prepared to extend our assistance to make sure that democracy, once gained, is not lost there.

An American foreign policy of engagement for democracy will unite our interests and our values. Here's what we should do:

• First, we need to respond more forcefully to one of the greatest security challenges of our time, to help the people of the former Soviet empire demilitarize their societies and build free political and economic institutions. Congress has passed five hundred million dollars to help the Soviets destroy nuclear weapons and for humanitarian aid. We can do better. As Senator Sam Nunn and Representative Les Aspin have argued, we should shift money from marginal military programs to this key investment in our future security. We can radically reduce the threat of nuclear destruction that has dogged us for decades by investing a fraction of what would otherwise have to be spent to counter that threat. And, together with our G-7 partners, we can supply the Soviet republics with the food and medical aid they need to survive their first winter of freedom in seventy-four years. We should do all that we can to coordinate aid efforts with our allies and to provide the best technical assistance we can to distribute that food and aid.

No national-security issue is more urgent than the question of who will control the nuclear weapons and technology of the former Soviet empire. Those weapons pose a threat to the security of every American, to our allies, and to the republics themselves.

I know it may be bad politics to be for any aid program. But we owe it to the people who defeated communism, the people who defeated the coup. And we owe it to ourselves. A small amount spent stabilizing the emerging democracies in the former Soviet empire today will reduce by much more the money we may have to commit to our defense in the future. And it will lead to the creation of lucrative new markets which mean new American jobs. Having won the Cold War, we must not now lose the peace.

• We should recognize Ukraine's independence, as well as that of other republics who make that decision democratically. But we should link U.S. and Western nonhumanitarian aid to agreements by the republics to abide by all arms agreements negotiated by Soviet authorities, demonstrate responsibility with regard to nuclear weapons, demilitarize their economies, respect minority rights, and proceed with market and political reforms.

• We should use our diplomatic and economic leverage to increase the material incentives to democratize and raise the costs for those who won't. We have every right to condition our foreign-aid and debt-relief policies on demonstrable progress toward democracy and market reforms. In extreme cases, such as that of China, we should condition favorable trade terms on political liberalization and responsible international conduct.

• We need to support evolving institutional structures favorable to countries struggling with the transition to democracy and markets, such as the new European Bank for Reconstruction and Development, whose mission is to rebuild the societies of Central and Eastern Europe. We are right to encourage the European community to open its doors to those societies, perhaps by creating an affiliate status that carries some but not all of the privileges of membership.

• We should encourage private American investment in the former Soviet empire. The Soviet republics, after all, are rich in human and natural resources. One day, they and Eastern Europe could be lucrative markets for us.

• We should regard increased funding for democratic assistance as a legitimate part of our national-security budget. We should support groups like the National Endowment for Democracy, which work openly rather than covertly to promote democratic pluralism and free markets abroad. I would encourage both the Agency for International Development and the U.S. Information Agency to channel more of their resources to promoting democracy. And just as Radio Free Europe and the Voice of America helped bring the truth to the people of those societies, we should create a Radio Free Asia to carry news and hope to China and elsewhere.

• Finally, just as President Kennedy launched the Peace Corps thirty years ago, we should create a Democracy Corps today that will send thousands of talented American volunteers to countries that need their legal, financial, political expertise.

Restoring America's Economic Leadership

Our second major strategic challenge is to help lead the world into a new era of global growth. Any governor who's tried to create jobs over the last decade knows that experience in international economics is essential and that success in the global economy must be at the core of national security in the 1990s.

Without growth abroad, our own economy cannot thrive. U.S. exports of goods and services will be over a half-trillion dollars in 1991—about 10 percent of our economy. Without global growth, healthy international competition turns all too readily to economic warfare. Without growth and economic progress, there can be no true economic justice among or within nations.

I believe the negotiations on an open trading system in the GATT are of extraordinary importance. And I support the negotiation of a North American Free Trade Agreement, so long as it's fair to American farmers and workers, protects the environment, and observes decent labor standards.

Freer trade abroad means more jobs at home. Every one billion dollars in U.S. exports generates twenty to thirty thousand more jobs. We must find ways to help developing nations finally overcome their debt crisis, which has lessened their capacity to buy American goods and probably cost us 1.5 million American jobs.

We must be strong at home to lead and maintain global growth. Our weakness at home has caused even our economic competitors to worry about our stubborn refusal to establish a national economic strategy that will regain our economic leadership and restore opportunity for the middle class.

How can we lead when we have gone from being the world's largest creditor country to the world's largest debtor nation—now owing the world four hundred and five billion dollars? When we depend on foreigners for one hundred billion dollars a year of financing, we're not the masters of our own destiny.

I spoke in my last lecture about how we must rebuild our nation's economic greatness, for the job of restoring American's competitive edge truly begins at home. I have offered a program to build the most well-educated and well-trained work force in the world and put our national budget to work on programs that make America richer, not more indebted.

Our economic strength must become a central defining element of our national-security policy. We must organize to compete and win in the global economy. We need a commitment from American business and labor to work together to make world-class products. We must be prepared to exchange some short-term benefits—whether in the quarterly profit statement or in archaic work rules—for long-term success.

The private sector must maintain the initiative, but government has an indispensable role. A recent Department of Commerce report is a wake-up call that we are falling behind our major competitors in Europe and Japan on emerging technologies that will define the high-paying jobs of the future—like advanced materials, biotechnology, superconductors, and computer-integrated manufacturing.

I have mentioned a civilian advanced-research-projects agency to work closely with the private sector, so that its priorities are not set by government alone. We have hundreds of national laboratories with extraordinary talent that have put the United States at the forefront of military technology. We need to reorient their mission, working with private companies and universities, to advance technologies that will make our lives better and create tomorrow's jobs.

Not enough of our companies engage in export—just 15 percent of our companies account for 85 percent of our exports. We have to meet our competitors' efforts to help smaller and medium-sized businesses identify and gain foreign markets.

And most important, government must assure that international competition is fair by insisting to our European, Japanese, and other trading partners that if they won't play by the rules of an open trading system, then we will play by theirs.

We have no more important bilateral relationships than our alliance with Japan, a relationship that has matured from one of dependency in the 1950s to one of partnership today. Our relationship is based on ties of democracy, but as we cooperate, we also compete. And the maturity of our relationship allows American presidents, as I will, to insist on fair play. As we put our own economic house in order, Japan must open the doors of its economic house or our partnership will be imperiled with consequences for all the world.

Now we must understand, as we never have before, that our national security is largely economic. The success of our engagement in the world depends not on the headlines it brings to Washington politicians, but on the benefits it brings to hard-working middle-class Americans. Our "foreign" policies are not really foreign at all.

When greenhouse gas emissions from developed nations warm the atmosphere and CFCs eat away at the ozone layer, our beaches and farmlands and people are threatened. When drugs flood into our country from South America and Asia, our cities suffer and our children are put at risk. When a Libyan terrorist can go to an airport in Europe and check a bomb in a suitcase that kills hundreds of people, our freedom is diminished and our people live in fear.

So let us no longer define national security in the narrow military terms of the Cold War. We can no longer afford to have foreign and domestic policies. We must devise and pursue national policies that serve the needs of our people by uniting us at home and restoring America's greatness in the world. To lead abroad, a president of the United States must first lead at home.

Half a century ago, this country emerged victorious from an all-consuming war into a new era of great challenge. It was a time of change, a time for new thinking, a time for working together to build a free and prosperous world, a time for putting that war behind us. In the aftermath of that war, President Harry Truman and his successors forged a bipartisan consensus in America that brought security and prosperity for twenty years.

Today we need a president, a public, and a policy that are not caught up in the wars of the past—not World War II, not Vietnam, not the Cold War. What we need to elect in 1992 is not the last president of the twentieth century, but the first president of the twenty-first century.

This spring, when the troops came home from the Persian Gulf, we had over one hundred thousand people at a welcome-home parade in Little Rock. Veterans came from all across the state—not just those who had just returned from the Gulf, but men and women who had served in World War II, Korea, and Vietnam. I'll never forget how moved I was as I watched them march down the street to our cheers and saw the Vietnam veterans finally being given the honor they deserved all along. The divisions we have lived with for the last two decades seemed to fade away amid the common outburst of triumph and gratitude.

That is the spirit we need as we move into this new era. As President Lincoln told Congress in another time of new challenge, in 1862: "The dogmas of the quiet past are inadequate to the stormy present. The occasion is piled high with difficulty, and we must rise with the occasion. As our case is new, so we must think anew, and act anew. We must disenthrall ourselves, and then we shall save our country. Fellow citizens, we cannot escape history."

Thank you very much.

One Nation Again

Macomb County Community College
Warren, Michigan
March 12, 1992

Clinton's campaign strategy for the general election counted on winning working-class white voters back from the Republicans, and Macomb County, Michigan, was the paradigm challenge. The white voters in the Detroit suburb deserted the Democratic nominees to support Wallace and Nixon in the 1960s and continued to vote Republican in the 1980s. Stanley Greenberg, the campaign's pollster, found that white working-class voters there abandoned the Democrats when they perceived the party as too concerned with social programs for blacks and its presidential candidates as no longer sharing the middle-class values of hard work and family.

Clinton had just swept the southern primaries by preaching racial harmony, personal responsibility, and welfare reform that would help people find jobs, and both black and white Democratic voters chose him overwhelmingly. He was now trying to deliver the same message for the pivotal Illinois and Michigan primaries. Speaking to an overflow crowd at Macomb County Community College, Clinton reached out to the "Reagan Democrats" in an almost intimate, talk-show format, telling them, "I'll give you a new Democratic Party which builds a new economic and social policy for the nineties based on mainstream American values—rewarding work and restoring the middle class." He said his platform combined "opportunity plus responsibility," but then he told the largely white, supportive audience, "You can't do any of this unless we are willing to give up some of the prejudices we all had in the eighties, or a lot of people did. The problems are not racial in nature. This is a crisis of economics, of values."

Then the following day, speaking to an enthusiastic gathering of four hundred and fifty black ministers at Pleasant Grove Baptist Church in Detroit's inner city, he delivered essentially the same message in an electrifying sermon on racial harmony, telling the audience,

"I said something politicians don't normally say in Macomb County. I said we can't get it done until you folks decide race is not the problem."

❖ ❖ ❖

Thank you very much. And thank you President Lorenzo and thank you all for being here.

I've looked forward to this day for a long time because, as I'm sure you all know, this county has become a very famous county in American politics: A county of people who were native Democrats who have basically been voting Republican in presidential elections. A county not unlike my native region, the South, and my state, which was a very Democratic state; a state that voted for Adlai Stevenson twice against Dwight Eisenhower; a state overwhelmingly white Protestant that still voted narrowly for John Kennedy against Richard Nixon; a state that voted for Lyndon Johnson against Barry Goldwater. And then we voted for Wallace in '68. Nixon got 69 percent of the vote in '72. Jimmy Carter won there in '76 because he seemed to be a lot like us. And then Reagan won, Reagan won, and Bush won big time in my state. And I was on the ballot all this time trying to stand up in the midst of all this.

And I think I know why a lot of people in this county and my state departed the Democratic Party and got involved with the Republicans. I heard it over and over again: "You know your party in Washington doesn't share my values anymore. They're not rewarding middle-class effort and middle-class values. They won't stand up for the country around the world." I've heard all of these things for so long. But, now we are sort of at a crossroads as a country. I hear that also where I live. We're coming to another presidential election at the end of the three slowest years of economic growth since before World War II and, more importantly, at the end of more than a decade of economic decline.

There were two stunning studies which came out in the last couple of weeks. You may have seen it, and a lot of you—even if you didn't see it—you won't be surprised because you have doubtless lived it. One of the studies said that over the last twenty years, the average family has worked harder and harder, not less and less; that in 1989 the average family was working one month per year longer than in 1969.

The other survey said, it was a study that the Joint Economic Committee released in Washington the other day pointing out that in the last twelve years, 60 percent of the growth in this country has gone to the top 1 percent of the people who live here. That's a stunning statistic: that the top 20 percent have gotten 30 percent of the growth; the next 20 percent have gotten 9 percent; the next 20 percent 4 percent; the bottom 40 percent nothing. They've fallen behind. If you are in the middle, if you've got the four or the nine, you don't even get anything, because we've spent so much more for health care, housing, education, and in taxes.

What that means is, for the last twelve years, basically all of the growth in this country has gone to the top 20 percent, 60 percent to the top 1 percent. So what has happened in this decade in which the American people voted for people who have promised to honor their values and stand up for everything that is best in this country?

The middle class is working harder, making less money. We've lost our economic leadership; our kids are in terrible trouble. The president goes to Japan and is humiliated at the end of a trade mission in which the Japanese prime minister says he feels sympathy for the United States. Sympathy for us! And then he says, showing that he doesn't understand it either, he says it's because we've lost our work ethic. But, that isn't true. We're working harder than we were twenty years ago. So, what did happen, and what are we going to do about it? Why am I running for president, and what's going to be different?

Well, first of all, I really believe that this election is not about the traditional divisions in Washington, D.C., between liberals and conservatives, and left and right, and even Republicans and Democrats. To me, this is a race between the eighties and the nineties, and whether we're going to have a new economic policy for the nineties and a new social policy.

I've been out here as a governor for eleven years, having a balanced budget, making tough decisions, trying to keep people's jobs for them, helping them educate their children, trying to solve problems, and getting very little help from Washington to do it.

If people, like people who live in this county, hadn't voted for me, I'd be doing something else today. I wouldn't be up here talking to you. I live in state with only two and a half million people, where even my enemies smile and call me by my first name. So, I have given a lot of thought to this. And here's what I think we ought to do: Number one, our economic policy ought to put our own people first again. It ought to reward work and family and effort and not just wealth and power. We ought to focus on education and training for a lifetime, so that people can always be competitive in a global economy.

We should give business incentive to invest, but only those incentives that will guarantee investment in our country. John Kennedy had an investment tax credit. You couldn't get it unless you bought plant equipment and put it into our plants. We have a tax system that today encourages you to move plants overseas rather than leave them at home. Let me just give you a couple of descriptions. Let's take a General Motors plant. OK? I want to come back to the General Motors situation. But, just suppose you are in the car business and you got about one hundred million dollars' worth of equipment. If you want to keep high-wage jobs in America and keep in production, under the present tax laws, you don't get any investment tax credit; that is, any real accelerated write-off for this equipment. So, suppose you say I think I'll take this old equipment and take it to another country where people work for wages we can't live on. So, you shut the plant down, you get a tax deduction for the cost of shutting the plant down, you move the plant overseas, and it costs you money the first year or so to set it up. You get to carry forward the loss in your American tax bill. Then you build up the money and you keep it over there, and as long as you don't put the money back here in a bank, you don't have to take those earnings and put those earnings here and pay taxes on them.

So, if you look at the whole framework of the tax system we've got, you would think your country was telling you, "We don't care whether you keep these jobs here or not." That's the tax system we have.

But, if we had a people-first economics, we'd be investing more in education and training, in incentives to keep jobs here, and we'd be organizing to deal with these changes. We have no automobile strategy. You know what your country's automobile policy is? Does your country have a policy for changing from a defense to a domestic economy? We're cutting defense spending all over America. We've got factory workers in the street, technicians without jobs, scientists and engineers who don't know what they're going to do. Do we have strategies for them? No. Somehow, this invisible market is supposed to figure out what happens to them. Because we have tried to put money first; that is, keep taxes low in upper-income people in corporations and forget about developing human capacity.

That's why I wanted to come here to give this talk today. Because the average young person will change work eight times in a lifetime. And if you don't have a continuous system of education, if you don't have a tax system that rewards investment in our country, and if you don't have a government that's trying to organize people for change, you get hurt.

The second thing we need to do, I think, is to recognize that we got killed in the 1980s by doing something as a nation most of you would never do in your families, and that is giving everybody something for nothing, starting at the top. I want to change that. Consider the case of General Motors. In the early eighties, they asked for tax cuts, and they got it. They asked for protection from imports, and they got it. They asked for regulatory relief, and they got it. They asked the auto workers to give them concessions, and they got 'em and they got 'em and they got 'em.

Look at this Flint, Michigan, plant—probably the most innovative plant in America for worker concessions—changing the work rules: No foreman people making decisions on the shop floor, an exciting productive place. They're going to close it anyway. And what do we get in return for that? All those concessions. They kept raising the price of cars and giving up market share. They didn't reinvest a lot of that money in the production process.

A lot of the inefficiencies in auto working in America are not due to labor; that's only 20 percent of the costs now. It's due to the inefficiencies in the production process itself and the fact that we use more scrap metal and we have more waste than our Japanese and German competitors. We didn't require them to fix that. That's a management problem, not a labor problem. And the executives continue to raise their pay and their perks, while the workers got the shaft. So we gave something for nothing, and we got what you would get if you ran your family that way.

And what I think we need to do in the nineties is say, "OK, we are going to try this a different way." We're going to have more opportunity and more responsibility. So, if you are at the top of the totem pole, more tax incentives to invest in our country—no more tax incentives to move your plants overseas or for unlimited increases in corporate compensation that don't have anything to do with whether or not you are putting people to work and making something people are buying.

If you are a worker, yes, we want you to change your work rules. But, you get in return for that: Lifetime education, affordable health care, and a sensible economic policy. If you are on welfare, we are going to do something for you. We will give you more education and training, child care for your children, health care for your children; and you've got to take a job.

If you are a student, we want to give you more opportunities. But there ought to be national standards—a national exam system that really means something. We've got some teachers here. They will tell you that all of these standardized tests we're giving in America today make money for the testing companies, and not much else. After you give them a couple of years, all of the kids in America are scoring above the national average, and the teachers are burdened down teaching to the test. So, you wind up seeming like you've got something you don't. I want to make it possible for every high-school graduate to either get two years of further training in an apprenticeship program if they behave themselves, play by the rules, and graduate, or to find the money necessary to go to college.

Let me give you another example. I don't know how many families I have talked to who have been told by their college-aid folks that they are too rich to go to college. Anybody here in that category? Been told that your family couldn't get any help? Here's what I think we ought to do: I want to scrap this student-loan program we've got and set in its place a national-service trust fund out of which any American could borrow the money to go to college. But you'd have to pay it back. And you couldn't beat the bill, like you can the student-loan bill sometimes. You'd pay it back in one of two ways: Either as a small percentage of income over time at tax time—not to the local bank at tax time; or you could work for a year or two in a form of national service—like a GI Bill at home. Come home after you graduate from college. Be a teacher, be a law-enforcement officer, work with troubled youth, work in a drug center. Do something to help solve the problems of our country to pay off your student loan. We could educate a whole generation of Americans and help solve a lot of our problems.

I'll give you another example. In Chicago, there's a public-housing program that gives tenants, who've never had jobs in their life, the opportunity to work in their own housing projects on twenty-four-hour-a-day shifts in partnership with police officers to clean out the drugs and the weapons in all of the housing projects and keep them safe. So that you get the right to earn a living if you work with law enforcement to keep your living environment safe. I could give you lots and lots of other examples.

I'll give you another example that I think is important. Look at all of these kids that are in trouble with drugs. I spent a lot of time in my life talking to people who were in gangs, talking to people who had gotten in trouble. Almost all of them have no education, come from broken homes, live in difficult neighborhoods, and grew up in an environment where the best money was in drugs. Whatever happens to them now? Now what happens to them is nothing the first two or three times. And then, after a while, they get into trouble and we send them to jail, where, at great cost to us, they learn how to be first-class criminals. Then, they get out after a while, and they do it again, and it goes on for life.

Why not try something different? Why not have in every community of any size in America a community-based, boot-camp-like facility, where people who get into trouble get discipline, drug treatment, real education, do community service work, and have a chance to develop some relationships with adults who will both give them love and discipline and give them a chance to get reconnected to society. These are the kinds of things I think we have to look at—opportunity plus responsibility, no more something for nothing.

Now, let me just make one final point. You can't do any of this unless we are prepared to give up some of the prejudices we all had in the eighties, or a lot of people did. The problems are not racial in nature. This is a crisis of economics, of values. It has nothing to do with race. This is the message, the message that I just gave you, that I just gave to the South. Over 80 percent of the black voters voted for me on Super Tuesday. Why? Because most blacks work for a living. Most of the working poor who are being ground down in the South are black Americans. There are more whites than blacks on welfare. The systems that are killing us are not racial in nature. This is a crisis of values, of education, and of organization.

One of the things that the Democrats I think have to stand and draw the line on, and one of the things that I have to tell you about, is that I do not believe we have any hope of doing what we have to do in America unless we can come together and cross racial lines again. One in four of our children is living in poverty under the age of six. One in two minority children under the age of six is in poverty. Most of the jobs in the 1990s will be filled by women and members of racial minorities. That's just the demographics. You can't repeal that. Nobody can change that. That's where the population growth is. And a lot of those folks are in terrible trouble. And people who give easy answers. Look at the Republican race baiting. Duke, even the Republicans got rid of him. Why? All he did, he talked about welfare reform. He was a state legislator. He never hit a lick to move anybody from welfare to work because he wouldn't have anybody to kick around anymore. It was a code word for race. Go talk to people on welfare. They hate it. But you've got to give them the power, the opportunity to go to work, and then impose the responsibility to work. You can't do one without the other. No more entitlement. But no more rhetoric without empowerment.

Take Buchanan. Buchanan comes to the South to campaign. He goes to a Confederate cemetery but won't walk across the street to the black cemetery —sending the signal one more time that that's the problem. And I'm telling you, that's not the problem. I grew up in an integrated society that was segregated. My whole region was kept poor and backward because the people who were running the politics knew as long as they could separate us by race, they could hold us down. A little moment in American history: Arkansas and Michigan were approved for admission into the Union at the same time. Did you know that? And we came in just a few months before Michigan did. We were approved under an agreement then available in Congress that both states had to be Andy Jackson Democratic states, but one would be a slave state, mine, and one would be a free state, yours. All right? One of the reasons that we never could get our act together in the South is that we were so polarized over race for so long.

Bush runs this Willie Horton ad on Dukakis last time. Now, Dukakis ran into it because he didn't answer it. But the federal government furloughs prisoners, too. Did you know that? I mean they had a furlough program. They were churning them out, too. All the time Bush was running this ad against Dukakis, there's this federal furlough program opening the jails letting people out. Why? Because we now have more people behind bars than any other nation in the world as a percentage of our people. So the answer is not Willie Horton. The answer is, who should you keep behind bars? what can you do about the others? and what are we doing about crime? This guy runs Willie Horton, scares the living daylights out of people, then cuts back on aid to local prosecutors, cuts back on aid to local law enforcement—ask the sheriff—cuts back on aid to the customs, the coast guard, the border patrol, all of the people who are supposed to keep drugs out of this country. It is not a racial issue.

And the one thing that is going to pull this country together is somebody has got to come back to the so-called Reagan Democratic areas and say, "Look, I'll give you your values back, I'll restore the economic leadership, I'll help you build the middle class back," but you've got to say, "OK, let's do it with everybody in this country."

In Chicago today, I went to a little business, one hundred and seven employees—blacks, Puerto Ricans, other Hispanics, a guy from Romania fixing to cast his first vote for me, Poles—all of them together. And you know what they said? They work and they went to school at work, at a big GED program. And they all talked about how the more education they got, the more secure they got in their jobs and the more productive they were. And the more their wages went up, the more fun it was to be working with all different kinds of people. It's amazing how, when your life works, you don't feel those resentments. It's amazing when you work with people who share your values, and who are winning, all the reservations that you might have kind of fade away. And that's the last thing I guess I want to say.

If I get elected president, maybe I'll give a few good talks, but I can't change this country unless the American people are willing to be Americans again. We've got to say we are going up or down together. So that's my message to you here. I'm trying to give you a new Democratic Party based on old values that will make you want to come home to the Democrats in this county. But I'm telling you, there is nothing I can do to get out of the fact that we have got to come together around values and across racial lines. And if we're not prepared to do it we are not going to make it as a country, because, if you look at who's going to be filling the jobs of tomorrow, they are people whose children are doing bullet drills instead of fire drills in school, who are working hard and are still poor, who are living in substandard housing, and who need these empowerment strategies.

So, I just hope and I pray that each of you in your own way and all of the people who live here will think about that. What would it take for this county to embrace a Democrat again based on opportunity, responsibility, people-based politics? And let's forget about race and be one nation again.

Thank you very much.

A New Covenant for Environmental Progress

Drexel University
Philadelphia, Pennsylvania
April 22, 1992

Speaking at Drexel University before an audience of more than one thousand cheering students on Earth Day, a week before the Pennsylvania primary, Clinton delivered his first major environmental policy speech of the campaign, outlining his proposed policies and contrasting them with those of the last twelve years. In an attempt to inoculate himself from future criticism while reminding voters that the election was about generational change, he acknowledged having made environmental tradeoffs during the 1980s to create new jobs during his tenure as governor, but said that in today's economy the nation need not be shackled by the view of past generations, that there must be a tradeoff between economic growth and the environment. Revising the speech only an hour before it was delivered, Clinton mentioned an article in the previous day's *New York Times* suggesting that pollution of the White River in Arkansas might be the political equivalent of the Boston Harbor pollution issue that damaged Dukakis in 1988, countered that the state was working to protect its natural resources, and suggested that federal policies were part of the problem.

With less than a week until the Pennsylvania primary and holding a comfortable 45 to 22 lead over Jerry Brown in the latest poll, Clinton did not mention Brown in the speech but referred to Bush or his administration's policies thirty-two times. One campaign aide said the speech was intended as an "in your face" environmental message to the White House and an outdated, sixty-seven-year-old president. White House spokesman Marlin Fitzwater responded to the speech by charging that Clinton had "the worst environmental record in America." As the campaign developed and Senator Gore joined the ticket, however, the endorsements of major environmental advocacy groups seemed to agree with Clinton that that honor belonged to the Bush administration.

❖ ❖ ❖

Twenty-two years ago today, thousands of Americans marched and met and spoke out across the country to raise a new concern onto our nation's agenda: the protection of America's environment. That first Earth Day in 1970 awakened our nation to the ticking of a different kind of biological clock—a clock that measured the careless degradation of America's air, water, land, and natural resources.

Many of you here were not even born yet. And it's worth recalling the whirlwind of change and progress that followed that day. Within two years, our nation created the Environmental Protection Agency, passed the Clean Air, Clean Water, and Endangered Species Acts, and banned DDT. For my generation, it was a heady, hopeful experience.

Two decades later, all those efforts seem dwarfed by the enormity of old and new threats to our communities, our resources, and our planet.

We restricted open dumping into our rivers, but now we see used hypodermic needles washing up on our beaches.

We banished lead from our gas tanks, but still find it concentrated where the children of our cities live and play.

We pinpointed the nation's toxic-waste dumps, but have only cleaned up a handful.

We confronted the acid rain killing our trees, but not the rush of development that is wiping out wetlands at home and rain forests abroad.

We stopped building nuclear power plants, but now see our addiction to fossil fuels wrapping the earth in a deadly shroud of greenhouse gasses.

We opened our eyes to the threats posed by oil-soaked beaches, smoggy skies, and burning rivers; yet we still struggle to comprehend less-apparent dangers, such as an invisible hole in a distant ozone layer that allows unseen rays to plant the microscopic seeds of cancer.

The question that falls to your generation is this: will the march that began twenty-two years ago move forward, or will we stand in place?

Over the past generation, much has changed in our thinking. Children now teach their parents to sort their garbage. Colleges like Drexel train young people in environmental engineering. A Big Mac at McDonald's comes in a recyclable cardboard container in a recycled paper bag.

Yet while the thinking of most Americans has changed, the thinking of our recent leaders has not. For more than a decade, we've had no national energy strategy, no environmental strategy, no economic strategy to capture the markets of the future with new technologies that are energy efficient and environmentally sound.

Within the past decade, climate change, ozone depletion, and other global environmental problems have emerged as threats to our very survival. Dependence on foreign oil has been the cornerstone of our energy policy, and oil imports now make up half our trade imbalance. The collapse of communism and the end of the Cold War have created new markets and a new urgency for environmental cleanup. We have an unprecedented opportunity to protect the earth and make our economy grow.

Too often, on the environment as on so many issues, the Bush administration has been reactive, rudderless, and expedient. Under George Bush and Ronald Reagan, presidential leadership on the environment has become an endangered species.

George Bush promised to be the environment president, but a photo op at the Grand Canyon is about all we have to show for it.

He made Boston Harbor a prop in his negative campaign in 1988, but four years later has done precious little to help clean it up.

He promised "no net loss" of America's precious wetlands, then tried to hand half of them over to developers.

He invoked Teddy Roosevelt's devotion to preserving our natural heritage, then called for opening the Arctic wilderness to oil drilling.

He talked about the need for an energy policy, then went to Detroit on the eve of the Michigan primary to promise American automakers that he wouldn't raise fuel-efficiency standards for American cars.

He called for an international summit on the environment but now is singlehandedly blocking a historic meeting in Rio de Janeiro of a hundred nations to control global warming.

And just yesterday, I read in the paper that he wants to make another attack ad, this time about problems along the White River in Arkansas. We're fighting the battle to clean up the White River, and I welcome the president's attention.

So, Mr. President, when you return from Rio, I hope you'll visit northwest Arkansas and the White River. I'll show you what the problems are and what progress we've made. I'll show you rivers you can fish in and streams kids can swim in.

And if you really want to clean up the problem, I'll make an agreement with you. We'll outline federal and state responsibilities, and we'll get results. Our people are tired of the politics of blame. But this is no Boston Harbor. If you want to place blame, you'll have to shoulder some.

Let me be clear. I don't believe President Bush is bent on destroying the environment. But his views were shaped in another era, when the world faced other threats, and economic growth and environmental protection were seen as mutually exclusive.

I've spent the last decade as governor of a poor state, fighting to keep jobs and make up for lost time. I know how much our people are hurting after the longest recession and slowest economic growth in the last fifty years.

In the eighties, I also faced the old short-term tradeoffs between jobs and the environment, made tougher by cutbacks in federal aid and the lack of clear policies in some areas which allowed states to be played off against one another. In this context, I've made the choice for jobs in a poor state without enough jobs or federal help for environmental protection and cleanup.

But over the years I've learned something that George Bush and his advisers still don't understand, to reject the false choice between economic growth and environmental protection. Today, you can't have a healthy economy without a healthy environment, and you don't have to sacrifice environmental protection to get economic growth.

Our competitors know that you can't have one without the other. One of the reasons German workers make 25 percent more than the average American worker is that their economy uses half the energy to produce the same amount of goods. Japanese companies enjoy a 5 percent competitive advantage in the global marketplace because of higher energy efficiency. Our competitors are rushing to develop new environmental technologies that will enable them to capture the markets of the future. Only the United States is heading toward the twenty-first century without a long-term strategy to achieve sustainable economic growth.

The Bush administration doesn't understand that perpetuating the false choice between environmental protection and economic growth is bad for the environment and bad for the economy. Our lakes will be dirtier and our air will be more dangerous because George Bush put Dan Quayle in charge of the Competitiveness Council, a group which lets major polluters in through the back door at the White House to kill environmental regulations they don't like. And the most disturbing thing is, they call that competitiveness.

Over the long run, the Bush administration isn't doing American business any favors by pretending that energy efficiency and improved environmental protection are at odds with economic growth. If we're going to compete and win in the world economy, if we want to improve our quality of life as well as our standard of living, we need to learn to use environmental protection as a tool for economic growth.

That is what I've tried to do in Arkansas. As governor, I've worked hard to pursue both environmental quality and economic growth. In my first term, I took on one of my state's strongest special interests when I tried to focus our utilities more on conservation than construction of new power plants. Today that approach is called "least cost planning," and nearly half the states use it to conserve resources and save ratepayers money. Back then, the name didn't exist, and the utilities fought it tooth and nail. By the end of the eighties they had come around, and Arkansas consumers and businesses will save lots of money in the future.

We did other things, too. We set up one of the nation's first state-level paper-recycling programs; helped establish nearly forty new wildlife preserves and parks to protect our rivers, forests, wetlands, and prairies; and created a new statewide reforestation program that has planted twenty-five million trees in the last two years. We've provided Arkansas business a 30 percent tax credit for installing waste-reduction and recycling facilities—a measure that is protecting Arkansas's environment and creating Arkansas jobs.

There was a time in this country when environmental protection was viewed as at best a necessary burden for industry to bear. Today that idea just isn't true. Technology has changed; the stakes have changed; and it's time for our thinking to change, too. In today's economy, there doesn't have to be a tradeoff between growth and environmental protection. We now have the tools and the need to choose both.

What we need today is a New Covenant for Environmental Progress. That covenant is built on a renewed commitment to leave our children a better nation—a nation whose air, water, and land are unspoiled; whose natural beauty is undimmed; and whose leadership for sustainable global growth is unsurpassed. This new covenant will challenge Americans and demand responsibility at every level—from individuals, families, communities, corporations, and government agencies—to do more to preserve the quality of our environment and our world. A new covenant for environmental progress will have three priorities: exerting new American leadership to protect the global environment; preserving the quality of our environment here at home; and finding ways to promote innovation and growth consistent with firm environmental goals.

The first part of a new covenant for environmental progress must be for the U.S. to exert international leadership for the health of the planet. The Cold War is over, and we have entered a new era in which threats to our security are less evident, but no less dangerous, than before. As Senator Gore has dramatized in his recent book, *Earth in the Balance,* if we do not find the vision and leadership to defeat the unprecedented new threats of global climate change, ozone depletion, and unsustainable population growth, then those threats may defeat us instead.

This June, the nations of the world will meet in Rio to negotiate reductions in their output of carbon dioxide and other greenhouse gasses, to end the destruction of the ozone layer, and to find rules for sustainable development to ensure that our species does not outlive its welcome on this planet.

Nearly a hundred heads of state have firmly committed to attend. But yesterday, the president said he can't decide whether or not to go.

We've seen eight of the hottest years in history in the last decade. The world's rain forests are disappearing at the rate of one football field a minute. An ozone hole is growing over Kennebunkport. And the leaders of nearly every nation on earth are waiting while the president of the United States makes up his mind whether to act.

I say this is one foreign trip George Bush can't afford to miss.

If the president does decide to go, simply showing up in Rio is not enough. Unless he makes the U.S. a leader against global warming and removes the obstacles he has thrown in the way of a climate-change treaty, nothing will come of the Rio meeting. President Bush should commit the U.S. to limit U.S. carbon dioxide emissions to 1990 levels by the year 2000 and to join in new efforts to protect the planet's biodiversity and preserve its forests. As Senator Gore says, this is now our most important global environmental challenge.

In a Clinton administration, the U.S. will take the lead in promoting sustainable development. We'll call on major banks and multilateral institutions like the IMF and the World Bank to negotiate debt-for-nature swaps that allow developing nations to reduce their crippling international-debt burden by setting aside precious lands. We should explore establishing the international equivalent of the Nature Conservancy, a fund contributed to by developed nations and pharmaceutical companies to purchase easements in the rain forests for medical research. These easements and the profits from new drugs could make not developing the forests more profitable than tearing them down.

We can also lead the quest for sustainable development by supporting efforts to stem global population growth. As Al Gore has noted, it took mankind ten thousand generations to reach a population of two billion. Yet we will likely see that number triple in my lifetime. The earth's resources and delicate ecosystems are straining and breaking under this unsustainable burden. President Bush was once a strong supporter of efforts to limit global population growth, and it is shameful that he blocked our contributions to those efforts to appease the anti-choice wing of his party. A Clinton administration will restore U.S. funding for the U.N.'s population stabilization efforts and allow U.S. foreign aid to support Planned Parenthood.

But we cannot lead the fight for environmental progress abroad unless we do more here at home. The U.S. constitutes just 5 percent of the world's population, yet we consume over a quarter of its oil. We need to reduce our oil consumption and increase our energy efficiency dramatically if we are to lead the fight against global warming, sharpen our competitive edge in trade, and reduce our vulnerability to cutoffs in the availability of foreign oil.

For the past eleven years, we have had no national energy policy. In a Clinton administration, we'll have an energy policy the day I take office.

We'll accelerate our progress toward more fuel-efficient cars and seek to raise the average goal for automakers to forty-five miles per gallon.

We'll increase our reliance on natural gas, which is inexpensive, clean burning, and abundant, and can reduce our carbon dioxide emissions. I'll start with an executive order to purchase natural-gas-powered vehicles for the federal fleet, following the lead of Governor Ann Richards in Texas.

We'll push for revenue-neutral incentives that reward conservation and make polluters and energy wasters pay. California, for example, has proposed giving purchasers of fuel-efficient cars rebates paid for by a special fee on those who buy gas guzzlers.

We'll invest more in the development of renewable energy sources. Federal funding for renewables has dropped from $850 million to $114 million in the last decade. There's no reason why 60 percent of the Department of Energy's money should still be going to nuclear weapons, with nuclear power and fossil fuels getting most of the rest. We'll encourage the use of new energy sources like wind and solar and new ways to get better results out of the sources we already have. In a Clinton administration, we will designate as wilderness the Arctic National Wildlife Refuge and stop the crusade for new drilling off our coasts.

As part of an effort to convert some of our Cold War military spending to civilian purposes, we'll use research and development funds to develop light rail, which can speed travel, save fuel, and provide transportation for people less able to afford it.

Finally, we'll make energy conservation and efficiency central goals in every field of policy—in designing our offices, planning our communities, designing our transportation systems, and regulating our utilities. My goal is to improve America's overall energy efficiency by 20 percent by the year 2000.

We also need a policy to prevent pollution. Since 1970, we've made great strides in controlling pollution "at the pipe"—regulating how much could be dumped and where. Now we need to expand our efforts earlier in the process and move from control to prevention.

One of our most urgent challenges is to reduce the amount of solid waste we generate. A Clinton administration will find new ways to prevent pollution in the first place.

We'll create a system of tradeable credits that will reward companies that recover a greater portion of their waste and penalize those that don't.

We'll create incentives for firms and government to recycle, and use federal purchasing power to create markets in recycled materials.

We'll pass a national bottle bill to encourage recycling by creating small deposits on all glass and plastic bottles.

To improve the quality of our water, we need to turn greater attention to the polluting effect of water running off our agricultural fields, city streets, and suburban developments. We need a new Clean Water Act with standards for non-point-source pollution and incentives that will unleash the creative and technological potential of our firms, farmers, and families to reduce and prevent polluted run-off at the source.

We also need to strengthen our efforts on toxic wastes. The Superfund program has been disastrously mismanaged. We've spent thirteen billion dollars to clean up only eighty of the twelve hundred deadliest dump sites—with much of the money squandered on legal fees and cost overruns to contractors who bought Rolex watches and art for their walls.

The Superfund program was a historic breakthrough in 1980. In my first term, Arkansas was the first state in the country to have an EPA-approved hazardous waste management program. Superfund enabled us to contain the most immediate risks and provided a powerful deterrent against toxic dumping. Now those of us who care about the environment must take the lead to explore every possible improvement that might get more sites cleaned up sooner for less, without letting responsible parties off the hook.

We also need to improve America's resources by preserving our natural heritage for future generations. As president, I will protect our old-growth forests and other vital habitats and make the "no net loss" promise on wetlands a reality. I'll rededicate the agencies that manage our national parks and wilderness lands to a true conservation ethic. And I'll expand our efforts to acquire new parklands and recreational sites with the funds already available under the federal Land and Water Conservation Fund. Every year, millions of American families vacation in national parks, from Yosemite to Yellowstone. They deserve an administration that cares about America's parks as much as they do.

All of our efforts to improve the nation's resources ultimately depend on enforcement and public awareness. In a Clinton administration, we'll stop shortchanging EPA's enforcement efforts and ensure that we hold companies and polluters responsible for their behavior. When corporate executives deliberately violate environmental laws, they must pay the price.

The third priority I want to speak about today is the need to bring powerful market forces to bear on America's pollution problems. Many of our environmental efforts in the past were based on a "command and control" approach to regulation that told firms how much pollution to produce and what kind of technology to use. While that approach produced important successes, it sometimes stifled innovation by locking firms into a specific kind of equipment and increased regulatory costs and burdens by taking such a detailed and inflexible approach.

I believe it is time for a new era in environmental protection which uses the market to help us get our environment back on track, to recognize that Adam Smith's invisible hand can have a green thumb. While we need to maintain tough guidelines and goals for reducing pollution, charging companies for their pollution would give them a daily incentive to find progressively cleaner technologies and manufacturing processes. In certain settings, this results-oriented approach can cut compliance costs, shrink regulatory bureaucracies, enlist corporate support, take environmental policy away from the specialists and lobbyists, and open it up more to the general public.

But freeing up our companies to find cost-effective pollution-control methods is not the only step we need to take. It is time we recognized that environmental technology will be one of the most vital and profitable economic sectors of the twenty-first century. The market for environmental technology and services is already around two hundred billion dollars a year, and developing nations will need to install a trillion dollars' worth of energy technology over the next fifteen years.

Unfortunately, we're losing that battle. In 1980, the U.S. had three-quarters of the world sales of solar technology. By 1990, German and Japanese competition had cut our share to 30 percent. We need to recognize that green economics is a booming business. And as president, I'll ensure that the nation that pioneered the environmental movement will be the world's foremost producer and exporter of environmental technology and services by the end of this decade.

As I have traveled across this country campaigning for president, I have been struck by the yearning I see among Americans of all backgrounds, incomes, and colors to be united again in common purpose. If there is one thing that has united Americans across dozens of generations, it is the feeling we have for this rich and expansive land. Our forebears were passionate about it. They were farmers and pioneers who made these two billion acres we call America the canvas of their dreams.

That stubborn, protective love of the land, which flows like a mighty underground current through our national character, is what burst to the surface of American life on April 22, 1970. And it was the well-spring for one of the most important marches for progress we have known in our time.

For over a decade, that progress has been arrested. And for too many of those years, we have walked backwards. Too many times we were told that trees cause pollution and that sunglasses are the best answer to the ozone problem. And far too many times we were divided against ourselves, falsely told to choose between our quality of life and our standard of living. I believe now it is time to move past the false choices, unite our nation again, and resume our progress for the land we cherish, the values we share, and the only earth we have. A generation ago, the conservationist Aldo Leopold wrote, "History consists of successive excursions from a single starting point to which man returns again and again to organize yet another search for a durable set of values." One of the starting points for America will always be our devotion to our natural heritage. And today I ask you to join me in beginning an excursion from that starting point anew.

Thank you.

Our American Community

Democratic Leadership Council
New Orleans, Louisiana
May 2, 1992

The Democratic Leadership Council had provided Clinton with a forum since he had participated in its founding, and its Progressive Policy Institute had helped develop alternative public-policies positions that were embraced by his campaign. His closing address to the group's annual convention at 11:15 A.M. in the ballroom of the New Orleans Convention Center was assured an interested and supportive audience.

The speech drew thunderous applause from a rapt crowd of one thousand conference participants, who were largely white, affluent activists from around the country and were not part of the Democratic Party's regular rank and file. They had come to hear Clinton deliver a traditional campaign speech, but it was for an entirely unexpected message for the DLC, once called the "Democratic Leisure Club" by Jesse Jackson.

Talking for almost an hour without a prepared text, Clinton improvised, scrapping a prepared speech and the teleprompter, speaking from hand-scribbled notes on a yellow legal pad. In a forceful, lectern-pounding performance, Clinton sought to offer a long-range vision of racial reconciliation that he and his staff believed was lacking in President Bush's response to the Los Angeles riots. The *Times* called it "one of the most powerful speeches of his career" in which he "took his inspiration not from the position papers that were piled all around in the hall but from the giant spring jazz festival that was going on at the racetrack outside."

The *Financial Times* was equally impressed, saying that Clinton's speech was "one of his finest oratorical hours . . . which defined as well as any why he wanted to be president and of what sort of country he wished to preside over. . . . While, after so much campaigning, no speech can be said to be wholly spontaneous, the performance served to remind how good a public speaker Mr. Clinton can be. . . . But it was also impossible to deny that Mr. Clinton spoke with real feeling. . . . The traditions of southern oratory are not lost on him." Even the domestic press that had been following his campaign for six months was impressed with his performance. The political reporter for the *Orlando Sentinel-Tribune* wrote, "Presidential campaign speechmaking often becomes a repetitive, empty buzz for speakers and listeners alike. But once in a while events and issues coincide to make a moment that tests a politician's grit. Bill Clinton had such a moment" in his keynote address in New Orleans.

❖ ❖ ❖

Thank you very much. To my good friends, Congressman Bill Jefferson, whose life has in so many ways paralleled my own; Daryl Landreau, who has been my friend and supporter; Senator John Breaux, who has done such a magnificent job in leading the Democratic Leadership Council; to all the delegates here assembled and especially those from my home state of Arkansas who have come down the way a little to cheer me on; to the staff of the DLC who has worked for so many years to try to put ideas back into the forefront of this party to change our party without giving up our values, to win elections without sacrificing principles, to change this country in ways that were good and decent and urgent: I am so glad to be here.

I can't help expressing a little bit of personal pride at the magnificent rendering of "God Bless America" by Earl Taylor, whose son, Earl Jr., works for us, and whose son, Ricky, introduced me in Georgetown when I first spoke there as a presidential candidate about my hopes for this country. He not only sings with a gift from God, he has raised two children that are testament to the enduring importance of a father's love.

All of you know that I believe deeply in the work of the DLC. I love the ideas we have espoused. I have searched for opportunity and responsibility. I have searched for means to empower people to take advantage of their own destiny. I have searched for ways to change government and make it work, to make it less bureaucratic and more entrepreneurial and creative, to have more partnerships with the private sector in ways that would generate explosive futures for America.

I know that we have been hurt by a leadership without a strategy to restore our economic strength. I know that we have been hurt by leadership that was irresponsibly divisive, denying of America's problems. But today I want to talk to you without the benefit of a prepared text and with some of my legendary scribble notes, which even I can't read once I write them down, about the other part of the DLC message which I have worked so hard to craft over the last several years. I want to talk about our American community.

Thomas Jefferson once said that the crisis of slavery is "a fire bell in the night." The crisis in Los Angeles is now our fire bell in the night. It is clear evidence once again of the profound divisions in our community—divisions that have been ripped to shreds in Los Angeles. People outraged by the Rodney King verdict who say the system does not work. People not voting because they have given up. People now who say they will vote for a third-party candidate because what he says sounds good, and he has the inestimable virtue of never having served in public office; because they believe all politicians have failed. People who are looting because they are not part of the system at all anymore. They do not share our values, and their children are growing up in a culture alien from ours: without family, without neighborhood, without church, without support, often finding that only in a gang is there an identity bigger than themselves and are they the most important person in the world to anyone.

We must begin with the hard truth that race is at the root of much of this. In the 1950s when I was a little boy I can remember the racial tensions beginning to flair in the open in my state. I had the virtue of being raised until I was four by a grandfather who had only a fourth-grade education, but who believed passionately in the cause of equal rights. But I watched my state sundered and torn when the president of the United States had to call out the National Guard simply to integrate Little Rock Central High School.

Then, in the 1960s I saw the civil rights movement lead to the burning of churches and the wreckage of lives in cities like Birmingham. I watched Martin Luther King shot in Memphis on the eastern border of my state. I was living in Washington when the city erupted in flames, and I remember as if it were yesterday sticking a red cross on my car and taking supplies into the inner city, where people were huddled in the basements of churches, waiting for food.

And now in the nineties we have what has happened in Los Angeles, and to a lesser degree, what has happened in other cities around the nation. In the 1950s and '60s there were arguments over equal access, over race, over poverty, over politics. To be sure, in the 1990s we have made a great deal of political progress. I was introduced today by a magnificent man who, if he were fifty years older, would not have been voting at this time in his life. Birmingham, Los Angeles, Memphis, the District of Columbia, and Atlanta all have black mayors. We have made a great deal of progress for those of us who live in the mainstream of America. But what has happened beneath that?

Beneath that there are those who are not part of our community, whose values have been shredded by the hard knife of experience, where there is the disintegration of family and neighborhood and jobs and the rise of drugs and guns and gangs. Since I started this campaign I have seen in New York City two little children, black teenagers, ripped off the streets of New York and beaten and painted white because God made them black. And then a few days later a girl was taken off the street and assaulted in retaliation, simply because she was white.

I was in Chicago when an eight-year-old child took his big brother's gun to school and shot another eight-year-old, barely understanding what he was doing. I was in Houston with the police who told me that they had found it necessary to put metal detectors in the front doors of eleven elementary schools to take the guns and the knives from the eight- and nine-year-old children as they came through the door to school every day. Little wonder that one of the most moving things that has occurred to me in the whole course of this campaign was an encounter I had with a man in a hotel uniform in New York as I was going in to give a speech. He grabbed me and said, "Governor, my boy studies politics in school. He is ten years old. He says you should be president, and since I trust my boy, I will vote for you." But he said, "I have to ask you something. Where I came from we were poor, but at least we were free. Here in America we are no longer free. When my boy cannot walk across the street to the park in my neighborhood and play unless I am with him, he is not free. When my boy cannot walk down the street to the school in our neighborhood unless I walk with him, he is not free. If I do what my boy asks and vote for you, will you make my boy free?" That is the cry of millions of Americans today, who know that they have no community day in and day out in this country. Let us face those fears.

White Americans often fear that violence has only a black face. They see it on the news. They see it in the movies. They are gripped by the isolation of their own experience where, especially in many of our larger areas, too many white Americans still simply have no friends of other races and do not know any differently.

Blacks fear that too often violence has a black face and no one cares. There was a memorial service in New Haven, Connecticut, a few weeks ago for children who were killed in the endless bout of drug wars in that city, and Reverend Jesse Jackson said that if white Americans killed white Americans like this, there would be an explosion of interest in the judicial system until the matter was solved; and if black Americans killed white Americans at this rate, there would be soldiers in the street everywhere until it would stop. But black Americans are leading other black Americans to the slaughter, and no one steps into the breach.

Oh, to be sure, most of us still love our country, and we are still capable of being a community. In a time of crisis during the Gulf War, we were one. I believe in our pain and anguish in the aftermath of the Rodney King verdict: After we had seen fifty-six blows rained in eighty-one seconds, we were one. When we lose a president, or a national hero, we are one. When Magic Johnson comes forward and, with courage, tells us he has AIDS, we are one.

But when the crisis passes, when we go back to the day-to-day ordinary living of life, I say to you: We are not a community. We have too many people who are totally disconnected, totally divorced from the mainstream of our life. We are raising a generation of Americans isolated, literally in a different culture, without family, often without home, without education, without jobs, without a future.

We should be afraid, my fellow Americans, but we must face our fears and stop running from them.

White people have been scared for so long that they have fled to the suburbs of America to places like Simi Valley and Macomb County in Michigan. I understand those fears. I live in a city, and my daughter goes to a city public school. She's a seventh grader in the public schools of Little Rock where we've had an incident of violence a year or so ago—a tragedy. Someone came onto school grounds, and death ensued. She tells me stories that sometimes cause me to fear, but I believe we must face our fears and not run from them, because she has gotten a good education. She revels in the biracial life she lives, and there has been more hope than fear in her experience. And besides, there is no place to hide.

When I was in Michigan, in Macomb County, the home of the Reagan Democrats, in a town meeting, one of the first things I was told is that there, in the place that people ran to, a fifteen-year-old had just shot another fifteen-year-old in another act of mindless, teenage violence. We have no place to hide. Rodney King said it well: "I never meant my verdict to be an excuse for this kind of behavior." But neither will his verdict make the streets safer for others, especially for black Americans. After all, more than any other racial group in this country, it is their children who are shot on the street, their neighborhoods that are savaged by crack cocaine, their businesses and dreams that are crushed. Let us not forget that we now live in a multiracial society, Los Angeles more than any other city in America. I spoke at the University of California at Los Angeles a couple of years ago to students from one hundred and twenty-two countries. What of the Hispanics, what of the Asian Americans, what of the other Americans who have come here from different nations? What is to become of them? Will they be part of the mainstream community or the other community of America? This situation cries out for leadership.

Last night our president made what I thought was a very fine statement on the security measures he had taken, on the action he had urged the justice department to undertake, and on the need for all of us to respect the law and honor the quiet heroes of the violence in Los Angeles who stepped in to save people's lives. But the truth is we must do more. You and I have to admit here today that one of the reasons we came to the Democratic Leadership Council is that we knew deep down inside that the political system, including both parties, had failed to reach some of the fundamental problems of the United States of America, and this, to be sure, is the most fundamental of all.

The Republicans, when they needed to prove that Michael Dukakis was soft on crime, brought out Willie Horton. The Republicans, when they need to cover up for their senseless economic strategy that is driving income down for most American families while they work harder, blame it on quotas, so that there can be racial resentment instead of honest analysis of our economic falsehoods.

Even if they plead for unity, the Republicans now send their vice-president out across the country to talk about welfare in a way that makes it clear that they intend to act as a wedge to divide the American people, instead of as an instrument to liberate the poor in the United States of America.

But we Democrats have also let the American people down, too. Those who sit on the sidelines don't want to vote for the president but don't participate in our primary. Too often they think we haven't paid as much attention to the victims of crime as we should have. Too often they think we have clung to putting their tax money into programs year after year, whether they work or not. Too often they have heard members of our party say that those who seek to reform the welfare system are the enemies of the poor. And so we have had too often a leadership in the nation's capital, paralyzed and divided, mirroring a country all too divided. And when that happens, my fellow Americans, we all pay. We pay when the crime rate in America spirals higher than any other country in the world. We pay for it when your taxes build jail cells, even as we're closing down schoolrooms. When other nations are investing more in education, we're spending more on jails. Oh yes, we pay. Every single one of us pays. We pay it when ignorance leads people to jails instead of jobs, when they take our tax money where it helps them instead of paying taxes into our system to educate a new generation of Americans, to build a new generation of high-speed rail and other high-technology infrastructure, to convert from a defense to a domestic economy in a way that explodes opportunity. Oh no, we pay. We have to put people in jail; we can't afford to build a future. We pay.

We pay when we live in the most violent country in the world, and so the emergency rooms of our hospitals are full every weekend with people cut up and shot. We all pay as the health costs go up, and we find it harder and harder and harder to compete in a global economy. We all pay.

We pay when we stick our heads in the sand instead of reaching out to these young children. We have the highest teen pregnancy rate, the highest low-birth-weight rate, the highest explosion of AIDS of any advanced country in the world. We will all pay for it because we refuse to face the underlying hard truth and go after these problems. We all pay when we are divided.

We pay when we blindly accept a permanent underclass in America, a culture of poverty where no one dreams of a better future, where people only wait for the next check or the drug deal on the corner, because they have no way of imagining that life can be different. We pay.

Abraham Lincoln once said in a very different context that it was his job to prove that government of, by, and for the American people had not vanished. I tell you that government of, by, and for the American people does not exist for millions of Americans today. Most people would hear this and say, "This sounds very good." That's what they say to me all over America. They say, "This sounds so good, but you are a politician. How can I believe you?" Well, I say you can believe me, but first you have to believe in you.

First, we have to begin honest talks about race, about culture, about values. We have to strip away all the intermediaries between the people who are elected and those they are supposed to serve. And we must honestly say: Here is what the leaders should do, and here is what the people must do. Unless we close the gap in understanding between what the leaders must do and only the people can do, we will go on and on and on in frustration after frustration. And anybody who wins an election will find his or her ability to change things drastically undermined.

So what would I do if I were president? Number one, I would start with the elemental proposition that the people in the other America deserve the same law and order that the rest of us demand, and I would work to make the streets safer. Through the reallocation of national resources, through the establishment of a national service plan that the Democratic Leadership Council has so long embraced, I would seek to put more police officers on the streets as friends—not enemies—of their neighbors.

I want to see everywhere in America what I saw in Philadelphia when I walked down the street with the mayor and two fine police officers. I saw the neighbors in a biracial neighborhood come out of their houses and welcome the police officers, knowing that they were working together, the neighbors willing to walk the street at two and three o'clock in the morning to run the drug dealers out. And the police were willing to be there twenty-four hours a day, the people working together to reclaim their rightful destiny to live in peace with their neighbors.

I have seen it in Chicago, in public-housing projects where twenty-four hours a day the police and the tenants work together. And believe it or not, not so very long ago, I saw it in Los Angeles. I have wondered so often what might have happened if that King incident had occurred in one of the neighborhoods I visited, where the police were there on two minutes' call for neighbors that had beepers and emergency phone numbers, where the citizens walked the streets and people treated one another as people. I have often wondered if it would have been different.

The second thing we ought to do is find something besides jail for our youngest and least-violent offenders who have no prospects. I believe in community punishment, in community boot camps. I believe the most urgent thing we have to do is to reconnect these children to the future we want them to live. If they go astray, leave them at home, give them discipline, education, drug treatment if necessary, let them do community service work and find one person who likes to work with one trouble child, so that at least the child can never say, "I never knew anybody who was a success who cared about me." Let's try that. What have we got to lose by trying?

We need to mobilize the energies of the American people in dealing with the troubled youth of our time. I saw a group called the "Untouchables" in Pennsylvania, a group of young black men, most of them junior-high-school age, who gave me one of their T-shirts that said, "Untouchables. We are untouchable by drugs. We are untouchable by guns. We are untouchable by crime. We have our life in our own hands." You know why they felt that way? Not because of a government program, but because one or two people loved those boys enough to give them a chance to live in a different kind of gang—a good gang, our gang—where the values were strong and the future was sound. There needs to be more of that in this country.

I met a judge in Texas during this campaign who told me that when he was on the trial bench he mobilized six hundred people in his own district, not just to go after the young men and women who came before him as violators, but to be with the seven-, eight-, and nine-year-olds when they first begin to show signs of trouble in their lives. I'm telling you, friends, if you want your country back, if you want those people to be in your community, if you want the next time a riot breaks out to see tens of thousands of poor people who say, "We don't steal, we don't loot, that's not our life"; you've got to go out to those kids and bring them back one by one, because that's the only way we're ever going to get them back.

Let me say one last thing about safe streets that it is somewhat unpopular in my part of the country and maybe in other parts. I live in a state where half the people have a hunting or a fishing license or both. But I don't believe ten-year-olds ought to have a license to kill. The people in Washington have played politics with the Brady Bill long enough. It is time to pass it, put it on the books, and stop people from buying guns who have no business with them. I can hear all the objections now. I've heard it over and over in the halls of my legislature. You cannot make a case for why a kid needs an assault weapon under the Constitution of the United States of America. It is insanity, and it has to stop. If we make our streets safer, we must then make our families stronger. You know what the agenda is as well as I do; we just have to have the will to implement it. We are the only advanced nation in the world where women regularly get pregnant and do not see the doctor six times before the baby is born. We ought to have preventive, primary, maternal health care in America. It would save us money. We don't do it because we don't have the will to do it. We ought to have preschool for every child who needs it, and we ought to involve the parents more in preparing their children to learn as we have tried so hard to do at home. We ought to have child care, and we ought to have family leave, and we ought to have the opportunity for the poorest families to work their way into housing.

I love going across America to these so-called "sweat equity projects," where foreclosed-on homes have been turned over to poor folks who stripped the lead paint out and built a house for themselves by working after work. It is a moving experience. But we also ought to remind ourselves that a big part of the problem of family income is people who bring children into this world and will not pay to support them. So I will say again that we need a much tougher system of child-support enforcement, because governments cannot raise children, people must.

The third thing we have to do is to make schools meaningful to our children. I will say simply this: I have been in more schools in more states than probably any other public figure in the United States. When I think of schools in cities, I do not think of those that fail. I think of the Thomas Jefferson Junior High School in Washington, D.C., or the Beasley Academic Center in Chicago, in a neighborhood with the highest murder rate in Illinois and the top 10 percent of all test scores, with a wonderful principal from the Mississippi Delta in my state, where the children in a public school have a dress code, strong values, seventy-five fathers and many more brothers volunteering in the schools, and there is a feeling that no one wants drugs or guns in the school because they don't want to leave the schools. The school is their gang. It's our gang. It's a good gang because it's about something good. And Cardozo High School in Queens. I could go on and on and on.

Why do these things work when so much is failing? What do they all have in common that America lacks? They have leadership that takes responsibility. They have rules by which all must live. They have responsibility for every person, from the principal, to the teacher, to the building maintenance people, to every single child that walks through the door. They have rewards for responsible behavior, and they have love. That's what they have, and it works.

If you look at that the next thing we have to do, which is to bring some jobs back into these areas, you will see that investment alone won't work. That's why the DLC's empowerment strategy is so important. There must be rules, responsibility, and reward. That's why this empowerment agenda of the DLC must be at the core of any serious attempt to revitalize the other America.

When you look at all this, at what I say about safe streets, strong families, good schools, and economic empowerment, if you're like me you ask yourself, "If it happens somewhere, why doesn't it happen everywhere?" I'll tell you why: Because there aren't enough of "us" and there's too much of "them." "Them." "Them" is the dread word in American politics. The Republicans blame all the problems on "them." Sometimes the Democrats say, "We're going to help 'them.'" People don't need help as "them"; they need to be part of "us," of defining their own future. We've got to stop blaming "them" or helping "them" and say, "Hey, come on, be part of us. Be part of our gang, it's a good gang. It will bring America back."

I want everybody here to think long and hard about this. Yes, I want to be elected president. I believe I can be a good president. I believe I've got a good plan. Many of you helped me to fashion it, and those of you from Arkansas helped me live it. Oh yes, I want that job, but first I want you to think about what kind of citizens you're going to be, what kind of life you intend to live, what kind of community you are determined to create. My life is a testament to the fact that the American dream works. Leadership, rules, rewards, responsibility, and love. I've come a long way from where I started. Whenever I come back to this city I think about what is perhaps my earliest childhood memory. When I was about three years old, my grandmother got me on a train, and we came from Arkansas to New Orleans, where my widowed mother was here studying to be a nurse. It was the first time I had ever been in a building with more than two stories, and we stayed high in the old Young Hotel. I can still remember being mystified by how people ever got so high off the ground. I remember, too, the first and most vivid memory of my mother: When we left after this trip, my grandmother and I, my mother kneeled down at the side of the railroad tracks and cried because her child was going, but she was here so she could make a living to support me. I got to live by the rules that work in America, and I ended up here today running for president of the United States of America, because I had the right kind of American community. It went beyond politics, it went beyond programs, it went to values.

Three years ago, before all these fights broke out, I went to South Central L.A., which you have seen in flames. I drove, hour after hour, up and down those streets watching all the buildings, some painted red, some painted blue for the gangs that had jurisdiction in the area. I went into a grade school where the sixth graders told me they dreaded growing older because when they got to the eighth grade, they had do crack and join a gang or be beaten. Those kids are in the ninth grade now. How often I wonder what has happened to them.

When my daughter was in her last month of school last year, I remember taking her to school one day and seeing a wonderful, handsome man walking his child to school. He had two other little children with him. The man happened to be a black American. He was a remarkable fellow. One of these little children came running up to me, holding his hands at me, jumped up in my arms, and held me so tight. Now any politician loves that, but if you know anything about child development, you know that's not a very good sign for a child that's two years old—to be indiscriminately bestowing that sort of affection. So I asked this boy, "You want to go home with me?" He said, "Yeah." And I said, "I don't have a boy. I'd kind of like to have a boy to go with my girl." We were joking, and then I said to the man, "How many children do you have?" And he said, "Five." I said, "You mean you have three others besides these two?" He said, "Oh no, these two are not mine. My wife and I had one child who died. And we thought that in her memory, we would always, for the rest of our lives, be foster parents for children in need. These two children were left alone by their mother for two days, and so the state gave them to us. And we are loving them, hoping that their mother can learn to be a good parent and take them back."

Those children are hanging in the balance. Will they be part of our gang or someone else's gang? I tell you today that, as Martin Luther King wrote many years ago in his "Letter from a Birmingham Jail," "we are caught in an inescapable network of mutuality, tied in a single garment of destiny. Injustice anywhere is a threat to injustice everywhere." The thing that is killing America today is not our problems, although they are immense: We don't invest enough. We're losing our productivity lead. We have enormous social problems. We have political gridlock. All those are immense problems, but the thing that is killing our country today is that millions of Americans, from New Hampshire to southern California, from southern Florida to Washington, get up every day and do not believe that tomorrow will be better. They do not believe anything will change. They do not believe politics can make a difference. They do not believe they can make a difference.

This campaign, as I have always said, is a crusade to change this country. But it requires political reform, economic leadership, and the reestablishment of the common bonds of community and humanity without which we can never, ever, hope to change this country.

And so I ask you, my fellow Americans, let a part of the new ideas of the Democratic Leadership Council be the old-fashioned wisdom that we have to return meaning and connection to the idea of being an American. There is nothing before us we cannot conquer if we can simply get the energy and drive and joy that will come back into the lives of our people if they can once again believe they matter to us and that tomorrow will be better.

Thank you very much.

The Tale of Two Mothers

Glide Memorial Methodist Church
San Francisco, California
May 10, 1992

Before a packed Mother's Day worship service at Glide Memorial Methodist Church, a multiethnic church on Ellis Street in San Francisco's "tenderloin district," Clinton spoke without notes and delivered this short emotional speech to an audience of two thousand in the cadence of a sermon. Although he never mentioned his primary campaign opponent, former California governor Jerry Brown, nor President Bush, his remarks were clearly a political narrative of public policy and in support of his candidacy, and during his appearance he received the endorsement of Rev. Cecil Williams. Following this speech and two others in San Francisco that day, Clinton returned to Arkansas where he said he and his wife would celebrate Mother's Day in Little Rock with their mothers and their daughter.

❖ ❖ ❖

I want to, if I might, say that my party and I are all grateful to be here today. I would like in particular to recognize one person who came here with me, your wonderful secretary of state, March Fong Eu. Thank you for being here.

I would also like to tell you that my wife said to me, privately, that this was the best Mother's Day present that I had ever given her—bringing her here today.

We have already heard the message. But, today on this Mother's Day, I would like to tell you that I think the decisions we confront as a people might be told in the tale of two mothers.

One I know very well. Forty-five years ago, as a young widow, she gave birth to me. And then, after I was born, she went off to nursing school so she could make a living for me and left me with my grandparents.

Over the course of her life, she has been widowed three times. But, through it all, she loved me and my brother. She gave us a mother's love—unconditional love—and discipline and values and the sense that we were the most important person in the world to somebody.

The world is full of people today who think that they are not the most important person in the world to anybody. But my mother, on this day, throughout all of the failures of my life, can look back and say she did a pretty good job because her son is in San Francisco looking at America's rainbow asking for the chance to bring a mother's love back to this country.

Let me tell you a story about one other mother—although there could be millions—who is grieving today. I read about her a week ago in Washington. Thirteen years ago she gave birth to a little boy; his name was Joey. He lived in a neighborhood that was not very well off, with a lot of gangs and shootings and drugs. But she took him to her church and taught him right and wrong and made him believe that he was the most important person in the world.

And by the time he was thirteen he was an honor student, and the Saturday before last he gave a speech in his own church. And on the way home with his brothers and sisters and his mother driving the car, they happened to drive through an area dominated by guns and drugs and gangs. And they were just in the wrong place at the wrong time. Two people were shooting at one another, and little Joey was killed.

The tale of those two mothers shows the gap between America's promise and its reality. It is an America denying its problems until they can't be denied and blaming other people instead of embracing the cause of change. And in the grip of a selfishness that would kill any nation—oh to be sure it was heartbreaking to see some little children going into the stores in Los Angeles and stealing from their neighbors.

But they live in a country where the top 1 percent of Americans have more wealth than the bottom 90 percent. For the first time in seventy years, that has happened. And we want people to be able to make money in this country. But we want people to be able to make money by putting the rest of us to work and healing the rest of our wounds and binding us up together—one nation under God. That is what we are facing.

The pastor mentioned AIDS. AIDS is a subject that comes up when a famous person gets it. When Magic Johnson has the guts to come forward or Arthur Ashe becomes the victim of a prying story, then we all talk about it. But every day, people die in silence.

And so it is time to embrace it. It is time to do more work in every way. And pastor, even those who say it is a behavior-modification problem, when

I try to get them to help me to modify behavior, by putting sex education in the schools and teaching the children to protect themselves and keep themselves alive, most of those folks can't be found.

Still, more women die of breast cancer every year. And if you look at the way we do our medical research, it is hard to find any attention paid to the medical problem of women, of mothers.

For all of the talk of family values of those who have governed this country for twenty of the last twenty-four years, we don't do anything like we should in the rearing and educating of children—society's most important job.

Nation after nation is better at it than we are. All of the people who thump their convictions and religions and pretend to be so righteous, where are they when the family values can't be found on the streets of this country? When there is no health care for pregnant women, when too many little children are born with low birth weight, when more die here than in twenty-two countries, when so many have no preschool, when they are coming from homes with no education and they get no individual attention when they begin their education, when we have a laughable system of child support so that people can bring children into this world and then cross the state line and hope that government will do what they should have done for their own children—where are they?

So, I ask you today, in this wonderful church, to remember the tale of those two mothers and all of the mothers that they might represent and all of the mothers in between.

The purpose of life is to live up to your God-given capacity. And that requires, according to the Scripture, change from the inside out, which is what the pastor talked about, and change from the outside in, which is what politics is all about.

Now, the pastor helped me today because people are always trying to define politicians, too, and it is usually not very pretty. Only you can do that for yourselves. But I am honored to be here today. I felt elevated. I thought of my favorite Old Testament Scripture when I was listening to this sermon, "Those that wait upon the Lord shall have their strength renewed. They shall mount up with wings, as eagles. They shall run and not grow weary. They shall walk and not faint."

That is what we should want on Mother's Day.

God bless you.

The Value of America's Families

Cleveland City Club
Cleveland, Ohio
May 21, 1992

The issue of "family values" had been addressed by Vice-President Quayle in a speech to the Commonwealth Club of California on May 19 and by President Bush in the commencement speech given at the University of Notre Dame on May 17. Clinton used this speech presented to several hundred business and civic leaders at the prestigious Cleveland City Club to reclaim family values as a Democratic issue and make clear he was not going to concede definition of the topic to the Republicans.

In a message that combined policies and politics, Clinton also took the opportunity to describe his own family values. His staff had been concerned that voters seemed to know little about him beyond the questions that had been raised about his character and had sought in recent weeks appropriate chances to reintroduce him to voters as a caring public servant. The forty-minute speech, which Clinton rewrote throughout the morning to include more personal connections to the policies he was discussing, drew heavily on his own experiences and programs in Arkansas and consolidated several of his previously stated policy positions.

President Bush was also in the city at the same time, partly because a new poll showed both Bush and Clinton trailing Perot in Ohio. The irony of the campaign situation was not lost on the press, which noted that while Clinton was describing his own family and its humble roots, Bush was eight blocks away, addressing three hundred Republican contributors at a thousand-dollar-a-plate lunch, en route to a four-day weekend at his seaside home in Kennebunkport, Maine.

❖ ❖ ❖

Thank you. Thank you very much. It certainly was a unique introduction, and it was partly true. Maybe you ought to run for president.

I have really looked forward to coming here today, and I thank you for the opportunity to appear. As has already been said, I want to depart from the standard message I normally give talking about my eleven years as governor and the work I've done to generate jobs and educate children and balance budgets and bring people together and try to ignore traditional Democratic and Republican solutions to problems when they are plainly out-of-date.

For several weeks, I have planned to come here to discuss what stands at the heart of America's dream and as much of the core of the disappearance of the American dream: the American family and its problems.

But this topic has acquired, as all of you know now, quite a bit more currency because of the recent speeches that the president gave at the Notre Dame commencement and the speech that the vice-president gave at the Commonwealth Club in San Francisco the other day.

The president's speech extolled the virtues of family life, lamented the breakdown of the family, said family life had more to do with what happens in America than what goes on in Washington. That's probably true, and thank goodness. But it offered no real action agenda for improving the plight of our most troubled families.

The vice-president's speech has become known by its reference to the television show "Murphy Brown"—and you've all probably had your laughs about that—but the fact is that the vice-president's speech had more substance than the president's.

While the president urged Notre Dame graduates to help solve our nation's social and family crisis, it typically offered no agenda and assumed no responsibility. Vice-President Quayle, while repeating the sad statistics of teen pregnancy and divorce and out-of-wedlock birth in America, reiterated the empowerment agenda that is most closely identified, among Republicans, with HUD secretary Jack Kemp, and among Democrats with the Democratic Leadership Council—a group that I chaired when we came here to Cleveland and met in national convention last year—more home ownership for poor people, urban enterprise zones, and welfare reform designed to encourage work and independence.

Unfortunately, the vice-president's speech also is, in my view, cynical election-year politics in that it ignores the relationship of our family problems to our national economic decline, holds out Murphy Brown as a bigger problem than TV's crass commercialism and glorification of selfishness and violence, and denies the administration's responsibility to face the full range of America's staggering family problems.

I want to talk about these issues today because family questions are terribly important to our nation and to me personally. As a public official, I have worked on family issues harder and longer than anybody else running for president this year. And I do believe that they are at the heart of our national discontent.

And as well as anyone, I know the importance of family values to personal growth. In 1946, I was born to a widowed mother. My father died in a car wreck three months before I was born. Shortly after I was born, my mother went back to nursing school to learn skills that would enable her to support me. Until I was four, I was fortunate enough to be raised by loving grandparents of modest means but great determination—who began teaching me to count and read when I was two.

My mother's extended family included great-grandparents and great-uncles and aunts, all of whom were poor or nearly so, but they were wonderful, old-fashioned country people who brought love and joy and values to my life.

When I was four, my mother remarried. And though their marriage was not free of difficulty—some of which has been reported in the press—my brother and I benefited from the love of my stepfather and his extended family. They enriched my life and my sense of what I could do with it. My mother has been widowed in her life three times, but luckily is married to a wonderful man who has also been a friend and inspiration to me.

Every year I ask all the relatives from all my extended families, and my wife's family, to gather at Christmas time. It's an amazing celebration of the different threads of family, a broad fabric of love and support that raised a child from modest means to a rewarding career in public service and a serious campaign for the presidency of the United States. I know the value of family.

Over twenty years ago, I met and fell in love with a wonderful woman in Law School who would become my wife and a lot of my life. It was Hillary, who, in 1971, was already concerned about the problems of poor children and their parents and who began to teach me about them then.

In 1975, we married. In 1977, after I became attorney general in my state, my wife founded a remarkable organization called the Arkansas Advocates for Families and Children. In that year, long before it was the national rage, she organized the conference called Parenting Is Primary.

In 1979, when I first became governor, with my wife's help, we began to try and build a pro-family policy for our state. In 1980, our one and only child, Chelsea, was born. She's been the great joy of our life, and watching her grow and flourish has given me a greater sense of urgency about the task of helping all of our children and their parents to do better.

Over the last twelve years, those efforts have evolved into initiatives to lower the infant mortality rate through expanded maternal and child health services; to reduce teen pregnancy through aggressive and often controversial but value-based sex education efforts; to enhance child care for working families through an innovative voucher system; to reduce long-term welfare dependence by aggressively promoting more education and training and child care and medical coverage for the children of welfare families, then requiring parents to take available work; to increase preschool programs for poor children with a special emphasis on involving parents as their children's first teachers through a remarkable program we borrowed from the nation of Israel called HIPPY—Home Instruction Program for Pre-School Youngsters—a program in which even illiterate parents are taught to spend twenty minutes a day, five days a week, thirty weeks a year preparing their children to learn.

And finally, we've worked to increase child-support enforcement through innovative efforts like reporting every delinquent parent who owes more than a thousand dollars to every major credit agency in our state.

The thrust of all these efforts is to find what I would call a third way to approach the American family—beyond the traditional politics of both parties, beyond the administration's cheerleading for family values on the one hand, and on the other hand, the old big-government notion that there's a program for every social problem.

There is a third way, a common-sense path that offers more opportunity to families in return for more personal responsibility and the assumption of more family values. Family values alone can't feed a hungry child. And material security alone cannot provide a moral compass. We must have both.

There is a way to embrace family values and enhance the value of America's families at the same time. A president should do both. President Bush is right to lament the high rate of teen pregnancy, yet he does not bring value-based sex education and health clinics into our schools to prevent pregnancies in the first place.

He is right to decry the high divorce rate, yet he has no national economic plans to help families under economic strains.

The president is right to speak out on the violence that stalks our children. And I believe he's been wrong to cut back the funds that cities like Cleveland can use to hire more policemen for their streets. And he is wrong to oppose the Brady Bill that your congressman sponsored and even President Ronald Reagan supports to require a waiting period before people can purchase handguns so that their criminal and mental health history and their ages can be checked.

Like any parent, I'm troubled by the gratuitous violence and sex and mixed moral signals we see on television. The same tough value questions for America's children and parents run from the affluent suburbs in New England to the poorest blocks of south-central Los Angeles. And they reach into our own family, too, with Hillary as a working mother and our daughter, Chelsea, who's about to become a teenager.

And if those questions are hard for us, with all the privileges that God has given us, think about how much tougher they are for most families who are working harder for less money these days, and how devastating they can be for those families confronted with layoffs, illnesses, alcohol and drug abuse, poverty, or a violent neighborhood.

The question is not are family values important? Of course they are. It's not are they under fire? You bet they are. It's not is TV destructive of family values. All too often it is. The question is, What are we going to do about it?

It isn't enough for America's leaders to blame past social programs or current TV programs. It isn't enough for Americans to change channels. We need to change course.

Family values can't simply be Washington code for Beltway Republicans who really mean, "You're on your own," or Beltway Democrats who want to spend more of your tax money on programs that don't embody those values.

If family values are going to mean something, we must offer our nation a third way. A nation that guarantees opportunity for every family, but a society that demands responsibility from every individual.

Of course there's a values crisis in America. But there's an action gap as well. Addressing one without the other isn't a plan of action, it's posturing to distract from inaction.

Today the dominant message from this administration is, "You're on your own."

Parents have to work two jobs and spend more hours at work and too little time with their kids because wages are declining in America; you're on your own. Parents without health care who live in deadly fear they won't be able to care for their children without going bankrupt, they're on their own. If poor, uneducated parents need preschool for their children so they'll have a chance to do better than their parents, well, they're on their own.

The problem is, nobody is on their own in this country; we're all in this together. The more we ignore these problems today, the more we'll all pay for them tomorrow in lost economic strength, in increased violence, in costlier jails, in poorer schools, and lost futures. As my friend Governor Ann Richards of Texas said of the looters and the shooters of the streets of Los Angeles: "These young hoodlums who burn and batter and turn our streets into killing fields were once our children—small and helpless and needing our attention and our love—and we let them go, tossed them aside like yesterday's news. Now they are making headlines that we don't want to read. God may forgive them, but we can't condone their action or reclaim their lives. They are lost to us. This tragedy must end with this generation. It must stop now."

A very great Republican president, Theodore Roosevelt, once called the presidency a bully pulpit. Then President Kennedy said that the presidency was the vital center of action. Both presidents were right. A president's words can move a nation, but talk must be backed up with action, or we risk diminishing the bully pulpit into a pulpit of bull.

When I was born in Hope, Arkansas, in 1946, our state's per-capita income was barely half the national average. Though my family and I later moved into a middle-class life, thanks to both my stepfather and my mother working, in the beginning, like most people in my state, we were poor.

But one of the values my family pounded into me was that if I worked hard and played by the rules, I'd be rewarded—and I have been, beyond my wildest dreams. We were taught to take responsibility for ourselves and for each other. And we were taught that if we did, we would do better.

I understand something about hard times and how hard things can get. My mother was widowed before I was born, and I lived with my grandparents when I was little, as I said. My most vivid memory of my mother and childhood was when I went to visit her at nursing school when I was three, and when my grandmother and I pulled out of the station, she knelt down by the side of the railroad tracks and cried. I remember that to this day. I remember how she bore her grief every day, because she believed that, if she sacrificed in the short run, in the long run she could build a better life for me.

Now there are millions of stories like that in America today. Remember, most poor people, those with and without jobs, did not loot and riot in Los Angeles, because their values kept them from doing so. They would not do wrong. Most Americans today do give their children love and discipline and respect for others and for the law.

There is a great deal of love in the poorest welfare families in America today. But we have to face the hard truth that too many Americans are cut off from these values and the life that we want them to live that reinforces those values. And too many Americans who live by their values are denied the progress they were promised—the progress that was real for the poor of my generation.

We simply cannot go on under these circumstances being the only major nation in the world without a family policy—one that enshrines family values by placing a value on family. We've tried to develop one in Arkansas, and I outlined it to you a moment ago. And I think we need one in America.

Here is a good beginning: First, we should reward work and family. Today millions of Americans work full time but don't make enough to lift their families out of poverty. That's wrong. No one who works full time and has children at home should be poor in America.

We should expand the earned income tax credit to guarantee a "working wage" to lift above the poverty line anyone with a family who's working full time. This initiative is not terribly expensive. It won't require us to spend one red cent for any public bureaucracy. Yet, it will reward work and lift one million working poor families and their children out of poverty.

Second, we need to reform our welfare system so that it puts people back to work and ends permanent dependency. In Arkansas, under the Federal Family Support Act of 1988, which I helped to draft as the governors' representative, we've created a system of training, and vouchers for day care, and medical coverage for children so that welfare families can return to the dignity of a job once again. As a result, our welfare rolls have grown less than the national average in the last three years, even in spite of the recession and high unemployment.

The truth is, most people on welfare don't like it anymore than you do. A few years ago, I asked the woman in our Welfare-to-Work program in Arkansas what she liked best about her new job. And she said it wasn't earning a paycheck, it was knowing that when her son went to school and they asked him what your mother does for a living, he could give an answer. People want the dignity of work.

We should give everyone the chance to have that kind of dignity. We should give everyone on welfare the education, training, child care, and medical coverage for their children they need. But I think we should go beyond the present law. After two years, if people can't find private-sector employment, I think they should be required to do public-service work in return for the income.

We can end welfare as we know it, not by punishing the poor, but by empowering them to take care of their children and to be role models.

Third, we need to do more to protect America's children from the consequences of divorce and absent fathers—and on some occasions, absent mothers. I was born to a single mother who was lucky enough to have the support of an extended family. Today, in the governor's office, I have old pictures of my grandfather and my great-grandfather. Unfortunately, too few children know who their great-grandparents were, and too many have parents who should pay for their upbringing but don't.

We need to get tough on child-support enforcement with a nationwide crackdown on deadbeat parents. In our state, if you fall more than a thousand dollars behind in your child support, we report you to every major credit agency in the state. People shouldn't be able to borrow money for other things before they take care of their children.

Because of that and other efforts, like putting the name and Social Security number of a father on a birth certificate if a mother shows up to give birth without a father—thus shifting the burden to the man to disprove his heritage—we collected more than forty-one million dollars from "deadbeat parents" in 1991, money that we didn't have to pay in welfare or other public spending. These are the kinds of things that we ought to do. We have to do more of them.

We must make the toughest possible child-support enforcement efforts in this country. We should enlist major credit agencies all across the country to follow the example that Arkansas and a few other states have. We ought to say to people everywhere, "Pay for your children first, or you shouldn't get credit." We ought to have a national system of child-support collection utilizing the Internal Revenue Service and tax records.

I'm tired of seeing custodial parents bear the whole burden for the problem of raising their children. Governments can't raise children, people do. And the people who bring children into this world should all bear a responsibility for raising them.

Fourth, we need to help parents do the best possible job of rearing their kids. Government can't create good parents, but it can make it easier for them to tend to their children's needs.

In 1988, George Bush promised to make sure, and I quote, "women don't have to worry about getting their jobs back after having a child or caring for a child during a serious illness." But when Congress passed the Family and Medical Leave Act, George Bush vetoed it. I would sign it. Other nations do the same thing.

Millions of Americans are already caught in a squeeze between taking care of their parents and taking care of their children. We should not now make them choose between work and family—not if we are going to be a pro-family country where most parents have to work.

Fifth, we can also bolster the family's crucial role in education. We should fully fund the Head Start program and quit delaying it. But in doing it, we should put increased emphasis on enlisting parents, even illiterate parents, as their children's first teachers. As I said earlier, the HIPPY program in Arkansas trains welfare mothers to teach their preschool children to read. The Head Start programs with the most long-lasting benefits for children are those in which the parents' role is greatest, no matter how limited the parents' own educational skills.

Our schools should also reinforce these family values and parental involvement by bringing more parents in. Schools all over America can follow the example of the Beasley Academic Center, a public junior high school in Chicago. It's located in a neighborhood with the highest murder rate in all of Illinois. But every week, seventy-five fathers and even more mothers regularly volunteer in the schools.

Against the odds, this school ranks in the top 10 percent of test scores in the state, with no guns, no drugs, no dropouts—in part because of a culture which includes a dress code, strong family values, and parental role models. Not just talk, action!

Sixth and lastly, I want to ensure that American families and individuals make the best personal decisions with their life with a full sense of personal responsibility and concern for the consequences of their behavior. That means letting teens know that it is wrong for children to have children and also providing them with the education about how to prevent that.

In Arkansas, my nationally renowned health director, Dr. Joycelyn Elders, and I fought for school-based health clinics and sex education. It wasn't popular, and it still isn't easy, but with teen pregnancy and AIDS claiming more and more of our young people, it is now a matter of life and death.

There are many other issues that we have to face: restoring economic growth to our nation so we can restore economic strength to our families, providing affordable health care to all of our families and their children, giving poor people more say over their own lives through initiatives like community policing and tenant management of housing projects, and preserving personal and family privacy—including, in my view, not repealing *Roe v. Wade.*

The president says he wants private-school choice even if it means taking public money away from public schools that are already underfunded compared to many other nations. He's willing to make it a crime for a woman to exercise her right to make the most private choice of all. I don't understand those priorities.

When my daughter was in her last month of sixth grade last year, I remember taking her to school one day—as I do every day when I'm home—and seeing a very handsome man walking his child to school. He had two other little children with him. And one of these little children came running up to me, holding out his hands, and jumping up into my arms. He held me very tight. Now, as you know, I'm a politician, so I love that—I mean, the baby wanted to kiss me.

But, if you know anything about child development—this child was almost two years old—it's not a very good sign for a two-year-old child still to be indiscriminately bestowing this sort of affection. So I asked this man, I said, "How many children do you have?" He said, "Five." I said, "You mean you have the one that went in there, these two, and two others?" And he said, "Oh, no, no, these two are not mine." He said, "My wife and I had a daughter who died. And in honor of her memory, we decided that we would spend the rest of our lives serving as foster parents for children in need. These two children I have are not mine. They were abandoned by their mother, alone at home, for two whole days. They were twenty months old. So the state gave them to us to care for for a while, and we're loving them and hoping that their mother can learn to love them and be a good parent and eventually take them back."

There are millions of children like that all over this country—hanging in the balance. They are part of our national family. Of course, we must exhort their parents to do a better job, and we must write into our social programs incentives for stronger family values. But we cannot ignore the plain need for a national policy to value families, to reconnect all Americans to our most cherished values and the idea of progress for those who live by those values.

Ultimately, it is up to each of us to build the bridge across that gulf that stands wide today between what we are as a nation and what we are meant to be. We must believe that we once again can make a difference, that tomorrow will be better than today if we build that bridge and make it so.

We have the tools. The question is do we have the vision and the will. This election will tell the tale.

Thank you very much.

On to the White House

Primary Victory Speech
Los Angeles, California
June 2, 1992

Thank you very much. Thank you. Thank you so much. On behalf of Hillary and on my own behalf, I want to begin by thanking the millions and millions of people who voted for this campaign and its promise of change all across this country.

I want to thank the people who volunteered literally millions of hours of their time to make this campaign work. I want to thank the friends of my lifetime who stood by me, the people from my beloved state of Arkansas who fought across this country for me, all the people who worked on our campaign across the nation and back home. And I want to say a special word of thanks to those who worked in my administration who kept our government going and working hard and made it possible for me to make this campaign.

All of you tonight, this is your victory. It is not mine, and I hope you're proud of it.

When I got into this race, the president was at a historically high point in popularity, and most people did not think there would be much of a race this year. But I was convinced then and I am convinced now that this country needs profound change.

For too long Washington has rigged our system for the benefit of the few, the quick buck, the gimmick, and the short run. For the first time since the twenties, 1 percent of the American people control more wealth than the bottom 90 percent.

For this we were promised jobs, but instead we got pink slips and insecurity, worries about health care and education and safe streets. We have tried it that way, and now we have to change. I am tired of seeing the people who work hard and play by the rules get the shaft.

And tonight, with this delegate count, we want to put the forces of the status quo and short-term greed on notice: the party is over, we are in for a change, we want our country back.

It's time to invest in this country again, reward those who play by the rules, punish those who don't, and get on into the future that the people in this country deserve. It is time to make sure that everybody knows, as grateful as I am for what has happened, that this campaign is not about delegate count; it is about making people count.

Tonight, I can't help thinking back over these last several months and all of the brave Americans I have met along the way. The people with whom I started in New Hampshire, Ron Macos Jr., who couldn't get a job with health insurance because he had a two-year-old child who had open-heart surgery. He played by the rules and was going to be punished, because he lives in the only advanced nation where the government stubbornly refuses to control health-care costs and provide affordable health care to all Americans. We are going to change that.

Tonight, I think of that wonderful immigrant father I met in New York, who grabbed me as I was walking toward a speech and said, "Governor, my ten-year-old studies politics in school, and he said you should be president, so I am going to vote for you. But," he said, "I came here because America is the land of the free. But my boy is not free; he can't even walk to school unless I go with him. If you become president, make my boy free." I'll tell you one thing, if this government helps cities put more police on the street in community policing, provided boot camps for first-time offenders, and passed the Brady Bill, that boy would be freer—and I intend to do that.

I think about the women that I met—the working mother in Livingston, New Jersey, in Sacramento, California—who worry about how they can balance the demands of motherhood and work, how they can do right by their children.

Well, I'll tell you one thing, if we had a president who would sign instead of veto the Family and Medical Leave Act, they'd be better off. And I am going to give that to them.

I think about that wonderful couple, Mary Annie and Edward Davis, I met and broke down and cried as I hugged them, telling me that every week they were choosing between food and medicine, because they live in the only advanced nation that doesn't have health care including a decent long-term health system. And I'm going to give it to them if you will help me be president of the United States of America.

For twelve years, Americans have tried to do the right things, and they deserve a government that will do right by them. Doing right by our people means rebuilding our economy by investing in their jobs, their education, in their health care. It means honoring work and demanding responsibility.

At the end of World War II, this great nation of ours did a wonderful job of rebuilding Europe and Japan. It's time at the end of the Cold War for us to rebuild America. That's where our work is today.

To do that, rebuilding America begins with a commitment to educate and train all of our people. It's the best investment we will ever make, and to do it, we need a real education president—someone who has paid the price and done the work.

I have heard all of the talk about what a wonderful program Head Start is. It's time we had a president who would fund it so the children in this country and their parents would know how wonderful it is.

And there needs to be something for these young people on the other end of school, too. For those who don't go to college but don't want to be in dead-end jobs, we should join the ranks of advanced nations and provide a two-year apprenticeship program to every noncollege-bound student so they can get those good jobs and we can restore the dignity to blue-collar work in this country.

Finally, I want to make it possible for every young American and every not-so-young American who wants to go to college to borrow the money to do it. We must end the attempt to make it impossible for people to go to college and provide the funds necessary for any American to go.

At the end of World War II, we rebuilt our country in large measure because we provided, through the GI Bill, the opportunity for any soldier who wanted to, to go to college.

When John Kennedy was president, we helped rebuild a lot of the rest of the world through the Peace Corps. I propose to take the best of both ideas. Let anybody borrow the money to go to college and let them pay it back by giving a couple of years of service to our nation here at home to rebuild America as teachers or police officers or nurses.

Investing in our people means also having the courage to take on the insurance companies and the health-care bureaucracies and the government and providing affordable health care to all Americans.

Tonight, even as we celebrate, there are thousands of people all across America lying awake wondering whether they are going to lose their jobs or their health insurance or whether the next illness will bankrupt them. That's because we have stubbornly refused to do what the competition does. Vote for me and together we'll provide affordable health care to the people of this country.

Investing in America also means creating jobs for the people who are educated and healthy to do. Every last dollar by which we reduce defense must be reinvested in America to build an economy for the twenty-first century—every dollar—for high-speed rail, for short-haul aircraft, for fiber-optics communication, for modern environmental systems, to clean up our water and to recycle our solid waste.

We can have growth and environmental protection if, but only if, we are committed to reinvesting in this country. That's the way we are going to create jobs, and we are going to do it by investing in America for a change.

Finally, if we want these changes, we are going to have to insist that all of our citizens accept the challenge to do their part and to be more responsible. There are millions of good people in business in this country today making the free-enterprise system go. But our tax system does not reward them.

It does not reward investment in new plant and equipment. Instead, it rewards unlimited executive compensation, even for companies that are losing money. It rewards moving plants overseas instead of moving plants here at home with new plant and investment.

And I tell you, we need a new responsibility ethic in our tax system—more incentives to invest in America, no incentives for executive compensation that is excessive or moving our plants overseas.

We also need a new family policy in this country—more incentives for child care and maternal and health care for the kids. We need family leave. But, we need the toughest possible child-support enforcement. I am tired of people running off and leaving their children for the government to raise, and we can stop it.

We need a new policy toward the poor. We need to lift those who work forty hours a week and have children at home above the poverty line. We need to say to those on welfare: we are going to end this system of welfare as we know it, we will invest more in your education and training and support for your children. But then you must work. We have got to end the system as we know it.

My fellow Americans, change is never easy, but I have worked hard for more than a decade to make change, and I have learned a few things about it. You have to be willing to take on organized groups and fight for change even if they are against you. You have to be willing to pay the price of time, and you have to know, that in the end, words have to give way to deeds.

I've got one opponent who says he'll do whatever it takes to hold on to the White House, then—wait a minute—then there's another person running who says he'll spend whatever it takes to get the White House.

Let me tell you, winning this election is not what's at stake here; winning the fight for America's future is what is at stake here. And what I came here tonight to promise you is that I will stay up late and get up early and work hard as long as it takes to turn this country around and give it back to the American people.

All of you have taught me a lot. I learned a lot about the American people that I didn't know but that I suspected over the last seven or eight months.

I've learned that from the farms to the factories, from the suburbs to the inner cities, we are not as different as we like to think.

Most people really do value work and family. Most people want to believe they are part of a bigger community. Most people know down deep inside we're all in this together and we are going up and down together, that all children can learn and that it is wrong for us to let so many of our resources, including our people, be wasted as we do. Most people believe that.

Most people are tolerant but not permissive. They are sick and tired of seeing this country be divided by age, by gender, by race, by ethnic group, by sexual orientation, by region, every way. We are tired of it. We want to be together again.

So if you ask me, "Bill, what did you learn from this primary?" I learned this is a very great country where we desperately want to win again, where we want to be one again, and where we know what we have to do again: invest in our people, be more responsible, and come together.

The election for America's future begins tomorrow. It is not about me; it is about all of you. I will fight every day in every way to make you proud, to make you believe that together we can make a difference.

Remember this, my fellow Americans, what kills a country is never the obstacles people face. There are always problems. This country is being decimated today by visionless leadership, by the politics of division.

I am going to give you a campaign with a vision of America that works again, that rewards work, that invests in people, that insists on responsibility, and that pulls us together as one nation under God.

Bless you all. Thank you.

Work, Family, and the Future

American Association of Retired Persons
San Antonio, Texas
June 4, 1992

While older Americans, the generations that lived through the depression of the 1930s, have historically been more likely to support Democratic presidential candidates, the AARP membership is generally the more affluent of that age group and often more insistent upon specific policy concessions affecting its interests. Not surprisingly then during Clinton's rather stern forty-minute speech, the several thousand retirees in the audience gave him mild applause at times, but for the most part they listened in polite silence.

Adapting his remarks to the convention's theme of "Generations Growing Together," Clinton called the Social Security system "a convenant between generations" and promised to honor that commitment and protect the system. As he looked out over a sea of elderly delegates in the Henry B. Gonzalez Convention Center, most of whom sat stiffly with their hands in their laps, he acknowledged that parts of his message calling for some sacrifice by everyone, including older Americans, might not be popular, but it was in the nation's best interest and that of future generations.

The text below outlines Clinton's views and is consistent with the overall theme of personal responsibility at the center of his campaign message, but it was also intended to strategically demonstrate that he would not pander to specific groups' demands nor duck the tough issues, even before a powerful lobby or a potentially wary audience.

❖ ❖ ❖

Thank you. Thank you very much. Thank you very much, President Burgess, ladies and gentlemen. I am so honored to be invited to be here with you today. I appreciate the warm welcome on coming in.

It is an amazing thing to be through this long string of presidential primaries where I learned a lot about not only how much we have in common, but how different we are as Americans. I'm always amazed at each day I learn something about how American people can look at the same set of facts and draw different conclusions from it.

And since I am here at the AARP, I thought I would tell you a story I heard the other day that illustrates this point so well—about a couple who'd been married just a little over fifty years.

They were sitting out on their porch rocking in their chairs, and the husband looked at his wife and he said, "Sarah, you know we've been together a long time."

And she said, "Yes."

And he said, "I'm really a man of few words—all these years there are so many things I should have said to you that I didn't."

She said, "Yeah."

He said, "You know, we got married in the depression and you believed in me, but it was the depression. And not long after we got married our little business went down and I was flat broke, but you hung in there with me."

And she said, "Yeah, I did."

He said, "Then I went off to World War II and I got that bad wound, and it took me a year to overcome it, but you hung in there with me every day."

She said, "Yeah, I did."

He said, "Then after the war, we finally moved into our own home for the first time, and six months later a tornado came along and blew it down. It took us six years to get in our house again, but you hung in there with me, didn't you?"

And she said, "Yes, I did."

And he said, "Well, Sarah, before it is too late, I just want to tell you one thing. Honey, you're bad luck."

So, if you want to be involved in this enterprise on which I have embarked, you have to be willing to have people see facts in a different way than you do. In that connection, I want to compliment your president for the theme of this conference: generations coming together.

As governor, I have worked hard to serve the retired people of my state—one of the states with the highest percentage of people over sixty-five in the United States. But, I want to be president to restore the promise of the American dream for our children.

When I was a freshman at Georgetown University twenty-eight years ago, I had a professor of Western Civilization who said that the very special thing about our civilization in general, and the United States in particular, is that we had always believed that the future could be better than the present, and that each of us has a personal, moral responsibility to make it so.

That's what I want to talk about today—beyond the talk of Democrats and Republicans, beyond pointing the finger of blame, to the assumption of responsibility. For the plain truth is that millions of our fellow citizens of all ages do not believe the future will be better than the present, and millions more do not believe they have a personal, moral responsibility to make it so.

I learned the American dream, and I lived the American dream as a child growing up in Arkansas. Nearly half a century ago, I was born in a little town called Hope. Somebody's here from there, probably. We're everywhere now. I have two delegates from Chicago who were born in Hope—one from Queens. We're way over our quota.

My father died in a car wreck three months before I was born. My mother went back to nursing school so that she could earn a living to support me. Until I was four, I was raised by loving grandparents of modest means but great determination.

They taught me to read and count when I was two and three. They taught me in their own way that our country isn't just another place, it's an idea—a solid covenant that spans generations, a commitment to uphold the values we learn in our families—to honor our parents and grandparents, to offer a helping hand to our sisters and brothers, to protect and provide for our children and our children's children.

I learned from my grandparents the basic contract of American life that if you work hard and play by the rules, you will be rewarded. That promise has come true for me beyond my wildest dreams. But as I have traveled across this great nation of ours, I've met too many good, hardworking people for whom that promise has been broken.

Coming over here today, I couldn't help remembering the encounter I had in Nashua, New Hampshire, with a couple named Mary Annie and Edward Davis, who broke down crying telling me how every week they had to choose between their food and the medicine they needed to stay alive and healthy. People like them have done right by America, and now it's time for America to do right by them.

One of the reasons I entered this race for president is that I was tired of seeing people being punished for their devotion to work and family, to country, and community.

If any Americans have kept faith with the American promise, it's the generation that worked their way out of the Great Depression, brought their way to victory over Nazism and fascism, led the way through the Cold War, and sacrificed to provide my generation with opportunities our parents never had.

I'm going to be a president who does right by older Americans, because you've done right by America. And your country owes you that.

Doing right means understanding that Social Security is a commitment that must be kept, not just for today's beneficiaries, but to today's working people who are paying into the system for their tomorrows. It's a covenant—Social Security—a covenant between generations, and I will honor that.

Doing right means understanding, that in spite of Medicare, most senior citizens still pay too much for health care. In fact, a recent study found that the average elderly person is actually paying a higher percentage of income for health care today than in 1965—just before Medicare was enacted in the first place.

During the first year of my administration, we'll send a national health plan to Congress to control the cost of health care by taking on the insurance and health-care and government bureaucracies that add tens of billions of dollars in unnecessary costs to our system. My plan will provide a comprehensive package of benefits and have measures to discourage excessive cost and especially to hold down the price of prescription drugs.

The plan will include long-term care for the elderly and the disabled—charging people based on their ability to pay—and will emphasize greater choice in care, from home to nursing-home service. After you've worked hard all of your life, you shouldn't be wiped out by serious illness, and you should have as much control over your own life as possible.

America is the only advanced nation in the world without a national health plan. We spend 30 percent more of our income on health care than any of our major competitors, and we do less with it. And we lag behind them as a result on many measures of health care from infant mortality, to heart disease, to life expectancy.

We also, I might add, are dramatically underfunding women's health research and development in areas from breast cancer to ovarian cancer to osteoporosis, and that's why the bill now in the Congress ought to pass for new health investment.

As you know so well, Americans pay more for prescription drugs than the citizens of nations who have national health plans. This is a special burden to elderly people who aren't poor enough to be on Medicaid but aren't rich enough to pay their bills themselves. Their numbers are legion. Mary Annie and Edward Davis are but two of the hundreds of thousands of them.

As the Senate Special Committee on Aging, chaired by my good friend and fellow Arkansan, David Pryor, found, prices of prescription drugs during the last decade have risen by three times the rate of inflation. And to add insult to injury, some American drug companies charge Americans more for the same products here than they charge people in other countries. That's wrong, and I want to change it.

That's why I support Senator Pryor's bill to take away tax breaks for drug companies to raise their prices more than the rate of inflation. When you go to the doctor or the drugstore or the hospital, your next stop shouldn't be the poor house.

These issues have long been a concern to me. Fifteen years ago, as one of America's youngest attorney generals, I created the Advocates for the Elderly Program to help older people with their legal problems. As governor of my state I led the nation's governors in fighting to stop the unfair termination of Social Security disability benefits.

In Arkansas, we started a long-term care program called Elderchoices, which let seniors use money normally reserved for nursing-home care for long-term care services of their own choice—from personal care to home health care to adult day care.

The country I want to lead will honor its obligations to people who've worked hard all their lives. But I also have to come here today to challenge you and all older Americans to honor our obligations to our nation's children, because our future depends on their strength, their intelligence, their skills, their citizenship.

Thanks to Social Security and Medicare, our country has made progress in reducing poverty among older Americans. We can all be proud of the fact that, beginning in 1985, for the first time in the history of America, the elderly were less poor than the rest of America.

By contrast, poverty has exploded among our children. Our new poor in America are young children and their mothers—most of whom are working mothers—and we cannot be proud of that. We can't be proud that 13 percent of America's children have no health coverage whatever; that 30 percent of all of our preschoolers are not immunized against mumps, measles, and rubella; that every year forty thousand babies born in the United States die before their first birthday. And many more are born with very low birth weights, imposing great costs on society and bearing mental and physical limitations which may dog them throughout their lives and further undermine their ability to be contributing citizens.

We can't be proud of the fact that 20 percent of all children under eighteen and 25 percent of all children under six are living in poverty; that teenage boys are more likely to die from gunshot wounds than natural causes; that each year a half million American children do not finish high school, and millions more stop there with no further education, thus condemned to losing out in the tough global competition in which what you earn depends on what you can learn.

It is astonishing to note that families under the age of thirty are earning more than 25 percent less than what their counterparts were seventeen years ago. We cannot be proud of this, because today's children are tomorrow's workers, tomorrow's taxpayers, tomorrow's parents, tomorrow's citizens. If they grow up malnourished, unhealthy, and unprepared to compete in the twenty-first century, then America will be neither safe nor solvent, neither prosperous nor powerful.

We must not neglect our children and let their decline be the legacy of our generation. They are the national-security issue of 1992.

As all of you know, we know what works. We know what works in raising children—how to help them grow up healthy and hopeful, loving and learning, and ready to build their futures and libraries and laboratories instead of giving their lives away to gangs and guns on our meanest streets.

Mr. Bush says when it comes to investing in America, we have more will than wallet. What I say, now that we've won the Cold War, we've got to find the will to invest in our people, in our jobs, in our education, in our health care and reclaim our own legacy.

We have the wallet to spend over one hundred billion dollars on the savings-and-loan bailout in this year alone. We have the wallet to let health-care cost go up two and three times the rate of inflation, with the money going straight to insurance and bureaucracy, while our competitors hold them down. We have the wallet to keep protecting Germany from the Soviet threat, while German factory workers earn 20 percent more than Americans for a shorter work week, and the Germans invest in the former Soviet Republics, while the former Soviet Republics slash their own defense budgets far more than we have cut ours.

And in the 1980s, we had the wallet to cut taxes on the wealthiest Americans and corporations, while raising taxes on the middle class, slashing our investments in the future, and exploding the federal deficit.

I know that the generation that won World War II and the Cold War has the vision and the will and the discipline to join this crusade to invest in our young people and reinvigorate our economy. Your generation has sweated and sacrificed and died for others. You've never had the attitude, "I've got mine, you get lost."

At the end of World War II, you led a strong America in rebuilding Europe and Japan. At the end of the Cold War, you must lead us in rebuilding America—in regaining our commitment to the future. You can teach all Americans lessons in patriotism and citizenship and responsibility.

As president, I must challenge you, and all Americans, to support a new national commitment to provide every baby born in the United States with a healthy start in life from health care and nutrition for expectant mothers and their infants to immunization for young children.

I will challenge you and all Americans to provide preschool for every child who needs it by finally fully funding Head Start so all our children can start school ready to learn. All this is in your self-interest and in our national interest. If we don't fully fund Head Start today, we may not be able to fully fund Social Security twenty years from now.

As president, I must challenge you and all Americans to help make every American school a model school, because all our children deserve the best. I will challenge you and all Americans to support a domestic GI Bill—a domestic peace corps that will offer college loans to every American of every age willing to repay the loan or give a couple of years of service back to our community here at home—not a peace corps for abroad, but a peace corps for America.

Think of it as we are here in San Antonio. If every young person from San Antonio or El Paso or Laredo or Houston or Dallas or Texarkana or Lubbock, if every one of them got a college education from a national-service loan and came home to work as a police officer, a teacher, in a drug rehabilitation program, with kids in trouble, we could solve the problems of America at home and educate a whole generation of Americans. It would be the best money we ever spent.

For those who do not want to go to college, we should follow our competitors and give every high-school graduate at least two years of further education and training on the job with a national apprenticeship program to restore the dignity of blue-collar work in America.

In order to do this, we must have the discipline to control health-care costs—which is the single most important force in the exploding federal deficit today—to reinvest all of our defense costs in rebuilding the American economy, and to ask upper-income Americans to pay their fair share of taxes. Those who received most of the benefits of the 1980s should shoulder more of the burden of the 1990s.

Let me be specific, although it may not be politically popular. If your income went up and your taxes went down in the last twelve years, if family income is over two hundred thousand dollars, you should pay more. We cannot ask the middle class to pay more. Their incomes went down and their taxes went up in the 1980s.

I support a higher rate for the richest Americans and a surtax on millionaires, such as that recommended in the recent tax bill sponsored by Senator Lloyd Bentsen and vetoed by the president. And if an older American on Medicare has an income in excess of one hundred and twenty-five thousand dollars a year, I think there should be a higher price for Medicare if, in return, you get control of health-care costs and a sensible system of long-term care. No one should be forced to pay for the same old system and just take money out of private pockets and send it direct to health-care companies or a bureaucracy that is out of control.

We didn't get into this mess overnight, and we won't get out of it without some sacrifice from those most able to make it. The days of something for nothing for a few at the top are over. To make America work again, we need more incentives for private investment and new plant and equipment, to start new businesses, to invest in the most depressed areas of our cities and rural America. We also need more direct investment in education and in health care in our future.

Unless those whose incomes went up while their taxes went down in the eighties pay their fair share, we simply cannot afford to increase these investments and bring down our huge deficit. These are problems we must all face.

I also hope you will support other policies which reinforce the values of work and family. For all of those working poor families I talked about, how about a simple tax system that says we will increase the earned income tax credit so that if you work forty hours a week and you've got children in the house, you will be lifted above the poverty line.

How about a welfare reform system that says we'll invest more in your education and training and child care and medical coverage, but you have to go to work. We have to end welfare as we know it.

How about providing more choices for elderly people in long-term care and more choices among public schools for parents and their children so there will be some competition but no private vouchers to deplete the limited resources of our public-education system.

How about the toughest possible system of child-support enforcement so people can't bring kids into this world, cross the state line, and leave them for the government to raise. That's the kind of thing we ought to be supporting.

How about a safe-streets initiative that will bring police back to the blocks every day, walking the same streets, working with the same neighbors, enlisting the energies of people to shut down the crack houses and open up the city parks. These are the kind of programs we need in America today.

And so I say to the AARP, I respect the theme of this conference. I ask you to live it. I ask you to go home and ask your fellow Americans to reach across generational lines.

As I said at the beginning, I was raised by my grandparents until I was four. I spent a lot of time with my great-grandparents, who lived out in the country in what would be called a shack today. They were poor, but they were loving and strong people. They made me feel loved and know discipline. They gave me self-esteem and respect for others.

In the governor's office in Arkansas, I've got a picture of my grandmother in grade school in 1916, a picture of my grandfather at the furnace of a sawmill in 1923, a picture of my great-grandfather holding my hand in a hospital room in 1952.

It's a long way in America from the photographs I have on my wall to our meanest streets where children don't know who their grandparents are, too often have to worry about their parents' own behavior and even drug abuse, and where too many join gangs to find the extended family I knew naturally as a child.

America's future needs an investment of your time as well as money. America's children need grandparents, even if they are not their own. I want to lift the earnings limit on Social Security, but I know our Social Security depends on your time being given over to more than earnings. The elderly people of this country could revolutionize the lives of the troubled children of America through volunteer programs in schools and communities all across this land. For America is a dream every child must cherish, a promise every generation must keep, a legacy we must leave to our children and our grandchildren.

And so I challenge you not only to fight and strive and struggle to save Social Security, but also to preserve, protect, and defend the security of our children; to fight not only to keep Medicare strong and stable but to make our economy grow and prosper; to work not only to keep older Americans out of poverty but to lift our children up as well.

Support programs that reflect our shared values, putting the future ahead of the present, moving people from welfare to work, establishing tough child support, lifting the working poor, creating a new system of national service for college education, and more. Work, family, future—that is what we must honor and reward.

Together we can end this era of every person for himself and begin the era of we're all in this together. Together we can do for America what America did for Europe and Japan at the end of World War II: build a prosperous and powerful new economy with millions of new jobs and dozens of new industries with people who are healthy and strong, and children who believe the future will be better than the present.

Most of all, we can leave our children a nation that is stronger, freer, and richer than the one we inherited. That must, in the end, be the true measure of our legacy as Americans: did we leave this world better than we found it? Today, the answer would be no; tomorrow the answer can be yes. It is that question on which this coming election depends.

Thank you, and God bless you all.

Rebuild America

Rainbow Coalition National Convention
Washington, D.C.
June 13, 1992

In remarks to about three hundred members of the National Rainbow Coalition's "Rebuild America" conference at the Washington Sheraton Hotel, Clinton addressed the concerns of the interracial group, and the speech is important for its exposition of his positions and his differences with the Bush administration on a number of domestic issues. In words similar to that delivered to other traditional Democratic constituencies, he said, "I pledge to you not that we will always agree but that I will work my heart out to make this country what it ought to be."

Clinton had received a relatively warm reception from the predominantly black audience as he delivered a thirty-minute speech that embraced much of the Rainbow Coalition's agenda, but the response changed markedly when, talking about racism and admitting mistakes of his own, he also criticized remarks made by rap artist Sister Souljah, who had appeared as a guest at the meeting the night before.

Press and broadcast news reports ignored the bulk of Clinton's message and focused on those few paragraphs near the end of his speech. Jesse Jackson stared straight ahead during these remarks and later told reporters, "You saw the chill that went across that audience. . . . The rippling effect through the conference has been traumatizing. . . . I do not know why he used this platform to address those issues. It was unnecessary. It was a diversion. . . . Perhaps he was aiming for an audience that was not here." Clinton defended his comments, saying, "This was the best audience for that message. If not here, where would have been better?"

Campaign spokesman and speech writer Paul Begala said that Clinton "had the courage of his convictions to say what he thought before this group," just as he had before other groups to which he had spoken. Undoubtedly, though, the remarks were intended to strategically demonstrate that Clinton was not a captive of the Democratic

Party's traditional coalition members, what the Republicans had successfully been able to label "special interests" in recent elections. The approach worked to maintain Clinton's image as an "outsider" or a "new Democrat" willing to challenge the party's main players, even at the cost of being able to fully mobilize those groups in the fall campaign, yet realizing that there was little chance they would support Bush's reelection campaign.

❖ ❖ ❖

Thank you very much. Thank you very much, Reverend Jackson, for reminding us of the biblical lessons applicable to the present. I want to thank you and acknowledge you and your wonderful family and the family of the Rainbow Coalition.

I want to say as the proud father of a daughter, I wish I had a dozen pictures of Jesse's face when his daughter was up here singing. There is no joy in life like the joy in the eyes of a father at a moment like that.

I also want to thank you for giving birth to this Rebuild America program. There is a remarkable commonality in the analysis you have of the last twelve years and the prescription you have for what we ought to do to rebuild this country, what I have been saying for years, and what I have said from the moment I entered this presidential campaign. And more than anything else I thank you for not just pointing the finger of blame but taking up the burden of responsibility.

This is an interesting presidential year in which it appears a person can come nearer the White House and its responsibilities by going on "Arsenio Hall" than by going on the offense in election states, if you can laugh when a man like Mr. Hall says that when I played the saxophone he was glad to see a Democrat blowing something besides an election.

An election which may be turned on such important findings as that discovered by the *Washington Post* reporter who traveled the thirty-five miles of farmland and cattle ranches and pine trees between my hometown of Hope, Arkansas, and Ross Perot's hometown of Texarkana, Texas, and concluded that after all I had even more humble beginnings than he did.

Or the reporter Chris Matthews in San Francisco, who somehow got me to speculate about whether I would be the last person ever to run for president who once lived in a home without an indoor toilet. He asked me what the worst things about it were, I said, "winter and snakes."

I don't know what all this has to do with being elected president, but I do know what you're here about has a great deal to do with what happens to this country. We have to rebuild America to bring our country together, to bring fundamental change, to go beyond the greed and special interests and paralysis of the last twelve years, to put our people first for a change and invest in them for a change.

The president used to talk a lot about the "New World Order." With the election just five months away he has decided on the five hundredth anniversary of Columbus's discovery of America to sail the ship of state here and discover America himself. But his ship of state lacks a compass and a vision.

And the Scripture says that where there is no vision the people perish. We are in the process of living out that admonition. Even after the riots in Los Angeles, the president could only discover one person in his administration, Jack Kemp, who had ever said anything about cities, and he had been kept in a closet until Los Angeles burned.

Now the centerpiece of their proposal is a program called "Weed and Seed." Now I agree, actually, with the goals of that program. I wish, for the sake of those struggling to be liberated from drugs, that it were properly funded and more extensive, but I can't help pointing out that notwithstanding weed and seed, we've gotten a lot more fertilizer than crop production from this administration.

This is an administration that promised us thirty million jobs and then vetoed a tax bill to invest in new plants and equipment, to encourage people to start new businesses, to encourage people to build housing in inner cities, because all those tax incentives would have been paid for by increasing taxes on the rich whose incomes went up and taxes went down in the 1980s.

This is an administration that extols family values and vetoed the Family Leave Bill so working people could be better parents.

This is an administration that promised us an environmental presidency and then vetoed the environmental agreement at Rio de Janeiro to reduce global warming in a way that could have improved the economy of America by investing in alternative-energy policies here at home.

This is an administration that promised us an education presidency and then with a straight face said nobody should get a scholarship from the federal government if they have an income of over ten thousand dollars a year, they were too rich. But if your income was over three hundred thousand dollars a year, you were still poor enough to need a capital-gains tax.

This is an administration that promised us a balanced budget amendment, while quadrupling the deficit and never proposing anything that approached a balance of investment and budget in America.

This is an administration that promised to make it easier for people to get health insurance but year in and year out made it more difficult by never, never taking on the health-insurance companies and the health-care companies that have exploded the price of health care and made it harder for people to get.

This is an administration that talks tough on crime but for one solid year has let the Brady Bill languish un-enacted in Congress because of its own ideological preferences when a simple bill could at least make it possible in every state in America to check for criminal history, for mental history, for age, in everybody who wants to put a gun in their hands in the streets of the cities of the United States.

We could go on and on in doing this. We could laugh, and then we could cry, but in the end we have to do what you have tried to do, not simply to rail against the night, but to build a new American order, a plan of action to put our own people first, to honor and reward work, to develop the God-given capacities of the American people.

Vice-President Quayle is now the hit person for this administration and their family values crusade. Reverend Jackson has already talked about that. He said the other day, Vice-President Quayle did, that I was leading a cultural elite; Jesse's part of a cultural elite; Mario Cuomo, specifically, singled out, is part of a cultural elite; Mario Cuomo, who graduated first in his class at St. John's Law School and did not get a Wall Street law firm to offer him a job because he was the son of an Italian immigrant grocer who worked his fingers to the bone. How dare Dan Quayle talk like that about anybody who knows what it's like to live the American dream and live by family values when there's no food on the table. I'm tired of people with trust funds telling people on food stamps how to live!

The real story of Los Angeles is in these people we stood up and clapped for. That's the real story. Let's not forget, folks, most people who live in that city did not burn or loot or riot. Most little children were home with their parents. Even the poorest children were sitting in their houses when they could have been looting goods because their parents told them it was wrong to steal from their neighbors. It violated the Ten Commandments. They could have gotten away with it, and they didn't and they were poor. They really live by family values. And we ought to honor that.

I'll tell you the families I'm worried about. I'm worried about the families that live by family values and play by the rules and still get the shaft. Those are the people we ought to be fighting this election for. They are the people whose future is at stake.

And that includes about 80 percent of the people who live in this country today. Well over two-thirds of us are working harder for less money than we had a decade ago, but what are we going to do?

At the end of World War II, when I was born, our country rebuilt Europe and Japan. At the end of the Cold War, we must rebuild our own nation, retrain our people, re-tool our factories, revitalize our business sector, restore our ability to compete. Surely we can do for America what we once did for Europe and Japan.

If we do not, make no mistake about it, we can go from being a military superpower to an economic has-been in one generation. When the president went to Japan last year, the whole trade mission ended with the Japanese prime minister saying he felt sympathy for the United States.

Now he did not feel sympathy for us because we lack ships or planes or weapons of war. We have missiles that will go down chimneys and through front doors. He felt sympathy for us because he thought our best days were behind us, because he believes that we do not have the discipline or the vision or the will to rebuild America.

Because the Japanese and the Germans know, even if the Americans do not, that national security begins at home. If you're not strong at home, you cannot be strong abroad. It is true for each and every one of us in our own families, and it is true for the family of our nation.

We didn't get into this mess overnight. We won't get out of it overnight. And we will have to change.

I want America to chart a new course, to depart from twelve years of dominance by special interests and big government that have given 1 percent of the American people at the top more wealth than the bottom 90 percent for the first time since the 1920s; that have cost us our economic leadership, our growth rates, and the reward for work which ought to be part of the American dream; that have undermined the strength of our families and have raised the awful specter that we may be rearing the first generation of Americans to do worse than their parents.

We should honor and encourage work, invest in our people, rebuild our communities. We should reward those who play by the rules and do the reverse for those who don't.

Don't let this election be about Willie Horton or Murphy Brown. Don't let this election be about the denial of the need for new directions by all people of both parties in Washington. Don't be prisoners of the past or the politically correct. Let us be bold and chart a new course.

Today I would like to talk about a few specific examples which will exemplify where I'm coming from, and you can measure for yourself how much it does or does not square with the program you have outlined.

One of the most striking things I heard when I was in Los Angeles, three years before the riots and three days after the riots, was the unanimous endorsement of community leaders at the grass roots for bold new steps to bring in money from the private sector as well as the public sector, venture capital, small-business loans, start up finances.

Most people I talked to in Los Angeles didn't want more big government. They wanted more jobs, and they wanted small business. Most people said what they really wanted was a Washington that would support their efforts at work, and they knew that Washington had failed them but also that their banks had not met their responsibilities to reinvest in their communities.

Risk alone cannot explain this. Surely, a small loan to a local entrepreneur is more sound than a lot of the loans the S&Ls made to go bankrupt in the worst financial scandal in the history of this country.

One community leader in Los Angeles told me that in that vast place we know as the inner city, there were one hundred and seventy-seven check-cashing stands in the neighborhood where the riots began and only thirty-three banks. In the Washington, D.C., area there are fifty major banks, but only two have branches in Anacostia and neither of them has a lending office.

If free enterprise can tear down the Berlin Wall, if we want to bring it to Eastern Europe and to the former Soviet Union, if we insist on restoring democracy and free enterprise in Haiti, if we press for it still and wait for the day it will return in Cuba, if the president is so eager to nurture free enterprise in China that he will put up with intolerable violations of human rights, why shouldn't we cultivate it in Baltimore or Washington or Detroit or Denver?

Part of a new American order ought to be a national network of community-development banks in all the cities of this country modeled on those which have worked, like the South Shore Development Bank in Chicago, operating under what today has become a radical premise: that banks ought to loan money to people who are in their neighborhoods and who deposit in them.

We ought to stake our future, in other words, with the people who butter our bread. Shore Bank's successes can be replicated. I know that. My wife and I, my administration, and others in our state helped established a similar bank in the Mississippi Delta region of our state. Today that bank has made more than twelve million dollars in development loans and investments in small, rural Arkansas towns way out in the country where people thought they would never get a bank loan again.

That money has generated more jobs, new businesses from summer camps to medical practices to farms and small factories. The bank also loans small amounts of money and large amounts of know-how to local people who lack experience and collateral, but have a lot of drive and determination.

Virtually 100 percent of the loans go to people who are poor and 80 percent are minorities. They're just the kind of people the present system has cast aside and cast out, and yet the loan repayment rate of these folks is 95 percent. If it had been that way for the S&Ls, we wouldn't be in the mess that we're in today.

Investing in our people is not simply the right thing to do morally and politically; it's also good economic sense. George Bush's economic policy is we're all in this alone. Our economic program ought to be we're all in this together.

Everybody, everybody, has something to contribute. We also have to recognize that we must invest more public money and more private money in other ways in this country. The president said years ago that we had all these problems but we've got more will than wallet.

I tell you one thing, one of my iron rules of politics is, when a politician says it is not a money problem, he's always talking about somebody else's problems. We're out five hundred billion dollars to the S&Ls this year and with all the deficit we've got, boom, overnight found another one hundred and five billion dollars but not five billion dollars so that every child can be in the Head Start program.

We have eighty billion dollars in tax reductions for the upper 1 percent of individuals in corporations but not a half a percent of that, four billion dollars, to lift the working poor above poverty. Anybody working forty hours a week, with a child in the house, ought to be lifted above poverty by our tax system. We can do it for one-half a percent of the tax breaks given to the top 1 percent in the last twelve years.

We have to have a plan that invests in our people again. Ask the wealthy to pay their fair share and really give us a chance to recover economic growth. We need more investment.

For the last eight months, I have gone across this country with the most detailed plan of any candidate. I promised at the end of the primary process, way back when I started, that I would learn something from the American people. I would listen to them. I would scan the landscape of this country and try to see what else needed to be done and that at the end of the primaries, I would review what we had recommended and update it and strengthen it. That is what I am doing now.

We need more investment in America. I know we have a four-hundred-billion-dollar deficit, and we must bring it down and I will do that. But we also recognize that one of the criminal aspects of this deficit is that in the last twelve years, we quadrupled our debt and reduced our investment in the United States.

Everybody in this room just about has borrowed money. If you borrow money to build a house or to buy a car or to start a business or to replace a piece of equipment, or if you are a mayor to build new streets, you don't feel bad about that because you think you will get more back in return on your investment than what you borrowed.

But if you have to borrow money to feed your family tomorrow, you worry about that because there is no return. Farmers call that eating their seed corn. That's what this country's doing. If we had borrowed this money to invest in America the last twelve years, we'd be the richest country on the face of this earth, and we could pay the debt back in a heartbeat. But we borrowed the money and spent it, because we did not have the discipline to invest in our country, to control health-care costs, and to put our priorities right.

So, I tell you, we will invest more, much, much, more in the next four years and have discipline to bring this debt down. In the next few days, I will be issuing my version of your program which will tell you exactly how much I think we can invest and where we will get the money. But don't let anybody tell you that we can grow this economy again without more investment. We're investing less in high-speed rail, and new airplane transportation, and new highway technologies, and new water and sewer and waste systems; things that would put millions of people to work and grow our economy, we're investing so much less than the Germans, the Japanese, and other nations.

We are told we cannot afford fifty billion dollars a year, but Taiwan—Taiwan, a country less than one-tenth our size—is spending fifty billion dollars a year in the next six years to build new roads, to build new industrial technology, to clean up their environment. They have decided that they want to be as rich as Germany and Japan and the United States, and you know something, they will be and then some, unless we do what it takes to invest in our country.

We also ought to give people who have money more incentive to invest in our country. I would change the tax code and say to people, "Hey, here's some money that you can take off your taxes if you will build your plants in America, if you'll start new businesses here, but we're going to stop this ridiculous outrage of having a tax code that will give you a tax break for shutting your plant down here and moving it overseas." That is wrong.

This nation is the only advanced nation that literally says especially to medium- and small-sized manufacturers: "We'll give you a better deal if you shut your plant down here than if you replace old plant and equipment and stay here. No investment tax credit for that modern machinery that will keep Americans working at higher wages, but take a tax deduction for the cost of shutting your plant down. Take the loss off it if you start a plant somewhere else and it loses money. Then when it starts making money, leave your money down here and we'll never charge you a penny of taxes." That's what we do in this country. Other countries think we're crazy. And they're right. *And they're right.* This is bad business.

We've got a lot of other things we need to do. We've got to have an education program that provides apprenticeship training for all the young people who don't want to go to college and don't want to be in dead-end jobs.

We ought to reverse the policy of the last twelve years and say, anybody who wants to borrow the money can go to college. The college dropout rate is more than twice the high-school dropout rate and part of it is money. So, we ought to say: we're going to try the best of two American ideas: the G.I. Bill and the Peace Corps.

The G.I. Bill educated a whole generation of Americans after the second World War, made us a rich country. The Peace Corps under President Kennedy sent America's best and brightest people out across the world to solve their problems. Here's what I want to do: abolish the present student-loan program and put a national-service trust fund in its place, and say to any American you can borrow the money to go to college but you've got to pay it back either as a percentage of your income after you go to work, or better, come home to Washington, D.C., and give two years of your life to a domestic peace corps. Be a teacher, be a law-enforcement officer, be a nurse, work with kids, keep them off of drugs and out of gangs. Solve the problems of America.

I want to reward work. This administration apparently wants to use welfare in this election as one of those divisive issues. Let's take that away from them. Let's set up a system that will make welfare a second chance, not a way of life, but in a way that rewards and empowers the poor instead of punishing them. Let's say we're going to give everybody education and training and child support and medical coverage for their children, then require them to take jobs when they can, and if they can't find jobs in the private sector, provide dignified, important, significant community-service work for people to do.

If we do that we can end welfare as we know it in a way that lifted all of our people instead of using welfare as a divisive issue. This crowd doesn't want to do anything about welfare; the communists are gone, and if poor people got fixed they wouldn't have anybody to kick around anymore. Let us do it.

Finally, let's give the American people a different kind of government. We may disagree on some issues, but I believe that we can agree that this government needs fundamental reform. I agree with Reverend Jackson that we need to open up the franchise and make it easier for people to register and vote. We ought to make the votes of the people in the District of Columbia mean more than they do now with statehood.

But, I also agree that the progressive party need not be the party of government. We, the Democrats, started as the party of the people not the party of government, and many of our most innovative leaders, from Governor Ann Richards in Texas to Mayor Kelly here in Washington, are people who have tried to make government work better, make it more efficient, spend less on bureaucracy and more on people. We ought to be out there on the front lines for that. We ought to be for programs that promote responsibility like boot camps instead of prisons for first-time nonviolent offenders; let them stay in their communities, get discipline, get education, get treatment, learn to deal with the community and work with successful adults.

Let's take those issues away from the do-nothing party and make it part of our do-something. And let's show a budget discipline. I think we ought to say we want to invest more; we'll have to consume less. Let's just say we're going to cut 3 percent across the board out of the administration of all the federal programs in the next three years and put it into direct delivery of services to people. We can do that.

I believe we ought to have a line-item veto so that we can stop some things that are pork barrel and put them into real growth and lasting jobs.

I believe we can prove that we can be the party of governmental reform.

I believe, in short, that we have to do things that will break the stranglehold that has kept America from being progressive. Let's us be for election reform, don't let a PAC give more than a person, cut the costs of the congressional campaigns, open up the airwaves to honest debates. If people want to stay in Congress, let them debate their opponents every two years on television and on the radio. Don't let them buy their way into another seat, whatever their party is.

Don't let people who are lobbyists have a disproportional amount of control, restrict the revolving door from government to lobbyist; we can be the party of opportunity again, not the party of government.

Finally, let's stand up for what has always been best about the Rainbow Coalition, which is people coming together across racial lines. You talked about Mr. Fields, from Louisiana, the other night, a great role model. We don't have a lot of time to do this. We don't have a lot of time.

You had a rap singer here last night named Sister Souljah. I defend her right to express herself through music, but her comments before and after Los Angeles were filled with the kind of hatred that you do not honor today and tonight.

Just listen to this, what she said. She told the *Washington Post* about a month ago and I quote, "If black people kill black people every day, why not have a week and kill white people? So you're a gang member and normally kill somebody. Why not kill a white person?"

Last year she said, "You can't call me or any black person anywhere in the world a racist. We don't have the power to do to white people what white people have done to us. And even if we did, we don't have that low-down and dirty nature. If there are any good white people, I haven't met them. Where are they?" Right here in this room. That's where they are.

I know she is a young person, but she has a big influence on a lot of people. And when people say that, if you took the words *white* and *black* and reversed them, you might think David Duke was giving that speech.

Let me tell you, we all make mistakes, and sometimes we're not as sensitive as we ought to be. And we have an obligation, all of us, to call attention to prejudice wherever we see it.

A few months ago I made a mistake. I joined a friend of mine, and I played golf in a country club that didn't have any African-American members. I was criticized for doing it. You know what, I was rightly criticized for doing it. I made a mistake. And I said I would never do that again.

And I think all of us have got to be sensitive to that. We can't get anywhere in this country, pointing the finger at one another across racial lines. If we do that, we're dead, and they will beat us.

Even in Reverend Jackson's new math of this election, it's hard to get to a 34 percent solution or a 40 percent solution if the American people can be divided by race.

I have seen the hatred and division of the South that Jesse Jackson and I grew up in. And I was just lucky enough to be raised until I was four by a grandfather with a grade-school education, who believed that all people were created equal, who showed me by the life he lived how to treat people without regard to race and told me that discrimination and segregation were morally wrong.

I was lucky. I learned more from my granddaddy with his grade-school education about that and how to live than I did from all the professors I had at Georgetown and Oxford and Yale. In the wisdom of a simple working man's heart I learned something that many of our youngest people today who are role models no longer believe.

We don't have a lot of time. And so I say to you, let's all, one more time, reaffirm the kind of life I'm trying to have my family live.

My little daughter is a seventh-grade student in a public school in Little Rock, Arkansas, where she is in the minority. But she's getting a good education, in life and in books. She's learning about the real problems of real people, but she's able to do what Martin Luther King said children ought to do, judge people by the content of their character.

So that is what I close with. We have to think big, be big, do big things in this election. We've got to give this election back to the people of the United States and reinvest in our country again.

But we also have to have the courage to make government work and to challenge people to come together. If we can win again and be one again, we can keep the American dream alive. That is our obligation.

I pledge to you, not that we will always agree, but that every day, in every way, from dawn to dark and beyond, I will work my heart out to make this country what it ought to be.

Thank you very much.

Putting People First

U.S. Conference of Mayors
Houston, Texas
June 22, 1992

Clinton presented his revised economic strategy—"Putting People First"—in an address before the sixtieth annual meeting of the U.S. Conference of Mayors at 11:30 A.M. in the ballroom of the Westin Galleria Hotel and won several rounds of vigorous applause when he declared it would remake America economically. Bush and Perot both had declined invitations to speak at the conference.

Running last in public opinion polls, short of money, and frequently criticized as lacking a clear message, Clinton made clear that he intended to claim the ground of a traditional Democrat seeking to create jobs through federal spending and to appeal to his party's traditional urban and working-class base. There was certain political danger in the specificity he offered regarding programs and their costs, distancing himself from the Democratic Congress and at the same time leaving him vulnerable to Republican charges that he was just another tax-and-spend Democrat; however, campaign aides said he had decided the risk was justified, with the need to get the campaign moving again taking precedence over his usual on-the-one-hand, on-the-other-hand approach to issues.

"As far as I'm concerned, the campaign in the cities began today. It's a bold political stroke," said Boston mayor Raymond L. Flynn, adding that Clinton's plan was "the first substantive issue that's on the table now in this presidential campaign," and that "George Bush not being here today is . . . really is a reflection of disregard for the people of American cities." Atlanta mayor Maynard Jackson called Clinton's strategy "a watershed day in the campaign," and Jesse Jackson praised Clinton for putting forth an economic plan, called "populist-Keynesianism" by the *Washington Post*, that would create jobs and improve the nation's infrastructure.

❖ ❖ ❖

Thank you very much, Mayor Riley, Mayor Flynn, Mayor James, and Mayor Lanier. We're glad to be in your city. I'd like to begin by acknowledging the person who came up here with me, my wife, Hillary, who is at least half of our campaign.

I'm a little jealous today. I was preceded on the podium by Jack Kemp and Bill Bradley, two great athletes. I was always a slightly overweight band boy, and I've resented them all my life. People still remember their heroic exploits.

When I went on "The Arsenio Hall Show" and played my saxophone, I got no respect. All he said was he was glad to see a Democrat blow something besides an election. They did make me think of a good old athletic story, though. Kemp, the football player, and Bradley, the basketball player, might remember the great baseball slogan that, when I was a boy, they said that Willie Mays's glove is a place where triples go to die. I think that Jack Kemp's office and Bill Bradley's office are places where good ideas go to die today, because we have no leadership to rebuild America, including urban America.

I want to talk to you today about, not only how our country is losing its way, we know that, but about what we can do about it. In the *USA Today* this morning on the front page of the second section, there's a little article that says, "USA Slides in Economic Rankings."

This is an international poll of business executives who, last year, said that we were only the second-best economic power in the world, compared to Japan. This year, that group of executives ranks Germany, Switzerland, and Denmark ahead of the United States in our economic vitality—because their work forces are better educated and better trained, because they do a better job of taking ideas and turning them into jobs in their country, because they invest more in their infrastructure in building an economy for the future than do we.

Our country has been in the grip of a false idea. And it has kept government from working for most people. It is an idea which has been written into our law and driven into our lives, not just by one party, but by both parties which permitted it to happen in the last decade. The idea was advanced by our presidents but has been ratified by our Congress, that if you just cut taxes on the wealthiest Americans and on our corporations at high incomes and got out of the way, they would invest, take care of all the rest, and we would grow. Well, it was a bad idea. And it hasn't worked that way.

Seventy percent of the economic growth for a dozen years has gone to the top 1 percent of our people. The contribution of our wealthiest corporations to the tax coffers has gone down. Middle-class taxes have gone up, and incomes have gone down. Most Americans, indeed, are having a tough time. They're working harder for less money to pay more for health care and education and in taxes than they were a decade ago.

We have a whole new class of working poor, many of them concentrated in the cities which you lead. People who are the true unsung heroes of America, who get up every day and go to work and play by the rules and raise their children. Their children most often don't break the law, and if they lived in Los Angeles, they didn't riot or loot or burn, but they're still falling behind.

The government doesn't work for most people, because we've forgotten what it takes to cooperate and to compete and to win in a global economy. You have to put your people first. You have to educate and invest and provide affordable health care to all. And make sure you're doing what it takes to develop the God-given capacities of everybody, because we don't have a person to waste.

I have given the American people, beginning on yesterday, this plan which I think you have a copy of, each of you, called "Putting People First." It has no necessary partisan connotation, although it does reject in the strongest possible terms the present state of play in our national government, and the present policies which have been put forward by this administration.

It is the right idea; it invests in people and their jobs and their education and their health care. It calls for us to cooperate, to be on the same team, to work together so we can compete and win in a tough global economy. It parallels, very closely, many of the recommendations already made by you in the report that you put out not very long ago, which your chairman, Mayor Flynn, and others have so vocally pushed to the United States and to me personally.

My plan is a bold plan. It offers fifty billion dollars in new investments over the next four years in each of the next four years. New incentives for the private sector, an investment tax credit, urban enterprise zones, new business tax incentives, research and development incentives, and others.

It offers twenty billion dollars a year in hard federal dollars every year for the next four years, to build an economy for the twenty-first century, to invest in new roads and bridges, and streets and rail systems, to develop high-speed rail and a national fiber-optic network, to develop new environmental technologies to clean our waters and our air, and to recycle more of our solid wastes. In short, to do those things which we are not doing today.

All of you know, as well as I, that our competitors for the future are investing far higher percentages in their income than we are. And it makes me sick inside to think what's going to happen to the incomes in the future of the American people if we don't make a commitment to invest in our capacity and our economy.

This twenty billion dollars will create a million jobs a year in each of the next four years, driving funds into your cities. It will help us to do the things you said you wanted, when you issued your call for a thirty-five-billion-dollar program in one year. This will do more over the next four years.

This will enable us to fund those ready-to-go projects you want funded. It will enable us to spend more in infrastructure and in law enforcement and in education and in social services. It will enable us to expand the community-development block-grant program, which, as a governor, I also believe strongly in. And this will happen without spending one red cent of state or local money or private-sector money.

When we leverage that, we can dramatically increase this program. The Rebuild America Coalition under the leadership of one of your number, Mayor Maynard Jackson, has recommended a number of things which can be done to leverage more local money and private-sector money with this twenty-billion-dollar commitment, including state revolving-loan funds for many projects and a federal infrastructure development bank, on-bank.

I support the recommendations of the Rebuild America Coalition, and I will work hard to leverage this money so that we can generate even more investments and create more jobs.

In addition to that, my program will help to make your streets safer. You have here, I know, Commissioner Lee Brown from New York, and Commissioner Bell from Atlanta, two of the nations most vocal proponents of community policing. I have been in many of your cities, and I have seen safer streets. I have seen closed crack houses. I have seen parks where children actually play in them again.

In Philadelphia, I shot baskets with Mayor Rindell and street kids who lived in the neighborhood at a city park which was once unsafe for anything but drug dealing. I know community policing works, but I also know that there are three crimes today for every police officer on the street, as compared with thirty years ago when there were three policemen for every crime. And so I have committed in this program to provide to the cities of our nation another hundred thousand police officers over the next few years, through a national police corps, which will be manned by men and women from two sources.

Number one, through our national-service trust, I want every American to be able to borrow the money to go to college and pay it back, either as a percentage of their income or in a domestic peace corps solving the problems of America here at home, giving a couple of years of service to our nation at home, just the way that many Americans have gone around the world in the Peace Corps.

The federal government would pay the salary, and anyone who worked for two years in a qualified public-service job would wipe off their four-year college loan. One of those jobs would be in the police forces of the cities of this country.

Number two, I want to embrace strongly the suggestion of Senator Sam Nunn, the chairman of the United States Senate Armed Services Committee, that we give men and women who won the Cold War for us something other than the cold shoulder, as we reduce our military forces.

Senator Nunn has suggested that we give men and women who are coming out of the service the opportunity to retrain and become certified as teachers or law-enforcement officers and then help to pay their way to work for the cities or for the schools, for a period of five years, during which time they can also earn credit on their military retirement.

These two sources together can give us another hundred thousand police officers, so that more of you can have community policing, and we can continue to drive the crime rate down. Chief Brown told me that in New York City, they have now had, because of community policing, reductions in all major areas of crime for the first time in thirty-six years. We can do it in America; we can get ahead of the crime problem. We can restore safety to your streets. There is no more important priority for many people.

When I leave you, I'm going to New York, and I'll never forget during the primary one night in a hotel there. A man who was working in the hotel came up to me, and he said, "Governor, I'm going to vote for you. My ten-year-old son studies all the candidates in school, and he says I should vote for you. And so I will." I thought, "What a smart boy."

But he said, deadly serious, he said, "Governor, where I came from, in my home country, we were much poorer, but at least we were free. Now we are not free. My boy can't go to school unless I walk with him. He can't walk across the street and play in the park unless I go with him. So if I do what my boy wants, and I vote for you, I want you to make my boy free." That's what I want us to do together, with the National Police Corps. They won't be national; they'll be your police. But we'll give you the people you need to do the job.

Finally, let me say that we have to have an education program. I don't know how many mayors have said to me we need Head Start, we need Chapter One, we need programs for our poor kids. We need something for our young adolescents to do. We need programs for them to be involved in if they drop out of school. This plan has those initiatives. Mayor Flynn and I once visited in Boston a program called City Year, maybe the best program of its kind in the country, in which young college students and young dropouts, kids from the top of the totem pole and kids from the bottom, kids who have had to drag themselves up from drug abuse, and kids who are the brightest kids in America, take time off and work together to help people in the city of Boston from all walks of life. These are the kinds of things that we need to do to bring this country back again. This is what I want you to support.

This has been an unusual election year. I noted in the paper yesterday, they're now alleging that Mr. Perot has spent a lot of time trying to investigate President Bush, and we know that Mr. Bush and the Republicans spend a lot of time investigating everybody. And I just spent my time trying to investigate these problems. That may not be the thing to do.

But I'll tell you one thing, this country deserves a plan; this country deserves a program; this country deserves action that goes beyond partisan politics. How do we pay for this? About half and half through raising money and cutting spending at the federal level.

We have to ask the wealthiest Americans to pay their fair share again. Their incomes went up in the 1980s, and their taxes went down. We can't ask the middle class to pay more. Their incomes went down, and their taxes went up. No nation would do what we have done willingly. For the first time since the "Roaring Twenties," the top 1 percent of Americans control more wealth than the bottom 90 percent. We must say to the wealthy, you have to give your fair share. We also have to say to foreign companies, there's something wrong with our tax code, if your income went up 65 percent in the 1980s, and your taxes went down 15 percent. And that's exactly what happened. You've got to pay your fair share if you want to do business in this country.

But we can't just do that. We also have to change the way the federal government operates, too. The General Accounting Office, Congressman Dorgan's commission on government waste, and my own experience as a governor, working, repeatedly cutting budgets, and restructuring government, tells me that there is a lot of money to save there.

I have recommended that we eliminate by attrition, not by firing anybody but by attrition, a hundred thousand people from the federal work force over the next couple of years.

We have in the United States still, even though we have very vigorous local governments and state governments, the federal work force still has more employees per capita than does Germany, Japan, or Great Britain. We have to do better.

I'm going to cut the White House staff by 25 percent, ask the Congress to pass a bill cutting congressional staffs by 25 percent. I'm going to stop handing down mandates to you and regulating you to death and not giving you the money to do it with.

We're going to reform the procurement and inventory practices of the government. We have 1.2 million little bottles of nasal spray in the Pentagon today. We have clothing going back to the fifties. No one is managing these things. We can change. We can do better. We're going to get this money to pay for this program by savings, by cuts, and by raising money where it can be fairly raised.

And we're going to adopt the toughest possible system to reform the health-care system and bring health-care costs under control. You will never be able to control this government spending until health-care costs are brought in line with inflation.

And you live in the only advanced country where your nation has not taken a national approach to controlling health-care costs by reforming the insurance market, by reducing bureaucracy, simplifying the billing procedures, and doing those things which other countries take for granted to keep costs in line with inflation. We must do that.

Now, a lot of people say to me, and this is an important big idea that you have to decide whether you agree with, they say, "Well, Governor, why don't you take all this money and reduce the deficit?" Because under my plan, we will increase investment and reduce the deficit by more than 50 percent over the next four years, but not eliminate it entirely. "Why don't you just take it all and put it against the deficit?"

I'll tell you why, because we have two deficits: a budget deficit and an investment deficit. And we cannot grow this economy until we put people back to work and until we invest in those things that will give us a high-wage, high-growth future. We cannot do it.

I am appalled at what has happened to the deficit. I can't believe it has quadrupled in twelve years and investment has declined. But every one of us has borrowed money at some time or another, for a car, for a house, to start a new business or buy a new piece of equipment, or in a city, to build a new sewer system or modernize the street system or build a new mass-transit system. So there are different kinds of borrowing, and when you invest in the future, you create wealth. And you create more wealth than the cost of the borrowing. So I say to you, we cannot afford to ignore the investment deficit.

This plan will dramatically reduce the deficit and dramatically increase investment. That is the only way to get economic growth. You must demand a four-year investment plan. You must go beyond what you have asked for. Go beyond your thirty-five-billion-dollar one-year plan and say we have to invest for four years.

Indeed, we have to invest for eight years until the end of this century, if we want America to enter the twenty-first century as the number-one economic power. We've got to do it, and you have to demand that it be done.

A lot of us have had many different emotional feelings in the last several months. A lot of us have had our own personal feelings in the aftermath of the Los Angeles riots. But in every city and town here represented, you see the stories of American lives undone, of American people who are not living up to the fullest of their potential, of people who break the law because they don't think there's any future in playing by the rules. America has always had problems, and we will always have problems. That's endemic to the human condition.

What is eating the heart out of this country today is that we have lost two of the things that always drive us to do better. First, a faith in the future. More and more of our people do not believe that tomorrow will be better than today. And when you don't believe that, it's pretty hard to get up every day and go to work whether you work in a plant or in a little business or on a farm or in the city hall. And their experience confirms that. We must restore the belief in the faith of the future.

The other thing that's killing this country is that most people don't believe they matter very much to their friends and neighbors. We don't have the sense of community that we need that embraces people across racial and ethnic lines and income lines. Most people really believe that, except for one or two folks, they just don't count for much.

And when people don't think they count for much, then they join a gang, because everybody wants to be part of something where they're important. I mean, when I was a kid coming up, I was in a gang, it's just we didn't break the law. It was a good gang. You come here to the Conference of Mayors and you commiserate to each how you got more mandates and less money. This is a gang. You all cry in your beer together and feel sorry for yourselves about how bad it is. We all have to be something where we matter.

So when you strip it all away, the reason I want to invest fifty billion dollars a year in America for four years—yes, so we can recover our economic leadership—but basically so people can feel inside again that tomorrow is going to be better, so they feel like getting up in the morning and going to work and being part of something important.

And so they can believe in the idea of America again, that this is the greatest country in the world because this is a place where everybody counts. And

I think that's what the Conference of Mayors was asking for, when it put forth its visionary bipartisan program. And that's what I'm trying to give this country.

We can all give our speeches, and we can all give our talks. We can all plead our cases; we can all tell our stories. But at the end of the day, what will matter is whether we have done anything to change the human condition of people in our country and the future of this great land. This will change the future.

Thank you very much.

An Administration That Looks Like America

NAACP National Convention
Nashville, Tennessee
July 11, 1992

Governor Clinton and Sen. Al Gore began the day in Carthage, Tennessee, where they spoke to twenty-five hundred people that morning at a campaign rally at the Smith County Courthouse and wooed the crowd of mostly rural white southerners. That afternoon, they both addressed a crowd of more than two thousand black delegates at the NAACP convention in Nashville, where they were equally at ease and equally well received.

George Bush had declined an invitation to speak at the convention, but that morning Ross Perot had addressed the group and upset some of the delegates with racial references that were considered insensitive.

Clinton and Gore entered the convention center to rousing applause and the strains of "When the Saints Go Marching In." Benjamin Hooks told reporters, "When they walked into the hall, you could feel the electricity." While Perot had received polite applause after his speech a few hours earlier, the *St. Louis Post-Dispatch* said that Clinton's "preacher-like rhetoric won enthusiastic reactions from the crowd," as he told the group, "We're going to give you an administration that looks like America."

After the speeches ended with standing ovations, Hooks said that Clinton and Gore were people "who eat the same cornbread," and that blacks would support the ticket because they genuinely like them and their civil rights records. Later that evening, Jesse Jackson also endorsed the Clinton-Gore ticket.

❖ ❖ ❖

Thank you. Thank you very much. Dr. Hooks and Mrs. Hooks, Chairman Dr. Gibson, and President Richardson, to all the distinguished board members and especially the two from my home state, Reverend Gaylord and Jerry Mauldin, two close friends and wonderful supporters. I hope they've been working this convention hard and telling stories about me from dawn till dark.

I want to thank Congressman Clement and Mayor Bradison and former mayor and congressman Fulton for their friendship and their wonderful work, and say to all of you, I am glad to be here today to celebrate all of us together. We the people of the United States, we're all in this boat together, we're going up or down together. And if I have one message, it is that we don't have a person to waste or a moment to lose.

You know, when I hear Ben Hooks preaching, it kind of makes me want to do the same thing. When I was about ten, I got carried away one day and started talking like that, and my grandmother looked at me and she said, "You know, I think you could be a preacher if you were just a little better boy." So I wound up in politics.

You know, I read today, Dr. Hooks, or yesterday that Senator Gore and I are the first all-Baptist ticket ever to seek the presidency. I have to tell you, though, I'm trying to be ecumenical. My wife is still a practicing Methodist. And those of us who grew up in these hard-shell Baptist churches, we know the difference between Baptists and Methodists. Methodists will call each other by their first name when they meet in the liquor store.

What I want to say to you is—I need to quit this, don't I? I'm reminded of the preacher who was one day preaching to his congregation and he'd worked so hard on his sermon and he knew that he would reach the magic moment in the sermon and everybody would raise their hand and stand up and shout. And he preached his heart out. He talked about the virtues of the good life, the hope of the afterlife. And when he reached the climax of the sermon, he said, "I want everybody who wants to go to heaven to stand up right now." And everybody stood up except one woman in the front row who had not missed a day in church in forty years. And he said, "Sister Jones, you have not missed a day in church in forty years. Don't you want to go to heaven when you die?" And she jumped and she said, "Oh, sure, Preacher, I thought you were trying to get up a load to go right now." Now, Al Gore and I, we're trying to get up a load to go right now. We don't think we can wait four more years.

I want to say, there are so many people here I want to thank, Hazel Dukes, who's been so wonderful to me in New York, and so many others. But I'd like to ask us to take a serious moment to remember the memory of Juanita Jackson Mitchell, who died on Tuesday, a great fighter for the cause of equal opportunity, a leader of real dedication and vision. I'm proud that she is a native-born Arkansan who is from Hot Springs, the town in which I grew up. And I just want to say a special word of appreciation for her life on this occasion.

I also would like to thank the NAACP for many things. But on one occasion in particular, the NAACP did something very special for me and for my state. In 1987, the board met in Arkansas on the occasion of the thirtieth anniversary of the crisis at Little Rock Central High School. And when the board came to the governor's mansion, I couldn't help thinking how we had finally closed the circle on a dark chapter in our nation's past because that mansion was once the nerve center of the fight to keep the school systems segregated. And in 1987, we celebrated that triumph of thirty years in the governor's mansion, the nerve center of our state's commitment to equal opportunity for all people.

I don't want to embarrass her, but I'm proud of my daughter, who's here with me. In 1992, the thirty-fifth anniversary of the integration of the Little Rock schools, my daughter has just finished her seventh-grade year there. Our school district is two-thirds African American, one-third white. But because we're working together, the enrollment of both white and black students went up in Little Rock last year. We can go forward together. We can do that.

I want to thank you for the warm reception you gave to Senator Albert Gore. I'm going to have to talk to him. If he gets to giving a better speech than I do, he'll be in deep trouble.

Many of you know my good friend Vernon Jordan, who was for many years president of the National Urban League. Vernon was on a committee with former governor Madeline Kunin of Vermont and Warren Christopher of California that worked on the vice-presidential search process with me, one that produced this wonderful public servant.

I want to tell you that, like Ben Hooks, I remember Al Gore's father when he was one of only two southern senators who wouldn't sign that Southern Manifesto, when he voted in the tough years of the 1960s as a senator from Tennessee for voting rights and open housing and opposed the then-president's attempt to pack the Supreme Court with justices who were not for civil rights. And I want to tell you that, as you heard today, he is in that mold. He didn't tell you, but he was one of the original cosponsors of the Civil Rights Act of 1991, and I'm proud of that.

Al Gore and I come here today with a simple message. We're going to give you an administration that looks like America. We're going to give you an administration that feels like Americans feel about the world we're living in, one that knows the promise and the pain of this country, one that will involve all other Americans in the struggle to make our nation the best again, one that will rebuild, reunite, and renew the spirit and the lives of the American people.

I pledge to you an administration that believes in and enforces the Voting Rights Act, an administration based on the principles of community and respect, not division and blame.

Last time we had a president promise us a kinder and gentler nation, it turned out he meant a meaner and harsher politics.

Last time we had a president who promised us—and I quote—"a new harmony and a great tolerance," turned out he meant he'd be the only president since Reconstruction, except for his predecessor, to veto a civil rights bill.

And the last time we had a president who promised us he'd listen to the quiet people when others don't, and he just vetoed a Motor Voter Bill that would make it easier for those quiet, hard-working people to register to vote because he doesn't want their voices heard.

In 1988, we were asked to renew our faith in an economic experiment we began in 1980. We were asked to vote for greater inequality in our country, make the rich a little richer, or a lot richer, put the burdens off on the middle class and the working poor and get out of the way and let investment take its course, and we'd all have more jobs and greater incomes; give us a little more inequality and we'll give you growth and opportunity.

Well, the first part of the promise came true. Last year, for the first time since the Roaring Twenties, the top 1 percent of Americans had more wealth than the bottom 90 percent. In the last twelve years, 70 percent of all the growth has gone to the top 1 percent of the people. Most people in this room, most people in this state, and most people in this country are working harder and spending less time with their children, for lower incomes and paying more for the basic necessities of life. We didn't get the other end of the deal, did we?

We gave them what they wanted for twelve years. And just a couple of days ago, the Children's Defense Fund gave us one of the most painful examples of what we got in return—in the decade of the 1980s, one million more children in poverty. It's harder now for the farmers and the small business people. It's harder for the factory workers and the people who get up every day and work hard and play by the rules. It's harder for the members of the NAACP in the big cities and in the rural areas. It's harder for people, without regard to race.

Senator Gore and I just came from his hometown of Carthage, Tennessee. It was so hot out there on the courthouse lawn, but people showed up by the thousands. And every one of them was nodding their head when I said it's harder now than it used to be.

What I want to do is to make economic empowerment and opportunity the civil rights issue of the 1990s.

I want to bridge the racial divide in this country by giving us all something to say yes to, not just things to say no to.

We've got a plan that's simple—more jobs and higher wages, affordable health care, excellence in education for everybody, safer streets and stronger families—a plan that puts our people first and puts government back on the side of ordinary Americans. That's what this election is all about, and you ought to be about it, too.

We ought to take every dollar by which we reduce defense and put it into building an economy for the twenty-first century here at home. You know, there are a lot of people in the service today and a lot of people in defense industries today who are members of the NAACP or who are their children. They won the Cold War for us, and we're leaving them out in the cold. It isn't right.

In California alone, there are five hundred thousand defense workers out of work, people who worked in those plants. And yet in southern California, they're trying to bid on a new high-speed rail network to take all those people around without having to get in traffic jams, and they had to look to Germany and Japan to try to find the trains, because we don't build them. I say let's build them here in America and put the American people back to work.

Let's give people incentives to make money the old-fashioned way. Let's change the tax code and give people more incentives to put their money into our cities, into our communities, into our rural areas, but no more incentives to move our jobs overseas. Make money by creating jobs in America again.

Let's join the ranks of the rest of the world and finally, finally, at long last, give the American people the chance to go to a doctor or a hospital or get the kind of medical care they need without breaking the bank and without breaking the economy—affordable health care for all Americans.

When we say we don't have a child to waste, let's act like it. Let's act like it. We have national education goals which are wonderful, but we're not doing enough to meet them. I say let's send every child who needs it to a Head Start program or another preschool program.

A study came out of Tennessee last year which makes it clear, painfully clear, that children who come out of poor or uneducated families do better in school if they have very small classes in the early grades. Let's give them those small classes and counselors so that these kids can get off to a good start in life. Let's provide apprenticeship programs for people who need it, so that those who don't go to college aren't in dead-end jobs. Give them two years of training and give them a chance at the brass ring.

And something I know that's important to you, let's give every child in America who wants to the chance to go to college. Every child. We're governed by an administration that thinks if your income is ten thousand dollars, you're too rich to get a college grant, but if your income's three hundred thousand dollars, you're still so poor, you need a capital-gains cut. I say give people a chance to go to college and make money and pay taxes and have success. I want to unite two of the best ideas this nation ever had—the GI Bill at the end of World War II, which educated a generation of Americans, that made us the wealthiest country in the world, and the Peace Corps, which President Kennedy put in, which gave us the chance to bring the benefits of liberty all over the world.

I want a GI Bill in the sense that I want every American to be able to go to college, but I want a domestic Peace Corps. Pay your college loan off by coming home to Nashville and being a teacher or a police officer or a nurse, working in a program to help troubled children.

The plan that Al Gore and I advocate will make our streets safer and less violent by helping to prevent crime instead of just to catch criminals. I'm tired of being twentieth in infant mortality and first in the percentage of grownups in prison. We can do better than that.

Our plan will put one hundred thousand police officers on the streets so that every city can have community policing, the same people in the same neighborhoods day in and day out, working to make their people safer. Lee Brown, the police chief in New York City, recently put in a community policing program, and listen to this, New York City for the first time in thirty-six years has had a decline in the crime rate in every major category of crime because they did it the old-fashioned way, by working with their neighbors, and we can do it in America.

I want to support local initiatives. You know, people think you can't make government work, but you can. You've got a mayor here in Nashville, Phil Bradison. He's here and I don't want to embarrass him, but he's given us a good example of how people can work together across racial lines to be creative and to be imaginative in the area of health care. And I want to wish him luck in his efforts and the efforts of other Nashvilleans in their work to merge the Meharry-Hubble Hospital with the General Hospital. And I'm glad you're clapping for him.

I just want to say one other thing. We want to be the family-values ticket. I've heard about that other family-values ticket. But I want you to know something. I think it's fine for the president and the vice-president to talk to us about family values, but they're not the nation's preachers, even though they have the bully pulpit. Politics is not just about doing right; it's also about doing better. You cannot raise a child without family values; I know that. Neither Al Gore nor I would be here today with our families if it weren't for the people who raised us with family values. But it's hard to feed a hungry child with a sermon.

So while I want the bully pulpit to be used to exhort the American people to be more moral and forceful and good in their behavior, I also want to use the power of the presidency to lift up the children and the parents of this country so that they can have decent and good lives and be rewarded for the work they do.

This administration found Murphy Brown out in California. But they ignored all those unsung heroes in the Los Angeles riots. You know, most people in Los Angeles did not riot. Most people's children stayed home. They didn't steal; they didn't loot. They did the right thing. Why? Because they believe in the Ten Commandments and the teachings of family values. But, what bothers me is too many of those folks are being punished. For the people who stayed home and did right, let's reward their work, let's reward their families, let's help them raise their children. Let's do this together. We don't have a person to waste. I want to find all the families of this country. I don't want any more "us" and "them."

If you vote for us, you'll have people who think you shouldn't lose your job if you've got to go home because your kid's sick or there's a child being born.

If you vote for us, you'll have people who believe if fathers run off and won't support their kids, I have a tough child-support system waiting for them so they have to pay to raise their children.

If you vote for us, you'll have people who try to help people move from welfare to work indicative of education and training and child care and medical coverage to liberate them.

If you vote for us, you'll have people that won't talk one way and act another.

I want to say just one personal word in closing. The feelings I have about civil rights are rooted very much in my background. When my mother was widowed shortly before I was born, she moved in, as so many people do, with her parents. And I lived with my grandparents till I was four. My granddaddy had a grade-school education, ran a country store in a little town called Hope across the street from the cemetery. Most of his customers were black. That was back in the late forties and early fifties.

I first got to know just about all I know about human nature sitting in that store trying to steal cookies out of the Jacksons' cookie jar, watching people come in and out who worked hard and did the best they could, sometimes needed credit. I watched my grandfather relate to people as people. And in

1957, '56, and '55 when all this tension was building up, my grandparents told me when I was a kid, they said, "This is wrong. We ought to integrate these schools, because all these kids need a good education."

I never knew why they were different from so many other people in my part of the country, but I've always been grateful that they were. I was raised to believe that if I didn't respect everybody and want everybody to live up to their God-given potential that some day somebody might not want me to, either. We are not playing games anymore.

You heard Senator Gore talking about the world we're living in. Ten years ago we had the highest wages in the world. And now we're tenth—not second, not third, but tenth. Even business leaders around the world recently rated us as only the fifth-best economy in the world, behind not just Germany and Japan, but also Switzerland and Denmark. There's nothing wrong with the people of this country. We're working harder than ever before, harder than twenty years ago. We're underorganized, we're undereducated, and we're underled.

So I want to thank you for letting me come today to share my vision with you. I want to thank you for letting me share a few laughs with you. I want to thank you for listening. What I want you to do is to go out of here and stand up for your country, stand up for its future, believe we can make it work again.

I'm tired of hearing people say this election doesn't make any difference and they're all the same and nobody can make it work. We've been around here for two hundred years.

It made a difference whether Abraham Lincoln won the election of 1860.

It made a difference whether Franklin Roosevelt won the election of 1932 or Herbert Hoover got reelected.

It made a difference whether John Kennedy was elected in 1960 or Lyndon Johnson was elected in 1964.

Go out of this hall today. I want you to be for Bill Clinton and Al Gore, but more than anything else, I want you to be for you. Cut through all this cynicism. Cut through all this skepticism. And ask the American people, all of us, black and white and brown and yellow, and all of us together to seize control of our destiny again. This is our country. It's still the greatest country in human history. There is no reason for us, none, to let this magic moment pass.

I want us to be singing together in the White House in a year or so. Lift every voice and sing till earth and heaven rings. Let's make America sing again.

Thank you.

God bless you.

A Vision for America: A New Covenant

Democratic National Convention
New York City, New York
July 16, 1992

On Saturday before the convention, relaxing on the campaign plane en route from Nashville to the Democratic National Convention in New York, Clinton studied a thick black notebook and a collection of acceptance speeches from past conventions. He told one reporter that he most enjoyed those speeches that told a personal story, especially Lyndon Johnson's speech recalling how, as a child, he wished he had the power to make the world a better place for the poor and underprivileged. The seasoned candidate admitted to being somewhat nervous about the upcoming speech, explaining, "Something like this, I don't know if I'll ever get finished with it. There are so many things I want to say."

Remembering his infamous convention speech four years earlier, Clinton spent most of the week working with Paul Begala, drafting and crafting his text to be delivered on Thursday night. Such situations are always difficult, for the nominee must speak to a diverse audience comprising the committed partisans in the hall and the merely curious watching television in their homes, invigorating the first with a rousing battle cry, while informing the latter and explaining policy positions that might capture their attention. In addition, challengers have the added burden of presenting their persona to a nation of citizens only beginning to give attention to and assessing the candidates in the upcoming campaign.

Preceding Clinton's appearance at the podium, a twelve-minute video campaign biography, "The Man from Hope," represented the campaign's attempt to "reinvent" the candidate after a brutal primary process and refocus his image by emphasizing his small-town roots, his difficult childhood, his solid educational background, and his experience in public office. Then, in the most important speech of his life, a chance for a defining moment on the national stage, Clinton elaborated on the video message to his national prime-time audience, saying, "Tonight, as plainly as I can, I want to tell you who I am, what I believe, and where I want to lead America."

Clinton, said the *Chicago Tribune,* "held himself up as a mirror of average Americans," the Americans "whose support he must have to win," and he also sought to weave some of the more detailed policies he has espoused into his broader theme of a "New Covenant," offering opportunity to the American people and demanding responsibility in return. Unlike many Democratic conventions of the past, however, he struck many populist notes and used frequent religious allusions, abandoning many liberal orthodoxies as he continued his effort to redefine the Democrats as a party of the middle-class center. Even the final scene of the convention broke with the traditional theme song, "Happy Days Are Here Again," and substituted the campaign's "Don't Stop (Thinking about Tomorrow)" by Fleetwood Mac, the anthem of the new generation of party leaders.

The *Atlanta Constitution* called Clinton's performance "a speech crafted more for America's living rooms than the passions of the hall," but the *Boston Globe* assessed it somewhat differently, saying, "His delivery was more earnest than outraged, often more ponderous than peppery. As an orator, Clinton has oscillated between populist passion and policy wonkery, but he suppressed his bureaucratic instincts often enough to deliver effective sound bites" that led the capacity crowd in Madison Square Garden to roar its approval. The fifty-four-minute speech captivated the delegates and brought eruptions of applause one hundred and twenty-two times during the address. Still, the *Washington Post* likened Clinton's delivery to "the slow-cadenced style of a southern preacher," though "it lasted almost an hour and dampened the cheering even in the partisan audience."

❖ ❖ ❖

Governor Richards, Chairman Brown, Mayor Dinkins, our great host, and my fellow Americans.

I am so proud of Al Gore. He said he came here tonight because he always wanted to do the warm-up for Elvis. Well, I ran for president this year for one reason and one reason only: I wanted to come back to this convention center and finish that speech I started four years ago.

Well, last night Mario Cuomo taught us how a real nominating speech should be given. He also made it clear why we have to steer our ship of state on a new course.

Tonight I want to talk with you about my hope for the future, my faith in the American people, and my vision of the kind of country we can build together.

I salute the good men who were my companions on the campaign trail: Tom Harkin, Bob Kerrey, Doug Wilder, Jerry Brown, and Paul Tsongas. One sentence in the platform we built says it all: "The most important family policy, urban policy, labor policy, minority policy, and foreign policy America can have is an expanding entrepreneurial economy of high-wage, high-skill jobs."

And so, in the name of all the people who do the work, pay the taxes, raise the kids, and play by the rules, in the name of the hard-working Americans who make up our forgotten middle class, I accept your nomination for president of the United States.

I am a product of that middle class. And when I am president, you will be forgotten no more.

We meet at a special moment in history, you and I. The Cold War is over; Soviet Communism has collapsed; and our values—freedom, democracy, individual rights, and free enterprise—they have triumphed all around the world. And yet just as we have won the Cold War abroad, we are losing the battles for economic opportunity and social justice here at home. Now that we have changed the world, it's time to change America.

I have news for the forces of greed and the defenders of the status quo: your time has come—and gone. It's time for a change in America.

Tonight ten million of our fellow Americans are out of work. Tens of millions more work harder for lower pay. The incumbent president says unemployment always goes up a little before a recovery begins. But unemployment only has to go up by one more person before a real recovery can begin. And, Mr. President, you are that man.

This election is about putting power back in your hands and putting government back on your side. It's about putting people first.

You know, I've said that all across the country, and someone always comes back at me, as a young man did just this week at the Henry Street Settlement on the Lower East Side of Manhattan. He said, "That sounds good, Bill. But you're a politician. Why should I trust you?"

Tonight, as plainly as I can, I want to tell you who I am, what I believe, and where I want to lead America.

I never met my father. He was killed in a car wreck on a rainy road three months before I was born, driving home from Chicago to Arkansas to see my mother.

After that, my mother had to support us. So we lived with my grandparents while she went back to Louisiana to study nursing.

I can still see her clearly tonight through the eyes of a three-year-old: kneeling at the railroad station and weeping as she put me back on the train to Arkansas with my grandmother. She endured her pain because she knew her sacrifice was the only way she could support me and give me a better life.

My mother taught me. She taught me about family and hard work and sacrifice. She held steady through tragedy after tragedy. And she held our family, my brother and I, together through tough times. As a child, I watched her go off to work each day at a time when it wasn't always easy to be a working mother.

As an adult, I've watched her fight off breast cancer. And again she has taught me a lesson in courage. And always, always she taught me to fight.

That's why I'll fight to create high-paying jobs so that parents can afford to raise their children today. That's why I'm so committed to making sure every American gets the health care that saved my mother's life, and that women's health care gets the same attention as men's. That's why I'll fight to make sure women in this country receive respect and dignity—whether they work in the home, out of the home, or both. You want to know where I get my fighting spirit? It all started with my mother.

Thank you, Mother. I love you.

When I think about opportunity for all Americans, I think about my grandfather.

He ran a country store in our little town of Hope. There were no food stamps back then, so when his customers—whether they were white or black, who worked hard and did the best they could, came in with no money—well, he gave them food anyway, just made a note of it. So did I. Before I was big enough to see over the counter, I learned from him to look up to people other folks looked down on.

My grandfather just had a grade-school education. But in that country store he taught me more about equality in the eyes of the Lord than all my professors at Georgetown, more about the intrinsic worth of every individual than all the philosophers at Oxford; and he taught me more about the need for equal justice than all the jurists at Yale Law School.

If you want to know where I come by the passionate commitment I have to bringing people together without regard to race, it all started with my grandfather.

I learned a lot from another person, too. A person who for more than twenty years has worked hard to help our children, paying the price of time to make sure our schools don't fail them. Someone who traveled our state for a year, studying, learning, listening, going to PTA meetings, school board meetings, town hall meetings, putting together a package of school reforms recognized around the nation, and doing it all while building a distinguished legal career and being a wonderful loving mother.

That person is my wife.

Hillary taught me. She taught me that all children can learn and that each of us has a duty to help them do it. So if you want to know why I care so much about our children and our future, it all started with Hillary. I love you.

Frankly, I'm fed up with politicians in Washington lecturing the rest of us about "family values." Our families have values. But our government doesn't.

I want an America where "family values" live in our actions, not just in our speeches; an America that includes every family, every traditional family and every extended family, every two-parent family, every single-parent family, and every foster family, every family.

I do want to say something to the fathers in this country who have chosen to abandon their children by neglecting to pay their child support: take responsibility for your children or we will force you to do so. Because governments don't raise children; parents do. And you should.

And I want to say something to every child in America tonight who is out there trying to grow up without a father or a mother: I know how you feel. You're special, too. You matter to America. And don't ever let anybody tell you you can't become whatever you want to be. And if other politicians make you feel like you're not a part of their family, come on and be part of ours.

The thing that makes me angriest about what's gone wrong in the last twelve years is that our government has lost touch with our values, while our politicians continue to shout about them. I'm tired of it.

I was raised to believe it's that the American dream was built on rewarding hard work. But we have seen the folks in Washington turn the American ethic on its head. For too long, those who play by the rules and keep the faith have gotten the shaft, and those who cut corners and cut deals have been rewarded. People are working harder than ever, spending less time with their children, working nights and weekends at their jobs instead of going to PTA and Little League or Scouts, and their incomes are still going down. Their taxes are going up, and the costs of health care, housing, and education are going through the roof. Meanwhile, more and more of our best people are falling into poverty—even when they work forty hours a week.

Our people are pleading for change, but government is in the way. It has been hijacked by privileged, private interests. It has forgotten who really pays the bills around here. It's taking more of your money and giving you less in return. We have got to go beyond the brain-dead politics in Washington and give our people the kind of government they deserve: a government that works for them.

A president—a president ought to be a powerful force for progress. But right now I know how President Lincoln felt when General McClellan wouldn't attack in the Civil War. He asked him, "If you're not going to use your army, may I borrow it?" And so I say, George Bush, if you won't use your power to help America, step aside. I will.

Our country is falling behind. The president is caught in the grip of a failed economic theory. We have gone from first to thirteenth in the world in wages since Reagan and Bush have been in office. Four years ago, candidate Bush said America is a special place, not just "another pleasant country on the U.N. roll call, between Albania and Zimbabwe." Now, under President Bush, America has an unpleasant economy stuck somewhere between Germany and Sri Lanka. And for most Americans, Mr. President, life's a lot less kind and a lot less gentle than it was before your administration took office.

Our country has fallen so far, so fast that just a few months ago the Japanese prime minister actually said he felt "sympathy" for the United States. Sympathy. When I am your president, the rest of the world will not look down on us with pity, but up to us with respect again.

What is George Bush doing about our economic problems? Now, four years ago he promised us fifteen million new jobs by this time. And he's over fourteen million short. Al Gore and I can do better.

He has raised taxes on the people driving pickup trucks, and lowered taxes on people riding in limousines. We can do better.

He promised to balance the budget, but he hasn't even tried. In fact, the budgets he has submitted have nearly doubled the debt. Even worse, he wasted billions and reduced our investment in education and jobs. We can do better.

So if you are sick and tired of a government that doesn't work to create jobs, if you're sick and tired of a tax system that's stacked against you, if you're sick and tired of exploding debt and reduced investments in our future—or if, like the great civil rights pioneer Fannie Lou Hamer, you're just plain old sick and tired of being sick and tired—then join us, work with us, win with us. And we can make our country the country it was meant to be.

Now, George Bush talks a good game. But he has no game plan to rebuild America from the cities to the suburbs to the countryside so that we can compete and win again in the global economy. I do.

He won't take on the big insurance companies and the bureaucracies to control health costs and give us affordable health care for all Americans. But I will.

He won't even implement the recommendations of his own commission on AIDS. But I will.

He won't streamline the federal government and change the way it works, cut a hundred thousand bureaucrats, and put a hundred thousand new police officers on the streets of American cities. But I will.

He has never balanced a government budget. But I have, eleven times.

He won't break the stranglehold the special interests have on our elections and the lobbyists have on our government. But I will.

He won't give mothers and fathers the simple chance to take some time off from work when a baby is born or a parent is sick. But I will.

We're losing our family farms at a rapid rate, and he has no commitment to keep family farms in the family. But I do.

He's talked a lot about drugs, but he hasn't helped people on the front line to wage that war on drugs and crime. But I will.

He won't take the lead in protecting the environment and creating new jobs in environmental technology. But I will.

You know what else? He doesn't have Al Gore and I do.

Just in case—just in case you didn't notice, that's Gore with an "E" on the end.

And George Bush—George Bush won't guarantee a woman's right to choose. I will. Listen, hear me now: I am not pro-abortion. I am pro-choice strongly. I believe this difficult and painful decision should be left to the women of America. I hope the right to privacy can be protected, and we will never again have to discuss this issue on political platforms. But I am old enough to remember what it was like before *Roe v. Wade*. And I do not want to return to the time when we made criminals of women and their doctors.

Jobs. Education. Health care. These are not just commitments from my lips. They are the work of my life.

Our priorities must be clear: we will put our people first again. But priorities without a clear plan of action are just empty words. To turn our rhetoric into reality we've got to change the way government does business—fundamentally. Until we do, we'll continue to pour billions of dollars down the drain.

The Republicans have campaigned against big government for a generation. But have you noticed? They've run this big government for a generation. And they haven't changed a thing. They don't want to fix government. They still want to campaign against it, and that's all.

But, my fellow Democrats, it's time for us to realize that we've got some changing to do too. There is not a program in government for every problem. And if we want to use government to help people, we've got to make it work again.

Because we are committed in this convention and in this platform to making these changes, we are, as Democrats, in the words that Ross Perot himself spoke today, a revitalized Democratic Party. I am well aware that all those millions of people who rallied to Ross Perot's cause wanted to be in an army of patriots for change. Tonight I say to them: join us and together we will revitalize America.

Now, I don't have all the answers. But I do know the old ways don't work. Trickle-down economics has sure failed. And big bureaucracies, both private and public, they've failed, too.

That's why we need a new approach to government—a government that offers more empowerment and less entitlement, more choices for young people in the schools they attend, in the public schools they attend, and more choices for the elderly and for people with disabilities and the long-term care they receive; a government that is leaner, not meaner. A government that expands opportunity, not bureaucracy; a government that understands that jobs must come from growth in a vibrant and vital system of free enterprise. I call this approach a New Covenant—a solemn agreement between the people and their government—based not simply on what each of us can take but on what all of us must give to our nation.

We offer our people a new choice based on old values. We offer opportunity. We demand responsibility. We will build an American community again. The choice we offer is not conservative or liberal. In many ways it's not even Republican or Democratic. It's different. It's new. And it will work.

It will work because it is rooted in the vision and the values of the American people. Of all the things George Bush has ever said that I disagree with, perhaps the thing that bothers me most is how he derides and degrades the American tradition of seeing—and seeking—a better future. He mocks it as "the vision thing." But remember just what the Scripture says: "Where there is no vision, the people perish."

I hope . . . I hope nobody in this great hall tonight or in our beloved country has to go through tomorrow without a vision. I hope no one ever tries to raise a child without a vision. I hope nobody ever starts a business or plants a crop in the ground without a vision, for where there is no vision, the people perish.

One of the reasons we have so many children in so much trouble in so many places in this nation is because they have seen so little opportunity, so little responsibility, and so little loving, caring community that they literally cannot imagine the life we are calling them to lead. And so I say again, where there is no vision, America will perish.

What is the vision of our New Covenant?

An America with millions of new jobs in dozens of new industries moving confidently toward the twenty-first century. An America that says to entrepreneurs and business people: We will give you more incentives and more opportunity than ever before to develop the skills of your workers and create American jobs and American wealth in the new global economy. But you must do your part; you must be responsible. American companies must act like American companies again—exporting products, not jobs. That's what this New Covenant is all about.

An America in which the doors of college are thrown open once again to the sons and daughters of stenographers and steelworkers. We'll say: Everybody can borrow the money to go to college. But you must do your part. You must pay it back—from your paychecks, or better yet, by going back home and serving your communities. Just think of it. Think of it; millions of energetic young men and women, serving their country by policing the streets, or teaching the children or caring for the sick, or working with the elderly or people with disabilities, or helping young people to stay off drugs and out of gangs, giving us all a sense of new hope and limitless possibilities. That's what this New Covenant is all about.

An America in which health care is a right, not a privilege. In which we say to all of our people: Your government has the courage—finally—to take on the health-care profiteers and make health care affordable for every family. But you must do your part: preventive care, prenatal care, childhood immunization; saving lives, saving money, saving families from heartbreak. That's what the New Covenant is all about.

An America in which middle-class incomes—not middle-class taxes—are going up. An America, yes, in which the wealthiest few—those making over two hundred thousand dollars a year—are asked to pay their fair share. An America in which the rich are not soaked—but the middle class is not drowned, either. Responsibility starts at the top; that's what the New Covenant is all about.

An America where we end welfare as we know it. We will say to those on welfare: you will have and you deserve the opportunity through training and education, through child care and medical coverage, to liberate yourself. But then, when you can, you must work, because welfare should be a second chance, not a way of life. That's what the New Covenant is all about.

An America with the world's strongest defense, ready and willing to use force, when necessary. An America at the forefront of the global effort to preserve and protect our common environment—and promoting global growth. An America that will not coddle tyrants, from Baghdad to Beijing. An America that champions the cause of freedom and democracy, from Eastern Europe to Southern Africa, and in our own hemisphere in Haiti and Cuba.

The end of the Cold War permits us to reduce defense spending while still maintaining the strongest defense in the world. But we must plow back every dollar of defense cuts into building American jobs right here at home. I know well that the world needs a strong America, but we have learned that strength begins at home.

But the New Covenant is about more than opportunities and responsibilities for you and your families. It's also about our common community. Tonight every one of you knows deep in your heart that we are too divided.

It is time to heal America. And so we must say to every American: look beyond the stereotypes that blind us. We need each other. All of us, we need each other. We don't have a person to waste. And yet, for too long, politicians have told most of us that are doing all right that what's really wrong with America is the rest of us. *Them. Them* the minorities. *Them* the liberals. *Them* the poor. *Them* the homeless. *Them* the people with disabilities. *Them* the gays. We've gotten to where we've nearly *them'd* ourselves to death. Them, and them, and them. But this is America. There is no *them;* there is only us. One nation, under God, indivisible, with liberty, and justice, for all.

That is our Pledge of Allegiance, and that's what the New Covenant is all about.

How do I know we can come together to make change happen? Because I have seen it in my own state. In Arkansas we're working together, and we're making progress. No, there is no Arkansas miracle. But there are a lot of miraculous people. And because of them, our schools are better, our wages are higher, our factories are busier, our water is cleaner, and our budget is balanced. We're moving ahead.

I wish . . . I wish I could say the same thing about America under the incumbent president. He took the richest country in the world and brought it down. We took one of the poorest states in America and lifted it up.

And so I say to those who would criticize Arkansas: come on down. Especially if you're from Washington, come to Arkansas. You'll see us struggling against some problems we haven't solved yet. But you'll also see a lot of great people doing amazing things. And you might even learn a thing or two.

In the end, the New Covenant simply asks us all to be Americans again, old-fashioned Americans for a new time. Opportunity. Responsibility. Community. When we pull together, America will pull ahead. Throughout the whole history of this country, we have seen time and again that when we are united, we are unstoppable. We can seize this moment; we can make it exciting and energizing and heroic to be an American again. We can renew our faith in ourselves and each other and restore our sense of unity and community. Scripture says, our eyes have not yet seen, nor our ears heard, nor our minds imagined what we can build.

But I cannot do it alone. No president can. We must do it together. It won't be easy, and it won't be quick. We didn't get into this mess overnight, and we won't get out of it overnight. But we can do it—with our commitment and our creativity and our diversity and our strength. I want every person in this hall and every citizen in this land to reach out and join us in a great new adventure to chart a bold new future.

As a teenager I heard John Kennedy's summons to citizenship. And then, as a student at Georgetown, I heard that call clarified by a professor I had, named Carroll Quigley, who said America was the greatest country in the history of the world because our people have always believed in two great ideas: first, that tomorrow can be better than today, and second, that each of us has a personal, moral responsibility to make it so.

That future entered my life the night our daughter, Chelsea, was born. As I stood in that delivery room, I was overcome with the thought that God had given me a blessing my own father never knew: the chance to hold my child in my arms.

Somewhere at this very moment, another child is born in America. Let it be our cause to give that child a happy home, a healthy family, a hopeful future. Let it be our cause to see that child reach the fullest of her God-given abilities. Let it be our cause that she grow up strong and secure, braced by her challenges, but never, never struggling alone; with family and friends and a faith that in America, no one is left out; no one is left behind.

Let it be our cause that when she is able, she gives something back to her children, her community, and her country. And let it be our cause to give her a country that's coming together and moving ahead, a country of boundless hopes and endless dreams, a country that once again lifts up its people and inspires the world.

Let that be our cause and our commitment and our New Covenant.

I end tonight where it all began for me: I still believe in a place called Hope.

A New Day for America

Bus Tour Campaign Rally
St. Louis, Missouri
July 22, 1992

The adventure began the morning after Clinton's acceptance speech to the Democratic National Convention in New York on a six-day, 1,250-mile winding tour of flag-waving crowds in the small towns of New Jersey, Pennsylvania, West Virginia, Kentucky, Indiana, Ohio, and Illinois. This toured an America usually forgotten in the mediated political campaigning of the era, before the eight-bus caravan rolled to a stop in Missouri.

In front of the main public library in downtown St. Louis, close to thirty thousand people—office workers, labor unionists, and curious onlookers—jammed the main staircase and lawns of the library and filled the streets for blocks around Olive from west of 14th Street to well east of 13th Street. The podium was on the south side of Olive facing the library. The temperature was in the mid-eighties, the skies were cloudy, the air was humid, and Clinton and Gore didn't show up until 12:40 P.M., but the crowd, which had been waiting for hours, greeted them with thunderous applause.

As he spoke, Clinton removed his suit jacket and rolled up his sleeves, but by the time he had finished, his blue dress shirt was soaked with perspiration. The *St. Louis Post-Dispatch* said, "Clinton turned on the crowd with an appeal brimming with old-fashioned populism," and *The New York Times* called it "an old-fashioned tub thumper of a speech." After the rally, Clinton and Gore moved through the throngs of people, shaking hands as they did repeatedly on the trip and throughout the campaign.

❖ ❖ ❖

Thank you. Thank you. Thank you very much. Thank you. Thank you very much. Ladies and gentlemen, this is the largest, most enthusiastic, most committed crowd of Americans we have seen on this great trip.

Al Gore and I today are ending the first thousand miles of our campaign to change America. We have gone from New Jersey to Pennsylvania to West Virginia to Ohio to Kentucky to Indiana to Illinois and now to St. Louis in a great crusade to give the American people their country back.

And all along the way, we have been reminded about what makes this country great, going through the farming communities and seeing the little children lighting sparklers along our way; seeing people hold out their American flags; seeing the Clinton/Gore banners draped across the combines in the fields; seeing America say we want to change this country and put our people first for a change.

This great state, the home of Harry Truman, is called the Show-Me State. One thing you cannot say about this administration, you can't say that Bush and Quayle haven't shown you; they have shown you. Look what they have shown you: the worst economic record in the last fifty years. Only Herbert Hoover in the twentieth century matched the economic record of this last administration.

When Reagan and Bush came to office, we had the highest wages in the world. We are down to thirteenth and dropping. In every measure of economic performance, we are falling behind.

Most people in this crowd today and most people in this country today are working harder today for less money than they were making ten years ago. Is it right?

And what have they given us? The same old, tired idea; they are in the grip of a failed theory. They believe passionately that the only way for America to compete and win in the world is for us to become more unequal and more divided, keep taxes as low as possible on the wealthiest Americans, raise them on the middle class, explode the deficit, and get the government out of the way.

What has it brought us? More decline, more inequality, an America that is the mockery of the world. This year, they got their way; the top 1 percent of Americans control more wealth than the bottom 90 percent. Did it make us strong? No.

What happened? The president goes to Japan and the Japanese prime minister says he feels sympathy for the United States. I say this to those who are holding up those "Jobs Now" posters, when I'm your president and Al Gore is your vice-president, people will look up to us with respect, not down on us with sympathy, because we're going to win again.

We want a new day for the Democratic Party and a new day for America. Here we are in St. Louis, Missouri, and you're having an election year here today. And I don't want to get involved in your elections, but I do want to say that you have two Democrats running for governor, both of whom are better than all the Republicans they can dredge up.

Al Gore and I woke up this morning, and Mayor Schoemehl said we could "have the run of" St. Louis. We ran up to Lafayette Square; we ran back. Neither one of us fainted, and we decided that this was a wonderful city, and Mr. Mayor, we're glad to be here.

And I want to thank your lieutenant governor, Mel Carnahan, for being one of the first people to endorse me when I was low in the polls, and now that we're up, we're going to change the country together, all of us working together.

Let me tell you something. In my announcement speech at the Democratic National Convention, I quoted one of my favorite verses of Scripture, "Where there is no vision, the people perish." George Bush mocked that as the "vision thing." He said, "I'm not very good on the vision thing." I hope you never leave a place without a vision; I hope you don't have to live tomorrow without a vision. I hope you never have to raise a child without a vision or plant a crop without a vision or start a business without a vision. That's what's the matter with this country today.

And I'll tell you something else. We have a plan. We have a plan. Mr. Bush said our plan was smoke and mirrors. Well, he's the world's expert on smoke and mirrors. You decide if it's smoke and mirrors. Here it is: it says, "For too long, our government has been dominated by special interests, our elections controlled by them, our process paralyzed by them. We're going to give the government back to the people again. We're going to invest in jobs and education and affordable health care for all Americans, not just a few."

Our plan says no smoke and mirrors. We're going to pay for it by taking every dollar by which defense is reduced and reinvesting it here in America to put those people back to work. Why should we throw people out to work, when we can create more jobs in the future?

It says, "We're going to open the doors of college education to all Americans. Let anybody borrow the money to go to college. And pay it back, either as a percentage of your income when you go to work, or, better yet, come home to St. Louis, come home to Missouri and work for two years. Be a police officer, be a nurse, be a teacher, work to help kids in trouble. Pay back your college loan by solving the problems of America at home."

Our plan says, "If you're a high-school graduate and you don't go to college, we want a hundred percent of you to have at least two years of further training in an apprenticeship program to get a good job, not a dead-end job." I'm tired of the dignity being stripped from blue-collar work in America.

Our plan says, "We're going to take on the health-insurance companies in the bureaucracy and the government regulation and strip the millions of dollars of waste out of the health-care system, to control the costs, to preserve industry and the decency and security of life for average Americans, and provide a basic package of health care to all Americans. We're going to get America in line with the rest of the world."

Our plan says, "Every American will have to be more responsible for the future of this country. We want to create more wealthy people in America than Reagan and Bush have, but we've got an old-fashioned idea. We want everybody to get rich by putting the American people to work, producing American jobs, American goods, American services."

And so we say, "New incentives for modern plants and equipment, new incentives to start new business, but no more tax breaks for moving your jobs overseas. We will help you to build America again, and we want you to get rich doing it the old-fashioned way."

Our plan says, "We're going to liberate the poor. We're going to change the tax system for all those working poor people who courageously get up every day, work forty hours a week, do their best to raise their children, and they're still in poverty. We ought to have a tax system that says, if you're working hard and playing by the rules, we're going to lift you up and out of poverty in this country today."

We're going to have a welfare system that says, "We want you to have more from your country in education and training, and health care for your children, but then when you can go to work, you've got to go to work." Welfare should be a second chance, not a way of life.

We're going to have a new idea. Put our people first. Invest in the revitalization of our cities and our countryside. Put this money back to where it belongs, in creating jobs and education, so we can compete. There is nothing wrong with this country, except that we're underorganized, undereducated, and underled, and we're going to change all that in November, if you'll help us.

Ladies and gentlemen, people say to me all the time, "Well, that sounds good. But how do I know you're serious?"

Well, I'll tell you one way you know I'm serious. Look at the first decision George Bush made and the first decision I made. Dan Quayle versus Al Gore. I win. I wanted Al Gore to be on my team because he knows more than I do about some things, not because he'll make me look good every day.

The first and greatest Republican president, Abraham Lincoln, said that you can never lift yourself up by putting other people down. Al Gore and I want to lift everybody in America up. We don't want anybody left out.

We think you can be pro-business and pro-labor. We think you can be tough on crime and, still, fair to all Americans. And we think you can preserve the environment and develop the economy, and the other side doesn't believe any of that.

Ladies and gentlemen, we didn't get into this mess overnight. And we won't get out of it overnight. But we will make progress.

The thing that kills a country is when people get up every day, and they don't think that tomorrow will be better, when they think nothing is going to change, when they think nobody cares about them, when it's every person for themselves.

We want to restore this country to a genuine sense of community and caring, to say we're all in this together. We're going up or down together, without regard to race or region or income. This is America. Let's start acting like it again.

And we want you to believe that tomorrow can be better than today. Don't let anybody tell you we can't make these changes.

There are countries in the world today where the people are not working as hard, and they're making more money, and they've got health insurance, because their governments put their people first. They know that if you don't take care of people, nothing else works.

So if you're sick and tired of the way it's been going, if you want people in control again, if you believe your country is still the greatest country in the world again, if you think we can compete and win again, if you're tired of being heartbroken when you go home at night, and you want a spring in your step and a song in your heart, you give Al Gore and I a chance to bring America back. We will lift the country up. It's time for them to go and time for us to rescue America.

God bless you, and God bless America. Thank you.

Expanding the American Dream

Urban League National Convention
San Diego, California
July 27, 1992

President Bush had turned down an invitation to address the national Urban League convention, but Clinton enthusiastically accepted the opportunity to speak that morning to more than four thousand delegates who packed the San Diego Convention Center. Bernard G. Watson, the Urban League's vice-chairman, introduced Clinton, saying that Clinton knows something about "our history," and that as "an old tenor saxophone player, I know what Governor Clinton is about."

His voice hoarse but his enthusiasm evident in an hour-long speech that was repeatedly interrupted by applause and standing ovations, Clinton endorsed the League's "Marshall Plan'" to rebuild cities and foster economic opportunities and compared it with his own. Quoting from the keynote address delivered by Urban League president John Jacob the previous evening, he embraced and repeated the idea that "Every African-American child should graduate from high school with the ability to do calculus; should be fluent in a foreign language; should be able to research, organize, and write a twenty-five-page essay on a challenging topic; should live by strict, high ethical standards. That's what it will take to make it in the twenty-first century, not just for African Americans, but for all of America's people."

Clinton's speech was evidence of his campaign strategy to win the White House by forging a coalition between disenchanted whites and traditional Democratic constituencies with appeals that emphasize the similarities in shared goals and economic circumstances. ABC news correspondent Jim Wooten remarked afterward, "One speech does not a campaign make, but Clinton's speech here today did seem to reinforce the basic blueprint of his campaign, which is to remove his party's liberal label, reclaim those white middle-of-the-road Democrats it lost over the years without alienating its liberal base."

❖ ❖ ❖

Thank you. Thank you so much. I came here today worried about how I could follow John Jacobs last night. Now I can't even follow my own introduction. I can't believe I got introduced by a saxophone player. Bird still lives; Train still rules; and besides that, for all of our jazz enthusiasts, Lester Young will always be "the Pres." You've got to be over forty to get that one.

Ladies and gentlemen, I am deeply honored to be here today. I meant what I said about John Jacobs speech last night. I have read it in its entirety. And I feel like he hit a grand-slam home run last night, and now I have to be the lead-off batter in the next inning. I want to associate myself with his remarks.

The Urban League has been a rich source of support to everything I have tried to do, and most recently, in this presidential campaign, because of the brilliant leadership of Ron Brown, who worked, not only to rebuild our Democratic Party after 1988, but on our great convention. And because of the wonderful job that Vernon Jordan did me, as the leader of my vice-presidential selection process with Warren Christopher and Madeline Kunin, I think that as a test of the first decision of the nominee for president in compared with my adversary, I did OK.

I'd also like to thank my fellow Arkansans who are here, who represent the Urban League, for the partnerships that we have had over the years—to improve our children's lives, to reduce poverty, to increase opportunity, to improve education.

I noticed the other side in the inevitable way has developed one of their negative campaign tactics, which they say, they're going to say, that I am the failed governor of a small state. That's their new slogan. And they run their little surrogates out every day to say that. Well, ask them. You know, this fellow is amazing in Washington. He wants to blame me for everything that's happened in Arkansas and not take responsibility for anything that happened in the United States of America for the last four years.

To all of you I say, we're proud of what we've done at home. A lot of you here have roots in my state. You know that, from its beginning, it's always been one of the poorest places in America. If you know anything about farming, you know that in 1980, the rural areas of America had an even steeper decline in income than the urban areas, and I think we, at least, can say in our state, we have moved in the right direction, which is something you cannot say about the nation as a whole. We're proud of our partnership, and we're going to keep working together, because that's what works—working together.

For eighty-two years the Urban League has been a leader in the fight for civil and equal rights and for economic empowerment and political empowerment. It has helped paved the way for opportunity for millions of Americans.

As John Jacobs said last night, the historic mission of the Urban League, and the cause we're fighting for in this election, is not simply to fight racism and end discrimination; though if you join with me, we will certainly do that.

It is not simply to close the opportunity gaps in our schools, in our factories, in our communities; though if you join with me, we will certainly continue to do that.

It is not even simply to rebuild our cities and bring new hope to urban life; though if you join with me, we will continue to do that.

Your mission and our challenge today are even bigger. For more than eighty years, the Urban League has stood, not only for making life better for American cities and those who live in them, but for expanding the American dream to every person in this country. And if you join with me, that is what we must do in 1992 and in the next four years.

The great French observer Alexis de Tocqueville came here in the 1830s to learn about democracy. He found, even then, much to admire—pride in individual work, a devotion to the work ethic, a government that then promoted the common good. But even then our young country struggled to make good on its promise.

De Tocqueville expressed one very troubling sentiment. He said, and I quote, "The most formidable of all the ills that threaten the future of the union arrives from the presence of a black population upon its territory." He didn't know if we could overcome our ignorance about each other and our prejudice toward each other and our fear of each other. In other words, in 1830, he didn't know if we could change.

But as John Jacobs said last evening, sometimes we get so hung up on what needs to be done that we've forgotten what already has been done. Until we find the strength in what we have done, it is hard to find the courage to meet the challenges of tomorrow.

Alexis de Tocqueville looked at America before we lived through the Civil War; before Lincoln gave the Gettysburg Address or signed the Emancipation Proclamation; before the Constitution was expanded to grant full citizenship to all Americans; before the birth of groups like the Urban League, who fight to empower all of our people; before Franklin Roosevelt from his wheelchair lifted up the spirits of America and put our country back to work; before the United States stood firm in World War II, and then afterwards, spread economic and political freedom throughout the world, leading a coalition against tyranny until the Cold War finished with the collapse of the Berlin Wall, the end of communism in Eastern Europe, and the end of the Soviet Union itself; and before the civil rights movement transformed the face of America.

In 1830, de Tocqueville didn't know if we could change. Yet we did, and we changed the world in the process, and we proved that we are the most remarkable nation in the history of mankind.

And yet a century and a half later, we are still dogged with the same doubt that gripped de Tocqueville. Even our own people, and certainly people around the world, now doubt that we can change.

Having won the Cold War, it is commonplace conversation all around the world among informed people that America is losing the peace.

Or it is literally true that most American families are working harder than they did twenty years for lower wages than they did ten years ago.

It is literally true that our economy is growing at an anemic pace, in the last couple of years, at roughly one-third and one-fourth the German and the Japanese rates.

It is true that as wealthy as we are, we are only twenty-first in infant mortality. A dozen countries have adult workers that read better than we do. We have fallen from first to thirteenth in the world in wages. And we're still number one in the percentage of our adults in prison.

And so, as people work harder for less, as the number of poor people explode, as the number of working poor people accelerate even beyond the number of the nonworking poor, as we see fresh evidence of our divisions by race, ethnicity, and income, many look upon our diversity and wonder whether it will be the instrument of our undoing rather than the source of our renewal.

And our own people are often so dispirited that they do not participate in elections, say that it doesn't matter, have no faith in the dialogue in which we are engaged, and wonder whether we can change.

I come here this morning with a simple message, not only from my heart, but from the experience of my lifetime. We have changed before, and I believe we are ready to change again.

I see the stirrings of hope in the astonishing crowds that are coming out to see Al Gore and me as we went across the country in our bus ride. We came in the dark to a little town of Vandalia, Illinois, where there were over twelve thousand people crowding the courthouse square. And we stood in front of the old state capitol where Abraham Lincoln stood as a state legislator, and I said to them in that little community, Abraham Lincoln gave his life for the Union, for the proposition that all people were created equal, for the notion that we could create a new America, and he would turn over in his grave if he saw what had happened to the Republican Party in our age and time.

I saw it when fifteen thousand people were in the streets of Seattle; well over twenty-five thousand in St. Louis; ten thousand people in Ontario, California, in the inland empire, the so-called home of the Reagan Democrats in California. They were there; they were there because they believe in change.

I have seen it because the crowds that come are not all true believers. They come not just to see me, but because they want to hope, and believe, and change again. Many tell me they are Republicans; many say they were for Ross Perot; many say that they are Independent. They are the elements that make up America.

But the most encouraging thing came to me, not in a big crowd, but in a small group. The day before yesterday, I was in Spokane, Washington. And before we went out to speak to a crowd of four or five thousand that filled the city park, I met with a group of eighteen Americans—African Americans, Hispanic Americans, Asian Americans, Native Americans, white Anglo-Saxon Protestants, Jewish Americans, Republicans, Independents, people for Perot. I don't see how they got so many categories into eighteen different people. We had a lot of twofers and threefers in that category. We covered all our bases.

And these people were selected last Thursday, to get together and read the economic plan I had put out, and then to meet with me to ask questions. Just eighteen Americans, people that weren't politically active, and we did it in front of the press corps where they asked the questions. And I could tell that these people had really come together; they were bonding even though they thought they had so little in common.

So after we had our conversation, which was exhilarating, in which they asked me all kinds of things from all kinds of directions, I asked two or three of them, I said, "What was the most remarkable thing about this experience, for you seemed to like each other?" And they were all so exuberant about having had the chance to meet each other. And I said, "What surprised you most about this?" And the three people I asked all said the same thing. They said, "We had so much more in common than we thought we would."

A Republican businesswoman said, "I've never voted for a Democrat before." But she said, "I am plagued by the thought that exploding poverty among working people, especially, is going to break the free-enterprise system to which I have devoted my entire life."

People ask me questions that people don't expect to come out of them, if all you have is preconception. I'm telling you the conditions are there to change this country, and give the government back to the people, and make it work again, and meet the challenges of this day and time.

I want a new day for America. I want a new day for America because I know if we don't change the present approach, we will continue to suffer decline. And because I know that we have within us the intelligence, the character, the knowledge, and the resources to revitalize America.

The central fact of our time is that we are now caught up in a global economy. A global economy in which opportunity is determined, not by things that used to shape our economy, but by what is inside our heads, what we are capable of learning, the natural resources God has given us, and then how we invest our money and our efforts here at home. Because production can be moved around the world, the world can change in an instant. And any public official that promises you the way things used to be should be run out the door. Nobody can make things the way they used to be.

The challenge to get our country moving again is to hook our country into the future and make change our friend not our enemy. How can we make change our friend and not our enemy?

When people work harder for less money than they were making ten years ago, they are playing by their rules, they are doing the right thing, but change is their enemy.

When people live in abject dependence, because they cannot break out of the cycle of poverty, even though they are dying to work and be independent, change is not their friend, change is their enemy.

When business people work as hard as they can, and still fall further and further behind, change is not their friend, change is their enemy.

What we have to focus on today, all of us, and this is what gives us the opportunity to unite, is that we need a new direction for America to make change our friend.

The first thing we'll have to do is to stop denying our problems and dividing our people. Deep in their hearts, people long to believe that hearts have been broken before. I have laid out the most detailed, aggressive plan I have ever seen in my lifetime from a presidential candidate. I am deeply devoted to it, but I don't believe in using phrases like, "Read my lips," because who knows what the future holds.

I have seen a president promise a kinder, gentler nation, and then practice a meaner, harsher politics. I have heard the promise of a new harmony, a greater tolerance, and then seen it manifested in a bitter fight against civil rights legislation.

I have heard a promise that this administration would listen to the quiet people others don't. And then I watched the president veto the Motor Voter Registration Bill, which would enable more quiet people to have a loud voice on election day.

I have seen the quiet people crushed under the burden of economic policies that favor the very rich at the expense of the middle class and the working poor and the broad public interest of America.

Having said all that, let's tell the truth. Change is hard. Change is not easy. In 1992, we have a chance to do what the Urban League has been fighting to do since its inception, to make economic empowerment and opportunity the number-one civil rights issue in this country. But to do it, we've got to fight for change.

To change the direction of the last dozen years, we need a plan to rebuild this country. You understand this only too well. You call your plan a Marshall Plan for America, to increase growth and productivity here at home. And I can tell you I am very impressed with it. I know that John Jacobs has been in touch with one of our congressmen, Ray Thornton, who has been working on what he calls a Marshall Plan to rebuild America.

I didn't call my plan by that name, but it has much in common with yours. I come here today to open a dialogue, to tell you what I believe should be done, and then to offer to work with you on your plan and mine to make one plan to make America great again.

Your plan and my plan, let us be clear, do not involve liberal versus conservative, left versus right, big government versus less government. That's the load of bull we've been paralyzed with for too long.

Your plan and my plan are about new ideas versus old ideas, the future versus the past, helping the many versus the few, making change our friend versus making change our enemy, having a government that is leaner and more effective, that invests more and consumes less, that builds people's hopes instead of playing to their fears. That is what we must do.

Your plan, also like mine, calls for investing more money in our people, but also requiring higher standards. And I want to emphasize that, because our adversaries in this election, in their eagerness to prove that they did nothing wrong by reducing investment, will say, "All they want to do is tax-and-spend."

Remember what John Jacobs said last night; I'm going to read this. Does this sound like a tax-and-spend liberal to you? "In the 1990s we need to recognize that our very existence as a people is on the line in a new challenging world that is being born. We need to ensure the continuous development of African Americans as a self-confident people, whose effective efforts can change our lives and our nation. And we must begin with our children. If Japan, Korea, and Taiwan can take people raped by poverty and devastated by war and move them into economic powerhouses in one generation, then a committed, dedicated African-American community can help its children to do the same."

Now, I want them to hear this in Washington. I want to say one other thing. Am I reading this as well as you did? This is important. I want the heartland of America to hear this. This is not about tax-and-spend. This is about progress or sink. Listen to this.

"What will it take for our children to develop into outstanding twenty-first-century citizens? Let me suggest four basic criteria. Every African-American child should graduate from high school with the ability to do calculus; should be fluent in a foreign language; should be able to research, organize, and write a twenty-five-page essay on a challenging topic; and should live by strict, high ethical standards. That's what it will take to make it in the twenty-first century, not just for African Americans, but for all of America's people."

Now, give him another hand. Do it. Now, those are goals worth fighting for. And when people in this election try to put on yesterday's broken record that sticks at the same old place in the song, "Tax-and-spend, tax-and-spend, tax-and-spend, tax-and-spend, tax-and-spend," and then the negative handlers, they push the arm a little further and it sticks again; it goes, "Liberal, liberal, liberal." You say, "We got standards, we got values, and we're going to change. And get of our way with all that stuff that's holding us back and dragging us down and dividing us."

When they recant those things, like mantras, they're chanting, say, "I don't want to hear that. We just had the three worst years of economic performance since the depression. I don't want to hear that, when we're dropping in wages and increasing in poverty. I don't want to hear attacks on new ideas and new approaches, when we're sinking in the rough of the status quo."

You know sometimes you've got to change just to survive. Change is the law of life. Change is necessary to preserve our basic values. Change today is the order, not just for people who think of themselves as liberal, that is open and reaching out and inclusive, but for people who think of themselves as conservative. How can you preserve the basic values? How can you conserve the fabric of your life if you do not have the courage to change, when what you're doing is tearing the heart out of your country? That is what we have to tell the American people.

My plan puts fifty billion dollars a year in private and public investment back into this economy, creates a million jobs each year in direct jobs, provides affordable health care for all Americans for a change, excellence in education, safer streets, and stronger families by putting the American people first again, and putting government back on the side of average American families.

My plan says let's take every dollar by which we reduce defense, and instead of just squandering it in the dark hole of the budget deficit, reinvest every last red cent in building jobs here at home to build an economy for the twenty-first century.

There are, in this state alone, hundreds of thousands of defense workers now out of work. People who have won the Cold War and now have been left out in the cold. High-wage workers, skilled workers, people who made the California dream a magnet that drove millions of people across the continent, out of the dust bowl of Oklahoma and the farm fields of Arkansas and Mississippi, looking for jobs in California, and now idled because there was nothing found for the defense workers to do.

When they took bids on a new high-speed rail network in Los Angeles County, with all these high-skilled workers out of work, did they get a bid from a company that was building trains with old defense workers? No.

Nobody was doing that; they had to look to Germany and Japan. Why aren't the defense workers building the national security of the future by building the national economy, building high-speed rail and roads and bridges and water systems and sewer systems and recycling systems? And why aren't those jobs in the inner cities where people can be put back to work and given the opportunity to go forward? That's what we ought to be about. That's about tomorrow. That's not about liberal or conservative. It's about the future.

And what about education? We need opportunity, we need investment, we need standards. I worked hard to develop the national education goals. And I have watched how our education president has embraced those goals, and then told us why they should be in the position of grading the rest of us with little responsibility to contribute to the effort we are making. And now they want to point the finger instead and say we did not do well enough.

In 1980, the federal government was contributing about 10 percent of the cost of public education, down to about 6 percent now. Think what a difference that would make in California today, just that. Think what it means to the poor states, like the delta states. Think what it means to the inner cities. Think what it means to the school districts who suffer from the savage inequalities that the great American writer Jonathan Kozel chronicled in his book.

I believe in high standards in education. I believe in accountability. I believe in standards for teachers and standards for students and standards for schools. I want to see a national exam system that's not a fraud, that really means something, that tells you whether your kids are learning what they're supposed to know.

I believe that we ought to do what John Jacobs said. I think every child needs to understand not just arithmetic, but advanced mathematical concepts, and needs to be able to read, write, and think and solve problems. Because we live in a world in which it's not so important what you know as what you can continue to learn. We live in a world where the average eighteen-year-old will literally change the nature of work eight times in a lifetime. Even if you stay with the same company, the world economy will force changes in the nature of work.

Being a bank teller today is not even what it used to be, is it? Working in most factories today isn't what it used to be. So we have to continue to re-educate people. It breaks my heart to see all these high-wage factory workers out of work, although we know mechanization will have to continue to be done. We've got to modernize plant and equipment if we want to pay higher wages here than people make south of the border or halfway around the world, which means you've got to keep creating new jobs, which means people have to know new things.

Well, you can't do that if you've got a vast sea of poor kids, and you don't even get them off to a head start so that everybody's starting at the same line when education begins.

We can't do that if we ignore the plain lessons that so many of our children come from poor families, undereducated families, that they need their parents involved as their children's first teachers. They need smaller classes; they need elementary counselors. We've got to do it right at the beginning. If we can give the kids the capacity to keep learning, we can move forward.

It's all very well to hold people to high standards, but they've got to be able to jump. And that involves doing it right at the beginning.

Then let me say, I like all this values talk except that it's coming from people who are telling us what we ought to do and making excuses for what they haven't done. I believe with John that there are certain basic values that we ought to impart through our school systems: respect for self, respect for family, respect for others, respect for community, respect for our natural environment, the obligation to honor truth over falsehood, the obligation to serve the larger community.

There are lots of things that we need to be imparting through the schools. That's why I want more partnerships with the private sector and more opportunities for kids to work with people who have succeeded.

That's why I know that Los Angeles can be rebuilt, if there are enough caring, successful adults that will support projects like the L.A. Conservation Corps and other things that give children the chance to see the nature of work working, to see connections with people, and imagine the future we want them to live.

I don't have any problem promoting good values, but the government ought to live by what it says, instead of having worse values than the families they're lecturing.

And if we know people are going to have to do eight different things in their lifetime, then a high-school education is not enough. I think you were telling me—no, not you—you were telling me that you served on the Grant Commission.

In 1987, my wife, William Julius Wilson from Chicago, Dr. Watson, and others served on a commission to look at what happened to the forgotten half of young Americans who don't go to college. We are the only advanced nation that does not have a system for guaranteeing all of them at least two years of further training. Result? Look at the 1990 census report. Younger workers with a high-school diploma only, or who dropped out of high school, had their earnings going just like this, dropping like a rock in a well. Younger people who got two years of further education beyond high school in apprenticeship programs, community colleges, vo-tech schools, or who went on to college, their earnings go up. I say we need a system in this country to restore the dignity of work by giving every high-school graduate two years of further education or training in apprenticeship programs.

And we need to adopt the national trust fund I have recommended, to offer every American the chance to walk through the doors of a college. Everyone, without regard to income, could borrow the money to go to college, everyone, and then pay it back, either as a small percentage of their own income after they go to work, or even better, by solving America's problems.

I want to combine two of the best ideas this country ever had, the G.I. Bill, after World War II, and the Peace Corps, under President Kennedy. We sent young people all across the world; let's send them back home. Let them work for two years as teachers, police officers, nurses, in a drug program, solving the problems of our cities, rebuilding America, and educating a whole generation of Americans. We can do that. We can do that. It would be the best money we ever spent.

And we need some special initiatives for our very poor areas in our cities. I know Secretary Kemp is coming here, and he's got some pretty good ideas. Trouble is, they only dust them off when there's a riot or some other problem. He's out there working all by himself and never even makes the newspapers until something goes wrong. And then the president discovers him and brings him up front again.

We must work together in these areas, and until we do, we're not going to turn them around. There's not enough government money in the world to fix the problems, if the private sector is not committed to liberating the potential of the people who are trapped in poverty and the lack of opportunity. You know that as well as I do.

But we have to make some specific changes in the laws. Let me just give you an example. There are lots of manufacturing enterprises that could be put into our inner cities again for relatively low-skilled and low-educated workers. But because we don't control health-care costs, and because we don't provide an investment tax credit for new plant and equipment, and because we don't have the incentives we should have for continuous training of our work force, we make it very hard for our workers, in real need, to be competitive with very low wages overseas, where they don't have to worry about health-care costs or environmental investments, and the cost of doing business is better.

So I say we need a national plan to make America a manufacturing power again, as well as specific incentives to work in our inner cities. We also need to understand that most new jobs are created by small businesses in units of under fifty, and that means a banking system that makes loans in the inner city again, for poor people who can do their work.

The president of the American Banking Association this year is a country banker from my home state, who works in the Mississippi Delta, the poorest part of America. And he said to me, "I realize now, Bill, most of our lending officers have no idea how to judge a loan to a poor person. They don't know how to do it."

And he said, "I want to work with you, and we can retrain and redirect the energies of our banking system." We can have banks cool their resources and create community banks like the South Shore Development Bank in Chicago. We can have people that understand that poor people are good loan risks, if you know what you are doing, and there's a market out there that's going to waste because we don't have enough businesses in the inner cities that are owned by the people who live there. And we've got to do a better job of that.

We've got to do a better job, too, of making our cities safer places. It's a big myth that most people in our cities don't want safety. It's also a big myth that you can't do anything about crime and drugs on the street.

New York City, for the first time in thirty-six years, has a decline in all major areas of crime, because Lee Brown, the police chief, instituted community policing.

Houston, Texas, dropped 15 percent in the crime rate in one year, because they put six hundred fifty-five more policemen on the streets working in community policing.

I walked on a street in Philadelphia and played basketball in a park with kids, where kids were, a couple of years ago, terrified to walk into the park, because of community policing and rapid prosecution of serious drug dealers. We can do this.

One of the things that my plan to rebuild America does is to provide a hundred thousand more police officers, not to be enemies of their neighbors, but the friends of their neighbors to walk the same streets every day to work to prevent crime, not just to catch criminals, and safer streets through community policing.

Finally, let me say something about family values. I kind of liked what you said about that last night, too. How in the world anybody in America can use family values to divide us is beyond me, but I can see it coming right down the tracks.

That's their wedge issue, family values, welfare. They got it; the message is, "Oh my gosh, don't." If we knew every family story in this room today, it would break the heart and lift the spirit of America at the same time.

I will say again, most of our families have good values, and they're a lot better than the governments today.

What does it say about family values when, in my bus trip, we were in Columbus, Ohio, and I met a single mother with seven children, which she bore in wedlock. She had a fifty-thousand-dollar-a-year job supporting her seven children, and she had to quit that job and go on welfare because one of those kids was sick, and she couldn't get any health insurance. So the only way she could take care of one kid was to give up a fifty-thousand-dollar job just to get Medicaid. What does that say of the family values of America?

I met a beautiful young African-American woman in her early twenties, big, tall, attractive, articulate woman, just got a college degree, had to stay on welfare, dying to go to work, because she had a child with spina bifida. And the only way that child could be taken care of is if she stayed dependent, instead of independent, because of the way our government system works in this country. Because we're the only nation with an advanced economy that's refused to provide a basic package of affordable health care to all Americans.

What does it say about family values, when we still have a welfare system that encourages some people to stay on welfare, not because the benefits are high—the benefits have dropped more than wages have in the last twenty years—but because they have children, and they can't afford child care or medical coverage for their kids, so they can't get the training they need?

I say to you, we ought to end welfare as we know it. It ought to be a second chance, not a way of life. But to do it, you have to liberate people. You have to educate them and train them and liberate their kids. Then you can require them to take jobs. That would be good family values, help people to succeed as workers and as parents.

And what about the fact that there are a million more poor children in this country than there were ten years ago. One million. And most of them are living in families where the parents work.

What does it say about our tax system? That in the 1980s we lowered taxes on the wealthiest Americans, while their incomes exploded, and we raised taxes on the rest of Americans, while their incomes declined. So that now there are millions of Americans who get up every day, work forty hours a week, and do their best to raise their children, and they're still in poverty.

I say the tax system ought to lift those people out of poverty. If you're working hard and playing by the rules, you ought to be taken out of poverty.

What does it say about family values? That we have a system of child support, which for millions of Americans is a cruel joke, where you go to court and you get your order, and then somebody crosses a state line or finds a lenient judge, and the kid never gets a dime; and where it is not confined by income and certainly not by race; where the problems in the system are just as prevalent among the middle class and the upper middle class as they are among the poor.

Why don't we have a system that says the government doesn't raise children, people do? And parents are going to have to help, whether they're home or not. And we're going to have a system to do that. You can't cross the line and beat the deal.

Oh, I think we know about family values. But let's be honest with one another. I had the privilege of spending some time in a two-parent household, and some time in a single-parent household. I never knew what it meant to be a foster child, but I sure knew what it meant to have an extended family. In the early years, I would have had a hard time making it with my single mother, if it hadn't been for my grandparents and my uncles and my aunts and my great-uncles and my great-aunts and my cousins so distant I couldn't count them. A lot of you know what I'm talking about, don't you?

So, tell them we know about family values. And we think our government ought to value families, help families, help families on welfare to liberate themselves, help the working poor with a tax system that lifts them above poverty. Pass the Family and Medical Leave Act, and don't veto it this time. Understand that child care and medical coverage for children and Head Start and programs to help parents become their children's first teachers.

These are not programs and expenditures of tax dollars. These are ways to help parents be better parents, kids be better kids, families be stronger families. Other nations of the world all make it easier for people to raise their children in dignity than we do, all the other advanced nations.

And one of the reasons a lot of these economies are growing faster than ours is that they understand they do not have a person to waste, and they are sickened when they see how we squander the human potential of America. We let people wind up in jail when they ought to be on the assembly line or in the offices leading this country into the twenty-first century.

And let me say, finally, we've got to do this together. Together, our diversity can be a source of our strength. A hundred fifty different racial and ethnic groups in America, in a world in which the global economy gets smaller and more interrelated every day, that should be a resource.

But we have to recognize that we have differences and we are different. But at the bottom, we want the same things for our children and our future.

Many of the feelings that I have about civil rights come from my southern heritage. I grew up in the segregated South with grandparents who believed in integration, not because they had a fancy education and had read all the books, but because they had personal experience with African Americans as people. And they knew what was going on was wrong.

I lived to see my daughter in a New South, a public school student in the Little Rock public schools, which are two-thirds black and one-third white, a student who learned what Martin Luther King wanted her to do, to judge people by the content of their character, not by the color of their skin. I watched her do algebra, play volleyball, dance ballet, argue politics, and dream dreams with children of both races. And I can tell you that's how America ought to work.

Everything I have tried to do as a governor—whether it was a minority business loan program or an aggressive effort to empower the parents of poor children to be successful teachers and get their kids off to a good start; to investing millions of dollars in isolated rural communities where people, literally, often have no sewage system or running water; toward trying to lift the vision of our state—all of it has been designed to let all of us live together and judge each other by the content of our character, not by the color of our skin; and all of us to live up to the fullest of our God-given potential.

There is nothing else to politics but that. Politics is about making tomorrow better than today and about making us all feel that we are a part of a larger community in which we matter to each other, in which all of us are better off because each of us is there.

That is the purpose of our common political life throughout two hundred years as Americans. But every generation, we are challenged to change, to meet the challenges of the time, so that we can preserve that.

That is the liberal mission of America, and that is the conservative mission of America. To make progress and to bind ourselves together.

If you vote for Al Gore and Bill Clinton, we won't solve these problems overnight, we didn't get into this mess overnight. We don't have all of the answers, no one does. But we know the old ways don't work. We know that trickle-down economics doesn't work. We know that investment economics and putting people first and putting government and business and labor and education all on the same side competing for opportunity in the world does work.

We know that America works best when our economy looks like a diamond, to use my friend Ray Marshall's shape; when we have the possibility of the great middle class to move up the ladder and do better, but knowing they'll be OK, if they just work hard and stay where they are; when the poor can look up and see a bigger group ahead of them, and they know that by their own efforts, they can get there.

But more and more and more, our diamond is becoming a triangle. What we have to do is to recover the diamond. What we have to do is to recover hope. What we have to do is to do it together.

The challenge of this time is very great, my fellow Americans. But I ask you, can we say, in good conscience, that our challenges are greater than Abraham Lincoln faced at the dawn of the Civil War?

Can we say, in good conscience, that our challenges are greater than Franklin Roosevelt faced, as he wheeled his wheelchair into the White House for the first time, at the beginning of the Great Depression?

Can we say, in good conscience, that our challenges are greater than John Kennedy faced when he feared that we would go to nuclear war with the Soviets?

We have always faced great challenges. All that remains for us in this election is to believe; to believe that we can do better; to believe that the future can be better than the present; to believe that we are important to one another, and that all of us can be more if we are together than we can if we are apart.

That is the mission of the Urban League. That is the challenge of America. That is the heart of my plan to rebuild America. That is the meaning of your Marshall Plan. And that, in the end, is our responsibility as citizens to bring about in this 1992 election.

Thank you. And God bless you all.

The Test for an Education President

American Federation of Teachers
Pittsburgh, Pennsylvania
August 11, 1992

Clinton delivered this major speech on education policy and called for long-term investment in education to a warm and cheering audience of almost four thousand sign-waving delegates to the Seventy-second American Federation of Teachers Convention at the David Lawrence Convention Center in Pittsburgh. He acknowledged past differences with professional education associations but stressed their common goals for improving public education, and he asked delegates to hold the Bush administration accountable for failing the test of educational leadership. The speech was loudly applauded, and hundreds of delegates approached Clinton following the speech asking him to autograph campaign posters. The AFT, which represents seven hundred and ninety thousand teachers, higher education faculty and staff, and school-related personnel, endorsed Clinton for president by a unanimous vote on the following day.

❖ ❖ ❖

Thank you. Thank you very much. Thank you. Thank you. Thank you very, very much. Thank you. Thank you. Thank you very much. Thank you. Thank you. Thank you. Thank you very much. Thank you very much.

President Shanker and ladies and gentlemen, it is wonderful for me to be here with you. I'm glad you've still got a few rowdy people here.

You know, usually when people talk about education lately, they make fun of the vice-president's unusual spelling of potato, but I want you to know that the other day, there was an allusion to it, I think, in what Mr. Shanker said, President Bush said that I came from a small state, somewhere between Texas and Oklahoma. Now, I want to ask the AFT to do something for this administration. I want you to promise that as soon as the November election is over, that you will personally offer the finest course in geography available to former president George Bush.

The Republicans are having their trouble today. They're trying to ride a platform, and they can't agree on how to characterize their record. The president said, "Read my lips" in 1988, and then in 1990, he signed that huge tax increase. And then, earlier this year, he said it was a mistake, and so the platform riders thought they were supposed to say it was a mistake. And then they decided it might be embarrassing to say that it was a mistake to break the principle promise of the 1988 campaign. So, they just said it caused the recession.

They took out their "No new taxes" pledge in this platform, but that wasn't enough for the right wing. They want them to promise to add four to five hundred billion dollars to the deficit over the next four years with another round of trickle-down economics, where you'd get a little and the wealthiest Americans would get a lot. And they can't figure out what to do with that.

Well, Al Shanker was right. I haven't always agreed with the AFT on all issues. I once had a very bracing debate in Chicago at an AFT-sponsored event on some issues relating to the testing question. And Joyce Elliot, who's here from our chapter in Arkansas, can tell you that, but we both believe in education, and we both believe in the laws of mathematics. And we, pretty well, learned to add and subtract, and I wish I could say the same for our adversaries in this election.

I will say this, no serious student of the last decade, in our common efforts in education, could doubt the steadfast commitment of the AFT for higher standards in our country for students and for teachers; for the belief that all children can learn; for the commitment to try to maintain a qualified and committed and highly motivated core of teachers who know they'll never be rich, but ought not to have to be poor to pursue their vocations.

My opponents on the other side, many of whom have worked with me for years in the cause of education reform, are trying to convince the average American taxpayers and parents that because you are for me and because the NEA has endorsed me and because most people who have worked in education are for me, that somehow, I'm not for reform. They think the only way you can be for reform is if nobody who teaches kids supports you.

Now, I think we all recognize that none of us has all the answers, that our problems are highly complex, and that we ought to have a continuing and vigorous debate over what we should do. But there are some things which are perfectly clear—some tests that we ought to have for someone who says he wants to be an education president. And that applying those standards, we need to make a change in the White House, so we can make some changes in the schoolhouses of the United States of America.

If I were you, with all the problems of your work, and they are many—more violence in our schools, more poor children, more children from troubled homes with difficult circumstances in their lives, the changing composition of our society, and the increasing burdens on our schools, the financial problems of so many school districts—and, by the way, let's have a parenthesis and correct one misapprehension that this administration continues to push. The United States does spend a higher percentage of its income on education that any nation in the world, if, but only if, you include higher education. On kindergarten through twelfth-grade education, we are nowhere near first. There are eight or nine or ten countries that spend a higher percentage of their income than we do on education.

And, it does not serve our debate, over what we ought to do and what changes we ought to make, very well to have this administration continually say that we are over spending on public education compared to other nations. The numbers simply don't bear it out. I think we're misspending a lot of the money we have, and so do you—so do you. But let's have a debate on that without clouding the issue.

Well, what is the president's job in education? What is the responsibility of the president? To lead? You ought to go down to Houston next week; maybe they'll listen to you.

We all know that the real magic of education is what goes on between the teacher and the students and the schools. That's where the magic is. And we all hope that the magic is reinforced by what goes on between the student and the parent at home, and that sometimes they are all together in the school.

We all know that most of the money for education comes from the state and the local level, regrettably a much higher percentage now than was the case a dozen years ago before this crowd got in. But there is a national responsibility to lead, to set standards, to create opportunity, to resolve the incredibly complex issue of pursuing excellence and equity at the same time. These are the things that the president must take a lead in.

Now, this president has got some pretty good people working in the Department of Education, but their whole deal in life is to tell the rest of us what we ought to be doing and to minimize their own responsibility of accountability for any of the results. And that is consistent with what they do in every other area. The maddest I've been in the last several weeks was when Mr. Darman, the head of the Office of Management and Budget, went up to the House Budget Committee the other day and he was asked why do we have the poorest economic performance in fifty years, the worst economy since the depression, the first decline in industrial output in the history of the country, the worst job growth rate and economic growth rate in fifty years? Why do we have it? And do you know what he said? He said, well, there are four reasons: the banks don't loan enough money, and the Federal Reserve didn't lower interest rates quick enough, and Saddam Hussein invaded Kuwait. Somebody else paid for that war, I don't know where he got that, but anyway it's what he said. And he said Congress won't do what we want them to.

So the Chairman of the Budget Committee said, well, how about the president? Do you and the president—do you have any responsibility for what's happened? Silence. And they refused to accept any responsibility. Can you imagine where this country would be today if Harry Truman had had a sign on his desk that said "the buck stops somewhere else"? If Franklin Roosevelt had said to a nation beleaguered by the Great Depression, the only thing we have to fear is my opponents and their nutty ideas? This crowd's been in the blame game so long they can't imagine what it would be like to take responsibility and establish partnerships and bind up the wounds and heal the divisions of the country and move us ahead together, but that's exactly what we are going to do in 1993.

I believe in the national education goals that I worked so hard to write. I believe in the call for national standards of what our children should know and a meaningful way of measuring whether those kids know it or not. You know as well as I do that most of the national testing we have today is a hoax and that once you give these tests, these so-called norm reference tests every two or three years, every child in America's making above the national average and we go around blathering happy talk about it. But that does not mean that we shouldn't have standards. It does not mean we shouldn't measure them. It doesn't mean that we shouldn't know the hard truth about whether we are or are not providing the kinds of educational environment and we're producing the kind of learning that our people will need to go into a global economy; where it's far more important to be able to learn than even to be able to know; where memorization is not as important as the ability to be literate and reasoning, to write and to discuss, and to grow, to have basic mathematics and calculating skills, to understand the world that we're living in. So we do have to know what the target is, and we have to recognize that it's a moving target, and we have to be willing to summon ourselves to the rigors of achieving it. But we have to also be very honest about what the best strategies are for doing that. We do need less bureaucracy and more school-based management, more decision making for teachers and principals and parents in the schools.

It is true that the administrative costs of public education in this country are too high in most districts. It is true, and you believe that, too, but it's also true that some of those costs which look so bad when compared to private schools are directly related to the fact that we take everybody, with all their problems, and that we have to deal with them. So, let us have an honest debate about how we can cut these administrative costs, how we can put that money back into programs and teachers and services for children. Let us say we know we're not spending all this money as well as it can be spent. Let's have some hard analysis and some cold truth and some real political pressure to change the spending priorities within public education. We can do that, and I think the teachers of this country want that to be done. I think you ought to have a Department of Education that supports reform at the state and local level and that recognizes that people ought to have some measure of choice in the public schools they attend. Most every big-city school system in the country now provides a wide range of choices for children and their parents. But that doesn't mean that in the present circumstances, with a school system that is already underfunded with radical inequalities among school districts in this country, that we ought to go for the private voucher system. I am opposed to that.

And let me say that I'm glad America has a strong system of private schools. I'm glad that people who have religious convictions can send their children to religious schools that also can teach them. When I moved, when I was a small boy, I moved from Hope, Arkansas, to Hot Springs. We were living way out in the country, and my folks didn't know anything about the schools that were out there. For two years I went to a Catholic school. It's an experience I will always treasure; I'm glad I did it. I learned a lot. We didn't have much money, but I'm darned glad the taxpayers didn't have to foot the bill for me going. My parents paid, that was a choice they made, and we were not wealthy people. I have signed a bill in my state to give parents the opportunity under rigorous conditions of accountability to do home schooling because it exists in every state in the country anyway, and we thought we ought to have standards for it. I am not opposed to competition for the public school system, I think that's a healthy thing. But I do not believe in a country which already is straining the financial resources of the public school system, that we ought to divert them when we know we can make reform work in the system if we've got the discipline to do it. That's my position, and that's the position I'll stick with as president.

I want to give you an education department that really works more on helping you to promote reform and spurring you to reform, and seeing that reform ideas travel across district and state lines, than just as an engine of paperwork and regulation. I feel very, very strongly, and you know this as well as I do and maybe better, that there is example after example after example of people solving problems in American education today. Virtually every problem you can mention, has been addressed extremely effectively by somebody, somewhere, in America.

Let's tell the truth, the real reason we don't need vouchers is there are public schools taking difficult situations and doing the best job of educating kids anybody's been doing anywhere, but the problem is—let's identify what the problem is—that we have not yet found a way to make ideas that work travel very well across district and state lines. We haven't done that. And that is our burden and our responsibility.

I have seen stunning things in schools in Chicago, in Boston, in Los Angeles, in the District of Columbia; all across this country I have seen things that any American parent of any income, any racial background, any social condition would be proud of. But we don't do a very good job of making those ideas travel. The bureaucracy, the resistance to change, is profound. And one of the things that the Department of Education ought to do is to provide incentives for continuing teacher training, continuing principal training, have an extension service to help these ideas travel across district and state lines and really work, so that all of us are comfortable in embracing the notion that we can learn from one another. We should be proud to learn from one another.

The Founding Fathers of this country set up state governments as laboratories of democracy, and I remember once a couple of years ago I told a reporter that I was always prouder to be the second state that adopted a reform than to be the first, because that meant I was stealing somebody else's ideas first and that was what the laboratories of democracy were all about. And that's the way we ought to view our schools. That is our challenge. We ought to have to answer to our parents and our taxpayers. If somebody solved a problem we haven't solved with a group of kids with the same level of problems that our kids have, in whatever district of the country, the burden is on us to change, but your national government should be helping to facilitate that. That is the sort of change that I see and that I will push.

In that regard, let me say that I have grave reservations about raising all this money for five hundred and thirty-five starved schools, which is the administration's main initiative in the Education 2000 program—the idea that we ought to go out here and put one new school in each congressional district and then two others in every state, one for each senator, one for every congressman, one for each senator, and build them from the ground up. It'll be interesting, but it's going to take a lot of time, a lot of money, a lot of energy. When we know today that there are strategies that work, why shouldn't we be trying to have bottom-up education reform instead of trickle-down education reform?

There are clearly some areas of total responsibility to provide opportunity, equity, and excellence. One, recognize that a president had not fully funded his Head Start; still only 36 percent of the eligible kids are in it. But I want to do more than fully fund that program. I want to do what I can to spawn an environment in which every child in this country, who needs to be in a preschool program can be in one, either Head Start or a school-based program, or a parent-based program, one that is most appropriate. I want to try to do what we can at the national level to alleviate those savage inequalities that Jonathan Cole wrote about, through funding the Chapter One program in ways that focus on smaller classes in the early grades and greater flexibility for the teachers, to spend the money in the most effective way.

I want a safe school initiative that will help all of our schools to be safe and drug free and gun free, an orderly environment. One of the things that we're going to do is to provide an initiative that will put another one hundred thousand police officers on the street to prevent crime from occurring, not just to catch criminals, to help school and areas around schools to be safe, to provide security equipment to schools, but also to try to help people to do those things which will make children want to be in a school that is a good school.

I visited a school in Chicago in the primary. It made a profound impression on me—the Beasley Academic Center, a junior high school in Chicago—and I want you to know the fact that the principal was from my home state had nothing to do with my going there. Here are these kids, in a neighborhood with the highest murder rate in the state of Illinois, consistently in the top 10 percent in all their test scores. No dropout rate, no drugs, no violence, a dress code—seventy-five fathers in that school every week volunteering—fathers, not just mothers. And we had a little meeting there and I asked the kids, I said, "Well, are there any guns in this school?" They said *no.* "Any drugs in this school?" *No.* "Any dropouts?" *No.* I said, "Why?" "We like coming here, and if we bring drugs or guns, then we'd have to go. Nobody wants to get kicked out of this school. We like being here. We want to be here." They also have security outside and support. We can do that, and we have to do it everywhere.

And one other thing I want to say about the schools, our children today are under more threats and more temptation and more duress than any generation of children before them, and some of these things are a matter of life and death. There have been any number of studies in the last few years which have shown that youthful sexual activity is not measurably greater in the United States than in European countries, but our teen pregnancy rate is twice as high. And there are now over one million Americans who are HIV positive, with the number going up exponentially, and more among traditional

American populations, rather than—it's no longer confined primarily to IV drug users and gay men. In fact, the rate is growing fastest among women—two chilling cover stories on two of our major news magazines just within the last month on this. We have got to have an aggressive program of health education and prevention in our schools. We have got to provide basic health services in our schools. It's the only place a lot of these kids can ever, ever get basic health services. And this is not just a city problem. In some of our poorest counties in my state an enormous percentage of the children go to school with infected teeth or gums because they've never seen a dentist. We're trying to get those clinics out there to them. It is not just an urban problem, it is an American problem—in the rural areas, in the suburbs, in the small towns, we've got to do it.

And I want to ask you to think about just three things that go beyond public schools which will involve the public schools. First, we've got to do something for the majority of the American kids who either don't go on to or don't graduate from four-year colleges. We've got to do something for them. The countries against which we compete for high-wage, high-growth jobs, almost all of them keep up with all of their students, and they try to see that they get at least two years of further training after high school. And in our—if you look at the census data, in our country, our young people who got at least two years of training after high school in the community colleges or vocational programs or working on a job in a training program tended to get jobs where their incomes went up. Those who dropped out of high school or graduated from high school but went no further got jobs where their incomes went down—markedly. Markedly.

We owe it to the children of America and to our own economy to establish the linkages necessary between the public school system and the vocational and community college network and the employer community to have a world-class apprenticeship system that restores the dignity to blue-collar work in this country. We've got to do that.

And for those who do want to go on to college, I'd say we ought to open the doors of college education to everybody. We ought to make access to college universal. Perhaps the most exciting idea that I have propounded in this election in terms of how it might affect other people's lives has been my notion of a national trust fund—kind of a domestic Peace Corps—out of which anybody can borrow the money to go to college and then pay it back with two years of service to our country here at home.

Think about it. Everybody—everybody—could borrow the money and pay it back as police officers, as nurses, as teachers working for kids in trouble. I mean, we could solve the domestic problems of America with the brightest of our young people and educate a whole generation of Americans. People could begin to think of college as a right, and you could start telling kids in the fifth grade or the sixth grade or the seventh grade or the eighth grade, "Hang in there. Look what's ahead for you. You can have a future. Do this. It can be yours."

We could really profoundly change the attitudes of our young people. We could restore hope to millions of children who cannot even imagine the life that we want them to live, and I want you to support that.

The last point I want to make about that is that if we really want to raise per-capita income in America in a hurry, the quickest and cheapest thing we could do is teach every American with a job to read and give every American with a job a chance to get a GED. It would raise the per-capita income of the country. It would raise the productivity of the work force.

We have invested an enormous amount of money in that in my state. I have only 2.4 million people in Arkansas, and it does border Texas, but it's not between Oklahoma and Texas, and we now spend as much money on adult education as Texas does, because it's money well spent. And I know it's beyond the purview of public education, but it will lift the productivity of the country, as well as restoring dignity and esteem to millions of American workers.

Now, let me say that that's my agenda, and you embrace the agenda and you know that and I know that and we're going to have a wonderful time if I win this election. Even when we debate and disagree, we're going to have a good time, because you're going to know that every day I'm going to get up burning with the desire to improve education in America. Because that's what I care about.

But, one of the challenges that we're all going to have in this election, and this is what I want you to think about as I close, is to get over the enormous dimension of skepticism, cynicism, and disbelief that exists in this country. There are so many people out there who live in your school districts who basically don't think things can be better. Isn't that right? And we're going to be very vulnerable to candidates who play on their fears instead of their hopes, who try to puncture any agenda that really offers the prospect of change.

And let me tell you something. I've worked for a dozen years in my state. When we put in those new standards, we became the first state, for example, to require eighth graders to pass an exam and go on to high school, they said, "Boy, this'll balloon your dropout rate." Guess what? The dropout rate went down, and we got the highest graduation rate in the region. I know we can make a difference. I've seen the college-going rate go up by 35 percent. I've seen just by scratching and clawing, a poor state like ours, we're fifth in the country now in the ratio of computers to kids in the public schools. I have seen the enrollment in foreign languages and computer science triple, advanced mathematics triple, physics and chemistry go up. I know that change can occur.

And what I want to ask you to do, because I know how easy it is for teachers to get burnt out and beat down and ground up, and coming to these meetings, you just wonder what's going to happen to help me get through tomorrow. What's going to happen to help me feed my children? What's going to happen to help me educate my children? I know how easy it is for all of us to be so ground down and so defensive that we just look right here, just this far in front of our noses. And I want to ask you to leave this convention today with a commitment to go back home and talk to your friends and neighbors who aren't teachers about the possibility of change in America.

I don't care what these polls say today. What these polls mean is that people long for change. They ache to believe in America again. But you know what's going to happen. Down in Houston at that Republican convention, they're going to say, "You elect Bill Clinton and Al Gore—those two kids are crazy. They're going to tax all your income away. They're going to take your guns away. They're going to—they're going to stomp on traditional American values. Oh, I know they're from Tennessee and Arkansas, but they're just great fakers. They've been hiding their true feelings for twenty years, waiting for this moment when they could burst upon the American political scene and crush the traditional values under some left-wing radical scheme of theirs. They've just been hiding away."

You know that's what they're going to do in Houston, don't you? It'll be ridiculous, you know, they—it's kind of funny—they don't even know what to say. They've just got to say their same old deal; they're too liberal and too that and too the other thing. But, the American people, if they do not believe that things can be better, if they will not permit themselves to hope, then they will be vulnerable to the fear tactic.

I talked yesterday at the Southern Legislative Conference about this, and Mr. Bush said my health-care plan would have the compassion of the KGB and the competence of the House post office, and, you know, as a politician, I appreciate a good speech line, and that's a good one, but it's just full of bull.

But let me tell you, there are a lot of Americans who cannot imagine that we could have an affordable health-care system that covers everybody, but other countries do it, and I don't think we're dumber than everybody else in the world. I think we can do it.

Don't kid yourself. There are a lot of Americans who have never been in any inner-city school that works. They cannot imagine that poor children or

African-American children or Hispanic children and other minority children can really learn, can master the complexities of modern life, can go on to win Nobel Prizes, can lift this country up. They don't believe that, and I'm telling you, if you really want to do something to help the Clinton-Gore ticket prevail in November, you go home and tell people progress is possible. You go home, and you make sure you believe progress is possible, because, on election day, if the American people believe that we can do better, we will win.

That's what I want you to do.

And God bless you all.

A New Direction for the Twenty-first Century

Southern Legislative Conference
Miami Beach, Florida
August 12, 1992

This speech, ostensibly on Clinton's plans for reforming the nation's health-care situation, was delivered at Miami Beach's Fontainebleau Hilton Ballroom on the final day of the annual meeting of the Southern Legislative Conference, and it was certainly a topic of interest to the group, which comprises lawmakers and staff from fifteen southern states. The immediate audience for the speech consisted of more than fifteen hundred people, including some eight hundred southern state legislators, most of whom were Democrats.

Clinton devoted most of the speech to health-care issues, numbing some of the legislators with statistics while detailing his plan, then, near the end of the speech, he previewed the GOP campaign tactics in the fall campaign. Combining humor with appeals to regional pride, he anticipated Republican efforts to paint him as a liberal out of touch with mainstream American values. This facet of the speech was intended to inoculate his supporters against the expected attacks to come from the Republican National Convention in Houston during the following week, but it was also a part of the larger strategy to recapture the South's electoral votes in the November election. He brought the audience to its feet—and drew what sounded like a few rebel yells—when he told them not to be "suckered" any longer by attempts to divide the people by race, and said, "Let's show 'em there is a new South and we're a lot smarter than they think we are."

❖ ❖ ❖

Thank you. Thank you very much. Thank you for that wonderful reception, and thank you for giving me the chance to be here today. I want to thank my longtime friend John Miller for that great introduction, and our present speaker, John Lipton, and the president of our senate, Jerry Bookout, who have been my friends and supporters, and all the members of our Arkansas legislature who are here. Without them, it is absolutely certain that I would not be here, because it was our partnership that enabled us to do whatever has been done in our state over the last dozen years.

And a lesson I think we ought to send to Washington is that the time for placing blame has come to an end, and the time for assuming responsibility is at hand, and we need to work together instead of dividing our people.

I want to say to the others on this platform, Senator Hankle, and Representative Williams, and my good friends from Florida, your speaker, and Ron Silver, who worked so hard for me in the primary here, and Senator Gwyn Margoles, and all of the members of the Florida legislature here, my campaign for president really took off on December 16, after the Florida straw poll, and without the help of many members of the Florida legislature, I doubt very seriously that we would have prevailed on that occasion. So I like working with legislators, and I hope I get a chance in January to do another job on that.

In eighty-four days, the American people will choose leaders that will take us to the edge of the twenty-first century. We will choose between two very different philosophies, whether we should continue with four more years of trickle-down economics and a limited, but out-of-control view of the national government, or whether we ought to adopt a new direction of investing in our people and organizing our country in partnerships to help America compete and win.

But we also will choose between two very different ideas of leadership, ways of getting things done and approaching problems. In a way, many of the decisions we must make are those which go beyond the traditional labels that we normally judge politics by. They really go beyond Democrat and Republican, and left and right, and liberal and conservative.

After World War II, we began a new era; some of you were part of it. We had to come home and deal with the dismantling of a vast military apparatus, and restructure our economy here, and at the same time try to rebuild Europe and Japan in ways that helped us all.

After the Cold War, it is important that we rebuild America. For during this period of forty-odd years when we stood up for freedom and democracy, and when our ideas came to triumph around the world, all Americans could justly take pride in our bipartisan commitment to those values and those ideas and that victory.

But for nearly two decades, we have been in the process of losing our economic leadership. And over the last decade, we have been in deep trouble indeed. In 1980, we had the highest wages in the world, and now we're thirteenth. In the last ten years, according to our own census reports, well over half of the American people are working harder for less money, and paying more for health care, housing, education, and in taxes.

We have unbelievably quadrupled our national debt since 1980, but reduced our federal investment in economic growth in education and economic development, in the environment, in infrastructure. We have not kept up with other nations in those things which create wealth and jobs and growth, even though we've quadrupled the debt.

There are new strains on state government all across America, and all of us know we have been asked to do more with less, and most of us have tried to support that. As the federal government said, "Well, we're in trouble. We want you to take over more of the responsibility for economic development, for education, for environmental protection, and here's less money to do it with."

And, obviously, the greatest financial burden of all in recent years has been the continued federal mandate in the area of health care, without any health-care cost control. So every year, we are told by the national government, both the president and the Congress, to cover more services through Medicaid, or cover the Medicare co-pay of low-income people. We are told by the administration how much we have to pay providers. And we are expected to come up with our share, even though unlike them, we can't run deficits. Certainly, even those who can run deficits can't really do it for more than a year without having disastrous or painful consequences.

All of this has occurred in an atmosphere of declining economic growth, the lowest economic growth in the last three years since before World War II, since the Great Depression, the first time in American history in the last three years when industrial output has actually declined. As a result of that, you have a rising tide of poor people, not only unemployed poor people, but working people. In 1980, 12 percent of the work force was still in poverty. In 1990, 18 percent of our work force, almost one in five workers, was living below the poverty line while going to work every day.

This has obviously led to a huge increase in the claims against the programs that we run, which are jointly funded by the federal and state government—the AFDC program, welfare, the food-stamp program, the Medicaid program. Now, there's plenty blame to go around for all this, I suppose. But do you want to blame it on trickle-down economics or borrow-and-spend economics?

But the main thing that I think all of us are interested in today is, what are we going to do tomorrow? Our greatest presidents have taken responsibility for seeing and solving our nation's problems, not by themselves, of course, but by charting the course to a better future and asking the American people to join in. Our greatest presidents have felt our pain and shared our hopes and challenged each of us to make a personal commitment to make tomorrow better than today.

Last week our president, Mr. Bush, spoke of an important lesson in life that he and I, and I'm sure everyone in this room learned growing up. And I quote, "Take blame when things go wrong, and share the credit when things go right." He spoke of the importance of personal responsibility, a value I believe everyone of us in public service deeply shares.

President Truman was the embodiment of that personal responsibility. He had a sign on his desk that said, "The buck stops here."

President Eisenhower said if he were elected president, he would go to Korea. He didn't say everybody in there now has made a mess of it. He said, "Vote for me, and I will go to Korea."

President Kennedy took full responsibility for the fiasco in the Bay of Pigs, even though it was an operation which began under his predecessor.

President Theodore Roosevelt reminded us, in one of his greatest statements, that the credit should always go to the person in the arena, even those who failed, if they dare and fail gracefully.

President Roosevelt, who lifted this country from the chains of his own wheelchair in 1933, and for twelve years thereafter, once told us that, "The only thing we have to fear is fear itself."

One of the greatest tests, perhaps *the* greatest test, for the president who will be elected in eighty-four days is whether that person can live up to that heritage—whether we can assume responsibility, wade into the problems, bring people together. And if it doesn't work, take responsibility for the failure and go back and try again.

Some of our problems are unprecedented. Nobody has all the answers. But I know what we've been doing doesn't work. And I know for sure that the politics of blame never solved a single problem.

The other day the president's chief economic advisor, Mr. Darman, went up to the House Budget Committee. And he was asked, "Why are we having the worst economic performance since the Great Depression?" And his answer was, "Well, it's easy. There are four reasons. The banks aren't loaning enough money, the federal reserve didn't lower interest rates quick enough, Congress won't do what we want them to, and Saddam Hussein invaded Kuwait." Now I don't know what that had to do with it. Other people paid for that war, but, anyway, that's what he said.

So the chairman of the budget committee said, "Well, what about you? Is the administration responsible for this crisis?" Silence. He said, "How about any responsibility? Would you believe five percent?" No, he refused to take any responsibility, blaming everybody else. Can you imagine where this country would be today if Harry Truman's sign said, "The buck stops somewhere else"?

I think we ought to keep what is best about our system. The fundamental right of people to have access to a private system of medical care, with providers who work for themselves, and who do a good job delivering health care. But we obviously have to change the system. We have to begin with a system of finance. Only in America are there fifteen hundred different health-insurance companies writing health insurance, thousands of different policies being written, and that is overlaid on the blizzard of government rules and regulations, different ones, I might add, from Medicare and Medicaid.

What is the result of that? Only eighty-four cents of the private health-insurance dollar in America goes into health care; in Europe, where it's private health insurance, ninety-five cents. What's the difference in eighty-four and ninety-five cents? That's eleven cents on the dollar on a five-hundred-and-eighty-billion-dollar private health-insurance bill. You figure it. That's not peanuts, folks. That is a phenomenal amount of money.

How do you squeeze that out of the system? You have to do two things, at least. Number one, require insurance companies to do what they do now in Hawaii and a few other states, and that is to rate people on broad-based community ratings. Put people back into large pools, so that millions of people are not prevented from changing jobs because of a sick family member or a prior health condition.

And let insurance companies make money the way grocery stores do, a little bit of money on a lot of people. Because otherwise, you're going to have more and more and more of this dividing up the health-insurance market where the very ideal thing you can do is to insure a group of fifty twenty-five-year-old women who spend two hours a day at the gym, don't smoke, don't drink, don't eat hamburgers, going to live forever. If you do that, you're laughing, this is the world we talked about; I know it's funny but you laugh to keep from crying. If you do that, then only 60 percent of the money goes into health care, and 40 percent of the money goes into profits and paperwork. You've got to have broad-based ratings.

Second thing we have to do is to develop an all-payer system that would have a national requirement of a basic package of benefits that would have to be provided either by the government or by private insurers, that includes preventive and primary care. If you do that, you simplify the paperwork dramatically. Instead of having every doctor's office keep up with thousands of different permutations of coverages, you'd have a very simple system, much simpler.

Now let me explain to you how important this is. In my state, and I expect my state is low, I interviewed hundreds of doctors year before last. The average doctor in my state is spending more than 30 percent of their income on paperwork. In America, the average hospital is hiring clerical workers at four times the rate of nurses.

A recent study done between a hospital in Canada and a hospital, and I don't favor the Canadian system, by the way, I just want you to get a flavor for the paperwork, a hospital in Canada and a hospital in Boston, same size, same number of beds, same average case load, there were six people in the bookkeeping department in the Canadian hospital, and two hundred people in the bookkeeping department in the hospital in Boston. This is a big deal, and it is wrong for us to be pouring this kind of money into this kind of system. We've got to change it.

If we do this, we can also modernize the system. We'll eventually move to a time when all of us will be able to handle it, carry a little health card that on a chip will have our health-care information. We'll be able to computerize the systems much better and eliminate billions of dollars in billing fraud every year. And we'll be able to simplify and rationalize the system.

Next thing we need to do is to give people real incentives to go into large health-care groups, where they can choose their providers within a large group, but where they have the option to have managed care, and managed competition, and to pay up front for a year's worth of health care.

I talked to a doctor—in Las Vegas the other night when I was out there giving a speech—who's part of a health-care group with several hundred doctors in it, and their costs for their participants has gone up or down in a range of 2 percent for five years now. It can be done. We can manage the system better.

There are all kinds of other things we need to do to reduce medical liability costs: have alternative dispute resolution mechanisms, give doctors some accepted practice guidelines all across the country that will raise the presumption that they perform properly, if they follow those practice guidelines.

We need to look, as my senator, David Pryor, has done in the Senate, at why some drug costs go up to three times the rate of inflation in America and drugs made in America cost more in America than they do in other countries, because of the marketing practices here. We need to address that.

There are all kinds of other issues we need to deal with, but you've got to deal with these big issues first. The states will have a role in this in designing the details of the package state by state and helping to set up state spending ceilings that we try to achieve. But the structure has to be changed, and it has to be changed nationally.

And let me just mention one or two other things. We have got to set aside some of the government money to put more clinics for primary and preventive care in poor communities, in rural areas, and in inner cities.

Again, let me remind you that almost everybody in America gets health care. But the people that don't have access to it get it when it's too late and too expensive, when the cow's out of the barn, and we spend a fortune. We ration health care in America on the front end, not on the back end. We do a great job of spending a fortune on people in the last six months of life, and, you know, I'm not criticizing that. Most of that is part of our humanity. There may be things that ought to be discussed here, but most of that is part of our culture and our humanity. But don't kid yourself. We ration health care in America. We ration it on the front end by denying basic primary and preventive health care, and that is what is costing us so much money.

Two more points I want to make about this. We've got to change. A lot of us have responsibilities, too. We've got to change our own behavior, and that means we need really aggressive health-education programs in the work place and in the schools of this country, to teach people what is and what is not good and acceptable healthy behavior to keep us alive. And I'm not just talking about the things that are somewhat controversial, but are life and death, like parenting education and sex education and AIDS education, but also what you eat and what you don't, whether you exercise or not, how much you smoke, what you do that will either lift you up or drag you down.

We have got to take more responsibility for organizing our own lives and making this country healthy, so that we don't have to spend money that we can avoid spending. That's not the insurance companies' fault. That's not the doctors' fault. That's not the hospitals' fault. We're going to have to do that.

And the final thing I want to say is there is a problem in any national system, which is, obviously, what do you do? Do you impose a burden? If you don't have the government pay for everything through a tax system, but everybody has to be covered to avoid cost shifting, what do you do with small businesses that are already operating on a thin margin? And that's a tough question.

But I want to tell you, first of all, I do not favor starting a health-insurance reform with a big tax increase on small business or anybody else. I think we ought to go for the savings first, reorganize the system, take the money we're saving, and put it back into the health-care system in phasing universal coverage, phasing it in.

Secondly, keep in mind, a lot of people are going to save money out of this system. The people that are paying for health insurance now will have their costs go down in future years, making the American economy healthier and stronger.

The third thing I want to emphasize is that I think small businesses ought to be able to be part of a very big pool, and if the private market still doesn't work, they ought to be able to pay into a public program that has a ceiling on the percentage of their income that has to be allocated to health care. But don't kid yourself.

Every one of us, even if you run a small business, and you don't insure your employees, you're still paying for it. Look at the deficit every year. You and your children and your grandchildren are paying for it. Look at the unemployment rate in America. Look at our lost productivity. Look at our lost competitiveness. Every American is paying for the system we've got now. No one can escape this.

So I am very sensitive to the small-business burden, and we're going to have to work into this, but we must begin now to change. I am convinced that if we don't do this, we're never going to be able to restore our country's manufacturing health.

We've got almost eleven hundred dollars a car in health-care costs now. If you want to sell American automobiles overseas, if you want to take back more than 66 percent of the American market, if you want to spot the foreign-car competitors six to seven hundred dollars a car in health-care costs, that's what we're doing today.

If you want America's manufacturing base rebuilt, if you want this federal deficit brought down. The entitlements are killing us; it's Medicare and Medicaid and the explosion of poverty. Contrary to popular belief, its's not middle-class people getting Social Security benefits. The Social Security tax fund is seventy billion dollars in surplus. It's paying for a lot of the debt. The problem is health care costs, and the rising tide of poverty, and people in low-income areas claiming the programs that were set up for them. We've got to deal with this.

So if you want your country's economic health restored, if you want the tensions between labor and management reduced at a time when it's clear that productivity requires cooperation between labor and management, if you want a healthy citizenry, if you want a healthy government, if you want a government that works, we've got to take a dramatically different approach to the health-care crisis.

Let me say that if you want to be able to go back to a legislative session and think about how you can help education, how you can move people from poverty to work through welfare reform, how you can take care of some of the needs of the elderly in your state, how you can do that even in a good year without raising taxes, we've got to get the burden of exploding health-care costs off your back.

You know as well as I do what's been going on for the last ten years. We've been backing into universal coverage by requiring states, through Medicaid, to cover more and more services. We've been backing into the unfairness of shifting costs by requiring states to spend more and more money reimbursing providers. We've been backing into more and more tax increases by having the national government require the states to raise the taxes when they don't, even though they have to. And let's quit backing into this, and face it up front, and do something about it. And that's what I think we ought to do.

And let me ask you one other thing. Even if you are a Republican legislator, let me ask you this. We've seen the South come a long way in the last few years. We've tried to open ourselves up to the global economy. Any reasonable person would say that most of our states have done a better job of reconciling racial tensions and opening up opportunities than many nonsouthern states have, something I think most of us are pretty proud of.

And I know we've got a long way to go, and I know our region still has a higher percentage of poor folks than other regions of the country. I know we've got a lot of things to do. But we've made a lot of progress.

And I want to challenge you to go home and talk to your friends and neighbors. And make sure this next eighty-four days, an election gets fought out on the real problems of America's future, on our hopes and not our fears, on the new ideas we need to take us into the future.

You know as well as I do what's about to happen. The other side's going to go down there to Houston. They're going to tell you that Al Gore and I may have been born in Arkansas and Tennessee, but we're just a bunch of crazy wild-eyed liberals. They are going to tell you that they took us to New York City in a safe that no one saw us in and incubated us for twenty years, and we got crazy ideas and came home and hid them for twenty years, waiting for the opportunity to spring them on the rest of the country once we got in national power. That's what they're going to say.

They're going to say every speech I gave on the Fourth of July in northeast Arkansas was a deliberate attempt to conceal my radical impulses. And that we just can't wait to get into power in Washington, so we can take your guns away and trample family values and raise taxes on every poor, working person in America. I can hear it now, and so can you. And the reason you're laughing is you know I'm telling the truth.

I just want you to think about this, whatever your party, whatever your philosophy, whatever your background. You think about what it's like to go home every night after you've been in a legislative session and you've worked your heart out trying to solve a real problem that real people have that you represent. And you ask the people you represent not to throw their vote away on the kind of rhetoric that people have gotten those of us in the South to be a sucker for over the decades.

Let's show them that there is a New South and we're a lot smarter than they think we are. And whoever is going to get our votes this time will have to respond to our hopes for our children, to the problems we really confront every day, and will have to give us a way to win again by being one again. That's what's working for us today in all of our states. When we can be one again, when we can work together again, when we can bring out the best, when we can honestly sit down across the table and air our differences, when we can imagine how far we have come, many of you in this room from share-cropper's shacks, slums without sewage systems, when we can think about how far we have come, that's when we're at our best.

You go home, I don't ask you to agree with me on everything, and I'm not going to be right on everything, and I don't know everything we should do. But I know one thing: we never got anywhere, anywhere, anywhere in our part of the country by being sucker-punched to appeal to our traditional values. Let us vote on our traditional values, let us live by our traditional values, let us lift up the whole country by starting in the South and saying, "Give us a new direction for the twenty-first century. Give us a real solution to our problems." Let's bring out the best in America, and let's start it here.

Thank you very much.

Strategic Security in a Changing World

Los Angeles World Affairs Council
Los Angeles, California
August 13, 1992

Clinton delivered this major foreign-policy speech to an audience of twenty-two hundred at a luncheon meeting of the World Affairs Council at the Westin Bonaventure Hotel in Los Angeles. "The 42-minute speech, which started late and ran long, drew a mixed reaction from the large audience. Like many of Clinton's prepared addresses, it sounded more like a laundry list than a crisp, integrated vision. Clinton himself showed little of the populist passion of his stump speeches, and he delivered some passages almost in a monotone," said the *Boston Globe*. Nevertheless, Clinton did show several rhetorical flourishes in the speech, declaring, "From the Baltics to Beijing, from Sarajevo to South Africa, time after time this president has sided with the status quo against Democratic change, with familiar tyrants rather than those who would overthrow them, with the old geography of repression rather than a new map of freedom."

The address, which was interrupted several times by polite applause, was his third major speech on foreign affairs, having spoken at Georgetown University's School of Foreign Service the previous December and to the Foreign Policy Association in New York in April. This time he was speaking as the Democratic nominee, and his remarks were addressed not only to his immediate audience but also to the national press. "Clinton's speech showed again that he is a policy junkie," reported the *San Francisco Chronicle*. "The political reasoning behind this approach is to make the Arkansas governor look like something much more than a foreign-policy novice. Clinton's inexperience in this area is sure to be a prime target for Republican orators at next week's GOP convention."

Clinton moved to raise the issue first and engage the Bush campaign, saying that while he had agreed with the president on some issues, "I do not believe he has a vision of our role in this new era. In a world of change, security flows from initiative, not inertia." The

Washington Post called the speech Clinton's "most comprehensive and critical assessment of Bush's foreign policy record, which is thought to be the president's strong suit in the campaign" and said he "made clear that he is prepared to go toe-to-toe with Bush on the issue of world leadership."

❖ ❖ ❖

Thank you. Thank you very much. Thank you. Thank you very much.

First, let me ask, can you hear in the back? People sitting right next to each other saying yes and no. How about that? Now can you hear? Better?

This has been an interesting day. We were a little late because we were feeding all this speech material that I've worked so hard on into a teleprompter machine, only to find out it is incompatible with the teleprompter we had here. So, by the end of this speech, you won't know whether I can spell or not, but you'll sure be able to tell if I can read. Then we got here slightly embarrassed about being a little late, and we had to wait until the sound system was hooked up. So, I thought to myself, "I will be reading in silence to two thousand people today."

Notwithstanding that, let me say how very glad I am to be here and how appreciative I am for the opportunity to address you. I appreciate the introduction which Dick gave me. I always enjoy speaking to people who are concerned about world affairs. Ever since I left my native state for virtually the first time when I was eighteen to go off to the School of Foreign Service at Georgetown University, I have been profoundly concerned with the role of America in the world and the impact of events around the world on our nation and the happenings within other countries with which we ought to be concerned.

Before I get into my remarks today, I would like to recognize the presence of two people who, one by example and the other by example and friendship, have been important to me. The first is your former governor, Pat Brown, who is sitting up here and a person I admire very much. The second is my very good friend, a former deputy secretary of state and the person who ran the vice-presidential selection search for me, Mr. Warren Christopher. And, as far as I know, he's the only person in this audience who has read the speech, so if you don't like part of it, blame him.

Ladies and gentlemen, it is always a hazardous enterprise to discuss foreign policy in the midst of a presidential election. I met yesterday in Washington with Prime Minister Rabin of Israel, and I assured him that I did not want anything that occurred in this campaign or afterward to interrupt the commitment of the United States of America to the peace process in the Middle East and that I intended to support the continuity of that process for the next eighty-two days and, if victorious in this election, beyond. That is, I feel that way about our attempts now to present a united front in dealing with the crisis in Bosnia and in our attempts to stand firm in the face of Saddam Hussein's flouting of the United Nations cease-fire resolutions in Iraq.

Nonetheless, it is important that a candidate for president, especially in a time of great change, set forth his or her views and distinguish them from the views of the opponent, and that is what I will try to do here today.

We stand blessed as the inheritors of a new world. It is a world of hope and opportunity, made possible by a half century of bipartisan leadership and unstinting sacrifice by the American people and our allies and, above all, by the courage of the women and men who tore down the walls of repression and stood down the tanks of tyranny. Now the Iron Curtain has collapsed. The Cold War has melted under the irrepressible flame of freedom. It is a cause for rejoicing.

But this new world we have helped create places new demands on the kind of presidential leadership America needs. The new world remains a place of peril. While the Soviet Union is gone, a president must still be ready to defy and defeat those who threaten us. Whatever else we expect of our presidents, we still need a resolute leader who will wield America's might and marshall our global alliances to defend our nation's interests. Yet today there are new tests of leadership as well.

The first is to grasp how the world has changed.

The second test is to assert a vision of our role in this dynamic new world.

The third test is to summon all our strengths—our values, our economic power, when necessary our military might—in service of that vision.

I do not believe President Bush has met these new tests, despite his effectiveness in organizing the response to Iraq's aggression. Too often the administration has held on to old assumptions and policies, trying to prop up yesterday's status quo, failing to confront our new challenges.

I have agreed with President Bush on a number of foreign-policy issues. But I do not believe he has a vision of our role in this new era. In a world of change, security flows from initiative, not inertia.

Next week, the Republican Party will gather in Houston to nominate Mr. Bush and praise his record abroad. The question will be: Do they paint a partisan portrait of the past, or do they render a vision of the future Americans can build together?

In their campaign, the Republicans already have tried to claim success for

America's Cold War victory. And they suggest that in their second term they will bring to domestic policy the same energy and expertise they say marked foreign policy in their first term.

Their argument misreads both history and current events. The notion that the Republicans won the Cold War reminds me of the rooster who took credit for the dawn. The truth is, from Truman to Kennedy to Carter, Democratic as well as Republican presidents held firm against the expansion of communism; and from Richard Russell to Scoop Jackson to Sam Nunn, Democratic leaders in Congress helped build the finest defense forces in the history of the world.

But even more flawed is the Republican claim that, just as they changed the world in their first term, they will change America in their second. We must understand that foreign and domestic policy are two sides of the same coin. If we're not strong at home, we can't be strong abroad. If we can't compete in the global economy, we'll pay for it at home.

The same president who refused to make changes as American wages fell from first to thirteenth in the world was slow to recognize the changes in Eastern Europe and the former Soviet Union. The same administration that did nothing as ten million Americans lost their jobs due to tired, old economic policies also stood by as courageous Chinese students were attacked with tanks in Tiananmen Square.

I believe global change is inexorable and can work to our advantage or to our disadvantage, depending on what we do. No one understands the opportunities and hazards of change better than the people of California. Your commerce and culture stand as testaments to the benefits we derive from our engagement with Mexico, Japan, and the other nations of the Pacific. Your economy has been hurt by the lack of a national economic strategy, especially the lack of a plan to convert defense cuts into domestic economic investments.

Last December at Georgetown University and last April in New York, I outlined the role I see for America in this era of change. I marked the steps we must take to meet our new challenges: to reestablish America's economic leadership; foster the spread of democracy abroad; and revamp our Cold War military to meet our new security needs. Today I want to expand on what leadership in this new era requires, particularly in rethinking our security strategy and modernizing our defenses.

Leadership for a Strong Economy

In this new era, our first foreign priority and our first domestic priority are one and the same: reviving our economy. America must regain its economic strength to play our proper role as leader of the world. And we must have a president who attends to prosperity at home, if our people are to sustain their support for engagement abroad. The world needs a strong America, and American strength begins right here.

This has been the administration's most glaring foreign-policy failure. An anemic, debt-laden economy; the developed world's highest rates of crime and poverty; an archaic education system; decaying roads, ports, and cities: all these undermine our diplomacy, make it harder for us to secure favorable trade agreements, and compromise our ability to finance essential military actions. Mr. Bush's economic neglect has invited foreign pity; it is time for economic leadership that inspires foreign respect.

Mr. Bush does not understand: the currency of national strength in this new era will be denominated not only in ships, tanks, and planes, but also in diplomas, patents, and paychecks. My first foreign-policy priority will be to restore America's economic vitality. I have laid out a strategy to raise our peoples' skills, boost productivity, spur innovation and investment, and make us the world's strongest trading power. I will elevate economics in foreign policy; create an Economic Security Council, similar to the National Security Council; and change the state department's culture so that economics is no longer a poor cousin to old-school diplomacy.

In a Clinton-Gore administration, presidential leadership will mean mobilizing our country for the global economic competition that is the hallmark of this new age. It will mean securing commitments from American business and labor to take on new cooperative responsibilities. It will mean championing open world trade that benefits American workers as well as American businesses—from the roaring markets of the Pacific Rim to the resurgent economies of Mexico and Latin America. And it will mean swift responses and stiff penalties to those who abuse the rules of trade.

One way we will strengthen our economy is through leadership for environmentally sound growth. President Bush abdicated that leadership, before and during the Rio Earth Summit. Al Gore and I will reclaim it. Someone recently noted there are only two groups in the world who still don't understand that economic growth and a clean environment depend on each other: the Bush administration and the former leaders of Eastern European communism. The fact is, if we steer toward cleaner ways of doing business, we'll create new jobs and make our firms more competitive. That's why I've proposed a strategy to boost U.S. energy efficiency and to use market-based incentives to prevent pollution before it's created. It's also one reason I picked Al Gore to be my running mate. We will put the U.S. back at the forefront of global efforts to achieve sustainable development, and in the process, leave our children a better world.

Leadership to Promote Democracy

The second imperative of presidential leadership in this new era is to reinforce the powerful global movement toward democracy and market economies. Our strategic interests and moral values both are rooted in this goal. As we help democracy expand, we make ourselves and our allies safer. Democracies rarely go to war with each other or traffic in terrorism. They make more reliable partners in trade and diplomacy. Growing market economies expand individual opportunity and social tolerance.

Yet Mr. Bush has been oddly reluctant to commit America's prestige on the side of people inspired by American precepts and example. When democratic reformers sought to break up the Soviet empire, Mr. Bush snubbed Boris Yeltsin, sided with the crumbling Soviet center, and failed to lead the call for aid to Russia until he was shamed into it by Richard Nixon and others.

When fifty million Ukrainians sought emancipation from a dying communist empire, Mr. Bush withheld moral support, and instead—in Kiev itself—publicly chided Ukraine's voices of independence for seeking a "suicidal nationalism."

When China cracked down on pro-democracy demonstrators, exported advanced weapons to radical regimes, and suppressed Tibet, Mr. Bush failed to stand up for our values. Instead, he sent secret emissaries to China, signaling that we would do business as usual with those who murdered freedom in Tiananmen Square.

And when it was clear to all that Yugoslavia was inexorably breaking apart, Mr. Bush and his secretary of state gave short shrift to the yearnings of those seeking freedom in Slovenia, Croatia, and Bosnia, and ignored warning signs that Slobodan Milosevic was emerging as one of Europe's bloodiest tyrants.

From the Baltics to Beijing, from Sarajevo to South Africa, time after time, George Bush has sided with the status quo rather than democratic change, with familiar tyrants rather than those who would overthrow them, and with the old geography of repression rather than a new map of freedom.

This pattern was most glaring in Mr. Bush's treatment of Iraq prior to its invasion of Kuwait and his failure to support Saddam Hussein's opponents after the success of Desert Storm. I supported the president's effort to drive Saddam out of Kuwait, and I respect his conduct of the war itself. But now we are learning how his administration appeased Saddam in the months prior to August 1990. Even after the conclusion of the Iran-Iraq War, after Saddam had gassed his own Kurdish population, this administration coddled Iraq with economic credits, licensed militarily useful technology, and offered an obliging silence about its savage human-rights record. In keeping with the president's directive to woo Saddam, the state department even wrote an apology after the "Voice of America" dared to criticize Iraq's tyrannical regime.

My administration will stand up for democracy. We will provide international assistance to emerging, fragile democracies in the former Soviet Union and Eastern Europe and create a Democracy corps to help them develop free institutions. We will keep the pressure on South Africa until its day of true democracy has dawned. We will stand by Israel—our only democratic ally in the Middle East—and press for more accountable governance throughout the region. We will link China's trading privileges to its human-rights record and its conduct on trade and weapons sales. We will create a Radio Free Asia, like the successful Radio Free Europe, to carry news and hope to freedom-loving people in China and elsewhere. We will buttress democratic forces in Haiti, Peru, and throughout the Western hemisphere. And we will make the U.S. the catalyst for a collective stand against aggression, the action I have urged in response to Serbian aggression in Bosnia, one with which the Bush administration now agrees after first calling it reckless.

Leadership to Modernize America's Defenses

No test of presidential leadership is more important than the president's actions as commander in chief. The threats to America may change, but a president's willingness to confront them must be unwavering.

The world remains a dangerous place. Moreover, the dangers are now different and less apparent. So as we scale down our military, we must also keep up our guard. U.S. military strength will remain a force for stability—and, yes, justice—as the old global order continues to collapse and a new one emerges.

We can never forget this essential fact: power is the basis for successful diplomacy, and military power has always been fundamental to international relationships. So a president must provide the American people with a clear explanation of our enduring security interests and a new estimate of the threats we are likely to face in the post–Cold War era. Mr. Bush has failed to supply either. His lack of a clear strategy for national security is fueling isolationism on both the left and the right.

Today there are two wrong-headed, dangerous approaches to adjusting our defenses for the new era. One is the administration's. It mouths the rhetoric of strategic change, but simply shrinks the existing Cold War force structure. Continuation of this policy runs the risk of weakening the two elements that were key to our victory in the Gulf: superbly trained and motivated personnel and world-class weapons technology.

At the same time, there are those—some in my party—who see defense cuts largely as a piggy bank to fund their domestic wish lists, with our defense structures and missions as an afterthought, rather than a starting premise. This policy could also weaken our technological superiority and the quality and morale of our personnel.

Leadership demands more than either "Cold War Minus" or "Domestic Spending Plus." A president must identify the new threats to our security, define military missions to meet those threats, adapt our forces to carry out those missions, and back up those forces with the training, technology, and intelligence they need to win.

We must start with a fresh assessment of the new dangers that could threaten our interests and potentially require the use of force. These include the risk of new threats from the former Soviet republics, should democracy fail; the spread of weapons of mass destruction; historic tensions in various regions, especially the Korean peninsula and the Middle East, and the related risks of terrorist attacks; and the growing intensity of ethnic, fundamentalist, and separatist violence, as in Yugoslavia and elsewhere, that can spill across borders.

The mission of containing an expansionist Soviet Union has disappeared. But enduring missions remain: to maintain nuclear deterrence even as we reduce our nuclear arsenals; to reassure our friends and democratic allies and discourage potential adversaries; to pursue our interests when possible through strengthened institutions of collective security; to preserve freedom on the high seas and protect our global economic interests; and to provide the superior technology and forces that are the ultimate guarantee of liberty.

House Armed Services chair Les Aspin is right: The administration's "base force" plan leaves us with a military that does not fit our strategy and cannot do what we ask. It is burdened with redundancy. Key parts lack flexibility and mobility. Just as you don't shoot gnats with a howitzer, we can't always respond rapidly and flexibly to far-flung regional conflicts with forces designed for warfare in Europe. In other words, we must understand the new world's threats, not merely to decide how much force we need, but to design the right forces.

To lead and build effective coalitions we must also have the ability to operate on our own if necessary. We need to base a larger fraction of our forces in the U.S. and maintain a modern and well-equipped navy and Marine Corps, so we can project power wherever we need.

Our new military must be more mobile, because the new world will not simply be one of fixed flash points. We need the additional sealift that the Bush administration refused for so long to build. We also need the capabilities of the C-17 airlifter, which can fly long distances and then land on short fields close to the front.

Our new military must be more agile, because, with the end of the nuclear standoff, the new battlefields will likely be dominated by maneuver, speed, and outthinking the enemy. That is why, for example, I support a technology the Bush administration has tried to cancel—the V-22, the only aircraft capable of certain special operations, including the rescue of Americans held deep in hostile territory. And as House Intelligence chair Dave McCurdy has said, we must have superior intelligence, to know where to apply force with best effect.

Our new military must be more precise and able to reduce casualties, because we may need to operate among civilian populations, and because the credibility of our threats to use force will often depend on our ability to limit the loss of life. We must upgrade the smart weapons that were so essential during Desert Storm and develop new systems that can help reduce American and civilian casualties.

Our new military must be more flexible to operate with diverse partners, because in the new world coalition operations will often be important for political legitimacy. New friends might be armed with former Warsaw Pact equipment, and new enemies armed with Western weapons. That is why we must find new ways to protect American and allied troops against the mistaken use of our own and allied weapons.

Our new military must be more ready, because the new world will be unpredictable. We must be ready in the future to reconstitute our forces if major new contingencies arise. And our new military must have deep roots in America, which is why it should make increased use of Guard and Reserve forces in regional contingencies, so that our use of force will be considered with utmost seriousness, maintained affordably, and supported broadly at home.

In all, by shifting from a force designed to win the Cold War to one better equipped to respond rapidly to regional flare-ups, the Clinton-Gore defense budget brings savings of about sixty billion dollars over the current Bush plan, through 1997, close to the numbers of Senator Nunn and Representative Aspin.

And our efforts must go further. I agree with Senator Sam Nunn that it is time to take a fresh look at the basic organization of our armed forces. We have four separate air forces—one each for the marines, army, navy, and air force. Both the army and marines have light infantry divisions. The navy and air force have separately developed but similar fighter aircraft and tactical missiles. We have at least three and in some cases four separate medical corps: chaplain corps, dental corps, legal corps, and nursing corps. Each service also has its own administrative, training, and logistics facilities.

While respecting each service's unique capabilities, we can reduce redundancies, save billions of dollars, and get better teamwork. In 1948, Secretary of Defense Forrestal convened a meeting of the military service chiefs in Key West to allocate responsibilities among the four services. It failed. As president, I will order the Pentagon to convene a similar meeting to hammer out a new understanding about consolidating and coordinating military roles and missions in the 1990s and beyond.

My administration will make security and savings compatible. We will reduce our forces, but maintain a credible presence in Europe and Asia, and make reductions in consultation with our allies. We will stand up for our interests, but we will share burdens, where possible, through multilateral efforts to secure the peace, such as NATO and a new, voluntary U.N. rapid deployment force. In Bosnia, Somalia, Cambodia, and other torn areas of the world, multilateral action holds promise as never before, and the U.N. deserves full and appropriate contributions from all the major powers. It is time for our friends to bear more of the burden.

Our new security strategy also will ensure our defense industry can supply the weapons and technologies America may need in the future. This administration lacks any such strategic sense. It is letting major production lines go cold, for everything from tanks to planes to submarines, often ignoring the capacities they represent.

We cannot keep every production line and military lab open. But we will define the core skills and industries for America's security. We will eliminate needless military specifications that make defense production so unique, separate, and expensive. We will pursue new technologies with both civilian and defense uses. And we will also pursue a strong upgrade program to keep current lines operating and start limited production of next-generation equipment.

We must not forget the American heroes of the Cold War whose lives will be turned upside down as our forces shrink. Mr. Bush has no serious plan to help our defense workers and military personnel to make the transition to a civilian economy. I do. For example, I support incentives for military personnel to earn military retirement by taking jobs as teachers and police. In my administration, we'll also help retrain defense technicians for work in critical civilian fields such as bio-technology, renewable energy, and environmental cleanup. The Pentagon stands as America's best youth training program, our most potent research center and the most fully integrated institution in

American life. It's time to put those assets to work at home. Senator Nunn has proposed work for military forces and the National Guard in solving the problems of infrastructure, education, and rural health—offering possibilities to serve as role models here at home, consistent with fulfilling their primary military mission.

Finally, we cannot make America more secure unless we act against a host of new threats that don't respect national borders, such as terrorism, drug trafficking, and global environmental degradation. As Al Gore has so compellingly argued, the damage we do to the earth can be more than a threat to our health and resources; it can also aggravate international tensions and raise the chance of war itself.

One of the most dangerous new threats is the spread of military technology, especially weapons of mass destruction. We can't afford to wait until a host of Third World nations acquires full arsenals of First World weapons. We all saw the enormity of that threat as Scud missiles arced across the night skies of Israel and Saudi Arabia. We need to clamp down on countries and companies that sell proscribed technologies, punish violators, and work urgently with all countries for tough, enforceable, nonproliferation agreements. We need better intelligence to identify at an earlier stage foreign nuclear, chemical, and biological weapons programs. We need to give informational nuclear inspectors the authority and means to make spot inspections. And a Clinton-Gore administration will not permit American firms again to sell key technologies to outlaw states like Iraq.

The ultimate test of presidential leadership, of course, is not defense budgets or battle plans. It is the judgment a president exercises in those perilous moments when countries are invaded, our friends are threatened, Americans are held hostage, and our nation's interests are on the line. When the American people choose a president, they want someone they can trust to act when those moments arise. Every president in the last half-century has had to confront the fateful decision to send Americans into combat. I do not relish this prospect, but neither do I flinch from it. I know we must have the resolve constantly to deter, sometimes to fight, always to win. That is why Al Gore and I supported the decision to use force to get Saddam Hussein out of Kuwait. And it is why we stand united with President Bush in sending this message to Saddam as he flouts the U.N.'s resolutions: toe the line or face the music.

Conclusion

Whatever the threat or opportunity, national security is and must remain a bipartisan task. As a nation, we have many opinions, but only one foreign policy.

Yet presidential elections are about choices. And one of the choices the American people must make this year is about the kind of presidential leadership we want in a fundamentally new era. In this election, President Bush will seek to establish his leadership by emphasizing the time he has spent, the calls he has placed, and the trips he has taken in the conduct of foreign policy. But the measure of leadership in the new era is not the conversations held or the miles traveled. It is the new realities recognized, the crises averted, the opportunities seized. I challenge him to set his vision of our nation's purpose in a dramatically new era against the one I am presenting in this campaign. For in the final analysis, I believe there is only one presidential candidate in this election ready to think anew as the world is new.

Today's leadership is rudderless, reactive, and erratic. It is time for leadership that is strategic, vigorous, and grounded in America's democratic values.

In 1960 John F. Kennedy told America that there was "a new world to be won." Today there is again. My vision is of a world united in peaceful commerce; a world in which nations compete more in economic and less in military terms; a world of dynamic market-generated growth that narrows the gap between rich and poor; a world increasingly engaged in democracy, tolerant of diversity, and respectful of human rights; a world united against the common enemies of mankind: war, poverty, ignorance, disease, and environmental destruction; a world we can pass on to our children and theirs with the knowledge that we rose to the new responsibilities of this new world and this new age.

I am running for president because I believe that a strong America—strong in arms, strong in values, strong in wealth, strong in will—remains the world's best hope for turning that vision into a reality.

Thank you.

We Have to Change the Rules of the Game

National Association of Police Officers Press Conference
Pontiac, Michigan
August 20, 1992

Clinton held a press conference and delivered these remarks to a small crowd of public officials and law enforcement officers on the tarmac of the Oakland-Pontiac Airport at 2:45 P.M. The scene presented a sharp visual contrast to the images and speeches from Houston during this same week, where the Democrats were being portrayed as liberal enemies of traditional American values. Declining to allow the GOP convention coverage to go uncontested and with a crowd of police officers in blue and brown uniforms crowded behind him providing a strategic media opportunity, Clinton was introduced by Michigan's law-and-order attorney general, Frank Kelley.

Then, Robert Scully, a veteran Detroit police officer and president of the one-hundred-and-thirty-five-thousand-member National Association of Police Officers that had twice endorsed Ronald Reagan, announced the group's endorsement of the Clinton-Gore ticket, saying, "In the last few days, the folks down in Houston put out an all-points bulletin for a pair of lunatics who they say are going to ruin our country. Well, let me tell you something: We have thought long and hard about Bill Clinton and Al Gore, and we just don't see the resemblance. It's a frame-up, and a bad one at that." Citing specific reasons for the endorsement, he added, "George Bush's promises haven't stopped any murders, but getting handguns out of the hands of criminals will."

Clinton then delivered this speech, outlining his perception of the problems, offering his proposals for what the federal government might do to reduce crime in the nation, and contrasting his positions with those of the Bush administration.

❖ ❖ ❖

Thank you. Thank you very much. Thank you.

I want to thank my long-time friend and colleague, Frank Kelley, for being here today and for being an inspiration to so many of us who have served as attorney general throughout this country. I want to thank Robert Scully and NAPO and all these fine police men and women who are here with me today to announce their support. I want to thank all of you for coming and ask you to wait after my remarks. I'd like to come out and shake hands with you after I see the police officers first.

I want to talk a little about the problem of crime and law enforcement today from the perspective of someone who has actually had to work in this area with grassroots people and practical problems, someone who's done a lot of things right and made a few mistakes and entered nearly two decades of effort to try to make streets safer and families more secure from the problem of crime in our country.

At the outset, I guess I ought to say that this is an issue, like so many others, where this administration says one thing and does another. They're down there in Houston talking about family values, and yet their number-one priority in the first two days of the convention was to attack my wife and my family. Nearly as I could tell, it didn't do 'em much good, and one reason is that for two decades, she's gotten up every day and tried to do something to strengthen the lives of children and family in this country, which is something I can't say for our opponents.

They talk tough on crime. And I understand that. I remember that 1988 campaign and the Willie Horton issue. And I understand how families are frightened and how governments make mistakes and people get hurt as a result in the criminal-justice area. I think it is important to be tough on crime, but it isn't enough. I have supported capital punishment in my state. People have been executed under my tenure, including people who murdered police officers in the line of duty. But I can tell you that the most important thing we can do to reduce the crime rate in America, besides improving the economy, is to change the environment in which law-enforcement people work, in which citizens live, in which we deal with people who break the law.

We have to change the rules of the game.

We have the highest percentage of people in jail of any nation in the world. We've fallen—in twelve years, we've fallen from first to thirteenth in wages, but we're still number one in the percentage of our people behind bars. We have more young people getting in trouble and committing violent crimes than any other nation. We have to try to find things that will change the environment. Not all of them are law-enforcement issues, but a lot are.

And I have found that one of the most important things you can do is to involve citizens in innovations, to try to get people involved in taking control of their own lives and keeping themselves safe and in making sure the system works. One of the things that I've been involved in for nearly a decade is the Victims' Rights Movement in America. And the National Association of Victims' Rights gave me a national award because I worked hard to bring victims back into the criminal-justice process, to let them be a part of the parole process, the sentencing process, the whole trial process.

Here are some of the things that I think will change the rules of the game. Number one, put more police officers on the street. Thirty years ago there were three police officers for every violent crime. Today there are three crimes for every police officer. You don't have to be a mathematical genius to figure out that more and more police officers are spending more and more of their time in cars going around trying to catch criminals, instead of walking the streets, working with their neighbors and friends, trying to prevent crime from happening in the first place, because they've been overwhelmed by numbers and resources. And we've got to redress the balance.

In this plan that Al Gore and I have offered to put the American people first, we offer a concrete and compelling way to provide one hundred thousand more police officers to our cities and counties over the next three or four years, from two sources: One, from people who will be mustered out of the military service as a result of the end of the Cold War. We think we should offer them proper certification to qualify as police officers and let them go in and work in law-enforcement agencies and earn military retirement at the same time as an incentive to help support law enforcement.

Number two, we want to offer any American the opportunity to get a college education, and then give anybody who borrows the money the opportunity to pay it back with service to our nation, including two years of service for a four-year college loan as a police officer in the streets of our cities, adding to the strength of our police forces throughout the country. Just think of it. If every community in America had enough police officers to have a genuine community policing system, where the same people worked the same blocks with their neighbors to keep crime from happening, to identify strangers, to work with families, we would be a safer country.

I know it works. In New York City this year, after an extensive effort to implement community policing, they had the first recorded drop in the crime rate in thirty-six years. In Houston, Texas, in one year, after the mayor hired six hundred and fifty-five new police officers, they had a 15 percent drop in the crime rate, not just because they were catching more criminals and processing cases more quickly, but because they actually prevented crimes from occurring in the first place. That's one of the reasons you ought to vote for the Clinton-Gore ticket—one hundred thousand more police officers on the street.

The second thing we have to recognize is that we need to keep people who are genuinely dangerous behind bars for appropriate lengths of time. And the only way to do that at an affordable price is to stop putting people in jail who don't represent a clear and present danger to the public safety and, instead, have first-time, nonviolent offenders, especially young people, working in community-based boot camps where they can get military discipline, education, drug treatment, and do community-service work.

Today, because of prison overcrowding, what normally happens to somebody when they commit a first offense is that nothing happens. They're put out with some poor, overworked probation officer and never given any supervision. And then the second or third time they wind up going to the penitentiary, where they learn to be first-class criminals at great expense to you. We need community-based punishment in this country, and our budget contains some incentive grants to help to set up boot camps all across the nation. Our boot camps in Arkansas show a repeater rate of only 13 percent—way below the average repeater rate of people who are sent to the penitentiary and paroled.

The third thing I think we should do is to pass the Brady Bill. And let me tell you, I know Michigan is a state with a lot of hunters and fishermen and women who love the out of doors and love the sporting life. And I can tell you, I come from a state where more than half of the adults have a hunting or a fishing license or both. It isn't easy to do or say anything that the National Rifle Association disagrees with. And I have worked with them on occasion and would welcome the opportunity to do it again. But we are crazy in this country for selling handguns to people who are underage, who have criminal records, who have mental history records, just because we don't have the discipline to wait long enough to check out their background. There is no reason for that.

There is no magic in a seven-day waiting period. If we had all the records in the country computerized and interconnected, we could have virtually no waiting period. But until we do, we have the obligation to check the backgrounds of people who are going to be carrying guns on our streets and threatening the lives and security not only of our citizens but of our police officers.

These are three things that I think we should do. There are lots of other ideas that I'll be developing at greater length during the course of the campaign, including ways to better go after big-time drug dealers through checking cash transactions and monitoring bank transactions and finding ways to deal with the finances of the drug trade, which is one of the things that you have to do if you really want to get the big operators instead of the small ones.

But let's begin where people live—on the streets. Let's begin with the Brady Bill. Let's begin with community-based boot camps. Let's begin with a hundred thousand more police officers on the street. Those are the kinds of new ideas which will help us to be a safer and stronger country and which will really promote family values.

Thank you, and God bless you all.

An Economic Strategy for America

Economic Club of Detroit
Detroit, Michigan
August 21, 1992

Outlining his detailed economic plan in a major policy speech to some two thousand business people at a luncheon meeting of the Detroit Economic Club, Clinton refined and consolidated the proposals he had developed during the ten months of his campaign. The candidate and his aides originally planned to make the speech and its focus on his economic proposals the centerpiece of their first day of the new campaign following the GOP convention, and the campaign organization did print and widely distribute glossy booklets of the speech.

In addition, Clinton used this speech, which had been billed as a major address on the economy, to mount a new phase of his campaign, to move from high-toned policy to hard-edged politics, and to recapture the public's attention from the Republican National Convention earlier in the week. Having been attacked harshly and seeing the Bush bump in the polls, Clinton revised the long-planned speech and raised the stakes by lamenting the betrayal of the nation. "Our leaders and their old ideas have failed us," he said. "We've heard it all before, seen it all before, tried it all before. It's 'read my lips' all over again, except this time, we can read the record."

❖ ❖ ❖

Thank you very much, Governor Blanchard and distinguished members and guests of the Economic Club of Detroit. I really appreciate that introduction Jim gave me. After the going over I got last night, I need it. But I'm always a little skeptical of those introductions where people talk about being born in a log cabin they built themselves. Most of that stuff was way overrated, and those of us who experienced it were glad to escape it.

I am delighted to be here today. I had looked forward to coming here for a long time. And I wanted to talk with you about my economic plans for the future. But, of course, now I also have to talk a little bit about what was said last night by my opponent in this election.

I want to talk to you about what's really at stake in this election: our nation's economic future and whether we can chart a new course in the world economy with an economic strategy that will create jobs and raise incomes.

We have to make a choice to create a high-growth, smart-work, high-wage economy or whether to continue to drift into a low-growth, hard-work, low-wage future.

That is the real issue. As the rabbi said, the test of presidential character is whether we use the power of this office to help the American people realize their potential.

The test of family values is not whether Al Gore and I love our wives and our children as much as George Bush and Dan Quayle do, but whether we get up every day worrying about your children and your future.

Today as we gather here in the city which was once the manufacturing capital of the world, our economy is struggling and the American dream is in trouble. I come here to tell you forthrightly that I believe that manufacturing is an important part of America's future, that the auto and truck and high-tech industries of Michigan are an important part of a national manufacturing and economic strategy that we must have, and that I'm here to commit to work, to strengthen our ability to grow and prosper.

Ten years ago, our nation had the highest wages in the world. Now we're thirteenth and falling. Last year Germany and Japan had productivity growth rates that were three and four times ours because they educate their people better, they invest more in their future, and they organize their economies for global competition while we don't.

Here at home, people who have jobs are working harder for lower pay. The United States census report documents that two-thirds of the American working people are making lower wages today for longer work weeks than they had ten years ago.

People who don't have jobs are looking harder and harder to find fewer jobs. Middle-class people are paying more for health care, housing, education, and in taxes, and at the same time, poverty is exploding.

There has been a stunning 50 percent increase in the percentage of our work force, people who get up and go to work every day, who are in poverty. Ten percent of our country is on food stamps. Welfare and Medicaid rolls are growing at record rates. Just last week we had the highest application increase for unemployment benefits in over a decade. And in spite of low interest rates, housing starts have dropped off.

Our leaders and their old ideas have failed us. In the last twelve years they have quadrupled the national debt and reduced our public investment in the future. For too long, the politicians in Washington have forgotten the people who elected them, and nobody seems to be looking out for the country and for the people who've made it great.

We desperately need a president who will take responsibility for getting this country moving again, provide the leadership to pull us all together, and challenge this nation to compete in the world and win again; a president who will leave behind the failed Republican experiment and trickle-down economics on the one hand, but will not embrace the old Democratic theory of tax-and-spend and regulate on the other.

We have to move in a radically different direction. The old economic ideas of the last two decades did not produce growth, did not create upward mobility, and most important, didn't prepare millions and millions and millions of our people to compete and win in this global economy.

And yet time and again in recent years what have our leaders told us in the most critical moments of need? Twelve years ago here in this city we heard a Republican candidate for president promise us he would cut taxes, raise defense spending, and balance the budget all at the same time. He won and brought us a decade where our country was left mired in debt, our economy declined, and inequality decreased.

The ten largest deficits in the history of the United States occurred during the last two presidents. Four years ago, we heard a candidate for president promise us in these four years fifteen million jobs, a balanced budget, never to raise taxes, no matter what. He promised an environmental presidency, an education presidency, and a kinder, gentler country. He won—and since then, we've have the slowest years of growth in fifty years—the slowest income growth, the slowest job growth in fifty years; the largest budget deficits in history; the highest middle-class tax burden; and the first decline in industrial production in the history of the United States.

Now we can see that those promises were hollow and betrayed us.

Last night, we heard that same candidate, desperate for reelection, promise another short-term capital-gains cut for the wealthy—the fool's goal of an across-the-board tax cut in the face of a four-hundred-billion-dollar deficit, and a balanced budget amendment with no serious specific proposals to balance the budget.

These promises, too, are false; and they, too, will betray us if we follow them.

In the words of the man who started all this, "There they go again."

We've heard it all before, seen it all before, tried it all before. It's "read my lips" all over again, except this time, we can read the record.

Mr. Bush said not long ago that he would do whatever it takes to get reelected. In his *USA Today* interview, he was asked why he wanted to be president, and he said, "Because I want it." Well, last night he proved that he wanted it and that he will keep his promise to do whatever it takes to get elected.

No wonder Americans hate politics when, year in and year out, they hear politicians make promises that won't come true because they don't even mean them—campaign fantasies that win elections but don't get nations moving again.

Last night proved something else: George Bush is a lot more interested in beating me than in helping you.

He couldn't say anything about his economic record, so he just says anything to stay in power. Three years and seven months into the presidency, he still has no agenda, no vision, no strategy—nothing to say about creating jobs in America. And in the last four years since he gave an acceptance speech without a plan, but full of promises and gimmicks, we've lost a million manufacturing jobs, wages have fallen further behind our major competitors, and just this week, as I said, a record number of Americans filed for unemployment.

Three times as many Americans have filed for bankruptcy as have gotten new jobs since the Bush administration began.

Again, last night there was no plan to create jobs or raise incomes—just more cynical read-my-lips promises.

For the first time in American history, more people are working in government than in manufacturing, since this administration took place. Now we have more government bureaucrats the president deplores than the factory workers he ignores.

Across the country people are eager for real answers about how we can create new jobs and save existing jobs, but the promises Mr. Bush made last night are intended to save one job: his.

In fact, the only new idea in his speech last night was to let people check a box on their IRS form to contribute a portion of their taxes to pay for the last twelve years of deficit or for someone else's capital-gains cut.

The president said last night this election is about trust. You bet it is. Four years ago, he said "read my lips." And then signed the second-biggest tax increase in history.

Last night he said some things about my record that he knew when he said them were not true. Read the *Wall Street Journal*. Mr. Bush says I proposed the largest tax increase in history. The *Journal* told the truth; it's one-third the size of the one he already signed.

Mr. Bush says I want to tax everybody with a job. The *Journal* told the truth. The richest 2 percent of Americans would be asked to pay their fair share, because their tax burdens went down in the 1980s. And there would be some modest tax relief to middle-class Americans who are overburdened, especially those raising their children.

Mr. Bush says I raised taxes in Arkansas one hundred and twenty-eight times in twelve years, and he just raised them once. The *Journal* told the truth when it said that attack is inaccurate. By Mr. Bush's own standard, he's raised taxes seventy-eight times in three years, and Arkansas still has the second-lowest state and local tax burden in the United States of America.

How can you trust someone who's a Republican and won't even honor what the *Wall Street Journal* says is the truth?

He says my program is bad for the economy, but in Arkansas, we have created manufacturing jobs at ten times the national average. And the average income has increased at twice the national rate since 1984.

In the last year according to the Bureau of Labor Statistics, we have led the nation in job growth. He talks about deficit reduction, but his own budget proposals in the last four budgets would actually have increased the deficit by one billion dollars over its present level, according to a study by the House Appropriations Committee.

Well, I balanced eleven budgets in a row and still kept the second-lowest tax burden in America. I know you have to make tough decisions. I've had to cut spending twice since I've been running for president.

He talks about education. But in Arkansas, we raised graduation rates from thirty-fifth to eighteenth in the country, the highest in the South, raised the college graduation rate from dead last to the national average, and ranked fifth in the nation now in the percentage of our children with access to computers in schools.

I am a Democrat who believes in entrepreneurship and encouraging investment, who understands and believes in market economics, who believes in individual choice and hates bureaucracy. We have a growth rate in manufacturing jobs that we're proud of. We have a tax burden that we're proud of. We also rank third in the nation in the percentage of our tax that we devote to education. We moved seventeen thousand people from welfare to work; we've given citizens more choices, in the public schools their children attend and in the long-term-care facilities their parents have available to them.

We started the state government's first, state government-wide quality management program to reduce bureaucracy and improve services. On the question of trust, I ask you to remember that notwithstanding what was said last night, and what has been clearly contradicted by the truth, one candidate for president was governor of one of the poorest states in the country and helped to move it forward.

The other candidate stayed with trickle-down economics, while American problems worsened. This election is about trust, and I hope you will look and see who can be trusted.

Last night the president took credit for every victory which has occurred around the world since he's been president and refused to take responsibility for any problem which has developed here at home since he became president.

I agree with him about one thing, the choice in this election is clear. For twenty years, going across administrations we have been losing ground in the productivity race in the world economy, but for the last twelve we have been in the grip of a failed economic theory.

This election is about whether we'll do what it takes to compete and win in the global economy, whether we will rebuild America and invest in our people, whether we'll build a high-skilled, high-wage, high-growth economy that offers opportunity and hope to all of our people. We know what works, investing in people, challenging the private sector to organize in new ways to increase productivity, by putting business and labor, education and government on the same side, and making an intense commitment to be competitive in the global economy.

I have issued a plan based on these fundamental principles. It's called putting people first. And it's been endorsed by six Nobel Prize–winning economists. It will create millions of jobs and cut the deficit by more than 50 percent in four years.

In degree and scope I believe it goes beyond what any presidential candidate has ever offered during an election season. It goes far beyond the little this president has done and far beyond the little he offered last night.

Not everyone in this room and certainly not everyone in our country could agree with everything that I say.

But my philosophy starts with the values that built America for all of us, providing opportunity, taking responsibility, rewarding work, encouraging entrepreneurship, investing in people and products, not paper and perks.

I reject brain-dead politics in both parties in Washington. The wrong-headed Republican notion that prosperity will trickle down if we just make the rich even richer, and get the government out of the way, and the old Democratic orthodoxy that there is a program for every problem and that we can tax and spend our way to prosperity.

Instead, I offer a new choice based on old values, opportunity, individual responsibility, faith in family, and hard work. I don't believe in big government, but I do believe in an effective government that promotes jobs and growth and gives people more choices and better services and inspires more personal responsibility.

I believe people on welfare ought to go to work, and I've been doing something about it in our state, where we've moved seventeen thousand people from welfare to work, and I have a plan to do even better, to end welfare as we know it and make it a second chance, not a way of life.

Mr. Bush didn't mention this in his acceptance speech last night, even though caseloads on welfare nationwide have grown five times faster in the last three and a half years than they did under Jimmy Carter or Ronald Reagan.

I believe in the toughest possible child-support enforcement.

I want a national system of national child-support enforcement, because governments don't raise children; people do. And I think—

I do believe that individuals should take responsibility for their own actions and that includes the president of the United States.

Of all the whoppers I heard last night, the biggest one wasn't even about me. It came at the end when Mr. Bush compared himself to Harry Truman.

Harry Truman had a sign on his desk in the Oval Office that said, "The buck stops here." If Mr. Bush had a similar sign on his desk, it would say, "Don't blame me, I'm just the president; the buck stops somewhere else."

The funny thing is, I've gone further than Mr. Bush in spelling out what I would do to change Congress, even though he's spent almost all his time blaming Congress. Some time ago I called for a 25 percent cut in aggregate congressional and White House staffs, an end to perks and privileges and pay raises while the pay of American workers is going down; a line-item veto of the sort that's helped me to balance twelve budgets in a row; a limiting of the influence of PACs, cutting spending in congressional campaigns, opening the airwaves to honest debate so incumbents don't have an automatic ticket to reelection.

But it will not matter who is sent to Congress if we don't put in a leader in the White House who will take responsibility for fashioning the direction this country must take.

More than any other Democrat in this election cycle, I have tried to be honest in my criticisms of Congress as an institution, even when it affected members of my party. But let's be honest about the present logjam. Congress passed an economic-growth package, fashioned largely by a pro-business Democrat, Senator Lloyd Bentsen from Texas, that included strong incentives for new investment in plant and equipment, and revitalizing the commercial real estate industry, getting small businesses off the ground, and Mr. Bush vetoed the package even though it contained a lot of things he had asked for, for one simple reason: It asked the wealthiest Americans to pay their fair share, raising maximum rates in the upper 2 percent to 35 percent, while giving modest relief to the middle class. And that was the ground on which it was vetoed, not because it didn't have incentives to get this economy going again.

We have got to have a president who will take responsibility for moving the economy, for putting Americans back to work. That's why I've offered a national economic strategy to put people to work so that we can have an expanding economy of high-wage jobs here in our country.

At the core of my plan there are four principles. First, we don't need more trickle-down economics; instead, we need more incentives for productive, job-creating investment. Mr. Bush's economic priority, the top one, is just what it's always been: an across-the-board cut in short-term capital gains, a tax cut that gives a better benefit to millionaires, about one hundred thousand dollars, but gives folks earning fifty thousand dollars a year or less an average of thirty dollars.

More importantly, it's a tax cut not targeted to long-term investment and activities that actually create jobs and emphasize new technologies. It doesn't distinguish between building a business and buying a race horse. It's just like the past twelve years of windfall without economic growth for most Americans.

Please understand me, I want to create more millionaires. But I want to do it the old-fashioned way: by investing in America and by having people reap a reward in return for their investment in American jobs and American goods and American services.

That's why I recommended that we go beyond what the Congress did last time and pass not a temporary, but a permanent investment tax credit to encourage continuous reinvestment in new plant and productive equipment here at home so that we can always be competitive in the global economy.

I also propose a 50 percent tax break for those who take risks in making five-year long-term investments in new business enterprises. A permanent research and development tax credit to reward companies which invest in groundbreaking technologies, from high-definition TV to high-speed computing.

I don't think we should subsidize the export of American jobs with tax breaks. And I favor getting rid of tax breaks for companies that shut down their plants here and move them overseas.

Again, I am not opposed to investment by American companies in other countries. I have sought the investment of foreign companies in my state. But I have also examined the tax codes of our competitors. And they don't subsidize foreign investment, they subsidize domestic investment. We do the reverse, and we should change policies and meet the competition.

I also favor closing the tax loophole that makes lobbying expenses deductible. And I do not believe that all executive compensation should be deductible without regard to the productivity of the enterprise.

For the last several years too many executives have failed to follow the example of the president of Delta who recently rescinded his 21 percent pay increase because his company was losing money. I don't care how much anybody makes, as long as it's related to the growth of jobs and incomes. But we shouldn't have another decade where executive compensation goes up at four times the rate of worker compensation and three times the rate of corporate profits. We ought to join hands and all go up or down together. If we do it, productivity and morale will increase in the workplace.

The second thing we need to do is to invest in our own people, in their education, their training and their health, to put our people first. Our economic future depends on our people's strengths and skills, their health and their hopes. If we're going to make America number one in the world economically as well as politically, we've got to put our people first for a change. I have a plan to invest in lifetime learning for every American, from preschool to college to job training and retraining. We should fully fund the Head Start program and provide a preschool opportunity for every child who needs it.

As a father and a student of education, I know that a life's work is done on children by the time they start school, and we have too many who are starting in unequal positions. For people who don't go on to college, we should provide—as our competitors all do—a two-year partnership between education, government, employers, and employees, an apprenticeship training so people can get good jobs, not dead-end jobs, even if they don't have a college education.

We should open the doors to college education again, to all the people of this country. The cost of a college education is about the only essential that's gone up more rapidly than health-care costs in the eighties. Under my plan, we would scrap the existing student-loan program and substitute for it a national-service trust fund out of which any American could borrow the money to go to college; but they would have to pay it back, either as a small percentage of their income at tax time so they couldn't beat the bill, as so many do today; or even better, by giving two years of service to our nation here at home, rebuilding America.

Just think of it: if every person from Michigan who got a college degree borrowed the money from the national service trust to get it and then worked for two years at a reduced rate as a police officer, as a teacher, as a nurse, in a housing program, working to keep kids out of trouble and off drugs, we could solve half the problems of this country and educate a whole generation of Americans. It would be the best money we ever spent.

I have a plan with a modest amount of money to establish a partnership with the states to teach everybody with a job to read and give everybody with a job a chance to get a high-school diploma or a GED in the next five years.

That normally doesn't get thunderous applause, but it might be the cheapest, quickest thing we could do to raise per-capita income and productivity in this country.

My state only has 2.4 million people, but we spend as much money on adult education as our neighbors in Texas do next door. And we do it because we believe it will help us to increase productivity and earnings.

And I do have a plan to get tax incentives or impose payments on businesses above a certain size—excluding small businesses—to retrain their workers. In the United States, as in all our competing nations, the average company spends 1 to 1½ percent of payroll on retraining. The difference between the United States and Germany and Japan, where wages are growing more rapidly and productivity's growing more rapidly, is that in our country 70 percent of the expenditures are spent on the 10 percent of the employees at the top of the corporate ladder. Our competitors spread those expenditures up and down and constantly retrain the work force. At a time when you can never guarantee anyone a lifetime job, and people will change work eight times in a lifetime, even if they stay with the same company, it is imperative that we have incentives to retrain the entire work force on a regular basis to guarantee productivity and worker mobility.

Lastly on this issue, I have a plan to tackle the single greatest problem facing America's families, our businesses, and our government—rising health-care costs. Entitlements now consume 43 percent of the federal budget, and the overwhelming culprit is exploding medical costs, now budgeted for the future at 11 to 12 percent a year, with an assumption that inflation will be under 5 percent. Unless we find a way to control medical bills and provide a basic system of affordable health care to all Americans, we are never going to restore the full health to the manufacturing economy, remove the biggest burden on small business, or get this government's deficit under control. Health-care costs are responsible for 80 percent of the strikes in America today, not wages—health-care disputes.

Health-care costs are adding well over one thousand dollars to automobiles. Health-care costs have now gone for the average American family from one thousand dollars to three thousand dollars a year. In 1980 we were spending $250 billion, this year we're spending $809 billion. If we don't do something about health-care costs they'll be over 17 percent of our GNP by the end of the decade; today they're over 13 percent, 30 percent higher than our nearest competitor.

And I tell you, my fellow Americans, that's one reason the average German factory worker can make 20 percent more than the average American for a shorter work week, because they kept health costs under inflation for the last six years.

Contrary to the assertion that Mr. Bush made last night, I want to preserve what's best in the present system—your family's right to choose the doctors and hospitals and medical providers of your own choice.

But if we're going to nurse this system back to health we are going to have to make some tough decisions. In America only eighty-four cents of the insurance dollar goes to health care, sixteen cents to administration and profit and paperwork. In Europe it's ninety-five cents. One reason is, there is a system to mandate broad-based community rating so insurance companies make money like grocery stores—a little bit of money on a lot of people.

Another reason is, there is a simple, basic package of comprehensive benefits which must be offered, either by private insurers or by the government so that you simplify paperwork and administrative burdens dramatically.

The third thing we've got to do is to give people incentives to engage in managed-care network so that managed competition can work to reduce the cost of health care.

Fourthly, we need to extend the availability of primary and preventive care and health education in the inner cities and the rural areas of this country. We are wasting a fortune because we don't do it.

Paperwork and bureaucracy and regulation alone add eighty to one hundred billion dollars in unnecessary costs to this system. The average doctor spends over 30 percent of income on paperwork; the average hospital is hiring clerical workers at four times the rate of nurses. We can do better. Lest you think we can't, I cite not only the German example, but the state of Hawaii, which has community rating, primary health clinics, broad-based groups of health-care providers, and which charges 50 percent less for health insurance than the American average. We can do it if we have the will to do it.

The third principle is that we have to invest today in the foundations of tomorrow. I was criticized last night for wanting to invest two hundred and twenty billion new dollars over the next four years. My opponent didn't point out that I also called for one hundred and forty billion dollars of spending cuts over the next four years.

We need to increase real investment of your tax dollars by fifty billion dollars a year, because all our competitors are doing more. Nine nations now spend a higher percentage of their income on kindergarten through twelfth-grade education than we do.

Virtually every country in the world with an advanced economy spends a much higher percentage of their income on infrastructure, on transportation and communications than we do. And we have got to compete. We've got to rebuild our railroads, our highways, our bridges, invest in a national information network to link every library and every laboratory and every classroom and every company and every home by the year 2015.

Wouldn't it be nice when our kids come home, if they could have computers that link them up to the Library of Congress, not just a video game?

We need to take every last dollar by which we reduce defense and reinvest it in an American economy for the twenty-first century, creating high-speed-rail networks, creating new environmental technologies, investing in new technologies that will permit us to retrain workers who do lose their jobs for even better jobs in the future, not leave them out in the cold just because they won the Cold War.

Every dollar by which we reduce research and development in the military should be reinvested in civilian research and development, and we should have similar partnerships in new high-technology opportunities in the private sector, in the commercial sector, that we have had for years in the military sector.

We've had a national economic strategy for high-tech growth in military weaponry, because we didn't want it produced overseas, and we have led the world. We need to do the same thing in the new technologies of the twenty-first century.

Fourth and finally, I propose a national economic strategy based on building America's team. Bringing together business and labor, government and education to compete and win. Mr. Bush sits at the head of a government that is the only advanced industrial nation in the world, the only one, which doesn't stand up for its businesses and workers and jobs with a national economic strategy.

I don't believe in government picking winners and losers. But our government should do what it takes to help American businesses and workers become winners in the world economic competition.

It isn't any accident that 28 percent of the Japanese work force and 32 percent of the German work force are in manufacturing, and we are all the way down to 16 now in the United States.

I want to promote American industry again. And I don't think there is a real choice to be made between trade and jobs if we have the right kind of trade policy. We need both. I am not a protectionist. But I don't want to be a pushover.

I want us to be able to expand trade. I want us to expand our trade and investment with Mexico. I want a big market. We may need it for defensive purposes as Europe gives signals of becoming more protectionist. But I know that we have to be fair to our workers, to our environment, and to our future.

We can do both if we are committed to growth through expanded trade and fair trade and if we realize that no nation on earth has free trade.

When rules are fair and markets are open, American companies can compete and win.

I want to use the powers of the presidency to make those rules fair. I think we should pass a stronger and sharper so-called Super 301 trade bill so that if other countries refuse to play by our rules, we can play by theirs.

I think our foreign policy should be focused much more on international economic policy, and I think we need an economic security council similar to the National Security Council, with responsibility for coordinating our economic policy. Maybe if we had had such a focus in the recent example, the treasury secretary, Mr. Brady, would not have given the Japanese a three-hundred-million-dollar windfall by reclassifying multipurpose vehicles as cars instead of trucks.

As much as I believe in expanded trade, I can't, and I shouldn't protect companies which won't organize to compete and win. But we shouldn't sit back and let companies that are increasing productivity at astonishing rates get clobbered in the world markets because of unfair practices and a president who won't stand up.

With a national economic strategy, we won't have to choose between clean air and clean water and good jobs. Mr. Bush's friends in Houston said that clean air and clean water are incompatible with a growing economy. I disagree with that. Reminded me of something a fellow from around here, Walter Reuther, used to say—that they may be looking at the future through their rearview mirrors.

The fact is, there is a growing market here in America and all across the world for equipment and services that can conserve energy and clean air and water and preserve the planet. The market for environmental technology and services is already over two hundred billion dollars a year. Developing nations will likely install—listen to this—a trillion dollars' worth of this type of gear—just in the developing nations—in the next fifteen years. That's why the Germans and the Japanese came to the earth summit at Rio, hawking their wares, doing their best to sell environmental technology all over the world, while the United States said we couldn't meet any of the targets that they can meet.

That may be why foreign companies now have 70 percent of the American market for environmental technology. All those defense workers should have been put to work doing that starting back in the mid-eighties when we began to make these defense cuts, and we'd be in better shape today if that had happened.

Let me say, finally, I don't have all the answers. I'm not a dogmatic person, but I am passionate about seeing this country fulfill its God-given capacities. Every day I wake up and worry about the people that can't educate their children or pay their medical bills, or the businesses that are doing fine but they're being crushed by the crazy elements in our system or by manufacturers that are increasing productivity at 4 percent a year and still can't make a go of that. I worry about that.

And I remember that the genius and greatness of America is that at crucial times in our history, we have always been able to reinvent ourselves. Sixty years ago, in the midst of a greater crisis, Franklin Roosevelt said this: "This country needs—and unless I mistake its temper—this country demands bold, persistent experimentation. It is common sense to take a method and try it, and, if it fails, admit it frankly and try another. But above all, try something."

President Roosevelt defined the ultimate test of economic leadership in an exciting and dynamic time: the willingness to take bold action to improve the lives of the people you serve. Six decades later, this administration's worst failure is not the devastating recession that has occurred on Mr. Bush's watch. It is that we have had this recession and he has done nothing but watch.

He has failed to meet the standard he himself set the day he took office to use the power of the presidency to help people. As Roger Johnson, the chairman of Western Digital Corporation and a Republican supporter of mine, said on national television ten days ago, "I think we've got some problems in our country. We've had them for some time. President Bush has had over three years to address them, and just hasn't shown the leadership to take us out of them. He spent a good bit of that three years telling us there wasn't a recession, as recently as a few weeks ago. Then we found out there was a recession."

I offer a vision of millions of jobs and thousands of new companies in dozens of new industries—a vision of economic growth that starts by investing in our people, their health, their education, and their skills; and a vision of presidential leadership that challenges every student and every worker and every business person to do their best so that we can compete and win again in the world marketplace of the twenty-first century.

Today if we put our people first, we can fulfill the historic obligation of Americans to always be prepared to recreate the strength of the American community and to reaffirm our belief that tomorrow can be better than today. We do not have a person to waste. And as my wife never tires of saying, "Life is not a dress rehearsal." We are letting too many opportunities and too many lives and too many futures go. We must have the courage in this election to change course.

Thank you very much.

Children and Family Values

Chautauqua Institution
Chautauqua, New York
August 23, 1992

Bill and Hillary Clinton and Al and Tipper Gore, having just completed a three-day Cleveland-to-Buffalo campaign bus tour, all made speeches at the Chautauqua Summer Forum on Social Issues, seeking not only to defend themselves against Republican attacks that they were undermining family values but also to capture the issue for themselves. They spoke on a beautiful afternoon before a crowd of more than ten thousand on the grassy quadrangle at the Chautauqua Institution, an educational facility in the scenic Victorian lake resort village whose fame is built on its annual series of summer lectures.

Following the GOP convention, a *Time*-CNN poll showed that more than 56 percent of American voters responded that Bush and Clinton should continue to address the issue of family values, and a *Newsweek* survey reported that Bush led Clinton by a margin of 48 to 37 on the question of promoting family values. Clinton appeared particularly incensed by attacks on his wife at the Republican convention during the previous week and responded by defending her work in defining and defending American families and children while also offering his own views on the related problems and opportunities within his national agenda.

❖ ❖ ❖

Thank you. Thank you. Thank you very much. Thank you. Thank you. Thank you so much, ladies and gentlemen. President and Mrs. Bratton, Governor and Mrs. Lundine, and Senator and Mrs. Moynihan, and Congressman LaFalce, ladies and gentlemen, I'm so elated to be back in Chautauqua.

I'm glad that our road show here was introduced by Pat Moynihan. Sometimes, I think when he walks into the chamber of the Senate, the aggregate knowledge of the body doubles. I told that to Al Gore once, and he said,

"Yeah, and when we both leave, there's nothing left." He didn't say that. I made that up. I'm not going to be like the other side. When I make something up, I'll tell you.

It is a joy for me to be back in this wonderful place, where I came first in 1988 by myself to speak to your second conference on the American family and where Hillary and I came last year to speak together about our family and American families.

The nice thing about batting cleanup in this group is that it doesn't much matter what I say, it's all been said. I want you to know how proud I am to be associated with Al and Tipper Gore. I think they represent something good and decent and important and wonderful for America.

And I can't help saying, as I heard my wife up here saying what I have heard her say so many times over the last twenty years, as I remembered how many years and how many hard days and long nights she has devoted not only to her own family, but to other people's families and their children and their futures, how funny it was to hear her attacked at the other party's convention on the question of family values by people who never even thought of the issue till they thought there were votes in it a few years ago. And I tell you that because I believe that there is genuine cause for us to be debating the condition of the American family, its problems, its discontents, its continuing wonders and great potential. And I think it is important to see it in the context of what is going on in the world today. The nice thing about what Al and Tipper and Hillary talked about is that there was really no partisan content to the nature of the problem. No one can dispute the problems with which they each dealt.

And I got into this race for president because I became convinced that we were at a historic turning point and that we were once again being called upon as a nation to go beyond the frozen rhetoric which normally dominates our public debate, to go beyond the labels of Democrat and Republican, of left and right, of liberal and conservative, and instead to ask ourselves questions about what it would take to regenerate the American dream and to propel our great nation into the future, a future brighter than our past.

It is clear to everyone who has studied the matter that our nation has been in severe economic distress for well over a decade, that real wages are no higher than they were twenty years ago, that our own census shows that over two-thirds of the American people are literally working harder for less money than they were making a decade ago, that there has been in the last decade a 50 percent increase in the percentage of working persons living below the poverty line, that we have responded to the pressures of the global economy in a way totally different from the response of any other major nation.

You heard Al Gore cite a couple of the areas in which we were different from the other advanced, high-wage, high-growth countries. We resisted taking the lead in global environmental leadership. We resisted doing our part to deal with global population control.

We are also the only major nation, to give you a couple of examples, where the national government has not stepped in to control health-care costs and provide a basic system of affordable health care to all of our people. Seventy-two, *seventy-two,* nations in this world provide protection for working people to get a little time off without pay when there is a baby born or a sick parent, but our country doesn't. And in spite of the best efforts of the Congress, on a bipartisan basis, this administration vetoed the Family and Medical Leave Act.

We are the only major country that has a strong economy that has no real national economic strategy to target areas of opportunity in emerging technologies, to invest a competitive amount of money in transportation and communication and in environmental cleanup, to have clear and defined partnerships between government and business and labor and education to create opportunity for our people. And most of the time, when we're on the stump, that's what I talk about, how we can put our people first and develop an investment-oriented economy, not trickle-down, not tax and spend, but invest, educate, organize, and compete.

Many of you are by now familiar with my views on these issues, but what I want to talk to you about just for a couple of minutes today is the other side of that coin. And that is the fabric and the potential of the people of America. For no matter how good our economic policy, no matter how strong our commitment to investment, our ability to flourish in this world depends upon our ability as a people to give birth to and to rear our children, to educate them, to give form and direction and character and fiber to their lives, to give them the capacity to be everything that God meant for them to be.

Our debate in this country over the condition of families and children, in my judgment, is long overdue, and I welcome that. Nearly every American family has fretted over the problems of modern life. All of us wonder and worry about the conflicting demands and obligations of the generations to each other, the fact that too many people have gotten too selfish for the moment and done things which were bad for their own children, the fact that too many children have been subject to too many temptations which led them to destructive paths in life. No person who has ever been a father or a mother, a grandfather or a grandmother, could have possibly watched the unfolding of American life for the last generation without feeling that kind of concern and caring and without knowing that unless we found a way to do a better job of developing all of our people, then the best economic policies in the world would still leave America short, divided, and falling behind.

The thing that bothers me is that the tone of the family values debate today is too polarized for short-term political purposes and too little imbued with a deep, profound concern for the welfare of the real people whose real lives will be affected by the real decisions of America in this election. The polarization comes in the form of something like this. One side says that, "What we really need to do is just exhort the American people, tell everybody to behave and do right and don't do such and such and do this and do that. Then, there's nothing left for us to do as a society." The other side says, "There's a lot of poor folks and disadvantaged people out there. All we need is another program of government assistance, and everything will be fine." Both are wrong. Both are wrong. You cannot feed a hungry child with an exhortation, but you can't raise a child without values successfully, either. We've got to find a way to pursue both. And that is the debate in which we ought to be engaged and which I seek for this election and which I challenge the other side to embrace.

I thank Senator Moynihan for scolding the Republicans for jumping on my wife. I think that what you ought to know is that, just like Senator Gore said about the population issue, what you really ought to know is that they know better. It wasn't so many years ago that the first lady put out a book featuring programs which helped to strengthen families, and one of the few she selected was one my wife brought to Arkansas, bragging on Hillary. It's a program you may have heard me talk about before, but it combines the best of helping families and imbuing family values.

It's called the HIPPY Program, Home Instruction Program for Preschool Youngsters. We brought it over to our state from Israel. Mothers are taught to work with their children for twenty minutes a day, five days a week, thirty weeks a year for two years to get them ready for school. Even totally illiterate mothers can be taught to do this. It strengthens family values. We have now the largest program in the world outside Israel in our state. And we had a reunion of some of those parents the other day. There was one woman in our back yard who used to be on welfare, forty years old, four children through the HIPPY Program, just got her college degree. Because we strengthened family values.

And I never will forget the time that Mr. Bush wrote my wife a thank-you note for opening his eyes to the problem of infant mortality in America. Because when she told him we ranked nineteenth in the world, he said she was wrong, but he promised to look into it. And then he thanked her, because he didn't know that. Well, while he didn't know, Hillary was leading an effort in our state to cut the infant mortality rate almost in half over the last ten years, and that's a family value. That is a family value.

I say this only to point out that we are not going to get anywhere in this election and we are not going to get anywhere in this country if we try to turn people who disagree with us politically into cultural aliens by distorting their words, misrepresenting their values, and dividing the American people when they ought to be reaching out one for the other to lift up all of our children and find a way to rescue our future.

The families of America are in crisis because of social and economic changes which are sweeping through this country. There are many, but let me just mention a few. The first is poverty among young parents and their little children. They are the new poor in America. One in four children under the age of five lives in poverty.

The second is the stress put on child-rearing by work. By 1995, two-thirds of the mothers of children under the age of six will be in the work force. And a study recently released documented what most of you know intuitively anyway, which is that the average American family is now spending more hours at work and less time with their children than they were twenty years ago because of the decline in our economic performance.

The third is that the structure of the family itself has changed, with the rising tide of divorce, which Senator Moynihan mentioned, which leads on average to a 40 percent decline in the standard of living of divorced women within three years after the divorce, most of them still having custody of their children; an enormous increase in out-of-wedlock births; smaller families for two-parent households; and a drastic increase in violence in the lives of our young people. There are policy responses to all this. A growing economy would reduce a lot of the problems of poverty. A better tax system could take the working poor out of poverty. Why shouldn't we at least say if you work forty hours a week and you've got a child in the house, instead of giving another tax cut to the wealthiest 1 percent of Americans, we'll spend a small amount of money and lift you out of poverty to reward work and family?

We ought to continue the welfare-reform effort that we began on a bipartisan basis, as Senator Moynihan said. Senator Moynihan in the Senate, New York congressman Downey in the House, the Republican and the Democratic governors, and the Reagan White House. We had a simple idea, that most people on welfare were young women and their little children, that most people stay on welfare because they were undereducated and they could only get minimum-wage jobs and they couldn't afford child care and their children would lose their medical coverage. So, we had this simple idea, we're going to spend more money on education and training, require people to go to work, but if they got jobs, we'd cover their child care and the medical coverage for their kids. And guess what? It works. We've moved seventeen thousand people from welfare to work in my state alone since that bill was passed in late 1988.

But we do have to break the chain of welfare dependency. There are people who are generationally dependent on welfare. But we've got to understand how it works. We need to go beyond that. I'd be in favor of changing welfare altogether, saying that if you don't have a job within a year after your education's completed, you've got to do community-service work, be part of rebuilding your community. But you have to do it. You have to do it consistent with a dedication to the best interests of the child. Poverty is a scourge of childhood, particularly against the disintegration of the family which is occurring today.

What can be done to deal with the work problem? Well, we at least ought to join the ranks of the rest of the advanced countries in the world and make sure we give enough support not just to the poor, but to working people so that they can afford to pick decent child care for their kids.

And we ought to stop saying as Americans, "We can't. We can't. We can't." I'm so sick and tired of hearing America can't do something that I can't stand it.

And if seventy-two other countries—if seventy-two other countries can figure out how to let parents get off of work without pay when kids are born, parents are sick, then we ought to be able to do it, too. That's pro-family. And by the way, it would increase productivity in the work force because the parents would feel more secure when they were at work and better about their employers and better about their lives and better about their future. And that is a family value.

What can we do about the changing structure of the American family? Are there laws we could adopt? There are some. We ought to have a national system of child-support enforcement so you can't cross the state line and beat your child-support bill. That would help.

Every state should look at its divorce laws and make sure that in every divorce proceeding, the judge really gives adequate weight to the interests of the children, even when neither parent seems to be pursuing it. That should be considered.

We ought to strengthen the adoption proceedings in this country and try to make it more attractive to adopt children, make it easier for people to adopt children across racial and ethnic lines, give support to people who will adopt children with health-care problems and other problems.

We ought to provide for more role models and mentors for kids who grow up without it in the home. Every child who makes it against all the odds almost always at least, almost always, has had a consistent relationship with a caring and successful adult. We need to try to do what we can to multiply that rule.

We can have stronger health education and parenting education programs in our schools. If you want to reduce teenage pregnancy and abortions and out-of-wedlock births, it does work to tell people how their bodies work and to give them some imagination of what kind of future they might have. So, there are programs we can pursue.

Are there values that we can promote in common with society? Sure there are. Listen, I'm a musician and I love the arts, and I believe in free expression, but I thought Tipper Gore was right. What's the difference in a record and a movie? I thought she was right to say that we at least ought to know what kids are listening to when they're eight, nine, and ten years old. That's what the movies are. What's the difference in a record and a movie? None. I do think we ought to be tough when our children are exposed to violence and pornography, and especially when the two things are put at us in tandem. That is a legitimate thing to do.

I do think that my wife was right when we worked out an opportunity for religious fundamentalists and others in our state to have the right to home school their children as long as they met certain standards. Because this is a big country, and we've got to have a big tent, and we need to be informed and enriched by people of different views and persuasions, and we ought to reward people who care about their parental responsibilities enough to put their kids first.

I do think our public leaders ought to be out there telling children they should avoid premarital sex, and they ought to, if they insist on having it, protect themselves against having children.

I believe we ought to be out there building the self-image and the capacity of our young people. But, remember, you cannot do one—that is, tell people how to behave—without the other, doing what you should do yourself to try to help promote the values you advocate. Those who advocate values have to behave in a way that is consistent with family values.

Not very long ago, the Children's Defense Fund did a study on young women who had babies out of wedlock. And they grouped them into two groups, those who had a second child out of wedlock and those who didn't. And guess what? The overwhelming reason for those who didn't have a second child out of wedlock was that they acquired basic learning skills, began to be successful in school, thought more of themselves, and began to imagine a different future for themselves. The two things are related. I believe with all my heart we can change the culture of America. I don't think that ten years from now, if we do what we should, we'll have the same rates of out-of-wedlock births. I believe we can drive that down. I believe we can bring down the number of abortions. I believe we can lift up the number of people who want to adopt children. And we can go forward together, but only if we have a consistent set of values and actions.

People aren't smoking as much as they used to, both because of advocacy and action. Heart disease associated with a lack of exercise is going down, because there's been a consistent effort over time. Cocaine use has gone down among all but the poorest of the poor who have no hope, no structure, no action to go with advocacy, who do not imagine that they can have a different future. Among those who do, it has gone down.

I'm telling you, my fellow Americans, we can do better. And we ought to be out there advocating what we believe in, but we also ought to know that we have to work together.

Let me close with just a couple of stories, to show you the great gap in this country between talk and action. I never will forget, when I was in New Hampshire at the beginning of this process, meeting a young man named Ron Macose, whose child had had open-heart surgery, a two-year-old child. He loved that little boy more than anything in the world. And nobody who had health insurance wanted to hire him, because the kid had had open-heart surgery and might get sick again. Is that a nation with family values?

I never will forget meeting a woman when the Gores and Hillary and I were in Columbus, Ohio, the sole support of her seven children. I believe she was a divorcee; she might have been a widow. Her youngest child was desperately ill. She made fifty thousand dollars a year and she was so proud that she could support these kids—wasn't a Democrat; was for Ross Perot for president till he dropped out. I'm not talking about politics here. She had to quit that fifty-thousand-dollar job and go on welfare because that's the only way she could get any health coverage for one of the children. The other six and that seventh were deprived of knowing their mother could support them, because of the system we live under in this country, and that's the only country in the world where it would have happened to her with any kind of an advanced economy. And I don't think that's family values.

When we were in Cedar Rapids, Iowa, the other day at a rally in front of Quaker Oats, I ran upon a lady, a white lady, holding an African-American child. And I grabbed that child in my arms, and I asked the lady whose child this was. And she said, "He's my child, and he has AIDS." And I said, "Well, where did you get him?" And she said, "I adopted him from another state." And by the way, she happened to have a pro-family, pro-choice button on. But she had adopted a child. She had stood up for life. And she said, "You've got to do something to help us get more of these kids adopted." She said, "Everybody's out here fighting over abortion. What about all these kids that are coming into the world and they're sick and they have AIDS and nobody's taking care of them and nobody wants to adopt them? Help me find a home for the children that are alive." And I think that's family values.

I could tell you stories like this all afternoon, but I know there's more you have to do. What I want you to think about is this: This is an election in which we must, we must, go beyond the frozen categories of the debate that has dominated American politics for the last twelve years. We can't just yell at each other across a big divide, with a line down the middle that says Republican/Democrat or liberal/conservative or family values or stomp on family values. It doesn't amount to a hill of beans, folks. The issue is, is America going to have the courage to make the changes necessary to adjust to the global economy, to adjust to the historic environmental developments that we have to face, and to recognize that unless we do a better job of lifting all of our people up, we're all going to be dragged down? Those are the issues that are facing us today.

Now, here, here at this wonderful place, people have come from all views and all parties and all parts of the country for decades and decades and decades. And when you leave this place this summer, I ask you to go home and do what you can wherever you're from, whatever your political party, whatever your preferences about politics, to be a good citizen as America once again seeks to recreate itself. No serious person could say that the problems we face today are greater than those faced by Franklin Roosevelt when he lifted the country from the chains of his wheelchair in 1933, faced by Abraham Lincoln when the country was coming apart and he literally gave his life to preserve the Union, or faced by the Founding Fathers when they had to deal with all those terribly difficult questions.

You know the other night—I will say this—the best line at the Republican convention was when President Reagan said he knew Thomas Jefferson and I was no Thomas Jefferson. I loved that. Now, I never compared myself to Thomas Jefferson, but Reagan never let the facts stand in the way of a good line. But I'll tell you this, and I close with this. I would never do that. Thomas Jefferson was one of the greatest people who ever lived, but he was subject to a lot of brutal, bitter, unfair, totally personal, totally irrelevant criticism in his public life, and he never would have tolerated a debate in which the personal attacks on the family of his opponent, or trying to alienate the people he was running against or debating with, dominated an honest consideration of the human elements of the issues of his day. And that's why, after two hundred years, we're still here.

You owe your children and grandchildren and generations of children yet to come that same effort in this year.

Thank you, and God bless you all.

I Will Honor Your Service

American Legion Convention
Chicago, Illinois
August 25, 1992

Just two hours before Clinton spoke, President Bush, wearing his Texas Legion life-member hat and standing behind the presidential seal, was introduced at the American Legion's seventy-fourth annual convention as an "honored veteran, a Legionnaire and a true, true comrade in arms," and used the occasion to remind the audience of his World War II experience and imply that Clinton was unfit to serve as commander in chief. Bush campaign staffers distributed a press release headlined, "Will Bill Clinton tell all about his draft record?" and another describing Clinton's policy positions as a threat to national security.

Addressing the Legion's twenty thousand delegates and family members at the Sheraton Chicago Hotel and Towers in arguably his most awkward speech of the campaign, Clinton's comments were his first before a national veterans' organization since questions about his draft record surfaced during the New Hampshire primary campaign in January. Campaign aides said the choice of venue and timing—back-to-back with Bush before a group representing twenty-seven million military veterans—demonstrated Clinton's ability to deal directly with criticism and compared his action to the courage of Kennedy's appearance before the Greater Houston Ministerial Association in 1960.

The veterans gave Clinton a polite hearing during the twenty-six-minute speech, and when he finished he received a standing ovation to the music of "Stars and Stripes Forever."

❖ ❖ ❖

Thank you, Commander DiFrancesco, and thank you all Legionnaires who have been so gracious in welcoming me here and inviting President Bush and me to address this convention.

I want to salute all my friends in the Arkansas Department of the American Legion. And I promised Al Gore that I would also recognize the Legionnaires from the Volunteer State of Tennessee, also.

I want at the outset to pay a personal tribute to two Legionnaires: First, my good friend Hershel Gober, a Vietnam veteran, former adjutant of the Arkansas Department of the American Legion, and current American Legion department service officer for Arkansas, who is my national campaign manager for veterans' affairs.

I also want to recognize Al Lynch, whose heroism in Vietnam earned him the Congressional Medal of Honor and who has volunteered for another tough mission: serving as my veterans' coordinator for Illinois.

I know it's become fashionable for some politicians to claim that they won the Cold War. But I know who won the Cold War—you did.

No American would be free today if it weren't for the heroic sacrifices of you and all the millions of men and women who have served America in times of trouble. I feel a special sense of gratitude. You not only gave me the freedom you won for all Americans on the field of battle. You gave me the opportunity to serve America myself in the arena of public service. It is literally true that I might not be here today if it weren't for the American Legion. Without your dedication to the youth of America—which gave me the opportunity to attend American Legion Boys' State and American Legion Boys' Nation—if that hadn't happened, I might not be standing before you as my party's nominee for president.

I still remember that July afternoon in 1963, in the Rose Garden of the White House as I was waiting eagerly, a young sixteen-year-old, to shake the president's hand.

I couldn't help thinking that only in America could someone like me be so fortunate as to meet the president of the United States.

I knew then that I wanted to answer President Kennedy when he said, "Ask not what your country can do for you, ask what you could do for your country."

Just three months before a lot of America's innocence died, when President Kennedy was assassinated, those warm and hopeful summer days, the American Legion taught me lessons I have tried to live by all my life, lessons about the greatness of America and the responsibility to stand up for what you believe; the strength of our people and the durability of our Bill of Rights; the nobility of public service. That summer I learned from the American Legion that being a citizen involves responsibilities as well as rights, including the responsibility to love your country even enough to right its wrongs; the responsibility to get involved, to make a difference, to serve.

I am not the only American whose life has been made better by your continuing service here at home. From baseball to the Boy Scouts, from keeping veterans' hospitals open to keeping kids off drugs, from addressing homelessness to preventing child abuse to instilling a deep sense of patriotism into still another generation of Americans, a grateful nation owes you a debt of gratitude.

Like any adult I have to take full responsibility for the mistakes I've made in my life. But the American Legion deserves a large measure of credit for whatever successes I have enjoyed.

The first group I introduced Al Gore to as my running mate was the Arkansas department of the American Legion.

Because of my respect for the American Legion, I am here to speak to you as a candidate for the presidency. But before I can speak in that role, I have to tell you something very personal—not as a governor—but as a citizen.

You know that I never served in the military.

You know that I opposed the war in Vietnam.

But I want you to know this: I was never against the heroic men who served in that war. I honored your service then, and I honor it still.

Although I have discussed my conduct during the Vietnam War in great detail, I feel I owe you one final statement, to set the record straight.

In 1969, while studying at Oxford on a Rhodes scholarship, I received a draft notice, which arrived late. My draft board postponed the induction date to give me time to finish my first year of study. That summer, I agreed to join the ROTC program and attend Law School at the University of Arkansas. But a few weeks later, I changed my mind and decided I should take my chances with the draft.

Not long after that, the lottery was initiated. My draft lottery number was 311. If it had been 3, or if my number had been called, I would have served, and gone to Vietnam if so ordered. But I won't lie to you: I was relieved when I saw my number was 311, not because I didn't want to serve my country, but because I believed so strongly that our policy in Vietnam was wrong.

I still believe that. It weakened and divided America and made us reluctant to use our strength in other parts of the world. But I know many of you then and many of you today disagree with me. I respect that.

If you choose to vote against me because of what happened twenty-three years ago, that's your right as an American citizen, and I respect that. But it is my hope you will cast your vote while looking toward the future with hope, rather than remaining fixed to the problems of the past. For in this critical year, if all of us vote our hopes and not our fears; if we use this election to bring our country together instead of keeping it apart; if, in short, we all begin to behave like Americans again, then I know that the greatest country in human history will make itself greater still.

The other question that arises, of course, is perhaps inevitable, not just in this election, but in other elections to come, as the post–World War II generation comes to leadership. And it is: Can someone who has never served in the military serve as commander in chief?

Lincoln might have thought the question odd. He used to joke about his lack of military experience, saying the only blood he lost in defense of his country was to mosquitoes. As a congressman, he had been a passionate critic of the Mexican War, and the sum total of his military experience consisted of a few weeks as a militiaman called to service during the Black Hawk War, in which he saw no action. And yet he had the judgment and the wisdom and the strength of conviction to lead America through its bloodiest and most painful conflict.

In our own century, the professorial Woodrow Wilson—a governor who was never in the service—led America and its allies to "make the world safe for democracy" in the First World War, and another governor, Franklin Roosevelt, proved himself one of history's greatest wartime commanders, though he had never served in the military.

In 1980, still another governor, Ronald Reagan, was derided for having spent more time filming *Hellcats of the Navy* than actually serving in the armed forces during Word War II. And yet he never wavered from the use of American might when he felt it was right.

In President Bush's administration, Secretary of Defense Dick Cheney, who had deferments during the Vietnam era, has served with genuine distinction, especially during the Gulf War.

Our history—and common sense—tell us that competent commanders draw their wisdom from the strength of our country—and our countrymen and countrywomen.

What makes a president fit to command is, in my view, faith in God, belief in the greatness of our country and the goodness of our people, a commitment to keeping America the strongest country in the world—militarily, economically, and morally—and an understanding of the essential character of the American people. We Americans love peace. But we will not shrink from force of arms if arms are required to keep the peace and defend our interests.

In the end, every decision must be guided by principle as well as experience. Just after his election, with the prospects of war appearing imminent, Lincoln told his neighbors in Springfield that defending the nation in a civil war was a task "more difficult than that which devolved upon General Washington. Unless the great God who assisted him shall be with and aid me," he said, "I must fail. But if the same omniscient mind, and Almighty arm that directed and protected him shall guide and support me, I shall not fail, I shall succeed."

No one knows better than those of you in this room the solemn responsibility of the decision to use force to protect our nation's security and interests. When the American people choose a president, they want someone who they can trust to act when those moments arise. Every president in the last half century has had to confront the fateful decision to send Americans into combat. I do not relish this prospect, but neither do I shrink from it.

I know we must have the resolve constantly to deter, sometimes to fight, always to win. And as commander in chief, I will fight to ensure that our troops who must go to battle are the best trained, best equipped, and best supported in the world. Good people ensure victory on the battlefield.

As we scale back the force structure, we must restructure those that remain to meet the new, less predictable threats in the post–Cold War era. Our forces must be ready and sustainable. They must be more mobile, more precise, and more flexible. And they must have the technologically advanced weapons they need to get the job done.

I will never allow a hollow army. My five-year defense budget over the next five years totals $1.36 trillion compared to the president's level of $1.42 trillion—a difference of only 5 percent.

There are differences between these proposals. This administration would keep more troops in Europe and spend more on SDI; I would shift the focus to real threats we are likely to face in the coming decade: aggressive tyrants like Saddam Hussein, new regional conflicts, terrorists, and the threat of nuclear proliferation. I would preserve a more limited SDI option and support more emphasis on some military weapons, including the V-22 and fast sealift ships.

I still believe we should strive for an American, not a Republican or a Democrat, but an American national-security and defense policy. I supported President Bush's efforts in Desert Shield and Desert Storm. I support the tough line the administration has taken with Saddam Hussein recently. I urged the policies the administration has adopted in Bosnia and Somalia.

The American people do not believe either political party has a monopoly on love of country. Patriotism is not partisan.

Nor does patriotism require a blind devotion to the status quo. Indeed, the risk of staying put; the costs of standing pat; the dangers of the status quo are far greater: for economic decline, more defense cuts without a conversion plan to protect those who won the Cold War and promote growth, more skyrocketing health-care costs.

From now on a large part of our national-security policy must be found in economic strength as well as military might. A country that is not strong at home cannot be strong abroad.

My economic plan will create millions of new jobs—for displaced defense workers, for veterans, for all Americans—by reinvesting in our nation's infrastructure, civilian research and development, for the highways jobs of the future, in retraining our workers and our servicemen and -women, and in redeveloping our communities.

As an American, I honor the service of every man and every woman who has served our country in uniform. As president, I will honor your service and sacrifice with deeds, not words. You've earned nothing less.

I will honor it first by giving veterans the kind of health-care system your country owes you. I will work to ensure the VA—the Veterans' Administration—gets the funding it needs to provide the excellent and timely care our veterans deserve—all our veterans.

I will work to see that once again our veterans' hospitals work for veterans. As long as I am president, we will not merge the veterans' medical centers into the welfare system.

Instead, we will simplify and reform eligibility and strengthen the VA's efforts to deal with the special problems veterans face—like post-traumatic stress disorder, complications from Agent Orange, drug and alcohol abuse. And we will honor America's unbreakable moral obligation to care for our veterans who were disabled in the service of our country.

And I will honor your service by appointing not a secretary of veterans' affairs, but a secretary *for* veterans' affairs—not someone appointed for political reasons, but a secretary I will choose after consulting with the American Legion and other veterans' groups—someone who will have your respect, your esteem—and mine. Of course, sitting even closer to me than the secretary of veterans' affairs will be your fellow legionnaire and my running mate, Al Gore, so you know your voice will be heard.

I will honor your service by cutting the VA bureaucracy to make sure you get the benefits you've earned without a lot of red tape and delay. It shouldn't take longer to get your VA benefits than it took to liberate Kuwait.

I will honor your service by carrying on your tireless struggle to account for everyone who has ever served this country. Back home I formed the Arkansas POW/MIA Verification Task Force to determine the status of the twenty-six Arkansans whose fates are still unknown. I do not know if there are still American POWs being held. But I do know this: when I am your president, the files will be thrown open, the roadblocks will be torn down, and the truth will come out.

America must never leave its warriors on the battlefield. If there are men being held captive still, I will not rest until they are returned. And if they are not, at least we will know the truth, and the truth will set us free.

I will honor your service by moving swiftly to address the special needs of the veterans who have been left out and left behind. Too many homeless shelters are bursting with veterans, including veterans of last year's victory in Desert Storm. Your family support program is an important and helpful step—veterans helping veterans.

But all Americans should help their fellow Americans. The fact that the American Legion is doing so much should not be used as an excuse for the American government doing so little.

And I will honor your service by making sure the heroes who won the Cold War are not left out in the cold.

Our people in uniform are among the most highly skilled in the areas of expertise we need the most. As gradual, sensible defense cuts take effect, we must transfer their talents and hard work to the civilian sector and ensure they receive the assistance to do so successfully.

For example, I support incentives for military personnel to earn military retirement by taking jobs as teachers and police, as Senator Nunn has recommended.

I want to add one hundred thousand police officers to help reduce crime and drug abuse.

I want to retrain defense industry technicians for work in critical civilian fields such as biotechnology, renewable energy, and environmental cleanup.

The Pentagon stands as America's best youth training program and our most potent research center. It's time to put those assets to work at home in the battle to make America strong once again.

We ought to encourage as many as possible to serve as citizen soldiers in the National Guard and Reserves. Our talented men and women in uniform are the best equipped to help solve the problems of infrastructure, education, and rural health, offering the possibility to our military personnel to serve as role models here at home, to many young people who never have good role models here at home, but still, all the while still meeting their obligation to fulfill their primary military mission.

How do you know I will do these things? Just ask my good friends from the American Legion of Arkansas.

I am proud of what we've done to honor the service of veterans at home. I appointed the first Vietnam veteran as director of the cabinet-level Department of Veterans' Affairs. We have a County Veterans' Service Officer Program, which is the backbone of our statewide outreach system, which makes sure no veteran is left out or left behind.

I am proud of the fact that Arkansas ranks first in the per-capita reimbursements we get for our veterans from the federal Department of Veterans' Affairs. And we were first last year, too, and the year before that.

I signed executive orders ensuring veterans' preferences in hiring. And I helped find the money to upgrade and expand the intermediate nursing facilities of the Arkansas Veterans' Home; I balanced eleven budgets in a row, but never on the backs of the veterans of my state.

In 1989, when the flag-burning controversy arose, I joined with the American Legion in taking steps to react. I signed legislation making it a crime to burn or deface the flag. But I also wanted to stop flag burning before it starts. So together with the American Legion we established one of the finest flag-education programs in the country. Volunteers from the American Legion launched an all-out assault in our grade schools, instilling in our young students the deep patriotism that gives you and I a lump in our throat and a stir in our hearts every time we see Old Glory go up the flagpole.

I am proud of my record of support for veterans. And I admire the American Legion's seventy-four-year commitment to what's best about America.

For three-fourths of a century you've been advising presidents—from calling for the GI Bill in 1944 to opposing the IRS's shameful attempt to tax cost-of-living adjustments to veterans' disability payments.

I will be a good president for America's veterans. After all, I've been taking advice from the American Legion for twenty-nine years.

Some of you may know, my father served in World War II. But he didn't die in the war. He was killed in a car accident three months before I was born, on his way home to Arkansas to see my mother.

He was killed just as he was about to start living for all the things he had risked dying for. And, when, many years ago, my mother showed me his service citation from World War II, I felt as proud as I've ever been.

I doubt he ever dreamed that, some day, the son he never knew would be standing here today as a candidate for president of the United States.

This could only happen in America.

And in my case, it might never have happened without the encouragement and assistance of the American Legion.

I know you are unlikely to base this important vote on the fact that I was in American Legion Boys' State twenty-nine years ago or that I have a good record on veterans' issues as a governor.

But I also hope you will not base your vote on the fact that I didn't serve in Vietnam twenty-three years ago.

This campaign must be decided on the future of our nation and on the issues—on jobs and health care and education and safer streets; on making the government work for all Americans, not just the special interests and the privileged few; on building a strong America at home and abroad.

In 1960, John Kennedy told the Greater Houston Ministerial Association that they should not oppose him just because he was a Catholic. He said, "If I should lose this election on the real issues I shall be . . . satisfied that I tried my best and was fairly judged."

Much changes, but much remains the same. What Abraham Lincoln called the "mystic chords of memory" preserve from generation to generation our hopes and dreams for our country. We have a chance, right here, right now—the chance of a dozen lifetimes—to fulfill those hopes, realize those dreams, and create the finest America yet.

For the next seventy days I will try my best. And I have confidence that you and all Americans will judge me fairly—on the real issues. Because that's the American way.

Thank you, God bless you, and God bless America.

A Partnership for Opportunity

Montgomery College
Rockville, Maryland
September 2, 1992

Speaking from notes before five hundred cheering students and supporters at 11 A.M. in the outdoor amphitheater at Montgomery College, a two-year school offering adult education and opportunities for students from working-class backgrounds, Clinton stressed his support for educational funding and the connection between education and jobs. The scene was fitting for the topic, and an MTV poll showed that the economy and education were the top-two issues for voters under thirty. Moreover, the state was an important one in the overall campaign plan. Although Maryland's ten electoral votes had gone for Reagan in 1984 and to Bush in 1988, a poll the previous weekend showed Clinton leading 48 percent to 39 percent.

Bush workers handed out a press release during the speech, charging that Clinton had presided over an educational "Bleak House" in Arkansas. The Bush headquarters responded to the speech by claiming that Clinton was a captive of the "educrats," and that afternoon Education Secretary Alexander held a press briefing to defend Bush's record on education.

❖ ❖ ❖

Thank you. Thank you. Thank you.

I ought to quit while I'm ahead, just rest on their speeches. I want to thank all of you for being here. I have enjoyed seeing the signs in the crowd, the report card over here. I like the "no more status quo, n-o-e-q-u-o-e" back there.

As I pulled up, someone gave me a piece of paper explaining a new club, along with a button, a Hillary Clinton Fan Club button. I appreciate that.

I want to thank you all for being here today. I want to thank the president and the chairman of the board of trustees and all the faculty and the students of this fine college for having me here, for all of you turning out, for your concern about our future.

Yesterday, I talked about the differences between me and the president in the way we would handle the health-care crisis and what his proposals will mean for the elderly of our country. Today I want to talk about the impact of this election on education, searching for ways to expand educational opportunity.

I was at the East Los Angeles Community College not very long ago, which is a big answer to what to do about the riots in Los Angeles—give those kids a chance to be part of that kind of two-year program that will guarantee them a better future.

And there I found young people, mostly Hispanics, some African Americans, some white, some Asian American, people you didn't read about after the riots, people who didn't riot, people who didn't burn, people who didn't loot, instead going to overcrowded makeshift classrooms bursting at the seams, dealing with all the cutbacks in student aid and programs and classes that all of you are experiencing here, struggling to make the American dream real for themselves, struggling to rebuild their communities.

The president has said many times that there is a fundamental difference between us in this election, and he is certainly right about that, especially on the issue of education.

The economic philosophy of this administration is that you make the economy grow by putting more and more wealth into the hands of fewer and fewer people at the top, getting government out of the way and trusting them to make the right decisions, to invest and to create jobs.

I believe the way to make our economy grow is to invest in our people, our children's education, our workers' skills, our families' health care, our plants and equipment, our best ideas in research and development.

They believe that you make an economy grow by putting money first. I believe you make an economy grow in a global economy by putting people first.

You can chart the differences between us by seeing who's won and who's lost; who's been helped and who's gotten hurt, while this crowd has run our government over the last twelve years.

For twelve years they have rewarded people who cut deals and cut corners; who make money by pushing paper instead of those who make money by investing in new plants, new equipment, new businesses; those who work hard, play by the rules, and pay their taxes.

And for the first time since the roaring twenties, the top 1 percent of the American people now control more wealth than the bottom 90 percent. But while the rich have been winners, no American would have begrudged them that, since we all want, in this free-enterprise system, to at least believe our children might grow up to be rich. No one would have begrudged that if the rest of us had been helped.

But in 1980, we had the highest wages in the world, now we're thirteenth. The census document itself shows that most Americans are working longer work weeks for lower wages; paying higher taxes on lower income; paying a bigger percentage of their income for housing and for health care; and yes for education.

Today, the United States Commerce Department issued its report on adjusted figures for 1991, in which it says that in 1991, there was a 2 percent real drop in the incomes of the American people—the first drop since 1982, the worst drop in over thirty years. I will say that again, inflation was 4.4 percent; incomes went up 2.2 percent; there was a 2 percent decline in the earnings of the American people, even though they worked more hours than the year before or the decade before.

And the average family is actually spending more hours on the job than they were twenty years ago. Now, that is a record.

I'm proud of the fact that my state, which has been at the bottom of America's per capita for a hundred and fifty years, ranked fourth in income growth in 1991 and first in job growth over the last year.

I say that only because of what I'm sure was an unintentional omission at the Republican convention to put that fact before the American people. But I can tell you that I got into this race for president because most of my folks are working harder for less, too. And unless we have a fundamentally different approach to what it takes for all of us to do better in America, to see the American dream, we will all fall further behind.

If you look at what they propose for the future as compared to what our competitors are doing, the differences are stark. For example, everybody in this audience knows in general, not specifically, that the high-wage, high-growth countries of the world—Germany and the rest of the European countries and northern European countries, countries like Denmark—which a group of international businessmen said earlier this year had a stronger economic performance than America now, or countries like Japan, you know what they do, don't you? They invest more in education. They invest more in continuous training. They have closer partnership between government, business, labor, and education. They continuously invest in modern plants and equipment and research and development. And everybody's on the same side, trying to figure out how to get the most out of every human being.

Now, that is their strategy. That is my strategy for America. That is what we pioneered.

If you contrast that to what we've been promised for the next four years, going back to the Houston convention, what did they say? Give us four more years and on top of this four-hundred-billion-dollar deficit, we'll give you another across-the-board tax cut, heavily weighed toward the wealthy, a short-term capital-gains tax cut for the rich, which makes no distinction between investment and buying race horses and vacation homes. And we'll tell you how we'll pay for it later. Give us until January, and we'll come up with a budget cut. Now, that was their line. *That* was their line. That's what they said.

And then when asked after Houston, well, how are you going to pay for it? We've got a four-hundred-billion-dollar deficit. How are you going to pay for more tax cuts? They said, "Spending cuts to be announced after January. Trust us."

Now, this is an administration that wants you to trust them about spending cuts with your future, that recently cared so much about protecting the wealthy that they asked the IRS to ease up on auditing the wealthy and spend more time auditing the middle class.

This administration, last week, and this president accused me of being a fearmonger. That's their word; because I want to crack down on tax evasion of foreign countries doing business in the United States.

Now, let me tell you this is not foreign bashing. I have actively sought foreign investment in my state. I welcome it as a way of integrating America into the global economy and providing jobs for Americans. And after all, that's where a lot of the money is today. Thanks to the policies of the last twelve years.

But here's what I ask for. You put yourself in my position. You've got a four-hundred-billion-dollar deficit. You have to figure out how to deal with that and increase investment at the same time.

And here are the facts: In the last ten years, foreign corporations doing business in America have had their incomes go up 65 percent and their tax payments go down by 15 percent.

Now, if *your* income goes up by 65 percent, will *your* taxes go down by 15 percent?

If you work for an American company, a small business here in Maryland, if your income goes up by 65 percent, will your tax liability go down by 15 percent? No.

No, just because you can't engage in some financial legerdemain and park some of your money somewhere else. I think that everybody who does business here, makes money here, makes a good profit here ought to be taxed on a fair basis. I don't think that's fear mongering.

But the main point is, these people want us to buy the same old thing we've been buying for twelve years, times two. Right?

Here we are with a four-hundred-billion-dollar deficit, and we cut our investment in the future, while we quadruple the deficit, and they want us to do it just one more time.

Yesterday, I talked about the specific recommendations that this administration had made to help veterans and the elderly instead of dealing with the fundamental causes of the health-care crisis and the deficit.

Today, I want to talk about what is going to happen in education, depending on the outcome of this election. And keep in mind, as Mr. Cornelius said, it's been a cutback, already, in the federal commitment to education. We're spending 30 percent less of the federal budget on education than we were in 1980. And every time I say this, the administration says we spend more on education than anybody in the world.

Well, the truth is that there are nine or ten countries that spend a higher percent of their income on kindergarten through twelfth-grade education than anybody in the world. We spend more on higher education than anybody in the world. But because of the way we spend it, the dropout rate from college is more than twice the high-school dropout rate, because we have priced it out of range for so many Americans. And that's what we have to change.

Look at the record of this administration in higher education. After a decade in which tuition costs were the only basis in the family's market basket of education needs, it went up faster than health care. This president tried to cut back on grants and loans that help millions of young people from poor and middle-class families.

If Congress had let him get away with it, George Bush would have cut off Pell Grants for over four hundred thousand students, this year alone. He tried to change the law so that if you make ten thousand dollars a year, you're too rich for a college grant from the federal government. Even though if you make three hundred thousand, you still need a short-term capital-gains cut.

He proposed to cut over four hundred thousand people off the Pell Grants Program. His '93 budget cut college aid seventy-nine million dollars. And he vetoed a bill which would let people deduct the interest that they pay on their student loan, from their tax burden, and let them use their IRA savings for college costs.

The bill, also, by the way, would have given new incentives for manufacturers to adopt new investments in plant and equipment; give a boost to small business; give a boost to research and development in a country that doesn't do enough of it.

Why did he veto the bill? Because it paid for all those investments by asking the wealthiest 2 percent of Americans to pay slightly more and giving middle-class families with kids a tax break. And so the bill was vetoed.

In his mid-session budget review, which he embraced eagerly, just a few days ago, George Bush recommended that over three million students who received federal loans pay over two thousand dollars more in interest on their college loans than they're paying under present law, starting even before they get their college diploma. And again, all of this is before they figure out how to pay for their across-the-board tax cuts, targeted to the wealthiest. Senator Mikulski and Senator Sarbanes down here, nodding, they know where that money is coming from, it's coming right out of your hide, if you do it.

Look what this college has already faced as a result of budget cuts and a weak economy. You know, first hand, that as federal money to the states has dried up and states have had less money because of the weakened economy, because we have no national economic strategy, budgets have been stretched thinner and thinner. And in Maryland, when something had to give, one of the things was this college.

You've seen class sizes increased, evening classes cut, staff reduced, and for the first time in history, you will have to limit enrollment.

Now, let me tell you how important that is, not just for those of you who will be affected, but for the rest of us Americans.

All of you know that we have a shorter school year in public schools than any country except Belgium—any advanced country. All other nations go to school longer.

So, not surprisingly, as the census documents prove, the only American workers, younger workers, who are really competitive in terms of global economy and who get good wages are those that not only graduate from high school but get at least two years of further training. The census proves that if you get two years of further training, you're likely to get a job with an income that goes up. And if you don't, you're likely to get a job with an income that goes down.

So, all of America's economic future, our total productivity growth, our ability to generate wealth, our ability to support one another, depends on now in this global economy, our capacity to offer 100 percent of our high-school graduates and our older workers coming back, the opportunity to come to a place like this. And we're cutting it off. And it's a mistake.

I want everyone of you to just think in your minds, if you had the chance with a four-hundred-billion-dollar deficit, with your country's economy growing much more slowly than many other nations, to decide the course for your country that included another across-the-board tax cut or an investment that would teach every adult with a job to read within the next five years; give everybody a chance to get a community college diploma—at least two years. And give everybody the chance to go to college and not drop out for financial reasons, which course would you choose? Anybody who understands the world would choose the course of education. Anybody. Thank you.

Ladies and gentlemen, as Shayla indicated in her introduction, if we were really to talk about everything I think ought to be done in education, we would be here until tomorrow at this time. And I won't do that to you. Let me talk about two things that could affect this college and every school in America and, most importantly, the people of this country.

I have recommended a number of educational advances, starting with fully funding Head Start and going into new technologies and new opportunities in our public schools. I want to talk about what we should do for those who are out of high school. And I just want to ask you to focus on one or two things.

Number one, we ought to set up a system where the federal government goes into partnership with the states in the private sector, both business and labor; in which everybody who graduates from high school who does not want to go to a four-year college at least has access to two years of further education and training, either in a community college, in a vocational program, or on the job. And we should share the cost. One hundred percent of the people need to do that.

Everybody who is at work today, who is willing to go back to school, should have the opportunity to be a part of this. You think of what would happen to America's per-capita income if everybody with a job today was taught to read at the high-school level and had access to a program at this college, here. Think what would happen. And it wouldn't be very expensive.

Number two, I have proposed a program that the president has criticized roundly—although, I don't think that they understand it. I saw a special on one of the television networks last night when I got to Baltimore to my hotel room—talking about the need to constantly retrain the work force. And the fact that American workers spend about 2 percent of their time in retraining as compared with 10 percent for the Germans and the Japanese.

Now, here is my proposal, a modest one compared to what our competitors are doing. The average American company spends 1 to 1½ percent of payroll on retraining. But in America, most of that money, 70 percent to be exact, is concentrated on the top 10 percent of the work force in any company.

In our competing countries, what they do is to push that money down to the front-line workers because they know that's where the money's made to productivity—improvement at the front line.

So, my proposal is take the money you're spending anyway and spread it across your work force, and we will help you by making sure you've got access to good training programs, good community colleges, making the linkages that we need. But if you don't want to do that, you can pay that amount of your payroll into a trust fund so that when your workers are unemployed, we can retrain them.

Now, we have an exemption for small business in the thing. So keep in mind, we're asking people just to spend money they're spending anyway in ways that are good for the company, good for the workers, and good for the country. We might not raise a penny out of this. Nothing would make me happier, if we did not collect one red cent because everybody retrains their own workers, making their own partnerships, supervising their own changes. That's what ought to be done. But it's a good idea. And it ought to be done in this country.

The final thing I recommend is just simply using the federal government to create a trust fund that would remove any barrier, financial barrier, for people going to school and staying in school. I want to see us continue to increase our scholarship programs and our work-study programs. But I want to change the student-loan program. It does not work. It costs too much money. It is too burdensome. It helps too few people.

It costs you four billion dollars a year now as taxpayers; a billion dollars in bank transaction fees and three billion dollars in busted loans, mostly from people who borrow the money to go to these make-shift operations that aren't training them to do things they ought to be doing. And everybody's picking up the tab.

So here's our idea, the campaign's idea that I've been nurturing for years now. It's one of the things I talked about on the day I announced.

I want to take the best of two of the greatest things we ever did, the GI Bill, after World War II, and the Peace Corps under Kennedy and create a national trust fund, a national trust fund out of which any American, without regard to income, could borrow the money to finance an education at either a two-year or a four-year school and then pay it back in one of two ways: either after you go to work as a limited percentage of your income, so you would never be discouraged from taking a job as a teacher, for example, just because of the size of the loan, because what you pay back would be limited to a percentage of your income.

Or even better, if you borrow the maximum amount, for every two years you could do one year of work at a reduced pay or for four years of loan at the maximum amount, two years of work at reduced pay here at home, rebuilding America, being teachers or police officers, work in housing programs, work with elderly people, work with children. You think about it. We could change the whole face of Americans with the brightest of Americans giving two years of their lives to building their country.

We need more police officers on the streets. You want to know one reason why the crime rate is going up? It's because there is now three crimes for every policeman. There used to be three policemen for every crime, thirty years ago. Go back to community policing. Put people on the streets, walking the streets. You'll lower the crime rate.

And by the way, don't take my word for that. Look what happened in Houston, where they hired the equivalent of six hundred and fifty-five more police officers, 15 percent dropped in the crime rate. They went to community policing in New York City, first time in thirty-six years, they had a drop in the crime rate, even while the national rates were going up. If you do that, you can prevent crime—*if* you do that. But the cities can't afford it. I say we help them in this way.

The same thing is true with children. There are clear studies now demonstrating if you get down to really small classes for disadvantaged kids in the early grades, their learning curve will improve, not only in the early grade, but forever. But the schools can't afford it. Put the teachers in the schools. Educate America. And put the teachers in the schools.

Now, let me say against all of this, I still think we have to bring down the deficit. And I have offered a way to do it. It doesn't take it out of education and the necessary investments to grow this economy.

The first thing we have to do is to bring health costs in line with inflation. And unless we do that, the deficit cannot be brought under control. But the way to do it is not simply to cut off benefits to the elderly under Medicare or reduce the payment to hospitals and doctors below the cost, because then those costs just get passed on to all of you who have private insurance and your premiums go up. Then more and more businesses stop insuring their employees and they get put on to some dole that they have paid for, and their costs are passed along.

What we have to do is to look at the areas in which American health care is totally out of line with any other advanced countries in the world: insurance, paperwork, regulations, regular drugs, steeper service no matter what, and the absence of primary, preventive health care in the inner cities and in rural America. If we dealt with those things, we could bring health cost in line with inflation.

The second thing we ought to do is to recognize, while the middle class had their incomes go down and their taxes go up in the 1980s, the richest 2 percent of Americans had their income go up and their taxes go down so that if 1980 tax rates were in effect, they would be paying seventy-six billion dollars more a year.

Now, what I have recommended is not that kind of tax increase. I want to leave the tax rates lower than they were in 1980, but I do think the upper 2 percent should pay their fair share, should make a major contribution to meeting our deficit needs.

I think we can improve the productivity of the federal government. We have a turnover of six hundred thousand a year. We have a higher percent of federal employees for our population than countries do that don't rely as much as we do on state and local government. So we can reduce the federal work force; but I want to do it by attrition—not by putting people in the street—by a hundred thousand in the next three years.

I think we can save money. And let me say this. This won't affect this community college very much, but I also think, while proposing billions more for schools and colleges and funding, we ought to cut the overhead cost that the federal government now gives to universities for federally sponsored research.

The abuses are unbelievable. We have examples where federal administrative dollars that ought to be spent in the laboratory for research and development to revitalize this country are being spent on parties, on civil services, on all kinds of administrative things, having nothing to do with economic growth. Those things ought to be cut out. You would spend the money better here. And we shouldn't keep spending the money on that.

And let me say one final thing; I want to set a good example. I've called for cutting the White House staff by 25 percent. And my opponent, who talks about how frugal he is . . . You need to know this. Between 1990 and 1991, when they were cutting everything else, like education, they increased the budget of the White House staff, now get this, by 23 percent in one year, ten times the amount of revenue growth. But they want you to believe that they are really tightening the belt up there.

So, I say to you, there are things we can do to bring this deficit down. And don't let anybody kid you, it is a major issue.

When George Bush gave his speech in Houston and said, "I'll give you one more tax break," the stock market fell and the American dollar fell against the German mark. Even the conservatives of the world knew it was a nutty idea. Everybody knew it was wrong.

But what I want to say to you is, in the nine weeks that remain in this election, we have to decide what we believe about our country. Do we want to stay with trickle-down economics for four more years? Or do we believe that there is nothing wrong with the American dream. It hasn't failed, but these policies have. And we've got to change them. We've got to put the American people first again.

I very much want this election to be about the education of our children and our adults. I wake up every day thinking about things I don't think crossed this administration's mind except at election time.

One of the things I think about is that the average eighteen-year-old will have to change the nature of work eight times in a lifetime; that most of our workers in the twenty-first century will be people who come from backgrounds—both racial and socioeconomic backgrounds—that we used to call disadvantaged; that I believe all people can learn. And I don't think that there is anything wrong with this country of ours except that we're undereducated, underorganized, underinvested, and underled.

Thank you very much.

Winners in the World Economy

General Board of the AFL-CIO
Washington, D.C.
September 3, 1992

Before Clinton's 10:45 A.M. speech to the AFL-CIO General Board, Bush campaign workers were at the Sheraton Washington Hotel in the foyer of the ballroom in which Clinton was to speak and were handing out flyers challenging Clinton to clarify his position on the free-trade agreement and citing a *Washington Post* article that said labor officials did not plan to confront him on the issue. Clinton acknowledged his differences with organized labor within minutes of taking the dais and told the union leaders, "While I know we have not always agreed, and we'll never agree on everything, I believe we share a common commitment to the working men and women and their children and their parents and most of all to the forgotten middle class."

Clinton addressed the NAFTA issue and said he supported the treaty in theory but would not sign it unless it contained strong labor and environmental standards for Mexico, but his main message dealt with reviving the American economy and other domestic agenda items. The speech was well received by a group that hasn't always been supportive of Clinton, regarding him as having a mixed record on labor issues in Arkansas and initially supporting Sen. Tom Harkin in the primaries.

Clinton and Gore received 99.8 percent of the 13,680,894 votes cast at the meeting by 178 delegates from 63 of the 88 unions that are affiliated with the AFL-CIO, including the 1.3-million-member International Brotherhood of Teamsters who abandoned Bush and endorsed a Democrat for the first time since 1968. Bush-Quayle deputy campaign manager Mary Matalin responded by calling Clinton "just another protectionist pawn of Big Labor," adding, "In this game of political chess, it looks like Clinton's the pawn and big labor's the king."

❖ ❖ ❖

Thank you very much, President Kirkland and all the men and women of the AFL-CIO, for your endorsement of me and of Senator Gore, of our common efforts to change this country. I am glad to be here today, grateful for your support, eager to embrace the next nine weeks of battle.

I'd like to begin by just saying one personal word and that is a special thanks to all of you along the way in this campaign who have taken some personal time to meet with me, to discuss issues with me, to frankly air disagreements with me in ways that were, I think, helpful to both of us and to our common cause.

I want to say a special word of thanks to one of my top staffers who's here today, my campaign manager, David Wilhelm, who worked very hard all during the primary process and is known to many of you.

My first meeting with Lane Kirkland was fascinating. He's not the easiest person in the world to have an argument with, and even lose with dignity, much less win. But it was sort of an example of a lot of what has happened over the last year to me as I have been crossing this country listening to people trying to come to terms with the realities of their lives. I wish that every one of you could have been on at least one leg of the bus trip, or the trips that our families have been taking across this country, seeing the people whose lives have been broken and the people who still live with hope; seeing the people who've lost their jobs or just the people who've lost their incomes; seeing the people who've lost their health care or who lost their health; seeing the number of people who desperately want to believe that this country can work again for them and for everyone, that we really can come together again and who are determined to make it happen—schoolchildren on a stagecoach in Soledo, Texas; a woman in Columbus, Ohio, who used to be for Ross Perot, who was a divorced woman with seven children and a fifty-thousand-dollar-a-year job, who had to quit her job and go on welfare because one of her children was terribly ill, and in this country that was the only way she could get any health care for that child. So she lost the power of supporting that child and the other six.

I could tell you story after story after story of Americans who are trying to pick up the pieces of this nation's neglect. And I say to you that while I know we have not always agreed and will never always agree on everything, I believe we share a common commitment to the working men and women and their children and their parents, the opportunity to dignity, to equality, and most of all, to the forgotten middle class. We're going to make Bush and

Quayle and their crowd remember those folks on November the third. I believe there's something wrong when the people who do the work, raise their kids, pay their taxes, play by the rules, and embody those family values our adversaries spent so much time talking about in Houston keep getting the shaft. That's the subject they didn't want to deal with.

By the way, could you believe that Republican convention? I mean, they spent the first two days running against Hillary. I was convinced Mr. Bush was going to walk out there on Thursday night and announce he was going to file for first lady and that Pat Buchanan would be his running mate, Pat Robertson and Jerry Falwell would be his secretaries of culture and appropriate behavior.

Mr. Bush says this election should be about trust, and I believe that's right. I trust the American people, and he doesn't. The election should be about who is to be trusted to get our economy moving again, to build a high-wage, high-growth, high-opportunity future instead of letting this nation drift, as it now is, into a hard-work, low-wage, low-growth future. The election should be about who can be trusted to talk straight, to take responsibility, to make tough decisions. Yes, the election is about trust, but for George Bush to say the election is about trust is about like me saying the election should be about making short speeches.

Yesterday—let's be real and serious for a moment—yesterday the commerce department reported that Americans' real incomes declined by 2 percent last year alone, the first decline in real incomes in ten years and the worst decline in real incomes in over thirty years. And just this morning, we're told that household income is down eleven hundred dollars this year over last year, median family income is down 2.4 percent, and 2.1 million Americans have fallen into poverty.

You can see that if you're in my business at the state level. Ten percent of this country's on food stamps now. The Medicaid rolls of states all across the country are going up by 12 to 15 percent a year, as more and more people are living in poverty and without health care.

Four years ago, Mr. Bush asked us to trust him when he said, "Read my lips—no new taxes." Then he signed the second-biggest tax increase in history, and it turned out what he really meant was "No new taxes for the wealthiest 1 percent."

Four years ago, he asked us to trust him when he said "fifteen million new jobs." Now he's more than fourteen million short. We've lost over a million manufacturing jobs in the last three and a half years alone. Less than one million jobs have been created, and only a hundred thousand of them have been in the private sector. The other eight hundred-plus thousand were in the government sector that he claims to hate so much. Our country now has only 16 percent of its work force in manufacturing, as compared with 28 percent for the Japanese and 32 percent for the Germans.

Four years ago, we were asked to trust Mr. Bush when he promised that the next century will be, quote, "an American century." But over the past eleven and a half years, while the Reagan-Bush-Quayle team have been in charge of America's economic policy, we have gone from first in the world in wages to thirteenth, and the latest census figures plainly show that over two-thirds of the American people are working harder for less money than they were making ten years ago.

Four years ago, Mr. Bush asked us to trust him when he promised us, and I quote, "prosperity with a purpose." But four years later, we have no prosperity, and this administration has no purpose except to win the election in November.

You know that this administration has compiled the worst economic record in fifty years, since Herbert Hoover was president, and at Houston we saw what their promise for the next four years is: more of the same. Two weeks ago in his speech at the Republican National Convention, Mr. Bush addressed an anxious people who looked for real answers in our economic crisis. But instead of a credible plan, he gave more incredible promises. In the face of a four-hundred-billion-dollar deficit this year, he made promises of another across-the-board capital-gains tax cut to the wealthy, and then promised everybody else an across-the-board tax cut, and then said, "We're going to pay for it with spending cuts, and I'll tell you about them in January." That's a typical thing for a former head of the CIA. Now he's got a secret plan for the economy.

And yesterday Mr. Bush made a series of election-year flip-flops only nine weeks before the voters vote, which would have gotten him a gold medal in Barcelona. After saying politics would never have any impact on national security, he dropped his long-standing opposition to the V-22 aircraft which is made in Texas, and strangely enough he announced it in Texas. I might say I was for that last year, but I would have paid for it with steeper cuts in troops in Europe and in Star Wars.

Meanwhile, Dan Quayle was announcing the administration had flip-flopped and will now support the M1 and the M1-A1 tanks which are manufactured primarily in Michigan and he made the announcement in Michigan. Then he told the good people of Fort Worth that he would interrupt for a moment his nonstop kow-towing to the communist regime in China and sell F-16s to Taiwan. Where do you think those planes were made? Fort Worth.

Then the president went to South Dakota—this is the most amazing thing of all—on September second and promised the wheat farmers he would expand the export subsidy program that on August sixth he recommended be eliminated. Now I'm a Baptist so I believe in deathbed conversions, but this is amazing. I'll tell you one thing, no matter what happens our campaign's done some good for some people in this country.

I think the American people are smart enough to see politics as usual and have been burned enough to know we've got to go beyond the gridlock which has characterized policy in Washington and which is only broken by the threat of the voters voting.

For the next few minutes let's try to get beyond what might happen in the next nine weeks and imagine what might happen in the next four years if Mr. Bush were to be reelected, to see what we can trust him to do. If you can trust the promises he made in Houston, he's going to cut another $294 billion in taxes over the next five years over and above the deficit we already have. That means that that's just the beginning. If you can trust him, he's going to cut taxes across the board, with the wealthy getting most of that, and cut the capital-gains tax. So he's promised $294 billion of spending cuts before Houston over the next five years, and now he wants to cut another $252 billion just for the tax cut at 2 percent, even if it's just a 2 percent tax cut.

Then, if only one-half of the taxpayers accept his little check off to put 10 percent of their taxes on the debt that's already been accumulated, that's another $139 billion.

Then he's going to increase the personal exemption which will cost another $182 billion over five years. Then he's going to pour at least $100 billion more into a health-care industry whose costs he has steadfastly refused to control.

And then he's going to pour $30 billion of public funds into private schools—if he prevails on that. Then his short-term across-the-board capital-gains cut will save the average millionaire one hundred thousand dollars but won't guarantee investments for new jobs. It makes no distinction between vacation homes and new businesses being started. That costs thirty-one billion dollars.

Well, to paraphrase the late Senator Everett Dirksen of Illinois, who was an old-fashioned Republican who would have been appalled by this, you take $252 billion here and $182 billion there, and pretty soon you're talking about real money.

When you put a price tag on all his promises, he's promising somehow to give us a trillion dollars worth of stuff over the next five years that he will make up for in budget cuts.

You know who he's going to send the bill to, don't you? The same people who have been taking a beating for the last dozen years—the middle class who are working harder for less, the working poor, and the poor.

You can see that future a little bit in a document he issued that most Americans never heard of called the Mid-Session Review. A couple of months ago, he spelled out the cuts that he would make now. That's before we get to the across-the-board tax cut, before we get to the capital-gains cut, just the cuts that he recommends now. He doesn't want most Americans to see this Mid-Session Review or to take it seriously, but he waved it in the air proudly when he gave a speech to the American Legislative Exchange Council on August the sixth, and he said, and I quote, "Here is the Mid-Session Review, and it tells exactly and specifically how to get the deficit down." And he pointed out it did have $294 billion worth of cuts over five years.

He wanted to make older Americans with incomes of under twenty thousand dollars, and many much lower than that, pay another four hundred dollars a year for Medicare or charge them two thousand dollars a year. That will save one hundred and twenty billion dollars by sending the bill to our parents and grandparents so we can in part finance the capital-gains tax on short-term gains by the wealthiest Americans.

He wants to save four billion dollars from federal student aid and lose tens of billions of dollars of untapped human potential in all those who either won't go or won't stay in college.

Perhaps cruelest of all, he's recommended taking 1.2 million disabled veterans off the disability rolls altogether to save ten billion dollars by sending the bill to the people who have sacrificed for our nation.

The Mid-Session Review tells in short how he's going to get all this money for $294 billion, and it gives you a sneak preview of what he'll have to do to pay when that bill goes to a trillion dollars to pay for all of his other tax cuts.

When he looks at the federal budget, there are some things he's promised to give away and some things he's promised not to touch. He says, no matter what, he won't raise taxes on the wealthiest 1 percent, even though their taxes have been lowered while your taxes have been raised. He's got his defense budget in place for the next five years, and he says he won't fool with Social Security.

But listen to this. If he covers the tax cuts with budget cuts as he says, here's what you get. If he gets rid of all veterans benefits; taxes all Medicare benefits as ordinary income; eliminates all the farm price supports while our competitors are refusing to do it—and that's one area where we're still competitive and making money in international markets; freezes discretionary spending, which means no more investment in education, in the environment, and economic growth; freezes cost-of-living adjustments on every program except Social Security; he'd still have another 344 billion [dollars] to cut—if he gets rid of all of that.

And then he'll have no choice. He'll be forced to cut, even to gut Medicare and Social Security, because if you don't raise taxes on the wealthy and you don't cut defense any more, and you can't get the economy growing again, then you just have to get all this out of spending cuts.

Now no wonder he doesn't want to say how he's going to do this. It's one more incredible promise. You've got, "Take the tax cut, and I'll tell you about the budget cuts later." If we trust Mr. Bush as he asks, it means we're going to have to do one of two things. We're going to explode this deficit, which is already too big, imperiling our future, or we're going to devastate America's middle class even further, increase the number of poor, and imperil our children's futures.

Now when this speech was given, the stock market got it. They didn't take it seriously and the stock market dropped the next day. Those are his constituents, and they're going to be—a lot of them—for Bill Clinton and Al Gore, because they know we've got a plan to get this country going again.

When he gave this speech, our allies got it—the dollar dropped dramatically against the German mark the next day because they knew he wasn't serious. They got it, and I think the American people are going to get it.

When George Bush first ran for president twelve years ago he called this kind of promise "voodoo economics." Twelve years later, he's become the high priest of voodoo economics, sticking pins in the middle class.

My fellow Americans, we can do better than that. We can do better than that. I've offered this country a plan that will really move us forward, a plan that challenges all of us to change. It gives us a chance to move beyond trickle-down economics on the one hand—between their borrow-and-spend policies on the one hand, and tax and spend on the other—to an invest-and-grow policy, one that asks the wealthy to pay their fair share but still keeps those tax rates well below what they were in 1980, one that disciplines federal government spending and consumption but increases what we invest in job generation, research and development, in education and training, in building an economy for the twenty-first century, one that builds cooperation between business and labor and government and education. You look at these other high-wage, high-growth countries. They've got everybody on the same side. They don't spend all their time fighting over how a shrinking pie will be divided because they are working too hard to grow the economic pie so everybody can have more money.

I would love to see the Clinton-Gore administration produce more millionaires than Bush and Reagan did, but I've got this crazy notion that it ought to happen the old-fashioned way, by putting the rest of America to work and letting the rest of America earn for the work that they do.

That's why when we say yes, we should raise taxes on the upper 2 percent of Americans because they're paying seventy-six billion less than they would had the 1980 tax rates stayed in effect, we still want to keep the tax rates at a modest level and use that money to pay for an investment tax credit for industry, for new plants and equipment, the same kind of tax credit that John Kennedy put in, the same kind of tax credit that our competitors have. In America we tell manufacturers you get more tax breaks for shutting your plant down and moving it overseas than you do for modernizing equipment here. We ought to reverse that in this country.

That's why we say, instead of getting a capital-gains break, if you hold a stock certificate for a year, you ought to get a break if you start a new business and invest in it for five years. Eighty-five percent of the new jobs in this country are being created in units of under fifty. Let's give people an incentive to risk, but to risk to put other people to work. The American people will support that. That's the American way.

That's why we say we ought to put more incentives into research and development, into low-income housing, into those things that will rebuild our country and put the American people to work. We cannot have another four years where 80 percent of the jobs we create are in the public sector. Even those of you who are public-sector employees know that you have to be supported by a vital private sector. This is a free-enterprise economy. Who ever thought we'd have a four-year period where 80 percent of the net new jobs in the country came from the public sector in a Republican administration that vows to hate government?

You know what those public-sector people are doing? You know what they're doing? They're running jails, because we're first in the world in the percentage of people we've got behind bars because we're undereducated and underemployed, because we haven't done enough to reduce crime.

You know what else they're doing? They're in health and human services programs where the government is taking care of exploding numbers of poor people because we don't have a national health-care plan that controls health-care costs and provides health care to everybody.

The policies of this country are shrinking the private sector and expanding the public sector because we're driving Americans down when we ought to be lifting them up, and it is a terrible mistake.

I want to have a vibrant public sector. I want to use the government to promote growth in the private sector.

That's why I want to spend twenty billion dollars a year for the next four years in defense cuts, in revenue increases on the wealthiest Americans, to build a transportation and a communications system and an environmental cleanup system that will put people back to work who lost their jobs in the defense business, who can be part of a high-wage, high-growth infrastructure economy for the twenty-first century.

That's why I want a policy that expands trade on terms that are fair to the United States. If you look at the last quarter of anemic growth, you will see that almost all of our low growth was because of a dramatic drop in exports. This administration says they really believe in that. You had a dramatic drop in exports. I believe, as all of you know, that if we had the right kind of trade agreement with Mexico it would be good for us, because if we have no agreement we'll still see jobs go on a fast track down there seeking relief from high health-care costs, thinking the only way they can make money is to drive wages down. I have seen manufacturing countries export more per capita than we do and still build a high-wage base at home, and we can do that. We ought to pass Super 301 trade authority. We ought to tell our trading partners we're going to open markets. And we ought to have the right kind of agreements with all of our partners. But with Europe becoming more integrated and maybe more closed, with Asia becoming more integrated and maybe more closed, we have to have some markets. And that's why I hope we can get the right kind of agreement with Mexico.

The president accused me of waffling on the issue, because I wouldn't trust him with an agreement I haven't read. He taught me four years ago I can't read his lips. I'm going to have to read the paper. I want to see the paper.

But we have got to be winners in the world. We've got to promote global growth. Because we've had an irresponsible policy, other nations have followed slow-growth policies, and the whole world has been winding down, because we have refused to lead in putting people back to work, in investing in our future, and in responsibly reducing the American deficit while increasing investments in critical areas to our economic growth. This whole election is going to be about whether we can really create an environment with a growing economy, with growing opportunities.

We say that we value families. All Americans do. But our administration does not act like it does. Most families have good values. What they want to do is have a chance to live by them. They know that there's nothing wrong with the American dream. The American dream hasn't failed, the policies of this administration have. And it's time to change them. It is time to change them.

What I want to say to you is, we have just about sixty-one days left—sixty-one days in which we have to unite the American people, in which we have to convince them that we are prepared to go beyond the policies of the past, beyond trickle-down, beyond borrow and spend—not back to tax and spend, but forward to invest and grow, that we are all prepared to do our part and all prepared to seize the future.

I have been terribly impressed with some of the things that I have seen in some of the work sites that many of you represent: workers working in new ways, taking more responsibility for the productive process, eliminating middle layers of regulation and management, recreating a high-productivity work force. The rest of America needs to follow that lead, but we have to first of all have a president who will lead the Congress and lead the country in a sensible—sensible—economic policy that will reward that kind of hard work.

I am tired of seeing Americans work harder for less. And if you give a chance to our team, we'll give you an economic proposal you can be proud of instead of this ridiculous list of promises and these election-year conversions that don't even start a year ahead of time, but only start two months ahead of time. Let's go out there for the next nine weeks and ask America to seize on something real, to have real hope over the fears the Republicans are putting out and to choose the future over a proven road of failure and to seize new ideas instead of things we know won't work.

I need your help. America needs your help. We can be together. We can do something wonderful. We can make all of the hope and aspiration that I have seen in the eyes of all of the men and women and boys and girls, that I have seen on these bus trips, in the inner cities, people of all races, in the rural areas on the big combines with their Clinton-Gore banners hanging off of them. We can be faithful to this hope if we will seize the next nine weeks. I am committed to it. I know you are. Let's go win this election.

Thank you very much.

The Working People's President

Labor Day Campaign Rally
Independence, Missouri
September 7, 1992

Forgoing the traditional Democratic Labor Day campaign kick-off with the national labor leadership in Detroit's Cadillac Square, Clinton chose to deliver his Labor Day speech at Harry Truman's hometown of Independence, Missouri, perhaps helping to establish an image of his own independence. He stood at the foot of a huge statue of President Truman in front of the Jackson County Courthouse and spoke to a cheering crowd of several thousand that packed the courthouse square and filled the downtown area.

Clinton's speech was delivered against the sound of thunder in the overcast skies, and, as rain began to fall midway through his talk, he departed from the script and told his audience, "I'll stay in the rain if you will. Folks, we've had twelve years of trickle-down. We can take twelve more minutes of it to turn our country around."

This speech is in the rally genre, visually crafting and rhetorically developing the perception of Clinton as an independent leader and defender of middle-class Americans by making an implicit comparison with Truman. Clinton noted that recently President Bush had tried to compare himself to President Truman, but he reminded the partisan audience that Bush had cast his first vote against Truman and said, "The truth is, the only part of Harry Truman's legacy that George Bush really wants is a victory in the election. And the only job he wants to save is his own."

❖ ❖ ❖

Ladies and gentlemen, on this Labor Day, I am proud to be in the hometown of the president who will always be remembered as the working people's president, Harry Truman.

I grew up in small Arkansas towns not so different from Independence, places where people know their neighbors. They know when the kids are born; they care when people die; they bear one another's burdens; and they live by their values instead of preaching at other people.

You know, Harry Truman's first job was at Clinton's Drugstore.

And if you read David McCullough's magnificent biography of Truman, he says one of the things Truman couldn't stand was all the hypocrites standing on the street corner telling everybody how good they were and then sneaking into the drugstore for a shot of whiskey. He said, if you want one, go to a bar and act like a person, quit being a hypocrite about it.

On Labor Day in Harry Truman's hometown, it's time for us as Americans to reaffirm who we are and to remember who George Bush is.

Harry Truman woke up every day dedicated to doing right by the people with whom he grew up and with whom he lived, the people who work hard, raise their kids, pay their taxes, and play by the rules. Harry Truman did not wake up every morning worrying about how to lower taxes one more time on millionaires.

Harry Truman's living legacy is the great American middle class, a living legacy of the generation of Americans who went to college because of the GI Bill, who were able to buy a home because of FHA and VA mortgages, who raised my generation with the hope and the opportunity that all things were possible.

George Bush's legacy is the destruction of that very middle class. Harry Truman's living legacy is the civil rights laws that guarantee people who are equal in the eyes of the Lord are also equal in the eyes of the law.

And Harry Truman's legacy, yet unfulfilled, is the dream that health care will be a right, not a privilege for every American.

George Bush's legacy is the use of the power of the presidency to divide us and the denial that it is possible to control health-care costs and provide health care for all Americans.

Yesterday I had a homecoming in Hot Springs, Arkansas, the town where I went to public schools and graduated. My teachers and my classmates, the people with whom I first worked were all there. They were good, solid, mainstream Americans.

And I said to them and I'll say to you now, many Americans have absolutely forgotten to believe that it's possible that someone who came from them could actually be president and that someone who came from them and cares about them could wake up every morning in the White House worrying about the lives of the American people. But that's exactly what I'll do if you give me a chance to serve.

Harry Truman said, and I quote, "If the working people of this country are well off, whether they work in factories or on the farms, in offices or in stores, this country will get along all right."

George Bush and Dan Quayle are the kind of Republicans that Harry Truman used to say he told the truth about them and they thought it was hell.

As Truman said, they honestly believe that prosperity begins at the top and would trickle down in due time to benefit all people.

Well, we've tried it their way for a dozen years now. In 1980, America had the highest wages in the world, and now we're thirteenth. For more than ten years, most Americans and most people listening to me today have worked longer work weeks for less money to pay more for the basics of life. Isn't that right?

And yet for the first time in seventy years, the top 1 percent of Americans control more wealth than the bottom 90 percent.

Can you believe that a man with this kind of record would be going around the country with a straight face comparing himself to Harry Truman?

George Bush cast his first vote against Harry Truman, and he has spent four years fighting against everything that Harry Truman fought for, and we won't let him forget it in the last eight weeks of this election.

Harry Truman's great legacy was taking responsibility for his job, making America strong at home and abroad, and building a broad middle class.

The Bush legacy is denying responsibility for the problems in the country, focusing on foreign policy and forgetting about the interest of the American people, and destroying the great American middle class. And we won't let them forget it in the next eight weeks of this election.

The truth is, the only part of Harry Truman's legacy that George Bush really wants is a victory in the election. And the only job he wants to save is his own. And we won't let them forget it in the next weeks.

This election provides Americans their clearest choice in a generation, a choice between hope and fear, between running in place and moving ahead, between more of the same trickle-down and embarking on a new course to guarantee old opportunities and the American dream.

George Bush wants to put even more wealth in the hands of those who are already wealthy, and I want to create opportunity for all the rest of Americans, too.

This election is a choice between two futures, four more years of broken promises, broken hopes, and broken dreams, or a different course. Just last week, we learned that the average American family has lost eleven hundred dollars in purchasing power, the biggest drop in over thirty years, that another two million Americans, including one in five of our children, sank into poverty, that we lost another one hundred and sixty-seven thousand jobs in the private sector.

And when this report came out, the White House said that was encouraging.

Since George Bush became president, the only growth we've had in jobs has come in the government he says he despises. There have been nearly forty thousand jobs dropped in the private sector. Think of it, a decline in the private sector.

They say that I have not been a good governor of your neighboring state, but my state ranks first in job growth in the last year.

And now it is clear that there have been more than ninety thousand private-sector jobs created in Arkansas since George Bush became president and over thirty thousand jobs reduced in the private sector in the country as a whole. And he wants us to believe that he is Harry Truman.

He wants us to believe that we're better off. He said yesterday—they said, can you really say we're better off than we were four years ago? He said yes.

It reminds me of the story of the fellow that fell out the ten-story window, and when he got to the third story, he looked down and he looked up and he said, so far so good.

In the last month, we've learned a little more about what the next four years will be like. With a four-hundred-billion-dollar deficit, the wreckage of trickle-down before us, Mr. Bush said, give me four more years, and even though we got a four-hundred-billion-dollar deficit, I'll give the rich another tax cut and I'll give you one, too.

I'm going to give everybody something. And I'm going to pay for it with spending cuts, and I'll tell you about them a little later.

Tune in in January.

But we know already from what he said that, while he won't ask millionaires to pay a penny more in taxes, he wants the elderly to pay two thousand dollars more for their medical bills.

I'll stay in the rain if you will.

Folks, we've had twelve years of trickle-down. We can take twelve more minutes of it to turn our country around.

George Bush wants an across-the-board capital-gains cut for the wealthy, but he wants to charge students two thousand more dollars in interest for their student loans.

He called me a fearmonger for suggesting that foreign corporations whose incomes have gone up should pay their fair share of taxes, but he's recommended cutting 1.2 million disabled veterans off of the roll of disability benefits.

On this Labor Day, his answer to the pain of America's working class is more and more pain for the working class.

Harry Truman gave the special interests hell. George Bush is giving it to you, and it's time you took your future back.

Today is the beginning of this general election campaign in earnest. And I hope to goodness that today is the end, the beginning of the end of George Bush's presidency of broken promises: fifteen million new jobs, read my lips, an environmental presidency, an education presidency, a kinder, gentler America.

Harry Truman had a sign on his desk—you remember what it said? The buck stops here.

But when George Bush became president, he put that sign in the basement and put another sign on his desk. It said: the blame begins here.

He has blamed his failures on everything from the Federal Reserve to Saddam Hussein, from Congress to consumers to the press. He says the recession is really over, we just don't know it. And if it's not really over, it's because we have an attitude problem.

The buck doesn't stop with George Bush. It doesn't even slow down there.

He wants you to believe that for the last four years, he's had to neglect America's problems because he's been so busy saving the world. He has taken responsibility for the courage of the Polish dock workers, for the courage of the people who stood in Moscow and stood atop those tanks. He says, I did that.

But when you say, well, what about the auto workers who lost their jobs in Michigan or the garment workers in New York or the computer workers in California, he said, I didn't have anything to do with that. What do you expect of me? I'm just the president of the United States.

Harry Truman knew better. At the end of World War II, he helped to lead us, to set up a political and military and economic framework that brought prosperity to America, that brought prosperity to the world, and that eventually led to the collapse of Soviet communism. But he knew that a country that is not strong at home cannot be strong abroad. And he gave workers more dignity, more security, and more opportunity than they ever had before.

And now I want you to know that if you give me a chance at the end of the Cold War, I will do what Harry Truman did at the end of World War II—more opportunity, more responsibility, an America strong at home as well as strong abroad.

I am tired of George Bush saying we can't compete and win; we can't have high-wage jobs; we can't control health-care costs; we just can't do what other countries do. I say we can.

Al Gore and I are a part of a "we can" campaign. That's what America is all about.

And you don't have to read our lips. You can read our plan. We're handing out ten thousand copies of this book to you today.

Not just something I cooked up for a campaign, but the work of more than ten years of my life trying to figure out what it takes to make sure every man and woman, every boy and girl can live up to the fullest of their God-given capacities.

I tell you, my fellow Americans, we've got to go beyond trickle-down economics, not back to tax and spend, but ahead to invest and educate and cooperate and compete and grow, putting people first. That is the economic philosophy that will prevail in the twenty-first century.

We want to give incentives to create jobs for small business people and industry and bring growth back to America. We want to put the American people back to work and educate them and control health-care costs, and that's what this plan does.

Before you drown, I want to tell you this one final thing. You read this plan, and you will see what it does to open the doors of college education, what it does to provide health care to your family, what it does to revive the jobs of America.

But you remember this: George Bush's message is, we could do worse; you can't trust Clinton and Gore.

They have nothing to run on but negativism and fear. We are running on vision and hope, and we're going to do what Harry Truman did, for the next fifty-seven days, go across this country, give 'em hell, and make America what it ought to be again.

Thank you, and God bless you all.

A Second Chance

Clayton County Department of Family and Children's Services
Jonesboro, Georgia
September 9, 1992

Portraying himself as a new Democrat willing to overhaul the nation's welfare system, Clinton renewed his campaign to capture the issue of welfare reform from Republicans and tried to present himself as one Democrat willing to use new ideas, neither conservative nor liberal, to make the system work as it was intended. On the same day that his campaign began airing a television spot on welfare reform, claiming that, as governor, Clinton had moved seventeen thousand people off the welfare rolls and into the work force in Arkansas, he delivered this speech on welfare reform to a mostly white audience of about two hundred social workers and mothers and children outside the Terrell Starr Resource Center, the main office of the Clayton County Department of Family and Children's Services, in Jonesboro, Georgia. The city is in a suburban Atlanta district that was represented until reapportionment by Newt Gingrich, an area of white "swing voters" that had previously supported Republican candidates in federal elections.

❖ ❖ ❖

Thank you. Thank you very much, Governor Miller and ladies and gentlemen.

I want to say a special word of thanks to the fine people who work in this PEACH program and to the people who participate in it, not only to those who are here with me but those with whom I met behind this building in the play yard. While you were out here suffering in the sun, we were playing in the sand. Don't you just resent it? We actually talked for a few minutes. There were several parents and their children who were either present participants in the PEACH program or graduates. Most of them are right back here. Would y'all raise your hand? Let's give them a hand. They were very helpful to me.

I'm here today to talk about this because I believe in the kind of work being done by the PEACH program and because I've worked with wonderful people back in my state, like the people who work in this program, to help move people off of welfare, out of dependency, to open their futures instead of to make them believe that life is a dead end waiting for another government check that is not enough to support your children or change your life.

I became first involved in the work of welfare reform way back in 1980, and since then, I have believed passionately that we ought to change the welfare system as we know it.

Most of what I have learned about welfare I have learned from the people who are on welfare or those who have been on it, or those who have worked with them.

I share a common belief that I heard from these mothers today and the counselors that the American people share, people on welfare are the people who dislike it most of all.

Most people on welfare are dying for another alternative, willing to seize it, and they'd like to end the welfare system as we know it.

Today, I want to share with you my plan to do that. It is more important today than it would have been a few years ago because of the alarming rate of increase in poverty. Here in Georgia and across the country there are more people who are working poor.

Last week the commerce department reported that average family income dropped eleven hundred dollars last year alone. Over the last decade, the percentage of hard-work low-wage jobs increased dramatically.

And now—listen to this—one in every ten Americans is on food stamps. America's welfare rolls are full to bursting, increasing five times faster under this administration than under the previous twelve years under Ronald Reagan and Jimmy Carter combined.

Three million more people have gone on welfare since 1988; three million more are out of work. When poverty and jobless rolls rise, we all pay. In the past year—listen to this—we spent eight billion dollars more than we were spending three years ago on welfare and food stamps alone.

A big part of the answer is obviously an economic program to put the American people back to work and to get our incomes going up again. And obviously that is what I have talked most about in this campaign. But the changing face of welfare, and the changing nature of it, and the enormous barriers to people moving from welfare to a productive life deserves special attention. Especially now that most people on welfare are young women and their little children. And the fact that only half of the people on welfare get off quickly.

That's just my musical background. It proves the point. In the mid-1980s, on behalf of all the governors, Republicans and Democrats, I co-chaired a welfare-reform task force. We worked in 1988 with the Congress and with the Reagan White House to write something called the Family Support Act of 1988, the first major, major reform in the welfare system in more than a generation.

The law gave the states some financial help and some marching orders. It said try to end welfare by giving more education and training to mothers, and then requiring those who can go to work to go to work, either when their children turn three or when their children are one if there is available child care.

The problem with the law is, as Georgia knows, it's never been fully implemented, and it didn't go far enough. But Arkansas wanted to be in the forefront of that law, and so, as Governor Miller said, we started Project Success, to give child care, health care, and education and training, and then move people off welfare.

In three years, seventeen thousand have moved from welfare to work, saving our taxpayers twelve million dollars, but far more important, opening a brighter future to parents and children.

Independent researchers from the Manpower Demonstration Research Corporation concluded it was one of the three best programs in the country. This PEACH program is doing a great job. It is not in every county in Georgia, and not every state in America has implemented welfare reform, because the 1988 act has not been fully implemented by this administration.

They talk a lot about moving people from welfare to work, but if you don't put the money in there for training, for education, for child care, for transportation, and you don't do it in every county in America, you cannot crack the welfare problem.

So the first thing I think every person with whom I have ever talked on welfare agreed that welfare ought to be a second chance, not a way of life. It's time to end this system as we know it, and to start with two simple principles: first, people who can work ought to go to work, and no one should be able to stay on welfare forever.

And second, no one who does work and who has children in the home should live in poverty, as too many are today.

I am running for president on a plan that would give everyone the funding they need for education, training, child care, and transportation. But after two years, or after the end of an education-and-training program, everyone on welfare would have to go to work, either with a private-sector job or, if none is available, with a job provided by the state or the local government in community service.

A strict time limit for AFDC recipients, coupled with a real commitment to help them support their children, provide them the education and transportation they need, would literally make welfare what it ought to be, a temporary hand to people who have fallen on tough times.

This is not a conservative or a liberal idea. It's both. It's different. And the people who have lived with the present system know it will work if we invest what we ought to and are firm in our administration of it. By the time we are through, we shouldn't have a welfare system in America; we ought to have a helping-hand program, followed by a jobs program.

The plan that I have offered sets money aside, up to six billion dollars over the next four years, up to six billion dollars a year, mounting up to that over the next four years, and pays for it from the cuts that we will make in wasteful government spending; in defense savings; and in raising taxes on the wealthiest 2 percent of Americans, whose incomes went up in America while their tax rates went down, the direct reverse of what happened to the middle class.

When you consider that if we do not change welfare, 25 percent of the people who are on welfare today will still be on it in the year 2000, you can be sure that we have to do it, and that doing it will save a lot of money down the road. Spending a couple of thousand dollars a year on a welfare recipient today; helping that person to become independent, to lead their children in a different direction; to open up new avenues of possibility; will mean more incomes and more taxes and less dependence in the future.

More important, it will improve the quality of life not only for people on welfare but for their friends and neighbors as well. We've heard a lot of talk this year about family values, and that's fine with me; most of us wouldn't be here today without them. But if we're going to be pro-family, we ought to be pro-child and pro-work, and that's what this plan is.

Today for people on welfare, going to work too often means taking a job that will never do anything, because you don't have any education and training; and you may lose it in a couple of weeks. It often means losing medical coverage and child-care benefits, giving up Medicaid. It often means struggling to find a job that will keep you mired in poverty forever.

I want to make work pay by simply expanding the earned income tax credit for the working poor. If you work forty hours a week and you've got a child in the house, the income tax system ought to give you a refund to lift you above the poverty line. It'd be the cheapest thing we could ever do to say we are for work and for family, and we'll reward the right values in this country.

We have to provide medical coverage to working people with children, and to control health-care costs while we're doing it. To do that, we'll have to take on insurance companies, the way the government regulates health care, the unbelievable paperwork and bureaucracy and waste in our system. But don't let anybody tell you we can't do it. Your nation spends 30 percent more of its income than any country in the world on health care, and yet we don't provide primary and preventive care, in poor rural areas in inner cities, and we don't do the things that other countries do to control health-care costs.

We're going to do that if I win this election. We also need to find a way for poor people to get into the free-enterprise system. There's a community development bank in Chicago called the South Shore Development Bank I've talked about all over this country that actually loans money to poor people to go into business for themselves or in small groups. And they've made money doing it, because they understand that poor people are like other people. Some are smart, some have skills, some have ideas, some can make money. And they've made money in a bank loaning money to people who are redlined in most communities in this country.

I want to set up a network of community development banks to bring free enterprise to poor people in rural areas and in inner cities.

The next thing we have to do is be pro-savings. Earlier this year, the government ordered a young woman in New Haven, Connecticut, and her family, to repay welfare benefits because she had scrimped and saved money from a part-time job to put herself through college.

I think we ought to raise the asset limit, and encourage poor people to save money for job training, for college, and for other paths to independence. And I recommend raising it from one thousand dollars to ten thousand dollars a year to encourage people to save who are in tough times. Finally if we believe in family values, we simply have got to toughen up our system of child-support enforcement and launch a nationwide campaign to get money from deadbeat parents who can pay and won't.

I might say, one of the most impressive things to me about the conversation I just had back there is, a lot of these young women who are here working in this program, taking care of their kids, said, if you want to run this program right, you're going to have to crack down on people who don't take care of their kids the way we do.

People who use drugs instead of feeding their kids with that money, you ought to take it away from them and take care of their kids; that's what they said, not me. I was impressed by that.

Today an awful lot of the money you as taxpayers spend on welfare goes for children whose parents should be giving them support, but who aren't. If we want to do something about the fact that one in five children plus is in poverty; almost one in four children under the age of five is in poverty; we can start by tracking down an estimated twenty-five billion dollars in owed and unpaid child support.

As president, I will push for the toughest child-support enforcement possible. In our state, if you fall more than one thousand dollars behind, we report you to every major credit agency in the state. If you don't take care of your kids, you shouldn't be able to borrow money for yourself.

And last year, we collected forty-one million dollars plus, money that we don't have to pay in welfare and other public spending.

Under my plan, we'll set up a national deadbeat parents' data bank; begin a national system of child-support collections through automatic wage withholding; and make an all-out effort to establish paternity in the hospital when the baby is born; not in the courts after the father has left. We ought to use our national data-collecting systems like the IRS to make sure that you cannot cross the state lines and meet your court-ordered obligations to take care of your children.

We ought to challenge major credit agencies nationwide to report on all people who are seriously deficient in their child support. You simply shouldn't be able to borrow money for yourself if you don't take care of your kids.

It's time to send a clear message to people who bring children into this world: governments don't raise kids, people do. In the end, this isn't about government. This is about people and their futures. There will never be a government program for every problem, and the government can never take responsibility for people that they ought to take for themselves.

The only thing that really holds us together as a nation, a free nation, is that most of us get up every day and do the right thing. We go to work; we do our best by our family; we honor the law; we treat our neighbor with respect; we just do the right thing. Nobody makes us do it.

We have got to empower people to assume that level of personal responsibility for themselves and for their children. It is one way we can bring people together. Surely every American, without regard to political party or religious faith or philosophical convictions, can agree that we can stop the division and blame and finger-pointing that has characterized welfare while things have gotten worse, and challenged people, then given them the means to make the most of their lives. That is what this is all about.

I want to tell you my favorite story. A few years ago when I started working on welfare reform, I brought some people from my state to Washington, D.C., who had been on welfare, and who had gone through one of our experimental programs before we went statewide. And one of these women was very articulate, and I was just questioning her. And there were all these governors just sitting around just absolutely fascinated listening to this lady talk. And I said, "Do you think that this ought to be mandatory? You think that people ought to have to be in this program to get a check?" She said, "I sure do, otherwise I might be home watching TV instead of up here talking to you." And I said, "Well, now that you've got this job, what's the best thing about it?" And you could have heard a pin drop, and that lady looked out at that crop of governors, and she said, "When my boy goes to school, and they ask him, what does your momma do for a living, he can give an answer."

The Georgia PEACH program is testament to the fact that these women behind me and those women who talked to me, and this fine lady over here who now works for the state senate, people want to take care of their kids, and they want to take care of themselves.

This is a crazy old world we're living in, and a lot of things happen to people that we wish didn't happen. But what brings us together today is the conviction that if we get up tomorrow, we can do better than we're doing today, and that life is full of potentials, and that we need to look at these folks on welfare, as potential, full blown, vibrant, active, constructive American citizens who are doing a great job raising their kids. And we need them.

We do not have a person to waste in this country. So I say to you that I hope that in the next fifty-five days all of you will reflect on this. Because one of the things that will chart the future of America as we move toward the twenty-first century is whether we can do a better job in making sure that every person lives up to the fullest of their potential.

Every person who's on welfare, and every kid who doesn't make it in school, is another person who's not out there in a job making America the strongest power in the world, and helping all the rest of us to see to our parents in their old age; our children in their youth; and our own lives in their full flower.

This is a very important issue for every American. It's time to end the welfare system as we know it and lift the people on welfare by providing more responsibility and more opportunity.

Thank you very much.

To Redefine Our Covenant

B'nai B'rith International Convention
Washington, D.C.
September 9, 1992

B'nai B'rith held its thirty-sixth biennial international convention at the Sheraton Washington Hotel, and President Bush had addressed the group in person the day before. He devoted his remarks almost entirely to Middle East issues and called Clinton an uncertain leader who would have jeopardized Israel's security by "waffling and wavering" on the Persian Gulf War. Bush, who got about 25 percent of the Jewish vote in 1988, received only mild applause during his speech.

Clinton addressed the fifteen hundred delegates representing all fifty states and fifty other countries at 10:45 via satellite on the final morning of the three-day conference from Jonesboro, Georgia, using a set with an easy chair and a U.S. flag and a B'nai B'rith banner in the background. He was introduced to the group by Democratic National Committee vice-chairwoman Lynn Cutler and delivered a speech that made the transition from the Middle East to problems at home, including education, the economy, health care, housing, and appointments to the U.S. Supreme Court, recognizing that Jewish voters were interested in domestic policy issues and constituted important voting blocs in several larger swing states.

Some audience members were disappointed that Clinton had not appeared in person for the speech, and many disagreed with his support for the sale of F-15 jet fighters to Saudi Arabia; nonetheless, he received more than twenty rounds of applause and one 35-second standing ovation during his thirty-minute speech.

❖ ❖ ❖

Thank you very much. It's an honor to join you today for your thirty-sixth biennial convention. For nearly a century and a half, B'nai B'rith has set the standard of this nation for community service, individual responsibility, and opposition to every form of bigotry and intolerance. I want to thank President Kent Schiner for his kind invitation to be with you today, and my long-time friend, Lynn Cutler, for her generous introduction.

A few years back, I was the honoree at the B'nai B'rith dinner in Hot Springs, Arkansas, where I grew up, so I'm an old friend of your organization. Today we join together once again to pay tribute to your extraordinary contributions to the struggle for justice here in America and around the world. You've been there to help those in need in your own neighborhoods, establishing local volunteer efforts, helping the blind, settling refugees from the former Soviet Union, combating the scourge of drugs, and working to strengthen the education of young Americans.

Even when I was growing up in Arkansas, I knew of the efforts of B'nai B'rith. Way back in 1914, B'nai B'rith opened the Levi Hospital in my home town of Hot Springs and today, because of your generous support, that hospital has become a major center for the treatment of arthritis and related diseases, as well as a center for the rehabilitation of a wide variety of ailments, serving hundreds of patients every year without concern for their ability to pay. There is also a B'nai B'rith senior citizens housing complex in downtown Hot Springs, two synagogues, and a thriving Jewish community. So I grew up with a keen appreciation for the work of B'nai B'rith. And I've always admired your commitment to helping others.

Wherever human tragedy strikes, at home or abroad, you've been there to provide assistance. You moved swiftly to address the crisis in Somalia, launched your own drive to help raise funds to stave off starvation of millions of Somalis. You were there to help the earthquake victims in San Francisco, Mexico City, Iran, and Armenia. You provided aid to cyclone victims in Bangladesh and pressed the world to act against the atrocities in Bosnia. And you moved very quickly to respond to the urgently needed assistance for the victims of Hurricane Andrew.

What guides each of you is a belief in a covenant that we all share, to enrich the lives of those around you, to fight bigotry, to protect liberty. At the high holidays—as the high holidays approach, each of you renews your commitment to your own covenant, and as the Shofar marks this period of reflection, let us join together to renew our dedication to the values we share in common.

America and Israel share a special bond. Our relationship is unique among all nations. Like America, Israel is a strong democracy, a symbol of freedom, an oasis of liberty, a home to the oppressed and the persecuted. Yet in this world where the Cold War has ended, peace is still a long way away in the Middle East. Israel is still surrounded by nations in pursuit of weapons of mass destruction, still at risk of Scud attacks by Saddam Hussein and now facing new, more advanced Scuds from Syria; still suffering the economic hardships of the Arab boycott; still waiting for an offer of peace from her Arab neighbors.

The current round of peace negotiations taking place in Washington is the best chance in a decade of bringing a lasting peace to the region. When I met with Prime Minister Rabin last month in Washington, I made clear to him my determination to continue the peace process if elected. I want to be very clear about this: there will be no hiatus in the current negotiations.

The recent elections in Israel have given this new government a mandate to move forward, and Prime Minister Rabin has wasted no time in breathing new life into the negotiations. He's agreed to stop all political settlement activity and shift the funds to spending on infrastructure and education in Israel. He's freed eight hundred Arab prisoners and reversed eleven deportation orders of Palestinians. He's pledged a gradual reopening of streets in what had been some of the most violent commercial and residential areas. He's eased restrictions on Arab laborers entering Israel. Israel has reaffirmed its recognition of the UN resolutions that are the foundations of the peace process and is specifically applying them to the negotiations with Syria and Israel. And it now has under consideration a plan for full autonomy for the Palestinians that includes early elections. Now it is time for the other side to reciprocate.

The peace negotiations will no doubt take time, but there is a simple step the Arabs should have taken long ago, an end to their illegal boycott against Israel. That boycott is economic warfare and that war must end now. It is time the administration made it clear that the United States will no longer turn a blind eye to this practice, by putting an end to U.S. government contracts with anyone who participates in the boycott. That is why I support Senator Al Gore's initiative to prohibit defense department contracts with any foreign companies that participate in the Arab League's boycott against Israel.

We need an administration that will promote action to stop the spread of dangerous missiles in the Middle East, and a strong international effort and tough sanctions to keep weapons of mass destruction out of the hands of nations like Iran, Iraq, Syria, and Libya. I do not believe we ought to pressure Israel into making unilateral concessions in the peace process as this administration has tried to do.

I believe we must stand by Israel in its historic effort to integrate thousands and hundreds of thousands of refugees into its society. And I believe the United States should serve as a catalyst and an honest broker in the peace negotiations. For in the end, only Israel, the Palestinians, and the Arab nations can make lasting peace with one another.

The United States must not waver in the meantime in its financial, security, and moral commitments to Israel. That is why I said early on in my campaign it is in our nation's best interest to continue military and economic assistance to Israel because this vital aid encourages long-term stability in the region and demonstrates United States commitment to Israel's security and sovereignty.

I am especially disturbed by the long-term outlook for the spread of weapons of mass destruction. It is very menacing. That means that our commitment must include not only an effort to reduce this spread, but a reaffirmation of our strong commitment to maintaining Israel's qualitative military edge over its foes. The sight of children huddled in basements with gas masks during the Gulf War brought home to every American just how vulnerable Israel is and just how volatile the region is.

Clearly, we must meet our security commitments to our coalition partners in the Gulf, but any of those actions must be taken in close consultation with the government of Israel, and any arms sales must not undermine our commitment to Israel's qualitative edge. As I have said repeatedly, any sale of F-15s to Saudi Arabia must only go forward in this context. I believe we can and should provide for the adequate defenses of our coalition partners in the region in a way that does not threaten Israel's security. As I have said, I would support the sale of some versions of the F-15s to Saudi Arabia, but we must not sell any offensive version of the F-15s to Saudi Arabia that could threaten Israel, tilt the military balance, or erode Israel's qualitative military edge.

There is another threat to Israel that has gone long unaddressed. It is a threat that can weaken Israel militarily, economically, and politically. It can hinder our ability to respond to crises that may affect Israel. That threat is the weakening American economy. Without a growing economy, without a strong, stable, and secure American middle class, America's commitment to Israel will always be under pressure.

It is time we had a president who will put our country back to work again, get our country moving forward again, have an America where our jobs are growing and our incomes are growing, not shrinking. Senator Gore and I have a plan to expand the economy, to create jobs and to strengthen our middle class and reduce poverty. It recognizes that our first foreign-policy priority and our first domestic priority must be one and the same, a revitalized economy, for we cannot be strong abroad if we are not strong at home.

Our plan creates millions of new jobs. We'll rebuild our roads and bridges. We'll convert defense-based industries into peacetime centers of cutting-edge technology. We'll take every dollar by which we cut defense and put it back into the economy to create jobs for the twenty-first century. We'll give new incentives to the private sector to create manufacturing jobs and jobs in small business. In short, we will put America back to work again, not with more trickle-down economics, not by going back to tax and spend, but by going forward to invest, to educate, to cooperate, to compete, and to grow.

Under our plan, health care will become a right, not a privilege. We must control the health-care costs that are crippling our economy, ballooning our deficit, weakening the private sector, and we must ensure that every American has access to quality care. And our plan will begin on the first day of our inauguration, not the last two months before our effort to secure reelection.

But you and I know this election is about more than the state of our economy and the government's responsibility to provide every American a decent chance at a decent way of life. It is also about the American spirit, about what kind of country we want to be and what kind of values we choose to cherish and to pass on to our children. Frankly, I'm deeply concerned by the cynicism, the intolerance, the ugliness that threatens our society today, and no one knows better than you the danger of bigotry, antisemitism, and intolerance that is on the rise not only in America but also abroad. Your own Anti-Defamation League has been at the forefront of the struggle against hatred and bigotry for nearly half a century. You understand the threat to our society of skinheads on the rampage, the surge of neo-Nazism at the extreme fringes of our own country, and the rise of hate crimes according to your own ADL statistics. And we're all aware of the troubling rise of anti-semitism in the former communist bloc. Across the region, neo-Nazis flourish, Jewish cemeteries are desecrated, and immigrants attacked. Within the last two weeks in Germany, a holocaust memorial and an immigrant center were bombed, and anti-semitic organizations like Pamyat in Russia are on the rise.

It is the responsibility of our leaders to counter intolerance, bigotry, and hatred. As president, my commitment to opposing fear and hate and prejudice will not bend with the prevailing political wind. It will be strong, steady, and certain.

President Bush's press conference on September 12, 1990, was one of the worst days in the history of our nation's relationships. His callous remarks against the American Jewish community and its efforts to participate in our system of democracy were an affront to the basic right of all Americans to speak freely. I think patriotism requires all of us to love our country enough to right its wrongs. Patriotism is not silent in the face of wrong-headed policy; it is vocal. And while others criticize you, I applaud your patriotism. A Clinton-Gore administration will never give sanction to intolerance and bigotry.

I must say I was also deeply disturbed by the tone of the first two days of the Republican convention in Houston, where it seemed that they were more interested in dividing the American people by claiming that some of us have values others don't than in uniting us in a common effort to overcome our problems. I will never do that, and you won't see a Democratic convention putting that kind of stake between the American people.

I was raised in a different faith than most of you here, but we were both raised in a tradition which champions tolerance and which defends freedom. We both have absolute faith in the primacy of each individual's conscience and judgment. We believe everyone ought to have the freedom to worship God in his or her own way. We believe in the strength of our country and our churches and synagogues to draw from the constitutional separation between church and state. That is why this election is so terribly important.

That's just another reason this election is so terribly important. We desperately need to bring this country together, to redefine our covenant to one another, to reaffirm the relationship of neighbor to neighbor, family to family, this generation to the next. We need to solve our common problems and move our nation forward together. We can and we *must* create a nation and a government we will be proud to leave to our children. We cannot have progress without restoring our sense of community. Whether we like it or not, we're going up or down together.

If we're serious about what this country means and can yet mean, then we know America is not just a place, it's an idea, an idea cherished and given life by Puritans and Catholics, by Jews and Baptists, by Republicans and Democrats, by women and men, by people of all colors, of all races, of all religions. That means an America where hatred and bigotry are not tolerated, an America where we have a Supreme Court which will respect our Constitution, protect a woman's right to choose, and protect the rights of all Americans. A Supreme Court that will free us of the need for Congress to overturn ill-advised rulings with legislation such as the Civil Rights Restoration Act and the Religious Freedom Restoration Act.

If we are serious about our covenant for a better America, then there is one sure place where all of us can meet, the one thing that most readily unites us across all the lines that divide us—it's our concern, our love, our hope for our children. So let us join now to give our children enough faith in the beauty of the idea of America that they can make it theirs, too. This is the mission that guided the founders of our nation. It is the responsibility of our generation to carry on that dream. It was that idea which brought me and my wife to embrace the HIPPY program from Israel in our state to make it the largest program outside Israel in the world so that we could give our poorest children a chance at a better future.

Let me remind you of an incident which occurred when the delegates to the Constitutional Convention gathered in Philadelphia in 1787, a time when most of the states still had laws requiring anyone who held public office to be a Christian. Some states even specified that they had to be Protestant, believe in the divine inspiration of the Scriptures, or believe in the Trinity. A man named Jonas Philips felt the injustice of this practice so strongly that he wrote a letter to the convention delegates. "I am one of the people called Jews of the City of Philadelphia," he said. He did not think it right, he said, that any American should be singled out because of his or her religion, especially since he and many other Jews had been, quote, "true and faithful patriots during the revolution."

Eventually, the framers of the Constitution agreed and declared that there should be no religious qualification for holders of federal office. One's relationship to God, they said, was and ought to be entirely separate from one's service to country. When Jonas Philips wrote to the Constitutional Convention in 1787, he ended his letter with a prayer: "May the people of the United States rise up as a great and young lion. May God extend peace to them and their seed after them so long as the sun and moon endureth."

We are closer to that dream because of the important and committed work of B'nai B'rith. Let us join together now in our common covenant to begin the work of changing and rebuilding our country. Let us build a nation that our seed will honor as long as the sun and the moon endureth.

Next year will mark the one hundred and fiftieth anniversary of B'nai B'rith. It's hard to predict the future, especially in my line of work. But this I'll promise: If you'll invite me, I'll be honored to celebrate your one hundred and fiftieth birthday with you in Washington.

Thank you, and God bless you.

Thank you.

Common Values and the Common Good

University of Notre Dame
South Bend, Indiana
September 11, 1992

Clinton's appearance was part of Notre Dame's election-year tradition of inviting presidential candidates and political figures to speak on campus, and in preparing his remarks he reread the speech that New York governor Mario Cuomo had delivered there in September 1984. While Clinton spoke to a mostly student audience at Notre Dame, he was also attempting to speak to the nation and to the larger community of ethnic Catholic votes in the industrial Midwest. He reminded the audience of his Georgetown education and was joined on the stage by Catholic public officials, including Sen. Harris Wofford of Pennsylvania and Mayor Raymond Flynn of Boston.

On the same day that George Bush addressed the Christian Coalition in Virginia Beach and reaffirmed his position against abortion, Bill Clinton received a standing ovation from an audience of two thousand at Notre Dame's Stephan Center when he declared for "freedom of conscience in matters of philosophy and family and faith." College Republicans outside the auditorium distributed flyers that read "No draft dodgers for president," and a small group inside heckled Clinton during his speech, sailing pictures of aborted fetuses into the audience. Clinton departed from his prepared text to respond to the protesters, quoting a woman he had met during the campaign in Cedar Rapids, Iowa, who said, "I respect this debate that's going on in our country about life, but how I wish we would all reach out and try to help the children who are living."

The Baptist candidate came to the nation's best-known Catholic university in a symbolic reversal of the fashion in which John F. Kennedy had spoken to Protestant ministers in Houston in 1960, seeking to overcome anti-Catholic prejudice. Clinton said he had been "appalled to hear the voices of intolerance raised in recent weeks," and, with reference to the harsh rhetoric at the recent Republican convention, declared, "America doesn't need a religious war; America needs a reaffirmation of the values that, for most of us, are rooted in our religious faith." The address continued his general theme of personal responsibility, adding that Americans also have a responsibility to each other. The *Los Angeles Times* called the speech "a somber and evocative address" that "frequently took on the air of a sermon" and the *New York Times* said the tone "was at times confessional and at times like a homily to the converted."

❖ ❖ ❖

Thank you. Ladies and gentlemen, we know that in this room at least our supporters can win the cheering contest.

I would hope that in this great university we could also prevail in the civility contest.

I hope if my opponent or his running mate shows up at this great university during this campaign that you will go there and quietly express your support for me, but I will hope you will let them speak and have their say.

I want to say a special word of thanks to all those who have come here to be with me today, to Governor and Mrs. Bayh, who are good friends of Hillary's and mine; to Mayor Flynn. Father Malloy was entirely too modest. He did not tell you that he and Mayor Flynn were great college basketball players together. Mayor Flynn played at Providence, another good Catholic university. And Mayor Flynn is still a great athlete. Al Gore went out jogging with him the other day, and he called me, out of breath, saying that the mayor had made him run for ninety-five minutes in the city of Boston.

I want to thank Mayor Kernan and Congressman Roemer for being here. I also want to note the presence in the audience of Congresswoman Jill Long and Congressman Jim Jontz. They are both here.

You have so many young people in politics here that it makes me feel like I am clearly in the tradition of Cicero, who said that of one thing he was certain—old age begins at forty-six. I want to thank my good friend Senator Wofford for coming and all the others who are here. And I want to thank Father Malloy and the Notre Dame family for giving me the opportunity to come here to help Notre Dame celebrate its one hundred and fiftieth birthday.

I know it's traditional for presidential candidates to stand up and tell you that they sprang from humble beginnings, even if they were born in log cabins they built themselves. But today I would like to turn that around, for Notre Dame literally sprang from humble beginnings, from a log cabin one hundred and fifty years ago when Father Edward Soren took over a log cabin on the snow-covered lake shore and dared to call it a university.

He came from France, but it must have been something out of the American ground that gave him the inspiration to dream dreams so that thousands upon thousands of young people could share his vision. Out of the vision came one of the greatest universities of this nation, in service to its students, to country, and to God.

I'm especially proud to be here with those of you who participate in the center for the homeless, those who have participated in the alumni service projects, those who have participated in the center for social concerns. Service is truly a way of life here at Notre Dame. I'm proud to be here because of the national leadership exhibited by the Notre Dame family.

Your former president, Father Hesberg, served with Hillary, my wife, on the Grant Commissions—Grant Foundations Commission—on the American family, work, and citizenship. And they dealt with issues which have deeply concerned all of us for many years.

Father Hesberg and Hillary and the other commissioners issued a highly acclaimed report, entitled, "Youth in America's Future—the Forgotten Half," which I believe detailed for the first time the sharp decline in earnings among young people with no education after high school and laid out a practical agenda to offer them hope, an agenda which is now deeply embedded in my presidential campaign.

A former Notre Dame law professor, Harris Wofford, here on this platform is now a United States senator from Pennsylvania. In the best tradition of Catholic social responsibility, he is leading the fight for health care for all Americans, worked for those without it, and national service for young people.

Your football coach, Lou Holtz, spent a lot of years at Arkansas before he came here. I want to tell you a story about that. In his first season he took our team to the Orange Bowl against what was then the number-one ranked team in America. But shortly before the game, he suspended three of the team's leading offensive players for serious misconduct. He was attacked and pilloried in the press. He was even sued. And as a young attorney general, it became my duty to defend him. Against overwhelming odds, Arkansas won the football game, but more important, Lou Holtz taught our state that high standards and values come before victory on the playing field.

I'm also proud to be here because I have personally benefited from Catholic education and from my state's tradition of religious tolerance. In 1928 Governor Al Smith of New York, the first Catholic to be nominated for president, picked as his running mate Senator Joe T. Robinson from Arkansas.

They lost the election to Herbert Hoover and, in part, to anti-Catholic prejudice. But they carried my home state.

In 1960, John Kennedy was the first Catholic to be elected president. And many Americans, especially in my part of the country, said that no Catholic should be elected president because of their views. But John Kennedy carried Arkansas.

If elected, I will be the first president to graduate from a Catholic college, Georgetown University. And long before that, I learned a lot about learning life in the second and third grades at St. John's School in Hot Springs, Arkansas.

On a hot summer afternoon, twenty-nine summers ago, I met President Kennedy in the Rose Garden of the White House as a sixteen-year-old delegate to American Legion Boys' Nation. That afternoon turned me toward public service. After President Kennedy was killed, another southerner, Lyndon Johnson, succeeded to the presidency with the promise to enact John Kennedy's program to get America moving again and to bring America together.

Because I wanted to be in public service, watch the Great Society unfold, and get a first-class education, I enrolled in Georgetown University, the nation's oldest Jesuit college. I wondered when I went there whether I would be out of place, a Southern Baptist who had rarely been far from home. Thankfully, both the students and the faculty there held to the scriptural commandment to befriend the stranger in their midst. And together, we found much common ground that Baptists and Catholics could walk together. And in the end, I felt completely at home in the Catholic tradition of Georgetown.

I was then, and I remain today, deeply drawn to the Catholic social mission, to the idea that, as President Kennedy said, here on earth God's work must truly be our own. I have seen it in the work that Catholic politicians like Mayor Flynn of Boston and Senator Wofford, whom I admire, have done.

I love the Catholic understanding of history and tradition, and how they shape us in our lives. And I love all the vigorous arguments. How I love those arguments.

I know that all of you here at Notre Dame will take from this wonderful place those same blessings, good friends, great and caring teachers, a strong sense of your place in history and your mission in the world, and a devotion to a lifetime of learning through honest debates and open, inquiring minds.

Both Baptists and Catholics in different ways are rooted in the spiritual richness of America's working people—people who know the pain of poverty and the bite of discrimination, people for whom life is a daily struggle in which they must sweat and sacrifice for themselves and their families, for whom life is made worthwhile not only through hard work and self-reliance but through opening their hearts to God and their hands to their neighbors.

Each of our faiths teaches that nobody makes it alone. Ben Franklin once said, we'll hang together or assuredly we'll hang separately. That is the heart of the Judeo-Christian understanding of what it means to be a member of the human society. Rabbi Hillel said two thousand years ago, "If I am not for myself, who will be for me? If I am only for myself, who am I?" Today America has wandered far from the lessons of our faiths and our history. Most people are working harder for less money. We are becoming a nation of greater poverty and much, much greater economic inequality. And that is straining the ties that bind us.

Today I want to talk about the America I see and seek, but most of all, about the values behind that vision of America. I want an America that values the freedom and the dignity of the individual. All of us must respect the reflection of God's image in every man and woman, and so we must value their freedom, not just their political freedom, but their freedom of conscience in matters of family and philosophy and faith.

I am grateful that I was born in a country where my faith can be powerful because it is a voluntary offering of a free and joyous spirit. As that great American Baptist, Roger Williams, understood so well, without the freedom to say no, the word "yes" is meaningless.

Here in our country more people believe in God, more people go to church or temples, and more people put religion at the center of their lives than in any other advanced society on Earth. And that is a tribute to the genius and the courage of the American experiment that our government can be the protector of the freedom of every faith because it is the exclusive property of none.

That is the promise of the First Amendment's guarantees of freedom of religion and separation of church and state, guarantees that my Southern Baptist church traditionally has supported strongly. Our freedom of conscience depends upon mutual respect.

Each of us must never forget that as John Kennedy reminded the Baptist ministers in Houston in 1960, when intolerance is turned loose, and I quote, "Today I may be the victim, but tomorrow it may be you. Until the whole fabric of our harmonious society is ripped." President Kennedy was right. To preserve our social fabric, we must always appreciate the wonderful diversity of the American tapestry. That is why like so many Americans I have been appalled to hear the voices of intolerance raised in recent weeks—voices that have proclaimed that some families aren't real families, that some Americans aren't—that some Americans aren't real Americans, and one even said that what this country needs is a, quote, "religious war." Well, America does not need a religious war. It needs a reaffirmation of the values that for most of us are rooted in our religious faith.

Like most Americans, I go to church on Sunday, and until I lost my voice early in this campaign, I sang in my choir. My faith is a source of pride to me, but far, far more important, it is a source of humility, because it teaches that none of us is a stranger to sin and to weakness. It is a source of hope because it teaches that each of us is capable of redemption. And it is a source of challenge because it teaches that we must all strive to live according to our beliefs.

We all have the right to wear our religion on our sleeves, but we should also hold it in our hearts and live it in our lives.

And if we are to truly practice what we preach, then Americans of every faith and viewpoint should look for ways to come together to promote the common good. That requires a much greater respect for honest diversity than we are hearing today.

It wasn't so long ago that some American voices suggested that Catholics weren't real Americans and invited the equivalent of religious wars against them. As Mario Cuomo said in his brilliant speech here at Notre Dame in 1984, "I protect my right to be a Catholic by preserving your right to believe as a Jew, a Protestant, or a nonbeliever, or anything else you choose."

We know Governor Cuomo said that the price of seeking to force our beliefs on others is that they might someday force theirs on us. This freedom is the fundamental strength in our unique experiment in government.

I want an America with those convictions to have a renewed sense of community, an America that is coming together, not coming apart. I want to bring back the American spirit that says we're all in this together, and we're going to rise or fall together.

It is that spirit that built America from the barn raisings on the old frontier to the immigrant mutual aid societies in the great society to the churches that have helped generations of African Americans make a way out of no way.

It is a spirit that draws upon our Judeo-Christian tradition. Everything in the Old Testament concerns not isolated individuals, but a people, a community. The books of law govern them. The books of history recounted their wanderings, their troubles, and their triumphs. And the prophets are the great poetic voice that recalled them again and again to the meaning of the people of God.

In the Christian tradition, that emphasis on community continues, since the Acts, the gospels, and the epistles all come from early Christian communities, and recount to us their problems, their failures, their strengths, but, above all, their unity.

Echoing down the ages is the simple but powerful truth that no grace of God was ever given me for me alone. To the terrible question of Cain—am I my brother's keeper?—the only possible answer for us is God's thunderous *yes.*

As I've traveled across this country, I've spoken with people whose daily experience testifies that a new sense of community is not just a moral imperative, but a practical necessity, people whose lives have been broken, even though they are doing the best that they can. And these people live everywhere. Crime and drugs are hitting our suburbs as well as our cities. Layoffs are hitting middle managers as well as assembly workers, and corporate bottom lines are suffering because our children's test scores are declining.

We are learning anew the wisdom of Martin Luther King, who wrote in his letter from the Birmingham Jail, "We are caught in an inescapable network of mutuality, tied to a single garment of destiny. Injustice anywhere is a threat to justice everywhere."

When I think of how I want to help change America during the next four years, I want, most of all, to restore the link between rights and responsibilities, between opportunities and obligations. The social contract that defines what we owe to one another, to our communities and to our country, as well as what we are entitled to for ourselves.

The American community should speak in a clear and certain voice that some things are wrong. On any day, at any time, in any place violence is wrong; bigotry is wrong; abandoning children is wrong. But our religious traditions teach of more than thou-shalt-nots. In our role as citizens, we should not see ourselves only as our brothers' and sisters' keepers, but also as our brothers' and sisters' helpers.

If we truly believe, as almost everyone says, no matter what they believe on certain issues, that children are God's most precious creation, then surely we owe every child born in the United States the opportunity to make the most of his or her God-given potential.

I want an America that offers every child a healthy start in life, decent schooling, a chance to go to college or job training worthy of the name.

Not only because that's essential for our common economic success, but because providing opportunities is how we fulfill our obligations to each other and the moral principles we honor.

Any community worthy of the name would do more than just tell its young people to say *no* to crime and drugs. It would give them something to say *yes* to, the opportunity for education and jobs and the sense of connectedness to society. Yes, we must insist that parents do right by their children, and that young people do right by their communities. But our American community must also do right by them, by offering them the opportunities that support families and children to do a good job with the lives they have.

We must move beyond the false choice between individual and social responsibility, because now more than ever we need both.

If I could select a watchword for America, it would be the title of the recent pastoral letter of the National Conference of Catholic Bishops, "Putting Children and Families First."

In the letter they offer the counsel of common sense and common decency, and I quote: "No government can love a child, and no policy can substitute for a family's care." But government can either support or undermine families. There has been an unfortunate, unnecessary, and unreal polarization and discussions in how best to help families.

The undeniable fact, the letter says, is that our children's future is shaped both by the values of their parents and the policies of our nation.

I want an America that does more than talk about family values. I want an America that values families.

I want an America that values families by recognizing that parents have the right to take time off from their jobs when a baby's born or someone's sick; an America that values families by freeing fathers and mothers from the fear that they won't be able to take a sick child to the doctor; an America that values families by helping every parent enjoy the dignity of a job that puts bread on the table, buys shoes for the children, and holds the household together in mutual support; an America that honors and rewards work and family not just in words but in deeds.

I want to see us share the values expressed in the bishop's pastoral letter on the economy, that every institution and every economic decision in our society must be judged by whether it protects or undermines the dignity of the person. And for everyone who can work, human dignity is first and foremost the opportunity and the obligation to support oneself and to contribute to society. When I talk about training workers today for jobs of tomorrow, when I talk about helping people move from welfare rolls to payrolls, when I talk about rebuilding America, I'm not just talking about economic policies. I'm talking about our moral obligation to help every one of our brothers and sisters enjoy the dignity of useful and productive working lives.

And if there is a dignity in all work, there must be dignity for every worker. We've got to make sure that no one who works a full week and who has children at home is condemned to a life of poverty. We've got to make sure that our families are assured a real family wage. If people work and have children, surely we should lift them above the poverty line.

I want to lead an America that fulfills its obligations to the future by upholding the traditional value of stewardship over the Earth.

When I was growing up, we were taught that soils and streams were not ours to waste, but a gift from God that we simply hold in trust for generations yet to be born. And I selected Al Gore for vice-president for many reasons, but one was his understanding of this.

His understanding of the obligations of this stewardship stated so eloquently in his book, *Earth in the Balance.* We must be our planet's caretaker.

Finally, I want an America where service is a way of life, as it is here at Notre Dame. I want Americans to learn in their own way the lesson that you've learned from Catholic social teaching, that our individual rights flow from our essential dignity as creatures of God, but that each of us reaches our fullness as human beings by being of service to our fellow men and women. Any of us who have traveled this land have seen these teachings embodied in Catholic social programs.

I think of schools where young people are called not only to academic achievement but to volunteer work in hospitals and nursing homes, tutoring programs, and homeless shelters, as a fundamental component of education.

I have in mind parishes where family values are not simply evoked but actively guided and supported, where young people are offered preparation for opportunities for adoption and sensitive counsel on how best to fulfill their parental duties as their children's first teachers.

And I see the work of Catholic relief services, the Campaign for Human Development, the National Catholic Rural Life Conference and so many other agencies, all deeply rooted in community service. Talking about service here at Notre Dame is the classic case of preaching to the choir. Your center for the homeless, your alumni summer service projects, your Center for Social Concerns—shining examples of the spirit of service that I want to see in every college and every high school and every community all across America.

I want an America where every young person and every not-so-young person understands what Marian Wright Edelman, the president of the Children's Defense Fund, tries to teach us when she says, "service is the rent we pay for living."

Throughout this campaign I've talked about my plan to open the doors of college to every American, to offer every person in this country the opportunity to borrow the money to go to college and then require them to pay it back either as a small percentage of their paychecks after they go to work or even better, by going back home and serving their communities.

And frankly, I'd much rather see everyone whether they're rich or poor or middle class pay back that debt by going home and working for two years in a Peace Corps here in America, to rebuild America. Just think of it. Think of it.

Millions of energetic young men and women serving their country by teaching the children, policing the streets, caring for the sick, working with the elderly or people with disabilities, building homes for the homeless, helping children to stay off drugs and out of gangs—giving us all a new sense of hope and real limitless possibilities.

I've offered this plan to help more young people go to college but I've also offered it because I want America to send a message that our society values and honors service to community, just as Harry Truman's GI Bill honored the service of my father's generation, who fought and won World War II, just as the Peace Corps, which President Kennedy created with the help of your former president, Father Hesberg and Senator Wofford, sent that message to my generation. Just as millions of Americans from all backgrounds and every walk of life are waiting for a summons to service and to citizenship, not just for young people that are going on to college but for young people in our high schools and people of all ages who want to do something for their communities and for their country.

And I would just give you two examples of the kind of thing that I hope will become a hallmark of America in the next few years. Recently I took a trip to Florida which was heartbreaking and heart lifting. I went down to Florida City after the hurricane to a predominantly African-American community that was almost wiped out. And as I walked down the street with the mayor, we came across a man who came all the way from Michigan with two of his friends with a truckload of food and supplies for the folks in Florida.

The gentlemen was a genuine American ethnic—burly and muscular and heavy set and so proud of himself he could split. And he was standing there next to an African-American woman whose home had been devastated by the storm. She looked at him and he looked at her and she said, you know, it was nearly worth losing my home to find out how well we can work together, but it's too bad it took a hurricane to prove it.

And let me tell you one other story. Hillary and I and the Gores were in Cedar Rapids, Iowa, at the Quaker Oats factory having a big rally. And I was working my way through the crowd, and I noticed there was a young white woman there holding an African-American child. And I went up to the lady, and I looked at this beautiful little girl, who came out and got in my arms, and I was holding her, and I said, "Whose baby is this?" And she said, "That's my baby. And my baby has AIDS."

And I said, "Where did you find this child?" And she said, "I adopted this child in another state." She said, "You know, Governor, I respect this debate that's going on in our country about life, but how I wish we would all reach out and try to help the children who are living."

We Americans are brilliant at doing right by each other at a time of crisis. All across this country, however, we must know we are in a quieter crisis of a fraying society and a declining economy, of an educational system unequal to the task of global competition, of an environment slowly coming apart at critical places.

But most of all, a crisis of community, a spiritual crisis that calls upon each of us to remember and to act upon our obligations to one another. The purpose of community, the purpose of our government, the purpose of our leaders should be to call us to pursue common values and the common good, not simply in the moment of extreme crisis but every day in our lives, starting right now, today.

That is the leadership I seek to offer America, and that is the America I hope to be able to lead.

Thank you very much.

A Healthy Nation

Merck Pharmaceuticals
Rahway, New Jersey
September 24, 1992

Although no Democratic presidential candidate had carried New Jersey since 1964, Clinton was leading in the state polls, and the campaign changed its earlier plans and decided to campaign there. Clinton's previous call for reforming the health-care system and controlling costs had resonated well among middle-class and suburban voters in states like New Jersey, but until now the campaign had been somewhat vague on the potentially controversial details. Deciding that one of his main strengths in the election was his ability to offer specific proposals for change, he offered a thoughtful analysis of the problems and offered specific proposals in a speech to more than fifteen hundred invited guests and the employees of the Merck pharmaceutical firm on the company's campus-like grounds in Rahway.

Bush campaign officials immediately attacked Clinton's proposals, as usual, arguing that it was too expensive and would require huge tax increases but ignoring the alleged problems and offering no counterplan.

❖ ❖ ❖

Thank you. Thank you very much. Dr. Vazilos, ladies and gentlemen, I am elated to be here at the headquarters of this magnificent company in such good company. I want to thank all those who are here with me. I want to thank Governor Florio for being here and for the work he has done in health care, and to remind those of you who received him in the beginning that state governments are not like the federal government. We don't get to print money, and we have to balance our books. And I thank him for his innovations in health care and other areas.

I want to say a word of thanks to Senator Harris Wofford, who has been an inspiration to me, and to Senator Jay Rockefeller, who used to serve with me as a governor. You need to know something else about these two people. Jay Rockefeller whispered to me when Harris Wofford got up to speak that America knows Harris Wofford now as the United States senator who put health care on the nation's agenda. "But many years ago," Jay said, "Harris Wofford personally convinced me to join the Peace Corps and give something to the world." Harris Wofford has spent a lifetime trying to solve the problems of this country and the human problems of human beings all over the world. And I think the work that he and Jay Rockefeller have done in health care is immensely commendable.

Let me say one other thing to you. I want to say a little more about Merck, but one of the things that impressed me about Merck that may not be so well known is that a magazine for working women declared that Merck was one of the top-ten family-friendly companies in the United States. And in that connection, I think I should announce that thanks to Senator Wofford and Senator Rockefeller, Senator Bradley and Senator Lautenberg and sixty-four others this morning the United States Senate overrode President Bush's veto of the Family Leave Act.

Merck has been for six years now declared by *Fortune* magazine the most admired company in the United States of America. I know something about admired companies. My wife was on the board of the Wal-Mart Corporation, Arkansas's fastest growing company for many years. I have been interested in quality management, running a big operation, which is what a government is. My state was the first state in the country to institute total quality management for the entire state government.

I know it's easy to talk about things and more difficult to get results. In 1987, as you heard Dr. Vazilos say, this company decided to give the drug to Africa to combat river blindness. In 1989, in the face of prescription drugs going at three times the national average in price, this company, without announcement, decided it would keep its drug prices in line with inflation, and it has done so since then.

I wanted to come here not because—I wanted to come here not because this— [Interruptions by hecklers in the crowd.] You know, one of the real problems—one of the real problems with the people who control the White House today is that they have such a lousy record and no vision, the only way they think they can stay in power is to stomp out free speech and honest debate and divert the attention of the American people. And I must say if they're that desperate to stay in, that may be the only way they can do it.

I want to say that I decided to come here to Merck today not because the management of this company or its employees will agree with everything I have to say about health care, but because this company represents what we can do as Americans if we set our minds to it. And I think we have to see this problem in the context of the overall American economic scene. This has to be part of our efforts to restore growth, improve education, and manage change in a tough global economy. It's part of a plan to create a high-wage, high-growth, high-opportunity society in America, to educate and train our people, to develop new energy policies, new environmental policies, to promote both personal responsibility and family security. And in that context, we have to do what we all agree we should do: promote control of costs, access to health care, and maintain quality.

I have offered this country a plan that maintains the promise of America's health-care system—groundbreaking research and development, excellence in providers, but deals with the problems that are well known but bear some repeating here. Since 1980, the cost increase in American health care has outstripped the rate of any other country and any previous decade in America, going from aggregate expenditures of two hundred and fifty billion dollars in 1980 to in excess of eight hundred billion dollars this year.

Family and individual spending on health care has tripled in the last decade. Out-of-pocket spending—listen to this—out of pocket spending by senior citizens as a percentage of their income will be greater this year than it was in the year before Medicare was adopted. Elderly people are spending a bigger percentage of their income on health care today than they were before Medicare came in. Companies are forced to move jobs overseas because of health-care costs, and people can't change jobs because they or someone in their family have preexisting conditions which would preclude them from getting health insurance if they changed. There are people in this audience today who either are covered by that or have someone in their family affected by that condition.

We have been losing one hundred—listen to this—in the last four years, we have been losing on average almost a hundred thousand people a month from any health-care coverage at all—over a million a year. A recent analysis estimated that two hundred thousand jobs have been lost in the last four years because of rising health-care costs alone in the private sector. We are spending 30 percent more of our income than any nation on earth on health care. And in our hospitals today, clerical employment is growing at four times the rate of health-care-giver employment.

All of this leads to heart-breaking stories, some of which have been mentioned, but let me just tell you that from the beginning to the end of this presidential campaign process, I have seen these people.

I met a young man in New Hampshire whose child had open-heart surgery, and he couldn't get anybody to hire him after his family business went under because they couldn't afford to take his child in the health-insurance system. I met a young couple in Columbus, Ohio, who had three children. And the youngest of their children was born with cerebral palsy. They were insured at the young woman's place of employment, a community nonprofit organization with only twenty employees. When the child was born, the company was left with the choice of either firing her or having premiums go up an average of two hundred dollars a month per employee.

I met a woman with seven children, a divorcee who was supporting her children with a fifty-thousand-dollar income. Her youngest child developed a serious health problem with monumental costs, and the only way she could get any help at all—the only way she could get any help at all—was to leave her job to qualify for Medicaid by becoming a welfare recipient instead of an American productive worker with a fifty-thousand-dollar income.

I met a young couple in Detroit a couple of days ago when I went to Michigan for the debate that didn't happen. In the midst of all the rhetoric that occupies the front lines of the newspapers, most of which has very little to do with how we'll live on the day after the election, this young couple stood up and the woman was in tears because she had gotten AIDS and her baby had AIDS, and these young people thought that no one really cared about them or whether the child particularly would have a chance to live.

Our infant mortality and low-birth-weight rates are too high. Our life expectancy, given our national wealth, is too low. We are not getting the system that we are paying for and nobody is paying as much as we are for health care. That's why I have pledged that within the first one hundred days of a Clinton administration, I would submit a comprehensive health-care plan for real change that deals with costs and coverage and access, with quality and the maintenance of consumer choice, one that would have less micromanagement by the federal government, but more effective control of costs, one that would encourage us to use market incentives to manage to get costs down.

Everybody wants change now, working families and businesses, states and cities, doctors and nurses. Eighty percent of all the strikes in America today are not over wages, they are over health-care benefits. We cannot afford to let any more time go by before we address this problem.

Last week the American College of Physicians, a group of seventy-seven thousand doctors, joined the American Nurses Association, a business group called the National Leadership Coalition on Health Care, and the American Association of Family Physicians in endorsing health-care plans remarkably similar to the one that I have recommended.

As has already been said, states all across America are trying to address these issues, Oregon, Minnesota, Vermont—the state with the only doctor in the governor's office in the country—has a comprehensive health-care plan under consideration, California. There are a couple of places which give us models in America that prove we can cover everybody and control costs. The state of Hawaii has a plan under which 98 percent of the people who live in Hawaii are covered by their employers, and health-care premiums there are much lower than the national average. And before you jump to the conclusion of saying, "Well, we all know they're more healthy out there," let me remind you that 20 percent of the people who are in the Hawaiian health-care system are native islanders who come to the Hawaiian islands for health care and they live in poverty.

Rochester, New York, because of the remarkable leadership of the business community in cooperation with health-care providers have developed a plan which provides virtually universal coverage for people who live in the city of Rochester and health-insurance premiums in that city are now only two-thirds the national average, covering everybody and stopping the cost shifting that is wrecking this country.

For the last five years, in Germany health-care costs have gone up slightly less than the rate of inflation, while they have gone up in this country at over twice the rate of inflation and government health costs have gone up at about two and a half times the rate of inflation. That may be one reason why the average German factory worker makes 20 percent more than the average American for working a shorter work week, gets four weeks paid vacation, family leave, and has comprehensive health care. We must do something about this problem if we want to preserve opportunity for all Americans.

The fundamental difference between my plan and the Bush plan has already been laid out. The Bush plan would put another one hundred billion dollars in tax credits through the same system between now and 1997, pouring good money after bad, with no plan for cost control. It would not mandate any kind of universal coverage. It would not deal with the very real problems of access that many of our people have in inner cities and rural areas. It would cut continually Medicare benefits, which would continue the cost-shifting that providers do now. When they get underpaid for Medicare or Medicaid, or when they have to deal with uncompensated care, they just shift the cost on to the employees of Merck and other companies that have health insurance, and that further adds to the administrative burden and drives prices up. This plan is too little too late, and everybody who has examined it knows it.

On the other hand, I do not want to further contribute to the rhetorical hot air today. I want to try to tell you exactly what I think we ought to do. Usually when this issue is discussed by my opponent, he says that I offer you a national system that will bankrupt small business and have all the compassion of the KGB and the confidence of the House post office. Now, those are very good lines, but I remind you that they are being uttered by a person who has enjoyed the benefits of socialized medicine for the last twelve years.

What we need to do is to cut through all the bull and ask ourselves, how are we going to address these problems—cost, coverage, access? How can we get cost in line with inflation and the whole American health-care system following the lead of Merck? We have to require change from all the major players in this system: change from the providers, from the insurers, from the drug companies, from the government, and from consumers. I think there ought to be the following points in national reform:

First of all, we have to change the system by which people are insured in this country. We must require insurance companies to go back to broad-based community rating, and we must require people not to be denied access to health coverage because of preexisting conditions.

Secondly, there must be national spending targets for aggregate health-care expenditures every year and a required comprehensive schedule of benefits offered at a minimum by employers. These two things should be done not by government, but by a board composed of consumers and providers, people who know what they're talking about.

If you did these two things, you could then drastically simplify the administrative costs of the American health-care system. Only the United States has fifteen hundred separate health-insurance companies writing thousands of different policies, all of which have to be kept up with by bookkeepers in doctors' offices and hospitals throughout America. And on top of that, they have to keep up with a blizzard of rules for Medicare and Medicaid and for different categories of people under those programs—constantly changing, irregularly enforced, and hard to understand. That is why health-care administrative employment is going up at four times the rate of direct care giver. Eighty-four cents on the health-insurance dollar in America goes to health care. In Europe it's ninety-five cents. The difference is over sixty billion dollars a year in administrative simplification alone that could be achieved if we had common agreement on comprehensive benefits and insurance reforms. We can do that, and that is where we ought to start. [Cheers, applause.]

Next, we should require employers to cover their employees, and the government to cover all the nonemployed, in a program which requires people to pay in accord with their ability to pay, and not more. We can do that and still be fair to small employers if we do three things. First of all, phase-in the requirement for small business to cover their employees over a period of years as savings are achieved so that the unit cost of covering the employees is less.

Secondly, provide opportunities for small-business people to go into large pools so that they can achieve the same cost per employee that large companies like Merck can achieve. And third, in the early years of transition, provide tax credits for those employees and businesses so we can make sure that no one loses their work by covering their workers.

Now, if we do this, let me point out something. Every time I say something like this people say, well, there you go again, you're going to really hurt small businesses. Most small businesses in this country insure their employees. They are being hurt by the system we have. They are going broke under the system we have. We have to think about them, too. And I want to point out—and I'll come back to this later—the major savings which will be achieved over the next decade with a comprehensive national health system like this will not be in tax dollars, they will be in private dollars. If we can cover everybody and bring costs within inflation, we will save hundreds of billions of dollars per year by the end of the decade to the private sector—money which can then be reinvested in growth, in productivity, in wages, in benefits, in making America a stronger country. It is very important.

The fourth thing we have to do is to give people real incentives to be in managed-care networks so that the costs can be held down by the forces of the marketplace and by companies that are well managed as this one is.

The fifth thing we have to do is to recognize that even if you cover everybody not everyone will have access in the world we're living in today. Some money has to be set aside, just as Hawaii now does, to establish primary and preventive health-care clinics in our inner-city areas and in our rural areas, either in health clinics, public health clinics, in schools, or in places of work so that people can actually reach the health care that we say they are entitled to.

Next, we have to emphasize health education and prevention in school and in the workplace. We don't do nearly enough of it. In areas like AIDS, it's a matter of life and death. In areas like maintaining a healthy physique to minimize heart disease and stroke, it can be a matter of life and death and is always a matter of productivity and costs to the American health-care system. The American consumers are going to have to do more in terms of education and prevention, and we have to do more in the schools and in the workplace to provide support for those efforts.

Over time, we should phase-in long-term care through the Medicare program so that people can purchase less-expensive but more-comprehensive options. Most people with disabilities and most elderly people today are under a system that requires them to spend themselves into poverty and then to go into a nursing home in order to get any help at all from their government. We should be moving toward a period of greater independence. With the fastest growing group of Americans being people over eighty, with more and more people with disabilities realizing the fullness of their God-given potential, we have no choice other than to build them a comprehensive long-term-care network that emphasizes in-home services, personal-care services, mobility to senior-citizen centers or to other adult day-care centers, and access to the workplace. We have all kinds of things that we'll have to do. People should be required to pay for these things, again, based on their ability to pay. But we cannot afford, in the direction we're going, given the population we have, to continue to have a long-term-care system that says spend yourself into poverty, then we'll put you into a nursing home. We have to do more and different things.

And finally, I think we have to do more with research and development. We have to continue to invest in health-care research. The pharmaceutical companies do a lot of it; there are a lot of incentives to do it. But there are all kinds of other health research that needs to be done. That's why I was so disturbed when the health research bill was vetoed a few weeks ago by Mr. Bush because of the fetal-tissue issue. And let me just say, that bill had three hundred million dollars for breast-cancer research. It would have done more for research on ovarian cancer. It would have done more for research in osteoporosis among women. It would have set up a women's health research center in our national government.

And I have a friend in Carolina who has a child that means more to him than anybody in the world who has terrible diabetic problems. The kid is very athletic, he does fine, but every now and then he goes into insulin shock and he knows, my friend, a conservative business person, that fetal-tissue research can do more to help solve the problems of his child's diabetes than any other known avenue of medical research. We should take the politics out of this and go back to a real commitment to research and development in our country.

So that's my plan, personal choice, private care, private insurance, private management, but a national system to put a lid on costs, to require insurance reforms, to facilitate partnerships between business, government, and health-care providers. These are the things that we have to do, and I think they are terribly important. Again I will say we have to have a national budget ceiling. That would be the most controversial thing across the country, I guess, but we have to have that, and we have to have a national comprehensive package mandated. We cannot go on with fifteen hundred separate companies writing thousands of policies and the blizzard of variations caused by the national government itself. We are spending nearly two hundred billion dollars a year in paperwork and bureaucracy alone, and it is too much. We have got to stop spending billions of dollars, having insurance companies trying to minimize risk instead of insure health care, deciding who to cover and who to overcharge. We have got to change that.

We need a single set of billing codes, a single national claims form, computerized claims. Eventually everybody will be able to carry a smart card which will save tens of billions of dollars in the billing alone. These things must be done.

Secondly, with a national health budget we will be able to keep costs within inflation. There is no starker example of these problems than what a lot of people face now in the curious mix of cost and coverage as it relates to prescription drugs. Over the last twelve years, prescription drugs, unlike the practice of the last few years at Merck, have increased at three times the rate of inflation. And according to the Department of Health and Human Services, many European countries, because of their policies, are paying half of what Americans pay for the same prescription drugs that are often actually made here in America. Three out of four older Americans say their highest out-of-pocket medical expense is for prescription drugs. More than eighteen million say they have trouble paying for their prescriptions, and eight million Americans over the age of forty-five say they have to cut back on essentials like food and fuel in order to pay for medicine.

When I was in New Hampshire I actually saw this in a senior citizens' living center where a couple named Mary Annie and Edward Davis actually broke down and cried talking to me because they had not one scrap of food in their refrigerator upstairs in the place where they were living because they had to spend their money every week to keep one of them alive on medicine. Why? Governor Florio mentioned it. They were eligible for Medicare, which doesn't cover medicine, and they weren't poor enough for Medicaid. But their medical requirements were not taken into account in determining whether they were poor or not.

Only a national system can solve mindless problems like this, and we need to have one. But we also must address the fact that not every company in this country has been as responsible as this one is in the runaway cost not of new, experimental drugs—I think the market should pay what is appropriate to cover all research and development costs of bringing those drugs to market, and they are enormous—but for regular drugs. That's why I have endorsed my—Senator David Pryor's proposal to end special breaks for companies that do not keep the cost of traditional, already established drugs within inflation. We spend fifty billion dollars a year in this country on prescription drugs. We must, we must get the cost of those that are already in the market in line with inflation.

But we have to do more. We have to decide what we're going to spend on health care and then spend it in a sensible way. Now, every time I say this, those people who attack me say, "There they go again, they want to ration health care." I don't want to ration health care; that's why I want a sensible system. We are rationing health care today. If you don't believe it, look at the infant mortality rate, look at the low-birth-weight rate, look at the people who don't have long-term care who need it, look at the people who don't get medicine who need it. We are rationing health care today—but we are doing it in sneaky, bureaucratic, confusing, absolutely indefensible ways. And we ought to change it.

I want to keep consumers with a variety of choices, including access to local health-care networks put together by insurers, hospitals, clinics, and doctors; managed-care networks that will receive the money they need to meet a consumer's full health-care needs over a lifetime. By limiting a network's total spending without interfering at all with its practices, the state-by-state budgets that I recommend will create real incentives for hospitals, clinics, doctors, and consumers to reduce bureaucracy, eliminate unnecessary duplicative technology and practices, and cut waste on their own.

This is very, very important. We've got to quit having the federal government try to micromanage health care and instead set up incentives for the private sector to manage the cost down within limits beyond which we absolutely must not go in spending.

These things will really help, especially when we provide the same incentives for small businesses to band together in large pools so we do not discriminate against small business. Eighty-five percent of the jobs in America in the last twelve years have been created in units of under fifty. We have got to promote that, but I remind you, over two-thirds of the small businesses in this country do today cover their employees, and they are getting murdered. The fair thing to do is to require everybody to have coverage, but to make that coverage affordable, manageable, predictable. That will lead to increased sanity, security, and productivity in the workplace and, as I said, over the next decade we'll free up literally hundreds of billions of dollars for reinvestment in the private sector.

Imagine what that can mean. Imagine what that can mean. We should start with covering the people that have to be covered: the uninsured, beginning with pregnant women and their little children, and helping small businesses to move into coverage. But by the end of this decade, we will have a health-care system that is the envy of the world, not only for the best doctors, the best pharmaceuticals, the best health care that the wealthy of us can afford, those of us that have the best policies now; we will have a system that also has American entrepreneurial ingenuity holding costs within inflation and providing basic, good quality, affordable health care to all of our people. I think that's what we should have, and I think that's what most Americans want.

This is a private system. It is not pay or play. It does not require new taxes. It will preserve what is best about the present health-care system, but it will also incorporate what we have learned about what is wrong. My fellow Americans, we are the only advanced nation in the world that does not provide basic health care to all its citizens. We spend 30 percent more of our income than any other country in the world on health care at a time when we desperately need to spend more on new plants, new equipment, new businesses, reinvesting in the education and training of our citizens, and rebuilding our cities and our depressed rural areas.

We cannot go on like this. This needs to be beyond partisan political debate, beyond the shallow and simplified rhetoric of hurling arrows at one's opponent. This is a matter that is critical for the future of this country's survival.

I ask you, in the next forty days, whatever your party or your position, whether you agree with the specifics that I have recommended or not, do not let this forty days go by without making a decision that you as an American voter will insist and demand that this problem be solved not in another ten years, but next year. That is a major, major, major factor, and that ought to determine the outcome of this election for president of the United States.

Thank you very much, and God bless you all.

A Grand Canyon of Differences

University of Connecticut
West Hartford, Connecticut
September 25, 1992

Several hundred people, mostly supporters but including some Bush partisans and antiabortion protesters, were waiting outside when Clinton's campaign motorcade arrived at the University of Connecticut's Greater Hartford campus in West Hartford at 11:45 A.M. The *Hartford Courant* seemed surprised that Clinton spent nearly twenty minutes shaking hands with the crowd and "seemed to be willing to mine every possible vote, even if that meant one at a time. When someone asked him a question, either friendly or hostile, he stopped and answered."

Clinton spoke under the auspices of UConn's Institute of Public Service in the auditorium of the campus's main building to an audience of invited Democratic officials, along with UConn students and faculty, that filled the three-hundred-seat auditorium to standing-room capacity, as several hundred more outside listened to the forty-six-minute speech over a public address system.

Shunning the usual campaign-rally theatrics, Clinton delivered a sobering message for tough economic times, and there were few laugh or applause lines built into the speech. He presented a somber analysis of the nation's economic situation and told the audience that there was a Grand Canyon of "fundamental differences in my approach and Mr. Bush's approach to the economy and to the role of government."

In addition to using the address for a major policy statement that he hoped would get national media coverage, Clinton also took advantage of local coverage that provided an opportunity to try to solidify his support in Connecticut, which had gone Republican in every presidential election since 1968, but where recent polls showed Clinton leading with 44 percent to 28 percent for Bush and 12 percent for Perot.

❖ ❖ ❖

Thank you very much. Thank you. Thank you very, very much. Thank you. Thank you very much, Mr. Aziretto. And ladies and gentlemen, thank you for that enthusiastic welcome. We also had a lot of people on the outside of this hall to say hello. Some of them were for Mr. Bush and were kind enough to engage me in the debate that so far he has refused, and I enjoyed that very much. And the thing I liked best about it was there was opportunity for follow-up.

I want to talk today, and I have prepared some remarks, about what I consider the fundamental differences in my approach and Mr. Bush's approach to the economy and to the role of government. But, before I get into them, I want to try to set the stage.

Our country has been in the grip of declining productivity and, therefore, declining wealth generation compared to other major countries for nearly two decades now, brought on in the early- and mid-seventies by the explosion of oil prices and by our being forced to compete with other countries around the world. That was a fact of life beginning in the mid-seventies. There was a general consensus among Republicans and Democrats alike, from Richard Nixon to Jimmy Carter, that something had to be done about it, that the national government had to respond to it, that there were differences in kinds of response, but most people acknowledged even that the path that had been taken in the past would not be enough to steer America into a global economy.

Twelve years ago, when Mr. Reagan was elected, the United States decided to set forth on a political and economic experiment that was unprecedented in the world of advanced countries, trickle-down economics, a very inactive government in most areas in which other countries, even those governed by conservatives, were active. Today, we are called upon to make a decision which will characterize whether that approach should be given four more years or whether the approach that I have taken should be given four more years. The president, Mr. Bush, has gone out of his way to try to characterize this choice in ways that I think are not accurate, and the major purpose of my presence here today is to try to tell you and, through you, the entire electorate of this country how I think this choice should be characterized. We are, after all, not choosing just between two people in the next thirty-nine days, but between two very different philosophies, two different ideas of the presidency.

George Bush says there is a Grand Canyon between us, and in that, he is certainly right. There is a gap between his economic policies and mine, between his philosophy of government and mine. There is also, in fairness, a gap between his rhetoric and reality; the reality of his positions as opposed to what he says, the reality of my record as opposed to how he characterizes it, and most importantly for you and your children, the reality of what I have advocated as opposed to what he says I have advocated—a gap so great that it seems to me that we really are in a canyon, because I so often hear the hollow ring of the other side's rhetoric.

I believe that my opponent is out of touch, out of ideas, and out of time.

Instead of debating me in East Lansing, he has run all across this country, flailing away at an imaginary opponent. Instead of a great debate about the future of our nation, Mr. Bush desperately wants this election to be a rerun of the past. He sincerely and passionately believes, however, in trickle-down economics. He really believes that the way to make the economy grow is to keep taxes as low as possible on the wealthiest Americans, concentrate as much wealth there as possible, and then let them make investments that will trickle down to the rest of us.

The problem is that that leaves very little room for tackling the real problems of our country, and this experiment has not worked. So when there is an emergency, or if the people who are supposed to be giving us the benefits of trickle-down need a reaction, then the government swings into action, whether it's the S&L bailout or another tax break for the wealthy. But mostly the government stands on the sidelines, when other governments around the world are moving aggressively on issues of economic development, preserving the industrial base, educating all the people of the country, controlling health-care costs, dealing with the problems that people face in new and innovative ways. I want that kind of government, a government that invests more but wastes less.

I believe first and foremost the way to make an economy grow in a global society is to invest in our children's education, our workers' skills, our families' health, so that our people can be the most productive on earth. Not trickle-down, but not tax-and-spend. Invest, educate, innovate, partnerships between government and business, doing what works. We've tried it their way for twelve years now. In a way, what they wanted to do did work. Almost all the economic gains of the last twelve years have gone to the upper 20 percent of our people, and most of that to the upper 1 percent. Indeed, for the first time since the Roaring Twenties, the top 1 percent of our people now control more wealth than the bottom 90 percent. Now, we would perhaps accept that in America because all of us want to be rich or want our children to grow up to be rich. I wouldn't mind trying it myself sometime. We would accept it if it worked. But the problem is we have tried it for twelve years and it doesn't work.

One of the reasons that my opponent has tried so hard to divert the attention of the American people from the problems before us is that he's having to run on the worst economic performance in the last fifty years. In the past two years alone, average family income has declined by almost sixteen hundred dollars. And while Mr. Bush has been in the White House, three people have gone bankrupt for every one person who has gone to work. Ten years ago, our nation was first in the world in wages. Now we're thirteenth and dropping. And the United States Census itself, concluded during the Bush administration, shows us that two-thirds of our people are working harder for lower wages, when adjusted for inflation, than they were making ten years ago.

With a record like that, Mr. Bush wants to run against an imaginary opponent with two diametrically opposing aspects. To hear him tell it, one day I'm a hayseed, the governor of a small southern state. The next day I'm an Oxford man who has an enormous advantage in a debate. To hear him tell it, one day I'm a big spender who would endanger the stability of the republic. The next day I should be attacked for not spending enough money on problems at home when we didn't have the money. To hear him tell it, one day I am an environmental extremist, depending on what state he's in. The next day I'm a big polluter. One day I'm reckless about Bosnia. The next day it turns out they all agree with my position. But make no mistake about it, at the core of the argument my opponent is making against this candidacy, is the position that beneath our southern accents and mainstream roots, Bill Clinton and Al Gore are yesterday's Democrats—old style, tax-and-spend, big government, anti-enterprise; people who have hidden their true impulses for twenty years in public life waiting for that moment when they could burst on the American scene and drag our country down. That is their argument.

But if and when Mr. Bush does actually debate me, he'll find that he's facing a different challenger, a different kind of Democrat who understands that the great issue of this election and our time is how we can help America in a global economy to build a society where the power of government is used to help people and to help the private sector create jobs and increase incomes, to solve problems like the health-care crisis instead of just talk about them, and to do it in ways that promote more innovation and less bureaucracy, and, finally, to educate and empower people to take responsibility for their own lives and their families' futures.

Mr. Bush says this election is a choice between private enterprise and big government, but there is a Grand Canyon between his rhetoric and the reality of his own record on that subject and my record, between his proposals and my proposals.

It's a fact that during the Bush presidency, the United States lost almost forty thousand jobs in the private sector, according to his own government's reports, last month, including 1.3 million jobs in manufacturing.

It's a fact that during the Bush presidency for the first time in the history of this republic, we have more people working for the government he deplores than we do going to work in factories every day.

It's a fact that during the Bush presidency, according to the conservative Heritage Foundation—not the Democratic Party—the Heritage Foundation, government regulation by the executive branch has gone up more during this presidency than in the previous twenty years under any president.

And for all Mr. Bush's talk about downsizing the government, the fastest-growing part of the executive branch, the White House staff, is up by 56 percent. Indeed, between 1990 and 1991, the budget increased by 23 percent, ten times the rate of revenue growth. Maybe he should take the beam out of his own eye before he plucks at the sty of others.

I know that the Democratic Party in Washington has been in the past too identified with tax-and-spend, big government, bureaucratic solutions, and I know that too often in the past twelve years, members of my own party have forcibly or willingly cooperated with the Republican presidents on failures ranging from the budget deficit to the S&L mess to allowing special interests in our nation's capital too much influence. But I have worked hard to be a different kind of Democrat and to give the American people a different kind of Democratic Party. If you want some evidence of that, look at the fact that we're proud this year to run on our platform, and they're running from theirs.

My fellow Americans, contrary to the rhetoric of my opponent, the issue is not more or less government, the question is what kind of government. I want a government that works to spur growth, create jobs, increase incomes; a streamlined government that still plays a central role, because in every advanced country in the world, whether governed by conservatives or liberals, there is an aggressive role for a government working to promote private-sector economic growth.

I want a government that, in the words of the author David Osborne, who has become something of an expert on what kind of government we need to create, "a government that steers more than it rows; a government that is a catalyst for action by others; a government that is market-oriented, less bureaucratic, and more entrepreneurial; one that favors empowerment over just handing out benefits; one that believes in opportunity and responsibility more than entitlement."

That is the kind of government I want.

That's why I believe in solving the health-care crisis through a system of managed competition and innovation and less regulation by government, but more cost control.

That's why I believe that we need fundamental changes in our education system that change the incentives for people to improve their own lot in life and give them the power to do it.

That's why I support things like boot camps for first-time, nonviolent offenders, and innovative programs to regenerate free enterprise in our depressed urban areas by setting up new banking systems that will actually work for profit to loan money to poor people to go into business. I could give you example after example after example.

That's why I have offered a national-security plan that won't just downscale defense but will give us a new and different kind of defense adequate for the twenty-first century.

And because of that, this campaign, in the last several weeks, has moved beyond the traditional bounds of party. Look what has happened. In Chicago, four hundred business executives, a third of whom were Republican, endorsing the Clinton-Gore ticket. In Northern California, twenty-one executives of some of the most fast-growing companies in this country, high-tech companies, endorsed our ticket. Two-thirds of them were Republican. Last weekend, Admiral William Crowe, the chairman of the Joint Chiefs of Staff under Presidents Reagan and Bush, endorsed Bill Clinton for president.

Why? Why? Why did this happen? And when you talk to these people they all say pretty much the same thing: "We are tired of a do-nothing president who refuses to acknowledge our problems. We want someone not that we agree with on everything, but someone who will roll up his sleeves, get up and go to work every day and face problems, whether it's national security or AIDS or education or job growth." That is what they're saying.

Now the other day—last week, when I went to Michigan for my debate—or earlier this week—Mr. Bush took an airplane and had little airport rallies in every stop around my state to tell everybody how bad Arkansas was. But you know, there are some things he neglected to tell all those voters.

He didn't tell them that since he's been president and I've been governor, my state has created seventy-two thousand private-sector jobs, while America has lost forty thousand.

He didn't tell them that his own secretary of labor, Lynn Martin, had to admit that our job growth in Arkansas—and I will use her word—was "enormous." He didn't say that *U.S. News and World Report* noted that not only did we lead the country in the last year in net private-sector job growth, but that we had the third-best overall economic performance in the country.

He didn't say that *Time* magazine a year or so ago said that Arkansas was one of two states showing the most improvement in its public schools in the last decade.

There were just all sorts of things that he didn't say. And while he railed about taxes, he didn't put out that, by his analysis, he's raised more than I have, and Arkansas still has the second-lowest tax burden in the country after he signed the second-biggest tax increase in history after saying, "Read my lips." He omitted to say all those things.

And amazingly enough, in the face of all this evidence that people who understand the economy know that what he is saying defies reality, from the eight Nobel Prize winners who have endorsed my economic program to all these Republican business people, he just offers us four more years of the same. He's been making and retracting promises about tax cuts again with the speed and agility of an acrobat. It reminds me of what Franklin Roosevelt once said about his Republican opponent. He said, "He seized the trapeze with the greatest of ease, and reversed himself in mid-air."

In the State of the Union address—listen to this: beginning early this year in his State of the Union address, when Mr. Bush was being sorely pressed by Pat Buchanan in New Hampshire, he asked Congress to raise the personal tax exemption for middle-class people by five hundred dollars per child. But just fifteen days later he presented his real economic program to Congress, and guess what? The proposal from the State of the Union address was nowhere to be found. And when reporters asked what happened to his middle-class benefits, one of his political advisers said, and I quote, "That was just a proposal for New Hampshire."

Two weeks ago, while campaigning in New Jersey, Mr. Bush said he was not going to raise taxes, quote, "again ever, ever." Just a day later, his press spokesman said that wasn't a pledge, no. No? Only in Washington can someone tell you that never, ever, is not a pledge. The next time Mr. Bush promises to cut taxes on the middle class or hold the line for the middle class, the people should ask him is this a promise for New Hampshire, New Jersey, or November?

Mr. Bush would have you believe that he's the candidate of fiscal responsibility in this campaign, but there again, the Grand Canyon between his rhetoric and reality is as big as the trillions of dollars of debt that's been piled up in the last twelve years. The fact is—and listen to this—the fact is that if every penny of the budgets that George Bush has recommended since he became president had been adopted by Congress, rubber stamped, the deficit would be a billion dollars bigger than it is. But he's tried to convince the American people that he was out there cutting spending, and the Congress forced him to do it. The fact is that he's never balanced a government budget; he's never come close to presenting one. He tells Congress there are all sorts of hard decisions they could make, but he doesn't want to advocate them. And interestingly enough, in the last year—now listen to this—three-quarters of the Republican members of the House of Representatives voted against the Bush budget. It was so bad, so ill prepared, so incredible.

I say this just to point out that you cannot permit this election to be about false choices from America's past, about the same old categories and the same old boxes we try to put people in. We are living in a new world at the end of the Cold War, and we have new challenges, and new opportunities, and we had better seize them, and we'd better be willing to park all this aimless hot-air rhetoric at the door and deal with the people's problems and the people's potential. That's what this election ought to be about, taking a new direction.

The central issue is this one, the economy. I do not believe, as my opponent does, that creating economic growth is a game played only by the favored few with the rest of us on the sidelines. I believe that in an international economic arena we must become one team, a dream team, a team of business and labor, of education and government, a team of men and women in which everyone has an important role to play, and we do not have one person to waste. I believe that our economic future must be built, yes, on the trading floors of Wall Street, but also on the factory floors of Main Street; yes, in the corner office, but also in every office; yes, in the board rooms, but more importantly, in the classrooms. Whether you're a parent who helps your child with homework, a worker who strives to make a better product, provide a better service, or upgrade your own education and training, an entrepreneur struggling to build a business from a dream, all these people have to be key players in our team and a crucial part of our economic future.

The differences are clear. Look what Mr. Bush offered when he finally came out with an economic plan 54 days before the election, but 1,327 days after he became president, during which time he denied that a recession existed. And then he said there is one, but it's all an attitude problem on our part. Compare those election-year promises with the economic plan that I began with last October, that I've worked hard to refine for months and months and months, that I have involved hundreds, indeed thousands, of Americans who understand our economy and its challenges, the one that I have put before the American people. It's not based on expedience in the final weeks of a campaign, but on my experience as governor for twelve years in a state where we're working hard to improve our schools and restructure our economy, to create new jobs and empower people to seize their destinies.

Mr. Bush's most important priority is still a short-term, across-the-board capital-gains tax for those who already have significant wealth. His important priority makes no distinction between investment and consumption by upper-income people. His capital-gains tax would give the average millionaire a hundred-thousand-dollar tax break and make the average family pay for it with cuts in government services.

If this were going to create jobs, we might buy it, but we have tried it their way. If this tax cut were targeted to long-term investments that actually create new businesses, new technologies, and new jobs, I would say hallelujah. But the tax cut doesn't distinguish between building a business and buying a race horse. It's just more of the same trickle-down economics like the past twelve years of windfalls for the wealthy and stagnation for the nation.

I don't want to give anybody something for nothing, but I want to give everybody the opportunity to make something for himself or for herself. Therefore, I support incentives for upper-income people, but targeted ones for their own incentive to create jobs. Let me just give you a couple of examples.

I want an investment tax credit, like the one John Kennedy put in in 1961, one which you can only claim if you buy a new plant and new equipment and you start new enterprises, and you either preserve jobs in a competitive global economy by doing it or create new jobs. That can only benefit people who invest in America.

I want to give people a long-term capital investment break, a 50 percent reduction in income for those who take risks to start new businesses or to expand enterprises and hold those investments for five years. There's a big difference between putting people to work and taking money in a short-term cash out for things that don't have anything to do with helping the American economy.

I want a permanent research and development tax credit to reward companies that invest in groundbreaking technologies, from high-definition television to high-speed computing.

I want investment, but no deductibility for irresponsibility.

You can measure the difference between Mr. Bush and me not only by the tax incentives we support, but by those we oppose. For example, I don't want any more tax breaks for dismantling our economy. I want to get rid of those tax incentives that literally offer small manufacturers more encouragement to shut their plants down here and move them overseas than to modernize plant and equipment and make them productive here. Why should we do that?

And I don't think the rest of the taxpayers should pick up the bill when we provide unlimited deductibility for executive salaries in companies, no matter how exorbitant, even when the companies are losing money. Now let me make this clear. I don't care how much people make in a free-enterprise system if the companies are making money. But tax deductibility means the rest of you pick up the bill. In the 1980s, executive salaries went up by four times as much as workers' salaries went up, and three times as much as profits went up—profits. What does that mean? That means people who are supposed to be setting the example are not.

I admire people like the head of Delta the other day who said, "We're having a lot of trouble in this company, and I'm going to give back my pay raise." And I'll tell you what, I'll bet morale went through the roof in that company, I'll bet it contributed to productivity, I bet they'll have a better year next year, if they possibly can, because of that kind of example.

The tax code today makes no distinction between a board's ability to reward somebody who is doing a good job or to subsidize someone who isn't. And you pick up the bill. We ought to make a distinction. We ought to be giving people more incentives to pay people more who are making money, raising wages, increasing products, and putting the American economy on the right path.

Now, Mr. Bush really doesn't believe this. On inauguration day, he said he would use the power of government to help people. But it turned out that he had a very narrow idea of what that meant. He really doesn't believe that he should do anything. Even when the economy sank into recession, I don't know if you remember this, just a few months ago and he acknowledged finally that there was a recession, he said he wanted the Congress to pass his economic-growth package with a capital-gains cut, but if they didn't do that, the next best thing would be to, quote, "do nothing." That's exactly what he said.

Now he believes that, he believes that. But I think we have learned, not only from our own painful experience but from what works in other countries and what has worked for America in the past, that government cannot do everything, but neither can it do nothing. And I believe we have to make investments to make our economy grow and to create an environment in which the private sector can flourish. So when it comes to investment, again there is a Grand Canyon between the two of us.

Mr. Bush and his predecessor have given us a dozen years of disinvestment. It is amazing to contemplate that we have quadrupled the government deficit in the last twelve years, but actually reduced in real dollar terms national investment in infrastructure, and research and development, in education, in environmental technologies, in the kinds of things that build a growing, high-wage economy and give people more opportunity. That is our challenge. We've got to find a way with discipline to bring the deficit down but to increase investment at the same time. Otherwise, in this critical last decade of the twentieth century, our competitors will run away with the new technologies and the high-wage jobs of tomorrow. We cannot permit that to happen, and government has a critical role to play.

When you look across the world at the high-wage nations that are spending a higher percentage of their gross national product on their infrastructure, on research and development, on kindergarten through twelfth-grade education, when you consider the fact that we are the only advanced nation that has no systematic plan for the people who don't wind up at UConn or the University of Arkansas, or Harvard, or someplace else—that is, those who do not go to four-year colleges—we have got a lot of investing to do.

When you consider the fact that we are the only nation that would have even dreamed of cutting defense as much as we already have with no thought to what would happen to the scientists, the engineers, the technicians, the factory workers from Connecticut to California, and when we need them to build the new economy based on new environmental technologies, new infrastructure investments, new communications and transportation systems, it is truly amazing.

I have an investment plan. It will conservatively create eight million jobs in the next four years by rebuilding America, from our roads and bridges, to high-speed rail and high-tech fiber optics.

It will give us a national information network linking our homes, our businesses, our classrooms, our labs, our libraries by the year 2015.

It will hook into the vast and mushrooming global market for environmental technologies.

It's amazing to me that this president went to Rio to the Earth Summit, for example, and devoted all of his energies to making sure we did not sign a global warming treaty or a biodiversity treaty. Meanwhile, our major competitors—Germany and Japan—signed off on them, and were there hawking their new technologies for the twenty-first century to other countries, so much so that now two-thirds of the American market in environmental technologies are occupied by foreign companies and foreign products, while we've got scientists, engineers, technicians, and factory workers walking around without a job in the aftermath of the Cold War. It is wrong. It is wrong.

But let me remind you that there are also limits on the ability of governmental policies and the private sector to create new high-wage jobs if our people are not able by the standard of global competition to perform high-wage jobs.

Make no mistake about it: one of the reasons for declining incomes of Americans over the last twenty years is that too many of our people were too uncompetitive if their job's income was set in a global marketplace rather than an American marketplace. We still have way too many adults in the work force who can't even read. We still have too many adults in the work force who are not capable of being retrained every year, even though we know that the average eighteen-year-old will change work eight times in a lifetime. We still have no system for moving people from high school to work with at least two years of training in a community college or a vocational program or on-the-job training. These are investments and opportunities we have to seize.

Now, our people are ahead of the politicians and the policymakers on this. Every community college in the country, just about, is oversubscribed. Older people are flooding back into educational institutions, including four-year institutions. The average age of a college student today is twenty-six or twenty-seven. So intuitively people know this, but we have no system to do things like teach everybody with a job to read in the next five years and give them all a chance to get a high-school diploma in the work force wherever possible, take care of the kids that don't go on to a four-year college, and open the doors of college education to everyone. Those are the investments that I want to make in education, because if we don't, it doesn't matter how good our economic policies are, our own people will not be able to get their incomes up.

And remember, there are two huge problems with this economy: unemployment is too high and too many people are insecure about keeping their jobs, but the other problem is the American dream is literally threatened when two-thirds of the people get up every day and go to work and think their wage is going to be lower today than it was yesterday, no matter how hard they work. So we have got to raise the skill levels of the American people, and we have got to have a system to constantly retrain our people. We've got to do it.

You know, the college dropout rate in this country today is two and one half times the high-school dropout rate, as bad as the high-school rate is. Why is that? Number one, too many people go to college without the real skills they need, which means we need to raise standards there and intensify our effort to get them ready to get in.

Number two, cost of a college education is the only essential thing that's gone up faster than health care in the last decade. That's why I favor the national trust fund to replace the student-loan program. Give anybody the money they need to go to college, no questions asked about income. Give them the option, including those of you who are still here, the option to pay it back either as a small percentage of your income after you go to work, at tax time so you can't beat the bill, or even better by doing, depending on how much money you borrow, one or two years of service to your country either before or after you go to college.

Now, consider this. Consider this. [Applause continues.] Consider this. If every person in Connecticut who wanted a college education signed up for the national service trust and paid the money back before or after, depending on what kind of job you want, by working a year or two as a teacher, a police officer, in a housing program, keeping kids out of trouble and being good role models for them, helping the elderly, helping people with disabilities, you just think about it. We could solve the problems of this country, not in a bureaucratic way, but from the grassroots up, and educate a whole generation of Americans. And it would be totally voluntary. But I think if you open that voluntary door, a flood would come through of Americans who want their country to work again.

I also want to emphasize this one more time. Working people's wages are going down. We have got to have a system, and I have offered it in this plan, where the federal government provides some money for incentives to every state to teach everybody with a job to read in the next five years and give them access to a high-school diploma.

My little state has 2.4 million people. We spend slightly more money than Texas next door, six times our size, on adult education. It's the best money we ever spent, sending people into these workplaces, teaching people to read, giving them their high-school diplomas, making them at least have access to training.

I also think we ought to have a system in which we give companies incentives to retrain their workers, and if they refuse to do it, we exact a small fee from them so that we can do it when those people are unemployed. We have got to retrain America's work force continuously. We cannot let this country go through another decade where people work harder for lower wages. It devastates the whole idea of what it means to be an American. And it is very, very important.

Let me just mention one other thing that I think is important, and a big difference between me and Mr. Bush. Since he's been president, one hundred thousand Americans a month have lost their health insurance. Now, the cost of health care is now responsible for 80 percent of the strikes in America. It is a major deterrent to American manufacturing being competitive. It is a back-breaker for small business, most of whom actually cover their employees at enormous cost. It's killing family farmers. It is the number-one headache in every state budget in the country today—the cost of health care.

I have spent over a year studying this on behalf of the governors. I've talked to literally hundreds and hundreds of providers and sophisticated consumers of health care. I am absolutely convinced that if we do not move to have a national solution to controlling health-care costs and providing basic health care to all Americans—and you can't do one without the other—that we will never get the government's deficit under control, and we will not restore our manufacturing health, and we will not be able to compete in the global economy.

Now, let me just give you one example. In Germany, they kept health-care costs under inflation for five years in the mid-1980s, and that's one of the reasons their factory workers make 20 percent more than we do for a shorter work week with a four-week paid vacation and family leave. We have got to address this.

Does that mean the government should provide health care? No. Does it mean we need a lot more bureaucracy and regulation? Lord, no. That's one of the reasons we're so expensive in this country. We have the most inefficient system of finance in the world. What it means is we have to have a national strategy to cap costs at inflation, giving states the opportunity to fill in the details, and a national requirement of a basic health-care policy that has to be offered by everybody so you can simplify the enormous administrative cost. In this country, eighty-four cents on the dollar goes into health care, sixteen cents to administration and profit, because we have fifteen hundred insurance companies writing thousands of policies overlaid on Medicare and Medicaid that have blizzards and blizzards of rules and uneven application. This is a nightmare. We have got to have a simple system. Once you do that, you can then give incentives for people to be in flexible managed health-care networks, and the government can regulate less than it does today; less regulation, more innovation. But you've got to keep the lid on costs. If we don't do it, we're going to bankrupt the country. And you've got to require that everybody gets some health care.

And let me say that we estimate that the private sector will save hundreds of billions of dollars in the next ten years. More than a capital-gains tax, more than an investment tax credit, more than any government spending program, bringing health costs in line with inflation would unleash capital to put the American people back to work. It is our most urgent spending priority.

Now I want to give you one last example of the difference in our philosophies. Last week, I went to Silicon Valley, and then I went down to the Sandia National Lab in New Mexico, one of our nation's major national laboratories, along with Los Alamos in New Mexico and the Livermore Lab in California, used in the buildup of our capacity as a nuclear power, used to make us a great defense power. This country has incredible brilliant minds in our national labs. And finally, because Congress has forced it—something they've done right—the labs are beginning to do more joint ventures with the private sector in new technologies for the twenty-first century to generate high-wage jobs and economic horizons that we can't even dream of. This president fired the head of the Defense Advanced Products Research Agency because he wanted to do more of that. He wanted to find ways for government to contribute to research and development in technologies that had national defense applications but could also create jobs for you here at home.

In my technology policy, we say we're going to spend 20 percent of all the money we give to government labs to let them work with the private sector on priorities determined by the private sector to generate jobs and new technologies for the future. That's a big difference in a small area of real significance.

Now, again I will say every time I talk about this, Mr. Bush says, "Well, Bill Clinton wants to give us a health-care system with the compassion of the KGB and the competence of the House Post Office." This is from a guy that's been on socialized medicine for twelve years. And then he says, "This is all heavy-handed government. This is what they got rid of in Eastern Europe." Let me read this to you. Sixty years ago, here's what Herbert Hoover said about Franklin Roosevelt. He said, "He has the same philosophy of government which has poisoned all Europe, the fumes of the witches cauldron which boiled in Russia." These guys haven't learned any new lines in six decades.

My view is it is time to try something different—not trickle-down, not tax-and-spend—invest, innovate, cooperate, compete, quit getting beat, let's start growing again, let's get jobs and incomes going again. This has always been a "can do" country where we tried things, and where the power of government was used to help people, not to be a heavy-handed bureaucracy, but to give some zip to our country, some direction, some drive.

I am tired of being told what we can't do. Every one of our competitors controls health-care costs better than we do, and provides health care to everybody. We're told, "Can't do it." We need to put another hundred billion dollars in the same broken system, that's his plan. He told us the other day when he vetoed the family leave bill that we weren't as good as seventy-two other countries—seventy-two countries have figured out how to give workers a little time off when there is a baby born or a sick parent. Have you ever met anybody that lost their job because there wasn't family leave? I have. I met a young couple in my state in a homeless shelter because they both had to give up their jobs because they had a child with cancer at our children's hospital. And they thought that child might die, and they wanted to be there. And so would you.

When Al and Tipper Gore's son was hurt so bad in a car wreck, he went to Johns Hopkins Medical School. They became friends with a young couple from the South who had to bring their child to Johns Hopkins to deal with a serious health problem, and they lost their jobs and their income.

I think this is a can-do country. This should not be an election about the stale, failed political rhetoric of the past. If we let this be about tax-and-spend and trickle-down, we ought to be ashamed of ourselves. This is about whether we have the courage to face up to the realities of modern life.

That is what has brought new support to this campaign. It's not about Bill Clinton and Al Gore. This is bigger than us. It's why Republicans and Independents and former Perot supporters and people who were military officers under Bush and Quayle and Reagan, people that care about their country and want to see something done for a change, are taking our course.

So I ask you in the next thirty-nine days, make that the choice in this election—not four more years, but a whole new future for America.

Thank you very much.

A Beacon of Freedom and Hope

Faneuil Hall Campaign Rally
Boston, Massachusetts
September 25, 1992

This speech was an example of Clinton's urban stump speech to energize the faithful in a state where recent polls showed him leading Bush by more than 2 to 1. It was not intended to generate media coverage outside of Massachusetts, because the campaign hoped the national press would focus on the major policy speech delivered earlier in the day at the University of Connecticut campus in Hartford.

Mayor Ray Flynn and Congressman Joseph Kennedy introduced Clinton at 4 P.M. at a boisterous rally that attracted a sign-waving crowd of forty-five thousand people outside historic Faneuil Hall in downtown Boston. The twenty-five-minute speech was described by the *Boston Globe* as "classic fire and brimstone," and the rally ended with the rock song "Revolution" blaring from the sound system.

❖ ❖ ❖

Thank you. Thank you, Mayor Flynn, for your leadership, your example and your support. Thank you, Reverend Stith for so many years of friendship. Thank you, Senator McGovern, for your eloquent words. Thank you, Congressman Kennedy. He did sound like a Southern Baptist preacher up here. I thought he was great. And thank you, Senator Tsongas, for your courageous campaign to restore America.

Thank you, Senator Tsongas, for being the conscience of the next generation for the last year while this administration has squandered the birthright of Americans repeatedly.

You know, President Bush says this election is about trust. That's what he was saying before the revelations of the last couple of days. But anyway, he says the election is about trust. Well, we've only made one decision in common—George Bush and I. My decision was Al Gore, and I think I did a pretty good job.

Anyway, Al Gore has got this line. He says, you know, in this country, poverty is up and jobs are down. Bankruptcies are up and incomes are down. Everything that's down should be up. Everything that's up ought to be down. They've got it upside down, and we're going to turn it right side up on election day.

You know, last Tuesday I went to East Lansing, Michigan, to debate George Bush.

Where was George?

I'll tell you where he was. Put yourself in his position. It isn't that he is a bad debater, but how do you explain the worst economic performance in fifty years? How do you explain after twelve years of trickle-down economics the fact that two-thirds of our people are working harder for lower wages than they were making ten years ago? How do you explain high unemployment and rampant insecurity? How do you explain one hundred thousand Americans per month losing their health insurance? How do you explain living with over a million people that are HIV-positive and never even mentioning the word AIDS while you're president of the United States?

How do you explain? I'll tell you how he explains it. He just doesn't. He gets in an airplane, and he flies around my state and tells everybody how bad Arkansas is.

Now, if he really believes that, of course, he could come and debate me and I could answer him.

You know, I was so interested the other day when Mr. Bush skipped out on the debate, instead skipped around the states that surround Arkansas, telling them all about how bad my state was. He forgot to tell them that we ranked first in the country in job growth this year.

He forgot to tell them that we had seventy-two thousand new private-sector jobs since he's been president and the country has lost forty thousand private-sector jobs since he's been president. He forgot to say all those things. Why? Because this is an administration that's run out of ideas, that's run out of vision, that's run out of commitment, and it should be out of time. It's time to change it.

My fellow Americans, increasingly as the days go by, the people in this country are moving beyond the comfortable categories of political debate. They are shedding all this useless rhetoric. They are beginning to wonder about what America would be like the day after the election, and they are more and more and more turning off the same old negative, tired, hackneyed, trite phrases that George Bush has used to stay in power.

They are saying no. They are saying no in every region of this country. They are saying no without regard to party or walk of life. In the last several days, in California, in Silicon Valley, twenty-one executives of high-tech companies, two-thirds of them Republicans, endorsed the Clinton-Gore ticket because George Bush has refused to face the problems of America.

In Chicago, four hundred business executives, one-third of them Republican, endorsed our ticket because the other side has no plan to revive the American economy and to make the business sector healthy and to provide jobs for Americans.

And last week, in one of the most moving encounters in which I have ever been involved, Admiral William Crowe, who was the chairman of the joint chiefs of staff for Presidents Reagan and Bush, endorsed Bill Clinton for president because he wants the problems of America solved here at home.

I ask you here, all of you in this crowd, to think about your responsibilities as Americans and the potential we have now to change this country. We cannot go on for four more years where most people work harder for less, where millions of Americans wake up every day waiting for a pink slip, where there is no sense of movement and progress. We have to stop saying no to our people. We have to stop trickle-down economics, no more across-the-board tax cuts, but instead incentives to start new businesses, to start new jobs, give people breaks if they put the American people to work and if for no other reason. Let's put this country back on the right footing.

We have to say in this state, which has long been thought to have the best system of higher education in these universities in the entire Western world—that we know, no matter how good our economic policies are, unless our people have the skills to compete in a global economy, they will be ground down. And so we have to say we do not have a person to waste, education is for everyone, and we will have a real commitment for that.

In this town of great universities, let us never forget that ours is the only advanced country in the world that has no system for dealing with the needs of all those young people who do not go to the four-year colleges and universities. They deserve help, too.

And if we prevail on November third, we will establish a system by which every young American not in college will have at least two years of further education and training to get good jobs, not dead-end jobs.

Let us remember here that the college dropout rate in America is more than twice the high-school dropout rate in part because the cost of a college education has gone up even more than health care.

So on November third, one of the issues in this election is opening the doors of college education to all Americans. That's what Bill Clinton and Al Gore represent.

In 1960, President Kennedy started the Peace Corps and gave young brilliant Americans like Paul Tsongas a chance to go around the world to help other people. In 1992, let us resolve to establish a domestic Peace Corps to rebuild America.

Let us say to every young American, we will loan you the money to go to college, no questions asked, no income limits—but you must in turn pay it back either as a percentage of your income after you go to work or even better, before or after you go to college, do something for your country. Be a police officer, a teacher, work with children, with the elderly, work with people with disabilities. Revitalize our housing markets, solve the problems of our country. That would be the best money we ever spent. We could educate a whole generation of Americans. That is what this election is all about.

Let us resolve—let us make it clear on November third that we are tired of being told what America cannot do. We have been told over and over and over again by this administration that there is something funny about America. We are the only advanced country that cannot bring health-care costs in line with inflation and provide basic health care to all Americans. I believe we can and with your help we will.

We do not propose, as George Bush says, a health-care system with the compassion of the KGB and the competence of the House Post Office. That's his line. And keep in mind, when George Bush criticizes my health-care plan, he's been on socialized medicine for a dozen years. We paid all his bills. We've taken good care of him.

I want you to have a health-care system where you can pick your doctor and your hospital, but where we control health-care costs, we reform insurance, we say to people, you will not be denied insurance nor the right to change jobs because someone in your family has been sick in the past and has a medical condition. You will not be able to have insurance priced out of your range because you're a small-business person or a farmer and if you do not work we will find a way to cover you, too. I have given this country a health-care plan that will save us hundreds and billions of dollars, enable us to bring the deficit under control and revitalize the American economy. Don't let George Bush take it away from you. Grab it on November third. Don't let him do it.

On November third, send a loud and clear signal that you did not buy the argument that George Bush and Dan Quayle have so passionately put forward, that every time you help the environment you hurt the economy. Tell them you've got it figured out.

Look what happened at the earth summit at Rio de Janeiro. Our president goes to Rio and spends all his time beating the global warming treaty, beating the biodiversity treaty. What did the Germans and Japanese do? They signed off on that the first day, and they spent the rest of their time selling high-technology, environmental-cleanup projects to other countries, taking markets away from us and jobs away from us, the work that ought to be done by the scientists, the engineers, and the factory workers that are thrown out of work by the end of the Cold War. We could use them to build a new and peaceful and cleaner world, and under our administration we will.

Tell George Bush, on November third send him a signal that we know something about family values and we want a president who values the family. On Tuesday, after Mr. Bush bypassed the debate, he spent the day flying around bad-mouthing me, he flew back in the dark of the night after the newspaper presses were down, after the evening news was over, to veto for the second time the family leave bill.

Now, what is the message there? Seventy-two nations—hear me again, seventy-two nations—seventy-two—guarantee working men and women a little time off when there is a baby born or a sick parent without losing their jobs. But once again, Mr. Bush says, we can't, we can't, we can't. I don't know if any of you have ever known anybody who lost their job because of a sick family member.

A couple of years ago, I was jogging in downtown Little Rock and I stopped at a local McDonalds, and this lovely young couple started talking to me about their child who was in our children's hospital suffering with cancer. They were two bright, fine young people who were fired from their jobs because they came to Little Rock because they wanted to be there if their child did not live, and they were living in a homeless shelter because we don't have a family leave law in America.

Al Gore tells the story that he and Tipper, when their son was in Johns Hopkins Medical Center, met a couple from one of the southern states who had to bring their child there for special medical treatment. They lost their entire income because we don't have a family leave law. I'll tell you something. I'll get up every day worrying about your families, and I will tell you we can, not we can't. I'm tired of we can't.

In thirty-nine days, you will be called upon to do what Americans have always done when they had to do it, to have the courage to change the course of this country. I want us again to be a beacon of freedom and hope. At the end of the Cold War, we have unparalleled opportunities to stand up for freedom and democracy and human rights all around the world, in our hemisphere, in Haiti, in Latin America, and in China and other countries in Asia and around the world. We should be a voice for freedom.

But never forget this. In 1960, President Kennedy hammered over and over and over again, go back and read the speeches and the debates, we cannot be strong abroad unless we are first strong at home. The American people must rise up from within.

So I ask you to think once again about the stories that Joe Kennedy told. We now take our great triumphs as a nation for granted. We take the triumph of the Boston Tea Party, of Paul Revere's ride, of the winning of the Revolutionary War, perhaps even more remarkably, of our decision to become one nation instead of thirteen separate colonies, we take that for granted.

But my fellow Americans, it was a miracle. It was a miracle. When George Washington and Thomas Jefferson and the other founding fathers said, we can't stay apart, we can't have thirteen armies and thirteen separate currency systems and thirteen independent economies, there was a whole crowd there that said, this is crazy, we could do worse. But Washington and Jefferson were in the we-can-do-better crowd and they prevailed, and so did we because of that.

At the outbreak of the Civil War, it was far from certain that this great nation would stay together. When Abraham Lincoln was elected, only 39 percent of the American people had voted for him. The finest military commander of his age, Robert E. Lee, had gone home to fight to break the Union apart. When Lincoln issued the Emancipation Proclamation, no one could have known for sure that it would become real in the lives of the black Americans who lived at that time.

It was a miracle. Lincoln's own wife lost three brothers fighting for the other side, but he gave his life to preserve the Union.

What we take for granted today happened because Americans had the courage to stay the course for change.

In 1932 when Franklin Roosevelt was elected president of the United States and lifted this country up from his wheelchair, Herbert Hoover said about him the same things that George Bush is saying about me. They haven't learned any new lines in sixty years. Herbert Hoover said he's trying to do what they're doing in Europe. It sounds like all that Russian socialism. It's just terrible what Roosevelt wanted to do. But Roosevelt said we have to change. We have to do what works. We have to use the power of government to help people and move this economy and face our problems, and he lifted the country from his wheelchair and the rest is history. But it was not foreordained. The American people made it happen. We made it happen.

The cause of change is always difficult to make. It is always easy to stay with a proven path even if it is failure. It takes courage to change. In 1960 President Kennedy was elected by one hundred and ten thousand votes, less than one vote per precinct. My fellow Americans, this election is about what happens to our children and grandchildren. It is about whether we'll have four more years in which we double the debt again or one in which we increase investment and bring the debt down and take a stand for our children's future. It is about whether we have four more years with an out-of-control health-care system or finally a system that provides affordable health care to all Americans.

It is about whether we have four more years of idle rhetoric about energy and the environment or we begin to sustain our energy and our environment and our education system for the twenty-first century. It is about more than whether these young children from Clinton High School have their namesake in the White House. It's about whether their children will have an America they can be proud to grow up in. That is what this election is about.

And so I ask you for thirty-nine days, every day in every way you can, think about your responsibilities as Americans. Talk to your friends and neighbors and family members. If you have friends in other states, call them and write them, ask them to be part of a crusade for change. It is our responsibility at this time to lift this country up, to move this country forward, to move beyond a vision to possibility. This can be the greatest age in America's history, and it is up to you to make it so.

Thank you, and God bless you all.

We Can Change the Future

Clinton-Gore Campaign Rally
Madison, Wisconsin
October 1, 1992

Clinton and Gore both spoke from the steps on the south side of the capitol to a sea of thirty thousand supporters covering the capitol grounds and stretching down Martin Luther King Jr. Boulevard. On that beautiful fall afternoon, the crowd didn't seem to mind that the 4:30 P.M. rally started late and lasted more than an hour. With a recent poll showing a lead of 43–36 over Bush in Wisconsin, Clinton gave a version of his standard stump speech of economic hope for the future. Then, he and Gore personally worked the crowd before moving to their next event at University of Wisconsin-Madison, where they sought the youth vote with an appearance and an hour and a half question-and-answer session on the national radio program "Rockline."

❖ ❖ ❖

Thank you. Thank you very much. Thank you. I am so glad to be back here in this wonderful city and at this wonderful state capitol, back in the state that has been so good to me for a long time, since I first came to Stephens Point over five years ago. Now I have been in the last two years to Madison three times, to Milwaukee several times. I have been up the Black River on our wonderful bus trip. This is a gorgeous place, full of good, level-headed, warm-hearted, determined, progressive people who can lead this country to a new future on November the third.

I want to say to those of you who take some comfort in the present polls to remember how you feel about the Brewers. It's not over till it's over, and we need your help all the way to the end.

Let me say also how grateful I am to be here with your attorney general and the leaders of your legislature and my friend of several years who ran such a remarkable campaign for the United States Senate, Russ Feingold, a person who will be a national figure.

Russ Feingold makes me feel like an old man. But I'm proud of him, and I'm proud of being able to run on a ticket with someone like Ada Deer, and if you send the two of them to the United States Congress we'll have a lot better chance to change this country in the way that we ought.

Let me say that once in a while the "read my lips," education, environmental, kinder, gentler, family-values president says this election is about trust. I ask you to consider this: the president and I have only made one decision in common, a profoundly important one, the decision of who should be the president of the United States and have all this awesome responsibility if anything should happen to us. And my decision was Al Gore. Who do you trust?

My fellow Americans, the indictment of this administration is not difficult. It is now widely known that not only has this administration and this president broken its major commitments to the American people in the election of 1988, but that its policies have produced the worst economic performance since the Great Depression, the first decline in industrial production in our history, an actual reduction in the number of people working in the private sector, and, as Senator Gore has said, even in states with relatively low unemployment rates, more than two-thirds of our people today are working harder for lower wages than they were making ten years ago.

I got into this race for president a year ago because I did not want my daughter to grow up to be part of the first generation of Americans to do worse than their parents, because I was sick of the politics of blame and denial and paralysis that has gripped our nation's capital for too long, and because I thought as a people we're better than that, and we can do better than that.

And so I ask the American people to join me on a journey to go beyond trickle-down economics, not back to tax-and-spend economics, but forward, toward the twenty-first century, with a commitment to invest in our people, to educate them, to face the crises that the health-care system and the AIDS epidemic and all the other problems we have imposed on us and seize the futures that is rightfully ours.

This has always been a "can do" country, and I am tired of being told what we cannot do.

None of us would be here today were it not for the fact that our forebears refused to say "we can't." They always said, "we can." I can't help pointing out today in this vast crowd the large number of our fellow citizens with disabilities who are here. They are here because they have waged a courageous battle for decades for the right to say, we can, we can live, we can do, we can have a life, give us a chance. That's what the Americans with Disabilities Act is all about, and that's what this campaign is all about. We can do better, and we must.

In the next few weeks, our opponents will do everything they can do to divert your attention. They will run ads that apparently have not even a close relationship to remote facts. The ad now running on taxation would be funny if it weren't so sad. The very idea that an incumbent president of the United States, at the end of four years, with no record, no vision, no plan, could resort to the debasing tactic of running an ad that has not one shred of truth in it about my record and my plan on taxation is embarrassing for our country. But I say to you, we won't have to put up with it too long if you will help us seize the future.

But what is more important, and what I liked about the way you spoke so loud and clear in this Senate race is that the American people now, led by people like those of you who live in Wisconsin, are saying that what matters is what happens the day after the election. What are we going to do to make America a better place? What are we going to do to change the future and open it up? Well, you don't have to look too far. Al Gore and I have said what we're going to do. It's on that big banner there, and it's in this book. We call it putting people first.

And I want to talk a little today, even to this vast crowd, in ways that go beyond the slogans of a political rally. What is the difference between our position and theirs? First of all, we're never going to turn this country around until we create jobs and raise incomes. We cannot have the American people working harder for less. What the other side wants to do is to give you four more years of trickle-down economics. It's a simple program. It says cut taxes on the wealthiest Americans and get out of the way and see what happens. All the benefits will trickle down.

Well, it hasn't worked. You know it hasn't worked, and I know it hasn't worked. Here's our program: raise taxes marginally and modestly on the wealthiest Americans, because we've got a four-hundred-billion-dollar deficit, and because their tax rates went down while middle-class taxes went up.

But then use the money—use the money to give modest relief to working-class Americans, especially those with children, and then say to the wealthy, if you want to pay lower taxes, here's a tax incentive. Invest in new equipment and new plants and start new small businesses and put the American people back to work and get rich the old-fashioned way. Then you can lower your tax bill by putting the people to work in this country. That is what we want, not trickle-down, but invest and create jobs and put us to work.

And we want to say that we want to invest more of your tax money. We have reduced the defense budget for three and a half years now, but all the money has been lost going into the S&L boondoggle and the higher health-care costs. What Al Gore and I say is, let's take every dollar by which we reduce defense and invest it in an American economy for the twenty-first century and modern transportation and communications and environmental clean up and other technologies that can create jobs for you and for people like you all across the United States. Let's build the American economy here at home.

We say we want to be involved in the world, we want to trade more, we want to sell more, we want to buy more, we want a fair and open and just relationship with the rest of the world. States like Wisconsin and Arkansas are great trading states. We sell a lot of things around the world, but we want fair access to foreign markets. And we also want jobs here at home. That means that I am outraged at the recent undisputed report that under the Bush administration the Agency for International Development has spent taxpayer dollars to shut plants down in America and move them overseas. That is wrong. Your money should not be spent that way. I am stunned to see that American taxpayer dollars have been used to pay for ads encouraging Americans to throw other Americans out of work so they can work people for fifty-seven cents an hour in Central America. That is wrong. We're better than that.

And now it comes out that we under this administration, this government, spent more money to train workers in Central America than it did to train unemployed workers in the United States of America. We can do better than that, and if you'll give us a chance, we will.

And we believe that it's not bad for the economy to help the environment. One of the reasons I put Al Gore on this ticket is that I wanted to make a clear statement that we believe with all our heart that having a sustainable, good, long-term environmental policy is a precondition to a strong American economy, not an enemy of it.

You think about the jobs we can make in America with a new energy policy, with more reliance on renewable resources and natural gas and energy efficiency. Think about the jobs we can make in America building light rail and high-speed rail. Think about the jobs we can make in America recycling our solid waste. There is a company here in Wisconsin, in Green Bay, that has a paper mill in my home state that takes newsprint and office waste paper to recycle to make products for the commercial market. They have saved us from environmental heartache and helped to create economic opportunities for America. And Bill Clinton and Al Gore are going to do that for four years, for eight years, and, by your will, for even longer.

We believe that we can never, ever reduce the government debt, restore health to the manufacturing economy, rebuild small business, or frankly provide basic security to the American people until this country joins the ranks of all other advanced nations and finally, finally moves to control health-care costs and provide basic health care to all Americans.

During the life of the Bush administration, almost one hundred thousand of your fellow citizens a month have lost health-care coverage. Think of it: almost a hundred thousand people a month. On our bus tours across this country, at every country crossroads, someone will come up to us with yet another heartbreaking story related to the absence of health-care coverage or the bankruptcy of a business or the pain of having to stop covering employees or the inability to change jobs because there's someone in the family who's been sick and you can't get new health insurance coverage. I tell you, my fellow Americans, it is the biggest problem with the deficit, it is one of the biggest drags on our economy. We spend 30 percent more of our income on health care than any other nation on earth, and we have less to show for it because we waste so much money on insurance, on administration, on bureaucracy, on the absence of primary and preventive health care.

We have a plan not to pour more money down the same old system, but to revolutionize the American health-care system to provide affordable health care to all. And only you can give us the chance to implement it.

Lastly, in the home of this great university, let me say that we believe America needs a real education presidency.

No candidate for president can promise you to reverse the march of time. No candidate for president can promise you to show the laws of change. The average eighteen-year-old will change work eight times in a lifetime. You live in a world where how well you do depends on what you can learn. It is time we had a commitment to educate people from preschool to all, to an education for a lifetime for every man and woman in this country. And we will offer you that sort of opportunity.

What does that mean? What does that mean? It means if you could see the faces of the people we see, Al and I, as we go along the road on this bus tour, the people who have worked like crazy all their lives, who are now making less than half of what they were making three or four years ago, it is obvious that we must make a renewed commitment to educate all our people. What does it mean? It means first teach everyone with a job to read and give everyone with a job a high-school diploma in the next five years. We can do that.

It means, second, for all the young people in this country who do not go on to four-year colleges, make sure they get at least two years of apprenticeship training in a community college or a work program to get good jobs, not dead-end jobs.

And finally, finally it means we must open the doors of college education to all our people.

I want to establish a national trust fund out of which any American can borrow the money to go to college, without regard to income, and then pay it back as a percentage of their income after they go to work, or even better, by working off their college loans by giving two years of service to our country here at home.

Think of it. Think of it here in Wisconsin. What if every person in this gorgeous state took a national-service loan and said I will pay it off. I'll be a teacher. I'll be a police officer. I'll work with people with disabilities. I'll work with the elderly in home care. I'll work with children to keep them out of trouble. I'll work in a housing program to solve homelessness. From the grass roots up, without government bureaucracy, we could sweep away many of our problems and educate a whole generation of Americans. It would be the best money we ever spent.

That is our agenda for change. But we cannot implement it without your help. You must also support our efforts to change this political system, for both parties in Washington have contributed to the paralysis. We want to reduce the influence of political action committees, control the cost of congressional campaigns, open the air waves to honest debate, limit the influence of lobbyists over legislation, and require them to disclose their activities. We want to clean up the system and open it up so that it will work in the progressive tradition of Wisconsin. The United States deserves no less.

And finally, we ask you to join us in challenging every American to be part of this change, challenging people on welfare to get more education and receive support for their children and move to work, challenging people who owe child support not to cross the state line to get out of paying for it and setting up a system to collect it, challenging people in the work force to be constantly ready to be more productive and to change, challenging people who get something from their government to give something back to their country.

It is time for all of us to be committed to change. Now we have just a little more than a month. In the next month, we will chart the course of America well into the twenty-first century. And there will be repeated pleas to you to remember that things could be worse, appeals to your fears, to your uncertainties, to your doubts. But let me tell you something: I remember when I was the age of the college students here, when America knew that if we could behave properly and not make mistakes, that the future would always be unlimited. Now we are gripped, not by the dimensions of our problems, but by the dimensions of our disbelief. It has been so long since we had a government that was on our side, a government committed to really working, a government that was not trickle-down and was not tax-and-spend, but that was lean and effective and committed to being in partnership with people in their private lives, to create opportunity, provide education, and solve problems, that many people do not believe it can be better.

But I tell you, it can be better. The thing that will determine the outcome of this election is whether we can in the end keep our courage up. At every critical juncture in our nation's history, the things-could-be-worse crowd have been there carping on the sidelines. And this crowd that's in there, they've had a long time. Their record is clear. They're running this economy down and shrinking our future when it ought to be expanding.

The end of the Cold War opens up unbelievable opportunities to all of you. I want your children and your grandchildren to be part of the American legacy, leading us to a freer, more democratic world, dealing with our global environmental problems, and giving richness and texture to the lives of every man and woman in ways that were never dreamed of before.

But it all depends on whether you can keep your courage up. And so I ask you this, on this beautiful fall night in this wonderful place: when you go home tonight and you think about what you want for the rest of your life, and you imagine what America will be like on the day after the election, resolve to do everything you can here in Wisconsin and with your friends around the country to say on November third we're going to take our country back, we're going go claim our future, we are better than we have been, we are going to be better in the future. It is our country, and on November third we're going to lift it up and move it forward.

Thank you very much, and God bless you all.

We Can Take Our Country Back

Girard Park Campaign Rally
Lafayette, Louisiana
October 27, 1992

During the last week before the election, Clinton made a concentrated effort to recapture the South for the Democrats, a feat that only Jimmy Carter had managed in the last twenty-five years and one thought necessary for victory. Polls showed Bush with a three-percentage-point lead among white voters in the region, and this tour was designed to remind voters of Clinton's message that he was a "new Democrat" and one of them. He had spent the previous day in North Carolina. Earlier on this Tuesday, Clinton began with a rally on the banks of the Savannah River in Augusta, Georgia, where he was introduced by Sen. Sam Nunn, followed by another in Tampa, Florida, where his words were supported by the music of Stephen Stills and Jimmy Buffett. He ended the evening at Houston, Texas. The next day he campaigned in Texas, Mississippi, and Tennessee.

This speech, delivered shortly after 6 P.M. on Tuesday during a traditional cajun *fais-dodo* in Girard Park, near the University of Southwestern Louisiana at Lafayette, illustrates Clinton's strategy of identification with southern voters through language, stories, and style. It is the southern version of the stump speech, designed to reinforce and secure favorable voters by reminding them of the campaign's themes. The festive scene and lively music provided an appropriate stage for the relaxed candidate to deliver his message and tell the audience of ten thousand—the "folks"—that he understood the region's problems and values and would govern in their best interest.

❖ ❖ ❖

You know, this has become an amazing election for me in the last few days. When I got into this race, my fellow Americans, I didn't have any personal ill will toward this administration. I just knew that trickle-down economics was a failure. I was tired of seeing people work harder for less. I didn't want to see my daughter and all the children in this crowd grow up to be part of the first generation of Americans to do worse than their parents, and I thought we could do better. And that's what drove me into this race.

But look at this last few weeks. Now, once again, my opponent, Mr. Bush, says we should trust him for four more years. After the worst economic record in fifty years, after a sixteen-hundred-dollar decline in family income, after unemployment going up, poverty going up, one in ten Americans on food stamps, one hundred thousand Americans a month losing their health insurance, I thought that was bad enough. But look what's happening now. They come to Louisiana, and they put an ad on the radio saying that I'm going to shut down offshore drilling.

Did I ever say that?

Did Senator Gore ever say that?

What happened? They made it up.

I was in North Carolina last night with the Louisiana agriculture commissioner and the agriculture commissioners of seven other states, representing seventeen states total, endorsing the Clinton-Gore ticket as good for farmers. And they've got an ad on in North Carolina saying we're going to make every farmer get a permit from a government agency to plant their crops and shut half of them down.

Did I ever say that?

Did Senator Gore ever say that?

They made it up.

This morning I was in Georgia with the chairman of the Senate Armed Services Committee, Senator Sam Nunn, the most respected person in the Congress on defense matters. And the day before, Bush people had been going all over Georgia saying that wherever there was a military installation, whatever it was, I was going to shut it down.

Did I ever say that?

Did Senator Gore ever say that?

They made it up.

You know, I'll say one thing: the politicians always jump on the media, but this year the media's done one thing really well. They've got a truth squad on all these ads, and everybody that's analyzed Bush's ads attacking my position on taxes, attacking my economic program, attacking all these things, says he made it up. There's no basis for it.

This is a guy that wants you to trust him with your future? He told you "read my lips" last time. He told you fifteen million new jobs. He told you you'd be better off than you were four years ago, and now he's telling you whatever he thinks you want to hear to scare you about me and get your vote on Tuesday. You know, when I was raised up the road in Arkansas, we had a saying: "Fool me once, shame on you. Fool me twice, shame on me." We're not buying it this time, Mr. Bush.

I get tickled. Look at what we're reading about in the paper. He says, "Trust me," and then you pick up the newspaper every day and look what you read about in Washington. This is your government. First, the justice department is investigating the FBI, and the FBI is investigating the justice department. They don't have any time for criminals anymore. They're too busy looking at each other.

Then there's a lawsuit in Atlanta over Iraqgate, over the deferral or the diversion of money that you paid for in your taxes to build up Saddam Hussein, and the CIA and the justice department under Bush are fighting about which one of them lied to the federal court to cover up this country's actions.

Then, as I live and breathe, the state department, in this high-toned administration, has three high-level employees that investigate my passport files to see where I went twenty-three years ago. They could have asked me; I'd have told them. Now, wait a minute. And I thought, well, that's all right; we know how political they are.

Then they go and investigate my mother? My mother. These guys—these three federal employees have got nothing better to do than to go look into my mother's passport file between six o'clock at night and ten o'clock at night. The one interesting thing about this is they waited, these three guys did, until the business office closed in the state department. They waited until all the government employees had gone home, and then they sneaked over to this building where all these files were, and they rummaged around for four hours, until ten o'clock at night, bumping into each other. And you know what was funny? I'll bet you that's the first time since Bush has been president that any of those buzzards worked till ten o'clock at night.

They violated the law. Have they been fired? Have they been reprimanded? No. They work for the most political administration in modern history that will do anything to stay in power.

You know—I hear these people—I hear them screaming over there. Just blow them off. We've only got to put up with them for one more week. One more week.

Let me tell you something, folks. Among the more bizarre episodes in this campaign has been the other two candidates charging that they, the other campaign, the other two guys in charge, that their campaign had investigated each other's children. Let me tell you something, folks. I ran for president because I was interested in looking into your children and their problems and their promise and their future, and that's what this election ought to be about. If this administration had a record it could run on and a vision of the future, they wouldn't have to spend all their time running me down. They could spend more time building you up. And that's what we ought to be doing.

I have worked hard with Senator Breaux and Congressman Jefferson and Mayor Landreau and a lot of other people in an organization called the Democratic Leadership Council to build a new Democratic Party, a party that could appeal to all Americans, a party that believes in promoting growth in the private sector, that believes in requiring more personal responsibility of people who get benefits from government, who believe that we are one nation, that we've got to come together across racial and income and regional lines and go up or down together, that we don't have a person to waste. And we have changed. We have changed the Democratic Party for the first time in a generation. You can tell it because we're running proudly on our platform, and the Republicans are running away from theirs.

And now I ask you to think about this. In the closing days of this election, when you hear all these mud balls thrown back at me, ask yourself this question: What difference will this make on the day after the election? You think about your life on the day after the election, and you think ahead to the next four years.

I stand for an economic program that will be good for Louisiana and good for America. I stand for the proposition that we ought to end trickle-down economics. No other country follows it. Our idea here under Bush and Quayle is to just lower taxes on the wealthiest Americans, raise taxes on the middle class, get out of the way and see what happens. Well, you know what happened. We've doubled the deficit. Income's down. Unemployment's up. We're in terrible trouble. What we ought to do is ask the wealthiest Americans to pay their fair share and then say we're not interested in hurting people with money.

We want to make more millionaires. But if you want to make money under our administration, you'll have to do it the old-fashioned way: Invest in factories, in small businesses, in new technologies. Put the American people back to work, and you can make lots of money.

We believe that we can revitalize the American energy industry by having a strong environmental policy. If this administration hadn't tried to gag the Clean Air Act with paralyzing amendments, we could have been producing more natural gas for use in America by Americans to clean up the air years ago, but they didn't believe in it until election time and we put the heat on them.

If you want a president who will really do something to revitalize the natural-gas industry and to move America away from dependence on foreign oil, vote for Bill Clinton. Vote for me. That's what we'll do. Folks, I come from a state that doesn't have as much natural gas as Louisiana, but we've got more than most. I am not going to become a president that will shut down the source of energy that can liberate our country from dependence on foreign oil and clean up our environment at the same time and put our people back to work. I'm going to push it forward.

The second thing I want to say is, if you want somebody who will take action on health care, you only have one choice. We ought to control health-care costs and provide affordable health care to all. Every other country does a better job at that than we do. I believe we can do better. We are going to go bankrupt in this country if we don't put a lid on health-care costs and find a way to provide basic coverage to all Americans. Our competitors do it, and so can we.

I believe that we need a real education president in this country. And here is our proposal: Teach everybody in the work force to read in the next five years and give them a chance to get a high-school diploma and lift the incomes of Americans. Give every young person who gets out of high school who doesn't go on to college the chance to get at least two years of further education in an apprenticeship program so they can get good jobs, not dead-end jobs. And open the doors of college education to all Americans. Don't let them be kept out because of money.

My friends, this is a big issue in your state and mine and in America. The average college dropout rate is more than twice the high-school dropout rate because of the cost. I say let's scrap the student-loan program and instead have a national trust fund out of which any American can borrow the money to go to college, but we should require people to pay the money back either as a small percentage of their income after they go to work, at tax time so they can't beat the bill, or even better, by asking them to serve in a domestic peace corps to rebuild America—to be teachers, police officers, to work with the elderly, to work with people with disabilities, to work in housing programs, to solve the problems of this country from the grassroots up without a bureaucracy and rebuild America to educate a whole new generation of Americans. We can do better than we're doing. We can do that.

The last thing I want to say about what I offer is this—not just opportunity but responsibility. I challenge all of you to face the fact that no person running for president can promise you to make the world the way it used to be. The average eighteen-year-old will change work eight times in a lifetime. Nobody can repeal the laws of change. The question is, how can we make these changes our friends and not our enemies? We have to require more responsibility. We have to say to our business executives, "We will give you more tax incentives to rebuild America, but no more tax breaks for moving your jobs overseas." I'm tired of that. We have to say to our students, "We'll pay your way to college, but you need to give something back to your country." We have to say to working people, "We'll provide you a system of training in a healthy economy, but only you can keep yourself well educated and well trained and more productive every year."

We will say, on the question of family values, we're going to say to people on welfare, "Here is more investment in your education and in health care for your children. Now you must go to work when you can, and you can support your children." We will say—it is a national scandal that too many people bring children into this world and try to leave them for the government to raise. We're going to have a much tougher system of child-support enforcement. You're not going to be able to get away with that if we're president. We will say to young people who get in trouble for the first time, "We're not going to leave you alone or send you to prison if it's not appropriate. We ought to have community-based boot camps where you can get discipline and education and drug treatment and work to rebuild your communities and get connected for a second chance in life.

My fellow Americans, that's what I represent, a new Democratic Party for a new America—job growth, income growth, education, health-care costs, personal responsibility. And I want you to know this: We're also going to change the way this government works. I want to reduce the influence of lobbyists, political-action committees, and special-interest groups, and I want to cut one hundred and forty billion dollars in unnecessary spending over the next five years.

We don't have a dollar to waste, either. Every dollar we can spend on a job for you is a dollar well spent. Every dollar we spend on a government program that doesn't work is unconscionably wasted with the deficit we've got.

And let me say this: There's been a whole lot of talk about change in this election. But of all your choices, there's only one person in this race that ever balanced a government budget. There's only one person in this race that ever did anything to limit the influence of lobbyists and interest groups. There's only one person in this race who has never been part of the Washington insider establishment, and that's the same person that made the best choice for vice-president, Al Gore, and he needs your help.

Folks, I don't know if you like the comic strip "Peanuts," but I do. And when you think about all these people chanting in the background and you listen to all the drivel they're going to put on the radio and television in the last few days, all these attacks that are bogus as a three-dollar bill, just remember what Lucy said in "Peanuts": "If you can't be right, be wrong as loud as you can." That's what they're doing.

I'm telling you, folks, you know what it's been like these last twelve years in Arkansas and Louisiana and Mississippi. You know what we have been through. We have suffered more from trickle-down economics than any people. And too many of our people have continued to vote for their side, for trickle-down economics, the politics for the rich and powerful, because the Democratic Party has not given them an alternative they could tie to, relate to, believe in, and support. That has changed now. That's what I tried to do in picking Al Gore and staking out a new direction and telling the American people the truth, that we're all going to have to change. And now you can be a part of that.

Let me tell you, from coast to coast, people are joining that person with a sign out there that says "Another Republican for Clinton and Gore." In many states, the people who organized the Perot petition campaigns have endorsed our efforts. In Oregon the other day, the state's biggest newspaper, in Portland, for the first time in one hundred and forty-two years endorsed a Democrat for president. In Connecticut, the Hartford newspaper, for the first time in nearly two hundred years, endorsed a Democrat for president. Twenty-four retired admirals and generals, including the deputy commander of Desert Storm and Admiral Crowe, who was the chairman of the joint chiefs of staff under Bush and Reagan, endorsed the Clinton-Gore ticket for president because they want a change.

But most important, folks, there are people who just walk around every day working hard and doing the best they can who need what we can offer. Yesterday in North Carolina, on our trip, a young man took out a dollar and gave it to me, a ten-year-old boy. And his daddy said, "My son wants you to have this to pay down the deficit. We're tired of seeing the economy go down and the deficit go up." A woman put her arms around me and cried. She said, "I've got a master's degree, and I can't get a job." In Grand Rapids, Michigan, a woman came up to me, a single mother with five children; she said, "I'm doing the best I can, and I fall further and further behind, because nobody cares about me."

Let me tell you something, folks: I care about you. I came from your roots. I understand what you're going through. I have represented a state not unlike yours, folks, and I will not forget where I came from. If you vote for me, I'll make some mistakes, because I won't wait until election time to do something. I'll get up every day trying to do something to move this state forward, this country forward, and our people forward.

I ask you to think about this: How are you going to feel on November fourth if you're stuck with four more years? How are you going to feel on November fourth if you've got the promise of a bright new day of change, of an America living up to its potential?

You've got a week. I ask you to talk to your friends and neighbors, to tell them there's a tired old Republican Party that many Republicans have abandoned. It's run out of ideas and energy and direction and passion. It spends more time looking into its opponents than it does looking toward the future. They've run out of everything good, and we ought to run them out of town. You can do it if you'll help me.

But most important of all, I ask you to remember this: I did not get into this race to run them down. I entered this race in the hope that together we could build you up. Let's make America what it ought to be beginning on November third. I need your help, Louisiana. Be there for me, and we can take our country back.

Thank you, and God bless you all.

A New Beginning

Old State House Victory Speech
Little Rock, Arkansas
November 3, 1992

Around the Old State House in downtown Little Rock, the trees were decked out in red, white, and blue lights, and everyone seemed to be in a defiant, festive mood. The wind and rain had passed, leaving behind a chill that did not deter the crowd from staying outdoors to watch four 20-foot-high mobile television screens, one tuned to each national network, as the polls closed and the results were reported. At 9:45 P.M., when the first network declared that Clinton had captured the two hundred and seventy electoral votes needed for victory, and again at 10:15 when Bush was shown making his concession speech, a deafening roar went up from the fifty thousand partisans in the sixteen-block area roped off for the watch party.

In a carnivalesque atmosphere, dubbed "Little Rock Around the Clock," movie stars, business leaders, just plain folks from across Arkansas, bigwigs from the Democratic Party, and the tireless staff and volunteers of the Clinton campaign stood crowded next to each other as sidewalk vendors peddled local favorites such as catfish and barbecued ribs and t-shirts with the campaign logo or proclaiming, "The Fat Lady Sang!" It was, said the right-wing *Washington Times,* "a scene to break the heart of the staunchest Yale crew team Republican."

Clinton finally made a dramatic entrance through the front door to the flag-festooned stage on the steps of the Old State House at 11:20 P.M., with his wife, Hillary, and daughter, Chelsea, followed by his running mate, Al Gore, and the Gore family, as choruses sang "The Star-Spangled Banner," "God Bless America," and "The Battle Hymn of the Republic." From the same spot where he had announced his first campaign for governor in 1978 and for the presidency in 1991, glancing occasionally at notes on a sheaf of wrinkled papers and with his voice noticeably strained from laryngitis, Clinton made the last stump speech of the campaign as he claimed and shared the victory.

❖ ❖ ❖

Thank you very much. Thank you. Thank you.

My fellow Americans, on this day, with high hopes and brave hearts, in massive numbers, the American people have voted to make a new beginning. This election is a clarion call for our country to face the challenges of the end of the Cold War and the beginning of the next century, to restore growth to our country and opportunity to our people, to empower our own people so that they can take more responsibility for their own lives, to face problems too long ignored, from AIDS to the environment to the conversion of our economy from a defense to a domestic economic giant. And perhaps most important of all, to bring our people together as never before so that our diversity can be a source of strength in a world that is ever smaller, where everyone counts and everyone is a part of America's family.

I want to begin this night by thanking my family, my wife, without whom I would not be here tonight and who I believe will be one of the greatest first ladies in the history of this republic. I also want to say a special word of thanks to our daughter for putting up with our absence, for supporting our effort, for being brave in the face of adversity, and for reminding us every day about what this election is really all about.

I want to thank my mother, my brother, my stepfather, my mother-in-law and father-in-law, my brothers-in-law, and my sister-in-law, who carried this campaign across this country and stuck up for me when others were trying to put it down. I love them, and I thank them.

I want to thank the people of this wonderful small state. Time after time, when this campaign was about to be counted out, the Arkansas travelers exploded out of this state around the country to tell people the truth about what we had done here together, how we had pulled together, what we believed in, and what we could do as a nation.

I had the best staff and cabinet you could imagine. They kept this state together. And even when we weren't here, we continued to lead the country in job growth, in keeping taxes and spending down, and in pulling the people of Arkansas together to show what we could do if the nation pulled together and moved forward, too.

I want to thank the people who were in that infamous group, the FOB's, the Friends of Bill and the Friends of Hillary. No person who ever sought this office was more aided by the friends of a lifetime, and I will never forget you. I want to thank the people in the new Democratic Party headed by our chairman, Ron Brown, the new members of Congress, the new blood, the new direction that we are giving.

And finally, I want to thank the members of my brilliant, aggressive, unconventional but always winning campaign staff, they were unbelievable. And they have earned this.

I want to say, if I might, a special word of thanks to two people who lost their lives in the course of this campaign, without whom we might not be here tonight, our friends Paul Tully and Vic Razor. Our prayers are with them. They're looking down on us tonight, and they're awful happy.

Not very long ago I received a telephone call from President Bush. It was a generous and forthcoming telephone call of real congratulations and an offer to work with me in keeping our democracy running in an effective and important transition. I want all of you to join with me tonight in expressing our gratitude to President Bush for his lifetime of public service, for the effort he made from the time he was a young soldier in World War II to helping to bring about an end to the Cold War, to our victory in the Gulf War, to the grace with which he conceded the results of this election tonight in the finest American tradition. Let's give Mr. Bush and his family a hand.

I heard tonight Mr. Perot's remarks and his offer to work with us. I say to you of all the things that he said, I think perhaps the most important that we understand here in the heartland of Arkansas is the need to reform the political system, to reduce the influence of special interest and give more influence back to the kind of people that are in this crowd tonight by the tens of thousands, and I will work with him to do that.

And finally, let me say how profoundly indebted I am tonight, beyond the folks at home, beyond the wonderful people that worked in this administration, Lieutenant Governor Tucker and others, to keep our government going, beyond all the others, I have to say a special word of thanks to my magnificent running mate, Senator Al Gore, and his family. I want to tell you that Al and Tipper and Hillary and I have become friends. I admire them for what they stand for. They're enjoyable to be with. They believe in our country. Al Gore is a man of almost unparalleled combination of intelligence, commitment, compassion, and concern to the people of this country, to our obligation to preserve our environment, to our duty to promote freedom and peace in the world, and together we're going to do our best to give you a new partnership for a new America. I want to thank Al's children, his brother-in-law, and his wonderful parents. They made about as many votes in some states as we did. I think we carried every state that Senator and Mrs. Gore campaigned in, and their percentage was the best of all.

I want to say that we have established a partnership in this campaign that we will continue into this new administration. For if we have learned anything in the world today it is that we can accomplish more by teamwork, by working together, by bringing out the best in all the people that we see. And we will seek the best and most able and most committed people throughout this country to be a part of our team. We will ask the Democrats who believe in our cause to come forward, but we will look, too, among the ranks of Independents and Republicans who are willing to roll up their sleeves, be a part of a new partnership, and get on with the business of dealing with this nation's problems!

I remind you again tonight, my fellow Americans, that this victory was more than a victory of party. It was a victory for the people who work hard and play by the rules, a victory for the people who feel left out and left behind but want to do better, a victory for the people who are ready to compete and win in the global economy, but who need a government that offers a hand up, not a hand out. That is what we offer, and that is what tomorrow we will begin to work to provide to all of you.

Today the steelworker and the stenographer, the teacher and the nurse had as much power in the mystery of our democracy as the president, the billionaire, and the governor. You all spoke with equal voices for change. And tomorrow we will try to give you that. You can trust us to wake up every day remembering the people we saw in the bus trips, the people we saw in the town meetings, the people we touched at the rallies, the people who had never voted before, the people who hadn't voted in twenty years, the people who'd never voted for a Democrat, the people who had given up hope. All of them together are saying, "We want our future back." And I intend to help give it to you!

I say to all of those who voted for us, this was a remarkable coalition for change. Many of you had to put aside this or that personal ambition to be a part of a broad, deep commitment to change in this country. I ask you to keep that commitment as we move from election to governing. We need more than ever for those of you who said, "Let's put the public interest over personal interest," to keep it right there for four years so we can turn this country around.

I say to all those who voted for Mr. Bush or Mr. Perot, those who voted for the president, those who voted for Ross Perot, I know you love your country, too. I ask you to listen to the voice of your leaders. I ask you to join with us in creating a "Reunited States," a united country with a new sense of patriotism to face the challenges of this new time. We need your help, too. And we will do our best to deserve it.

When we seek to offer young people the opportunity to borrow the money they need to go to college and the challenge to pay it back through national service; when we challenge the insurance companies, the drug companies, the providers, and the consumers, the government to give us a new health-care system; when we offer those on welfare new opportunity and the challenge to move to work; when we ask companies to take the incentives we offer to put American people to work and export American products, not American jobs, all of this is a part of a new patriotism, to lift our people up and enable all of us to live up to the fullest of our potential.

I accept tonight the responsibility that you have given me to be the leader of this, the greatest country in human history. I accept it with a full heart and a joyous spirit. But I ask you to be Americans again, too, to be interested not just in getting but in giving, not just in placing blame but now in assuming responsibility, not just in looking out for yourselves but in looking out for others, too.

In this very place, one year and one month ago today, I said we need more than new laws, new promises, or new programs; we need a new spirit of community, a sense that we're all in this together. If we have no sense of community, the American dream will continue to wither. Our destiny is bound up with the destiny of every American. We are all in this together, and we will rise or fall together. That has been my message to the American people for the past thirteen months, and it will be my message for the next four years.

Together, we can do it. Together, we can make the country that we love everything it was meant to be.

I still believe in a place called Hope.

God bless America. Thank you all.